2/1/12
#85.00

CRITICAL INSIGHTS

Emily Dickinson

CRITICAL INSIGHTS

Emily Dickinson

Editor
J. Brooks Bouson
Loyola University Chicago

Salem Press, Inc.
Pasadena, California   Hackensack, New Jersey

Cover photo: The Granger Collection, New York

Published by Salem Press

© 2011 by EBSCO Publishing
Editor's text © 2011 by J. Brooks Bouson
"The *Paris Review* Perspective" © 2011 by Jascha Hoffman for *The Paris Review*

∞ The paper used in these volumes conforms to the American National Standard for Permanence of Paper for Printed Library Materials, Z39.48-1992 (R1997).

Library of Congress Cataloging-in-Publication Data
Emily Dickinson / editor, J. Brooks Bouson.
    p. cm. — (Critical insights)
    Includes bibliographical references and index.
    ISBN 978-1-58765-695-8 (alk. paper)
    1. Dickinson, Emily, 1830-1886—Criticism and interpretation. I. Bouson, J. Brooks.
    PS1541.Z5E385 2010
    811'.4—dc22
                                        2010029178

Contents

Career, Life, and Influence

Critical Contexts

Critical Readings

Resources

CAREER, LIFE, AND INFLUENCE

On Emily Dickinson _____

J. Brooks Bouson

Variously portrayed as a nineteenth-century mystic dressed in white, as a rebellious New England nonconformist and eccentric recluse, and as a great and original American poet whose enigmatic verse is a precursor to the experimental works of modernist and postmodernist writers, Emily Dickinson (1830-1886) continues to be an iconic figure in the popular American imagination in the twenty-first century, even as her notoriously difficult poetry has generated a seemingly interminable and ever-intensifying critical debate, leaving the laconic poet awash in a virtual flood of words. The spare but also sensational facts about Dickinson's life are well known. Born in 1830, Dickinson spent an unremarkable girlhood in Amherst, Massachusetts, as a member of a prominent, well-to-do family, and she was an eager student when she attended first the Amherst Academy and then Mount Holyoke Female Seminary. Despite her ordinary beginnings, Dickinson ended up living a reclusive life as she not only withdrew from society and secluded herself in her family's home but also isolated herself in her room. The self-secluded poet who would famously write disembodied, depersonalized poetry and who, in one of her well-known poems, referred to herself as "A Woman – white – to be –" (307), dressed only in white and, instead of having face-to-face contact with her visitors, spoke to them from behind screens or closed doors. Even as Dickinson became a kind of local legend—indeed, her contemporaries in Amherst called her "the Myth" (Sewall 216-17)—she produced hundreds upon hundreds of poems, which she refused to publish. After her death in 1886, Dickinson's sister Lavinia found almost eighteen hundred poems locked in a dresser drawer in Dickinson's room, most of them contained in hand-bound and hand-sewn volumes, which are called "fascicles," and the rest in loose-leaf booklets called "sets." "Publication – is the Auction / Of the Mind of Man –" (788), Dickinson wrote in one of her poems, describing her aversion to publication. And yet, as scholars have pointed out, Dickinson did engage in a form of self-publication, for she circulated hundreds of her poems by including them in letters to family members and friends.

Despite the current scholarly attempts to situate Dickinson as a nineteenth-century woman and as a product of her time and place, the central biographical mysteries of Dickinson's life continue to vex critics. Why did she seclude herself? Did she do this, as some scholars suggest, both as an act of female submission and as a sign of rebellion, since in her self-seclusion she became an extreme, if not parodic, version of the domestically confined woman? Or did she suffer from agoraphobia? And how are we meant to interpret what seems to be a clearly symbolic act, Dickinson's dressing only in white? Did her white dress represent the abandoned bride's gown? Or was it a sign of her nunlike seclusion, her desire to rise above the body and devote herself wholly to her transcendent and bodiless art? And why, even though she refused to publish her poetry and even asked that her poems be destroyed after her death, did she, in effect, self-publish hundreds of her poems by circulating them among her friends, and why did she carefully collect her poetry in her hand-bound fascicles and loose-leaf sets? Did she not wish for a larger audience, and did she not see herself, as she suggests in her verse, writing a sublime and immortalized poetry for posterity?

Even as the biographical puzzles surrounding the life of Emily Dickinson continue to vex scholars, her poems present a series of unresolvable and formidable poetic mysteries wrapped in the larger enigma of her elusive verse, which demands and yet resists any easy form of understanding or interpretive closure. In Dickinson's verse, what may, at first glance, appear personal veers off into metaphysical abstractions as the poet seemingly invites intimacy and then withholds herself from her readers. The poet who says of her poetry "This is my letter to the World / That never wrote to Me –" also writes of her seclusion from the world: "The Soul selects her own Society – / Then – shuts the Door –" (519; 409A); indeed, for Dickinson, "Renunciation – is a piercing Virtue – / The letting go / A Presence – for an Expectation –" (782). Called to her poetic vocation, she is "Adequate – Erect, / With Will to choose, / Or to reject," and she chooses "just a Crown –" (353). As a contemplative poet, she is in touch with the deeper sources and mysteries of life—"Behind Me – dips Eternity – / Before Me – Immortality – / Myself – the Term between –" (743)—and thus through the narrow life necessitated by her poetic seclusion, she gains an expansive awareness as she dwells "in Possibility – / A fairer House than Prose –" and spreads "wide" her "narrow Hands / To gather Paradise –" (466). In her secluded but chosen life as a kind of priestess of the imagination, she writes for posterity:

> The Poets light but Lamps –
> Themselves – go out –
> The Wicks they stimulate
> If vital Light
> Inhere as do the Suns –
>
> > (930)

But if in her isolation Dickinson can experience the "Certainty" of her "Columnar Self" and assert that "Much Madness is divinest Sense – / To a discerning Eye –," she also has moments of profound mental anguish and fear, for there are times when she feels "a Funeral" in her "Brain" or a "Cleaving" in her mind (740; 620; 340; 867). Indeed, going deep within the self can be a dangerous endeavor, for

> One need not be a chamber – to be Haunted –
> One need not be a House –
> The Brain – has Corridors surpassing
> Material Place –
>
> > (407)

"When I try to organize—my little Force explodes," Dickinson once said of her poetry (L 271). Writing verse that is notoriously opaque and difficult but that also exposes the painful costs of her poetic seclusion, Dickinson has been described by Jed Deppman as a poet whose work is a "thoughtful production of, and reaction to, extreme states of being" and by Harold Bloom as a poet who had "a mind so original and powerful that we scarcely have begun, even now, to catch up with her" (Deppman 85; Bloom 1). Dickinson scholars sometimes openly confess, as does Shira Wolosky, to the "difficulty and obduracy" of Dickinson's poems, which "require the closest textual attention" yet "cannot easily be cited as evidence in an argument, since closer textual work almost always uncovers further readings and implications not easily resolved or subsumed into a summary statement" ("Being" 130). While the Dickinson poem, writes Domhnall Mitchell, may "challenge" readers to "arrive at a meaning," it also "refuses to confirm or deny if it has been touched by any of our promiscuous speculations" (81). If, as some Dickinson scholars claim, the critic-reader "becomes akin to a poet, in that her [critical] performance is a kind of re-'writing' of the poem," and if the critic-reader, in entering Dickinson's "volatile" intellectual and emotional works, is invited to "join and repeat" Dickinson's thought experiments as she thinks "about and beyond thinking," her poetry nevertheless remains elusive (Juhasz and Miller 125; Deppman 95, 100). Indeed, her works "both say and unsay, claim and disclaim . . . define and circumvent definition" so that "whatever stance a poem seems to pursue, by the end it seems no less to unravel" (Wolosky, "Being" 132). A poet who confronts readers with "authentic cognitive difficulties" and whose "strangeness . . . still causes us to wonder at her," Dickinson "compels us to begin again in rethinking our relation to poems" (Bloom 1, 8).

Dickinson's poetry, which offers daunting interpretive challenges to critic-readers, has also compelled scholars to think and rethink not only how best to approach her work—a discussion that has intensified with the publication of the manuscript versions of her poems—but also how to situate Dickinson within both nineteenth-century poetry and the canon of American literature. Fred D. White, in his detailed analysis of the scholarly methods used to analyze Dickinson's poetry—which include feminist and cultural studies approaches, biographical and psychoanalytic criticism, and textual criticism and manuscript studies—explains the complexity of contemporary approaches to Dickinson by describing how a particular study, "like a set of Chinese boxes . . . might contain a strict formalist reading of a poem within a framework of a psychoanalytic approach that purports to advance a cultural-studies perspective on Emily Dickinson's oeuvre" (2). In tracing the recent history of Dickinson scholarship, White notes that following the feminist criticism of the mid-1970s, which "marked the beginning of an Emily Dickinson renaissance," there was a "rich . . . critical outpouring" in the 1980s and 1990s that has persisted into the present time as feminist and postmodernist critics, cultural and historical critics, textual scholars and historians of the book have investigated Dickinson's poetry (189, 191). And if, in early editions of Dickinson's poetry, editors attempted to "correct" or "clean up" the seeming irregularities of her verse—her use of dashes of various lengths, heights, and angles, her unusual capitalization, her inclusion of variant word choices and canceled words in many of her poems—many contemporary critics engaged in manuscript studies assume that what Dickinson chose "to do with her writing is significant" and that Dickinson "allowed herself experiments in the fascicles that would have been impossible in the world of print publication, most famously by indicating variant readings for many fascicle poems—alternative word choices that keep the poem in suspense as to a final meaning" (Smith and Loeffelholz 4, 5).

As researchers have gained access to various print and digital editions of Dickinson's manuscript writings and both the study and interpretation of Dickinson's manuscripts have intensified, scholars have become involved in a new critical debate—what some call a "war"—on what should count as a poem in Dickinson's work. Thus when contemporary critics quote from Dickinson's poetry, as Cristanne Miller remarks, they "implicitly manifest their theoretical position as to what constitutes a Dickinson poem," for if they quote Dickinson's poetry "without variants in metrically lineated stanzas," they suggest that Dickinson "shared major nineteenth-century assumptions about fixed poetic form," and if they quote her poetry "with variants, cancellations, scriptural lineation, and in some cases even with attention to the particular slant of dashes," they suggest that Dickinson was "a proto-modernist poet, anticipating the spatial or visual focus and free-verse line breaks of later writers" (45). And such readings also argue for or implicitly support "postmodern readings of plurality, visual intentionality, and the poet's deliberate construction of fluid texts of one form or another, linking this understanding of Dickinson's texts to the primacy of manuscript study and visual attention to her handwritten pages" (45-46). While some scholars argue for the poetic intentionality of the material found in Dickinson's manuscripts, others, including R. W. Franklin, the editor of the variorum edition of Dickinson's poetry and the facsimile edition of the manuscripts, argue that there is no special significance to Dickinson's lineation, word variants and dashes, or the organization of her poems into fascicles.

Even as an intense critical "war" has erupted over the meaning of and intentions behind Dickinson's manuscripts, other critics have questioned what they see as "a flight from history . . . in order to fetishize [the] fascicle manuscripts" and "ponder lost and irrecoverable intentions in new hypertextual scriptures" (R. Smith 15). In the view of Betsy Erkkila, rather than measuring "the blank space on Dickinson's manuscript pages as a means of gauging her poetic intentions," critics instead "might want to examine her manuscript production in relation to the cultural production, poetics, and writing practices of her place and time" (26). And as scholars such as Margaret Dickie have come to question the "long line of literary historians who have banished Dickinson from history" and isolated her "from her own times," there has been renewed attention to the cultural and historical, as well as literary, contexts of Dickinson's art (186, 185). Thus, critics have argued, variously, that "Dickinson was throughout her lifetime actively immersed in nineteenth-century American literary and religious culture"; that she "directly and indirectly wrote poetry that detailed the psychological reality" of the Civil War years; that she was expressing, through her "stylistic and public reticence," her class-based "sense of gentility"; and that she had a "keen eye" on the American popular culture of the nineteenth century and "drew poetic sustenance from it" (Smith and Loeffelholz 3; Dickie 196; Mitchell 78; Reynolds 167).

Yet even as there has been a renewed focus on the historical and cultural contexts of Dickinson's art, some scholars have expressed reservations about such approaches to Dickinson, arguing, as Paula Bennett does, that the recent attempts of critics "to relocate Dickinson's poetry in history, although illuminating in themselves, run counter to Dickinson's own assiduous attempts to place her poems outside 'space & time'" and to "dematerialize her art" (232). If scholars, by "relocating Dickinson's poetry in the material circumstances of her daily life, and in her social relations with others," have, in effect, "sought to fill in what appears to be the empty space around and within Dickinson's poems," so those involved in the new manuscript studies of Dickinson have sought to rematerialize Dickinson's poetry by creating a Web site containing all of Dickinson's "drawings, cutouts, and visual manipulations of paper shape and type and assembly (from stationery to shopping bags, to affixed stamps and illustrations scissored from other books" (Bennett 219; M. Smith 132). While the joining of the "artifact with the work, the document with the baked goods, the textual with the cultural," may promise "plenitude, presence, and a return to origins," it may also, in the view of Shawn Alfrey, "place Dickinson's discourse within a space of fictional plenitude that, while treating her as the sublime, quiets the sublimity within her own texts" (17, 13, 17).

As Virginia Jackson writes, "The exposure of Dickinson's private hand to the public gaze has thrilled readers since the nineteenth century, and though new Web technologies may provide more spectacular means for such exposure, it is not technology itself that determines interpretation" (148). Indeed, as Shira Wolosky has observed, while

Dickinson's poems are "pages of script," they are also "cultural representations, rhetorical fields, spiritual contests, personal expressions, aesthetic compositions, linguistic theorizings, power struggles, woman's voicings, and no doubt much else" ("Manuscript" 96). Even as twenty-first-century scholars engage in an ongoing debate not only about the meaning of Dickinson's poems but also about the very conception of what constitutes a poem in Dickinson's work, a new generation of readers is grappling with Dickinson's elliptical, elusive, and obdurate poetry. "[S]pace & time are things of the body & have little or nothing to do with our selves. My Country is Truth," as Dickinson once remarked of her poetry, which is often described as disembodied and otherworldly—as bereft of other people and as scene-less and history-less (qtd. in Sewall 427). Described as an author who strove for "an entirely dematerialized linguistic state" and as the "ghost that haunts American literature" (Bennett 234; Martin 609), Emily Dickinson, a "Woman – white – to be," continues to invite us to "dwell in Possibility" with her as we enter her poetry's strangely disembodied and selfless—and thus forever open—world of haunting possibilities.

Works Cited

Alfrey, Shawn. "The Function of Dickinson at the Present Time." *The Emily Dickinson Journal* 11.1 (2002): 9-20.

Bennett, Paula. "Emily Dickinson and Her American Women Poet Peers." *The Cambridge Companion to Emily Dickinson*. Ed. Wendy Martin. New York: Cambridge UP, 2002. 215-35.

Bloom, Harold. "Introduction." *Emily Dickinson*. Ed. Harold Bloom. New York: Chelsea House, 2008. 1-8.

Deppman, Jed. "Trying to Think with Emily Dickinson." *The Emily Dickinson Journal* 14.1 (2005): 84-103.

Dickie, Margaret. "Emily Dickinson in History and Literary History." *Challenging Boundaries: Gender and Periodization*. Ed. Joyce W. Warren and Margaret Dickie. Athens: U of Georgia P, 2000. 185-201.

Dickinson, Emily. *The Letters of Emily Dickinson*. Ed. Thomas H. Johnson and Theodora Ward. 3 vols. Cambridge, MA: Harvard UP, 1958. Citation by letter number.

_____. *The Poems of Emily Dickinson: Variorum Edition*. Ed. R. W.

Franklin. 3 vols. Cambridge, MA: Harvard UP, 1998. Citation by poem number.

Erkkila, Betsy. "The Emily Dickinson Wars." *The Cambridge Companion to Emily Dickinson*. Ed. Wendy Martin. New York: Cambridge UP, 2002. 11-29.

Jackson, Virginia. "Dickinson Undone." *Raritan* 24.4 (Spring 2005): 128-48.

Juhasz, Suzanne, and Cristanne Miller. "Performances of Gender in Dickinson's Poetry." *The Cambridge Companion to Emily Dickinson*. Ed. Wendy Martin. New York: Cambridge UP, 2002. 107-28.

Martin, Wendy. "Emily Dickinson." *Columbia Literary History of the United States*. Ed. Emory Elliott. New York: Columbia UP, 1988. 609-26.

Miller, Cristanne. "Controversy in the Study of Emily Dickinson." *Literary Imagination: The Review of the Association of Literary Scholars and Critics* 6.1 (2004): 39-50.

Mitchell, Domhnall. "Northern Lights: Class, Color, Culture, and Emily Dickinson." *The Emily Dickinson Journal* 9.2 (2000): 75-83.

Reynolds, David. "Emily Dickinson and Popular Culture." *The Cambridge Companion to Emily Dickinson*. Ed. Wendy Martin. New York: Cambridge UP, 2002. 167-90.

Sewall, Richard B. *The Life of Emily Dickinson*. 1974. Cambridge, MA: Harvard UP, 1994.

Smith, Martha Nell. "Dickinson's Manuscripts." *The Emily Dickinson Handbook*. Ed. Gudrun Grabher, Roland Hagenbüchle, and Cristanne Miller. Amherst: U of Massachusetts P, 1998. 113-37.

Smith, Martha Nell, and Mary Loeffelholz. "Introduction." *A Companion to Emily Dickinson*. Ed. Martha Nell Smith and Mary Loeffelholz. Malden, MA: Blackwell, 2008. 1-7.

Smith, Robert McClure. "Dickinson and the Masochistic Aesthetic." *The Emily Dickinson Journal* 7.2 (1998): 1-21.

White, Fred D. *Approaching Emily Dickinson: Critical Currents and Crosscurrents Since 1960*. Rochester, NY: Camden House, 2008.

Wolosky, Shira. "Emily Dickinson: Being in the Body." *The Cambridge Companion to Emily Dickinson*. Ed. Wendy Martin. New York: Cambridge UP, 2002. 129-41.

_____. "Emily Dickinson's Manuscript Body: History/Textuality/Gender." *The Emily Dickinson Journal* 8.2 (1999): 87-99.

Biography of Emily Dickinson_____

Gerhard Brand

Early Life

The sparse facts of Emily Elizabeth Dickinson's external life can be summarized in a few sentences: She was born in the town of Amherst, Massachusetts, on December 10, 1830, spent almost her entire life in her family home, and died there on May 15, 1886. She graduated from Amherst Academy in 1847, then attended nearby Mount Holyoke Female Seminary for one year. She traveled occasionally to Springfield and twice to Boston. In 1855, she and her family visited Washington and Philadelphia. She never married. Yet her interior life was so intense that a distinguished twentieth century poet and critic, Allen Tate, could write, "All pity for Miss Dickinson's 'starved life' is misdirected. Her life was one of the richest and deepest ever lived on this continent." It is a life that has proved a perplexing puzzle to many critics and biographers.

What led to Dickinson's monastic seclusion from society? Was it forced on her by a possessive, despotic father? Was it self-willed by her timid temperament, by rejected love, or by her neurotic need for utmost privacy while she pursued her poetry? Speculation abounds, certainty eludes; nothing is simple and direct about her behavior. Perhaps the opening lines of her poem 1129 are self-revealing: "Tell all the Truth but tell it slant – / Success in Circuit lies"

When Dickinson was born, Amherst was a farming village of four to five hundred families with a cultural tradition of Puritanism and a devotion to education as well as devoutness. The Dickinsons were prominent in public and collegiate activities. Samuel Fowler Dickinson, Emily's grandfather, founded Amherst College in 1821 to train preachers, teachers, and missionaries. Edward Dickinson (1813-1874), Emily's father, was the eldest of nine children. He became a successful attorney and, at age thirty-two, was named treasurer of Amherst College, a position he kept for thirty-eight years. He served three terms in the Massachusetts legislature and one term as a member of Congress. Even political opponents respected him as forthright, courageous, diligent, solemn, intelligent, and reliable; he was the incarnation of responsibility and rectitude. In a letter to her brother, Dickinson mocked him (and her mother): "Father and Mother sit in state in the sitting-room perusing such papers, only, as they are well assured, have nothing carnal in them."

Emily's mother, Emily Norcross (1804-1882), was born in Monson, Massachusetts, twenty miles south of Amherst. Her father was a well-to-do farmer who sent his daughter to a reputable boarding school, where she behaved conventionally, preparing herself for the respectable, rational marriage that ensued after Edward Dickinson had courted her politely and passionlessly. The mother has received adverse treatment from most of Dickinson's biographers because of several statements the daughter wrote to her confidant, Colonel Thomas Wentworth Higginson (1823-1911): "I never had a mother. I suppose a mother is one to whom you hurry when you are troubled."

Richard Sewall indicates in his magisterial two-volume *The Life of Emily Dickinson* (1974) that Emily's acerbic remarks should not be taken at their surface meaning in the light of the poet's continued preference for remaining in the familial home. To be sure, Dickinson's mother read meagerly and had a mediocre mind, but she was a tender-hearted, loving person who committed herself wholly to her family and to the household's management. While she never understood her daughter's complex nature, she also never intruded on Dickinson's inner life.

Dickinson's brother Austin (1829-1895) was closest to her in disposition. Personable, sensitive, empathic, and sociable, he became an attorney, joined his father's practice, and succeeded him as Amherst College's treasurer in 1873. He shared his sister's wit, taste in books, and love of nature; his vitality was a tonic for her. He married one of her schoolmates, Susan Gilbert, who was vivacious, worldly, and articulate.

Dickinson and her sister-in-law, living next door to each other, were in each other's homes frequently during the first years of this marriage. Dickinson had a near-obsessive concern for her immediate family and greatly desired to make of her sister-in-law a true sister in spirit. She sent Sue nearly three hundred of her poems over the years—more than she sent to anyone else. Yet a satisfyingly soulful friendship never quite materialized. To be sure, Sue's parties did keep Dickinson in at least limited circulation in her early twenties. The two women exchanged books and letters, with Dickinson occasionally seeking Sue's criticism of her poems. Dickinson, always fond of children, was particularly delighted with her nephew Gilbert. Tragically, he died of typhoid fever at the age of eight; Dickinson's letter of condolence called him "Dawn and Meridian in one."

Yet the two women's paths ineluctably diverged. Sue had a husband and, eventually, three children and was an extroverted social climber. For unknown reasons, Dickinson and Sue quarreled in 1854, and Dickinson wrote her the only dismissive letter in her correspondence: "You can go or stay." They resumed their friendship, but it proved turbulent, as did Sue and Austin's marriage. In 1866, Sue betrayed Emily's confidence by sending her poem "A narrow Fellow in the Grass" to the *Springfield Republican*, which published it but mutilated it by changing its punctuation. "It was robbed of me," Dickinson bitterly complained.

With her natural sister Lavinia (1833-1899), Dickinson was intimate all her life. Like her older sister, Lavinia (known as Vinnie) remained a spinster, remained at home, and outlived her family. Dickinson and Lavinia were devotedly protective of each other. The younger sister was relatively uncomplicated, steady in temperament, pretty, and outgoing. Their only quasi-serious difference was that Vinnie adored cats, while Emily cared for birds. It was Lavinia who organized the first large-scale publication of Dickinson's poems after her death.

Outside her family circle, Dickinson had only a few friends, but they mattered greatly to her—she called them her "estate" and cultivated them intensely. While still in her teens, she established a pattern that was to recur throughout her life: She sought to attach herself to an older man who would be her confidant and mentor or, to use her terms, "preceptor" or "master." These pilots would, she hoped, teach her something of the qualities she knew she lacked: knowledge of the outer world, firm opinions and principles, sociability, and intellectual stability.

Dickinson's first candidate was Benjamin Newton (1821-1853), only nine years her senior, who was a law student in her father's office from 1847 to 1849. He served her in the roles of intellectual companion, guide in aesthetic and spiritual spheres, and older brother. He introduced her to Ralph Waldo Emerson's poetry and encouraged her to write her own, but he died of consumption in his thirty-third year, before she became a serious poet. Her letters to him are not extant, but in a letter she wrote to Higginson in 1862, she probably refers to Newton when she mentions a "friend who taught me Immortality—but venturing too near, himself—he never returned—."

Dickinson's first mature friendship was with Samuel Bowles (1834-1878), who inherited his father's *Springfield Republican* and made it one of the most admired newspapers in the United States. Bowles had a penetrating mind, warmth, wit, dynamic energy, strongly liberal convictions, and an engaging, vibrant personality. Extensively seasoned by travel, he knew virtually every important public leader and was a marvelous guest and companion. He, and sometimes his wife with him, became regular visitors in both Edward and Austin Dickinson's homes from 1858 onward. Thirty-five of Dickinson's letters to Bowles survive, and they show her deep attachment to—perhaps even love for—him, even though she knew that he was out of her reach in every way—just as her poetry was out of his, since his literary tastes were wholly conventional. In April, 1862, Bowles left for a long European stay. Shortly thereafter, Emily wrote him, "I have the errand from my heart—I might forget to tell it. Would you please come home?" Then, in a second letter, "[I]t is a suffering to have a sea . . . between your soul and you." That November, the returned Bowles called at Amherst. Dickinson chose to remain in her room, sending him a note instead of encountering him.

Life's Work

The turning point in Dickinson's career as a poet, and hence in her life, came in her late twenties. Before 1858, her writing consisted of letters and desultory, sentimental verses; thereafter, particularly from 1861 to 1865, poetry became her primary activity. As far as scholars can ascertain, she wrote 100 poems in 1859, 65 in 1860, at least 80 in 1861, and in 1862—her *annus mirabilis*—perhaps as many as 366, of a prosodic skill far superior to her previous achievement. What caused such a flood of creativity? Some biographers attribute it to her unfulfilled love for the Reverend Mr. Charles Wadsworth (1814-1882).

Dickinson and Lavinia visited their father in Washington, D.C., during February and March of 1855, when he was serving his congressional term. On their return trip, they stopped over in Philadelphia as guests of a friend from school days and heard Wadsworth preach in the Arch Street Presbyterian Church, where he served as pastor from 1850 to April, 1862. Married and middle-aged, of rocklike rectitude, shy and reserved, Wadsworth nevertheless made an indelible impression as a "Man of sorrow" on Dickinson. He was generally regarded as second only to Henry Ward Beecher among the pulpit orators of his time. A contemporary newspaper profile described him in these terms:

> His person is slender, and his dark eyes, hair and complexion have decidedly a Jewish cast. The elements of his popularity are somewhat like those of the gifted Summerfield—a sweet touching voice, warmth of manner, and lively imagination. But Wadsworth's style, it is said, is vastly bolder, his fancy more vivid, and his action more violent.

It is presumed that Dickinson talked with Wadsworth during her Philadelphia visit. Few other facts are known: He called on her in Amherst in the spring of 1860, and again in the summer of 1880. She requested his and his children's pictures from his closest friend. In April, 1862, Wadsworth moved to San Francisco, becoming minister to the Calvary Presbyterian Society. Dickinson found this departure traumatic: She used "Calvary" ten times in poems of 1862 and 1863; she spoke of herself as "Empress of Calvary," and began one 1863 poem with the words, "Where Thou art – that is Home / Cashmere or Calvary – the Same . . . ." It may be because of this inner "Calvary" drama of loss and renunciation that she began at this time to dress entirely in white. By 1870, and until his death, Wadsworth was back in Philadelphia in another pastorate, but the anguished crisis he had caused her had ended by then.

After Dickinson's death, three long love letters were found in draft form among her papers, in her handwriting of the late 1850's and early 1860's. They address a "Master" and have therefore come to be called the "Master letters." Their tone is urgent; their style, nervous and staccato. In the second of them, "Daisy" tells her "Master": "I want to see you more—Sir—than all I wish for in this world—and the wish—altered a little—will be my only one—for the skies." She invites him to come to Amherst and pledges not to disappoint him. Yet the final letter shows the agony of a rejected lover, amounting to an almost incoherent cry of despair. For whom were these letters intended? Thomas Johnson and most other biographers designate Wadsworth. Richard Sewall, however, argues for Bowles on the evidence that some of the images in the unsent letters parallel images in poems that Dickinson did send to Bowles.

In 1861, Dickinson composed the most openly erotic of her poems, with the sea the element in which the speaker moors herself:

Wild Nights – Wild Nights!
Were I with thee
Wild Nights should be
Our luxury!

Futile – the winds –
To a Heart in port –
Done with the Compass –
Done with the Chart.

Rowing in Eden –
Ah! the Sea!
Might I but moor – Tonight –
In Thee!

Is this poem derived from autobiographical experience—or, at least, intense longing for such experience—or is the first-person perspective no more than that of the poem's persona or speaker? Again, Dickinsonians divide on this question.

On April 15, 1862, responding to an article in *The Atlantic* by Thomas Wentworth Higginson, Dickinson sent him four of her poems and a diffident note, asking him if he thought her verses were "alive" and "breathed." Trained as a minister, Higginson had held a Unitarian pulpit in Newburyport, Massachusetts, then resigned it to devote himself to social reforms, chief of which was the abolition of slavery. He had made a reputation as a representative, influential midcentury literary critic, with particular interest in the work of female writers. The four poems Dickinson mailed him were among her best to date; in his evaluative replies, however, he showed an obtuse misunderstanding of them, as he did of her subsequent submissions, which were to total one hundred.

Dickinson undoubtedly felt a strong need for another "preceptor"— Wadsworth had just departed for San Francisco—and especially for a literary rather than romantic confidant. Higginson was to prove her "safest friend" for the remainder of her life. A warm, courteous, sympathetic man, he regarded her with mystified admiration. After their correspondence had been under way for several months, he asked her to send him a photograph of herself. Her response was, "I had no portrait, now, but am small, like the wren, and my hair is bold, like the chestnut bur, and my eyes, like the sherry in the glass, that the guest leaves." After Higginson had met her eight years later, he confirmed this self-portrait and added to it that Dickinson was a "plain, shy little person, the face without a single good feature."

Dickinson's poetry, unfortunately for both of them, was simply beyond Higginson's grasp. He immediately and consistently advised her not to seek its publication because it was "not strong enough." His critical judgments were invariably fatuous, showing deaf ears and blind eyes to her original language, syntax, meter, and rhyme. She resigned herself to his recommendation against publication but gently yet firmly ignored his strictures concerning her poems' construction. Thomas Johnson summarizes the relationship as "one of the most eventful, and at the same time elusive and insubstantial friendships in the annals of American literature."

In the late 1870's, nearing her fiftieth year, Dickinson fell in love with Otis Phillips Lord (1812-1884). He was a distinguished lawyer who, from 1875 to 1882, served as an associate justice of the Massachusetts Supreme Court. He answered Dickinson's constant need for a settled, senior friend-tutor, intellectually gifted and personally impressive; he became her last "preceptor." She had first known Judge Lord when he had called on Edward Dickinson; like her father, Lord was vigorous, conscientious, commanding, and highly disciplined. Their affection developed after December, 1877, when Lord's wife died. Fifteen of her letters to him survive and indicate that, over the objection of his nieces, Lord apparently offered to marry her. With her father and Bowles now dead and her mother an invalid requiring many hours of her time each week, Dickinson found considerable solace in their correspondence. Yet she also knew that her reclusive life was too rigidly established for her to adapt to the major changes that marriage would require of her.

On April 1, 1882, Wadsworth, the man she had called "my closest earthly friend," died. On May 1 of that year, Lord suffered a stroke; on May 14, Dickinson wrote him a fervent letter of joy at his (temporary) recovery, assuring him of her "rapture" at his reprieve from impending death; on October 5 came news of her beloved nephew Gilbert's death; on November 14, her mother finally died, after years of serious illness. It is not surprising that Dickinson then underwent a "nervous prostration" that impaired her faculties for many weeks.

After an 1864 visit to Boston for eye treatment, Dickinson did not leave Amherst for the remainder of her life. Her withdrawal from society became gradually more marked. By 1870, she did not venture beyond her house and garden, preferring to socialize by sending brief letters, some of them accompanied by poems, flowers, or fruit. She retreated upstairs when most visitors came to call, sometimes lurking on an upper landing or around corners. While strangers regarded her eccentricities as unnatural, her friends and family accepted them as the price of her retreat into the intensity of her poetry. In perhaps her most self-revealing poem, the first lines declare, "The soul selects her own Society – / Then – shuts the Door –." Emily Dickinson died of nephritis on May 15, 1886.

From *Dictionary of World Biography: The 19th Century.* Copyright © 1999 by Salem Press, Inc. Reprinted with permission of Salem Press.

Bibliography

Boruch, Marianne. "Dickinson Descending." *Georgia Review* 40 (1986): 863-877. Boruch, a gifted writer and poet, pays tribute to Dickinson in this lively, conversational discussion. She criticizes the parasitic "cottage industry" that feeds off speculative details of Dickinson's life and praises and explains Dickinson's heavy use of dashes. Includes a good explication of "I heard a Fly buzz – when I died –" and notes to other criticism throughout.

Carruth, Hayden. "Emily Dickinson's Unexpectedness." *Ironwood* 14 (1986): 51-57. This essay, one of seven in a special Dickinson issue, declares Dickinson's significance in Western literature and urges readers to read her as a poet, without constant reference to useless biographical information. Carruth explains four poems with great skill and sincerity, without overusing intellectual jargon.

Dickenson, Donna. *Emily Dickinson*. Oxford, England: Berg, 1985. A well-researched and accessible literary biography meant to fill the gap between the detailed scholarly criticism and the outdated popular image of Dickinson as a lovelorn recluse. The author does not try to make the poet's life explain her poetry, nor does she stretch the poetry to fit the life. The notes after each chapter indicate useful avenues for further study.

Dickinson, Emily. *The Complete Poems of Emily Dickinson*. Ed. Thomas H. Johnson. Boston: Little, Brown, 1960. A single-volume condensation of Johnson's three-volume *The Poems of Emily Dickinson Including Variant Readings Critically Compared with All Known Manuscripts*. The variant readings are omitted.

_____. *The Letters of Emily Dickinson*. Ed. Thomas H. Johnson and Theodora Ward. 3 vols. Cambridge, Mass.: Harvard University Press, 1958.

_____. *The Manuscript Books of Emily Dickinson: A Facsimile*. Ed. R. W. Franklin. 2 vols. Cambridge, Mass.: Harvard University Press, 1981. Facsimiles of Dickinson's manuscript books and unsewn fascicle sheets, arranged as much as possible in the order and groupings in which they were found after Dickinson's death.

_____. *The Master Letters of Emily Dickinson*. Ed. R. W. Franklin. Amherst, Mass.: Amherst College Press, 1986. Reproductions of Dickinson's "Master letters" with Franklin's commentary.

_____. *The Poems of Emily Dickinson Including Variant Readings Critically Compared with All Known Manuscripts*. Ed. Thomas H. Johnson. 3 vols. Cambridge, Mass.: Harvard University Press, 1955. The first comprehensive, scholarly edition of Dickinson's poems. As much as possible, the poems are arranged in chronological order and numbered. Variant readings are also included. Johnson was the first Dickinson scholar to make a serious attempt to reproduce accurately Dickinson's unusual jottings, scribbles, and semifinal drafts in printed text. Even so, his choices of alternative language have sometimes been questioned by other Dickinson specialists, prompting R. W. Franklin to publish two second editions of Dickinson's poems, *The Poems of Emily Dickinson: Variorum Edition* and *The Poems of Emily Dickinson: Reading Edition*.

_____. *The Poems of Emily Dickinson: Reading Edition*. Ed. R. W. Frank-lin. Cambridge, Mass.: Harvard University Press, 1999. A condensed version of Franklin's variorum edition, here Franklin selects one variant of each poem, usually the one appearing to be the last variant Dickinson composed.

_____. *The Poems of Emily Dickinson: Variorum Edition*. Ed. R. W. Frank-lin. 3 vols. Cambridge, Mass.: Harvard University Press, 1998. The second comprehensive, scholarly edition of Dickinson's poems. Franklin, like John-son, arranges the poems chronologically, but dates them differently. The vario-rum edition includes variant readings, publication history, and editorial notes.

Eberwein, Jane Donahue, ed. *An Emily Dickinson Encyclopedia*. Westport, Conn.: Greenwood Press, 1998. Edited by a founding board member of the Emily Dickinson International Society as well as a professor of English. Covers a wide range of topics, from people important in Dickinson's life to her stylistic traits.

Farr, Judith. *The Passion of Emily Dickinson*. Cambridge, Mass.: Harvard Univer-sity Press, 1992. Provides both a portrait of Dickinson as an artist and a guide to understanding the poet's work.

Ferlazzo, Paul, ed. *Critical Essays on Emily Dickinson*. Boston: G. K. Hall, 1984. This collection, edited and introduced by a leading Dickinson scholar, contains thirty-two essays that range in publication date from 1890 (Thomas Wentworth Higginson's "Preface to Poems by Emily Dickinson") to 1984. Includes a solid gathering of writings by well-known critics, Dickinson scholars, and both nine-teenth century and contemporary fellow poets.

Grabher, Gudrun, Roland Hagenbüchle, and Cristanne Miller, eds. *The Emily Dick-inson Handbook*. Amherst: University of Massachusetts Press, 1998. A collec-tion of up-to-date essays covering Dickinson's poetry, poetics, and life. Useful reference with extensive bibliography.

Habegger, Alfred. *My Wars Are Laid Away in Books: The Life of Emily Dickinson*. New York: Random House, 2001. Biography demonstrates the development of Dickinson as a poet, answers many of the questions that her enigmatic life and career raise for readers, and confirms her poetic genius.

Juhasz, Suzanne, ed. *Feminist Critics Read Emily Dickinson*. Bloomington: Indi-ana University Press, 1983. The title essay is a twenty-page introduction by the editor, who explains how feminist criticism can correct some partial or "false" criticism that has always split Dickinson into "woman" and "poet"—elements that should go together. The feminist perspective is based on the assumption that gender informs the nature of art.

McNeil, Helen. *Emily Dickinson*. New York: Virago, 1986. In this short critical bi-ography intended for the general reader, as well as the student or specialist, the author reveals how strongly Dickinson distinguished between oral expression, which is restrained by convention, and written self-expression.

Robinson, John. *Emily Dickinson: Looking to Canaan*. Winchester, Mass.: Faber & Faber, 1986. Accurate facts, deft insights, and a readable prose style make this volume of the Faber Student Guide series a useful introduction. Robinson re-veals a Dickinson who sought to escape from history and time and whose work was satiric, yet defined by Protestant ethics.

Sewall, Richard B. *The Life of Emily Dickinson*. 2 vols. New York: Farrar, Straus and Giroux, 1974. By far the most comprehensive Dickinson interpretive biography. Sewall devotes his first volume to Dickinson's family, his second to her friends, and intertwines her life with both circles with great tact, sympathetic understanding, and impressive learning. The prose is clear and often eloquent. One of the most admirable modern literary biographies.

_____, ed. *Emily Dickinson: A Collection of Critical Essays*. Englewood Cliffs, N.J.: Prentice-Hall, 1963. A rich and diverse collection of critical essays, displaying an almost bewildering range of interpretive views. Such important critics and scholars as Charles Anderson, R. P. Blackmur, John Crowe Ransom, Allen Tate, and George Whicher are represented.

Wolff, Cynthia Griffin. *Emily Dickinson*. New York: Alfred A. Knopf, 1986. Well-written, insightful biography stresses the interior life of the poet, especially her struggle with Trinitarian Christianity and nineteenth century notions of womanhood.

The *Paris Review* Perspective _____

Jascha Hoffman for *The Paris Review*

While Emily Dickinson was alive only a handful of her lyrics saw print, mostly anonymously and against her will. After her death, Dickinson's room in her father's house in Amherst, Massachusetts, where she lived in seclusion for most of her adult life, was found to contain piles of poems scribbled on the backs of letters, flyers, even wrapping paper. There were more than 1,750 of them in all.

For the reader who sets out to wade through these poems in sequence, there is an initial sense of lightness and speed. The early years pass quickly, as a hail of simple exercises produces the occasional gem worth copying over in longhand. But then, shortly after her thirtieth birthday, as the Civil War begins to split the United States, something cracks inside the poet. A torrent of exquisite poems comes out, a steady tide of suffering and transcendence. In a four-year span nearly a thousand poems emerge, accounting for more than half of the poet's lifetime output.

In this period Dickinson's stubbornness is impressive. One sees her repeating the same handful of motifs (gardens, oceans, sunsets, bees) and preoccupations (hunger, pain, death, divinity) in search of the perfect formulation. When she hits the mark—and she does so quite often— her strength lies in the sharpness and rightness of how her lines move, in their singsong patterns but also in their terminal and vigorous crookedness.

After this astonishing wartime run, Emily Dickinson's output reverted to a trickle for the remaining twenty years of her life. But that four-year explosion of spirit, that freak distillation of loneliness and nerve, that suspiciously charmed streak—it is not a job for a timid reader. If you try to plow through it you might hurt yourself.

Forget the poems themselves; Emily Dickinson has single lines that are meals on their own. Take the menace that resides in a simple opener like "The Sky is low – the Clouds are mean" (1121). Or the clean action of this windowsill thriller: "A Sparrow took a Slice of Twig" (1257). Or the Shakespearean richness of "A full fed Rose on meals of Tint" (1141). Each introduces a world with its own landscape, actors, laws, and logic.

It is sometimes forgotten that Emily Dickinson was also a storyteller. Edgar Allan Poe and Nathaniel Hawthorne would have trouble competing with the gothic suspense of "'Twas just this time, last year, I died" (344). One is struck by the threat inherent in warnings like "My Life had stood – a Loaded Gun –" (764) and even "I've got an arrow here" (56). Not to mention the pathos of confessions like "I am afraid to own a Body –" (1050). The dramatic range of these rhetorical effects is impressively wide.

Dickinson also knew how to tell a story about the great internal struggles: men and women aging and falling sick, lovers plunging to the edge of despair, and, most of all, mortal souls reckoning with the divine. The result is that, especially in her later years, she often managed to condense a lifetime of spiritual anxiety into a line or two. One can see this in a group of poems some might call her maxims. Take this frosty couplet, which could be read as a crystallization of the poet's craft:

> Winter under cultivation
> Is as arable as Spring
> (1720)

Or this delightfully ambiguous dictum, which seems to carry some wisdom about the merits of language and love:

> The Blood is more showy than the Breath
> But cannot dance as well –
>
> > (1558)

It would be hard to deny that Emily Dickinson was a master of the miniature. But when she exercised this gift on the cosmological scale, the effects could be truly vertiginous. Her command of proportion and perspective is apparent in the early poem "Safe in their Alabaster Chambers," in which she takes a God's-eye view of entombed souls awaiting resurrection:

> Grand go the Years,
> In the Crescent above them –
> Worlds scoop their Arcs –
> And Firmaments – row –
>
> Diadems – drop –
> And Doges – surrender –
> Soundless as Dots,
> On a Disc of Snow.
>
> > (124)

The visual effect of these stanzas is not unlike an aerial camera pulling away from a cemetery to reveal the town, the wilderness, the continent, until all human exertion narrows to a single point, then vanishes.

Above all else, Emily Dickinson was a poet of suffering, with an impressive catalog of poems dedicated exclusively to pain, its anticipation and recollection:

> There is a pain – so utter –
> It swallows substance up –
> Then covers the Abyss with Trance –
> So Memory can step

Around – across – opon it
As One within a Swoon –
Goes safely – where an open eye –
Would drop him – Bone by Bone

(515)

There are many others: "After great pain, a formal feeling comes" (372); "Pain has an element of blank" (760); "I measure every grief I meet" (550). One feels the pain most forcefully not in the words but in the dashes between them. With these the poet halts and interrupts herself, lending her lyrics the quality of a controlled seizure—or an act of self-strangulation.

These dashes allowed Dickinson to mimic the native rhythms of thought. One sees this most clearly not in the poems but in a trail of letters to siblings and trusted friends in which she abandoned the constraints of verse to speak intimately (but still obliquely) of her own private longings. Take this passage from an unsent letter to an unidentified correspondent she calls "Master":

> I am older—tonight, Master—but the love is the same—so are the moon and the crescent—If it had been God's will that I might breathe where you breathed—and find the place—myself—at night . . . I used to think that when I died—I could see you—so I died as fast as I could . . . I waited a long time—Master—but I can wait more—wait till my hazel hair is dappled—and you carry the cane. . . . Have you the little chest—to put the alive—in?

That last question stands out for its skillful simulation of innocence. Is the poet asking for a birdcage? A coffin? Some obscure medical aid? It is hard to say. We might as well assume that she is pointing us back to the poems, that city of scraps her sister found after Emily died in 1886. Each poem was a shelter for a spirit in hurt, a paper house for a suffering angel. Each poem a little chest, perhaps, to put the alive in.

Bibliography

Dickinson, Emily. *The Master Letters of Emily Dickinson*. Ed. R. W. Franklin. Amherst, MA: Amherst College Press, 1986.

_____. *The Poems of Emily Dickinson: Variorum Edition*. Ed. R. W. Franklin. 3 vols. Cambridge, MA: Harvard UP, 1998.

Linscott, Robert N. *Selected Poems and Letters of Emily Dickinson*. New York: Anchor Books, 1959.

Oates, Joyce Carol, ed. *Essential Dickinson*. New York: Ecco, 1996.

CRITICAL CONTEXTS

Emily Dickinson and Her Culture_____

Elizabeth Petrino

Countering the view of Dickinson as a recluse who was isolated from her nineteenth-century social and political world, Elizabeth Petrino, like other contemporary Dickinson scholars, argues that Dickinson was, in fact, engaged with her culture, in particular with New England religious life and the Civil War.

While Dickinson, as Petrino shows, was indebted to and shaped by her Puritan heritage, "her entire body of work might be interpreted as a rebellion against the structures and dictates of Puritanism." If from the Puritans Dickinson learned the habit of introspection, she was also formed by the romanticism of her time, with its reliance "on intuition and feeling to access spiritual knowledge," and, in particular, she was influenced by the "heady ideas of transcendentalism," which she absorbed by reading the works of Ralph Waldo Emerson. Despite being "steeped in the progressive Christian evangelicalism of her age," Dickinson shared with writers such as Emerson, Herman Melville, and Walt Whitman "a distrust of doctrine" and a "sense of alienation from her spiritual culture."

The great test of Dickinson's faith came during the Civil War, which "was not a minor disturbance but a major preoccupation" for the poet. While some critics have claimed that Dickinson's war lyrics should be read as personal meditations on her own inner struggles or as a response to the "political theology" of the era that offered religious justifications for the war, Petrino argues instead that the speakers in Dickinson's war poems "often occupy a position that resists taking a single political perspective, but rather provide an incisive critique of the era's political discourses." Dickinson, who "felt a disjunction between the accounts of the Civil War and the personal tragedy of its victims," emphasized in her poetry the difficulty not only of representing the trauma of war but also of "inhabiting another person's experience of the war." While Dickinson, if removed from her social and political context, can appear as "a rare and original poet who dropped almost fully formed into the literary tradition," once we situate her writings in her culture and time and in the print context of her age, according to Petrino, "her poems take on new resonances as we discover their connections to important issues of her day."   J.B.B.

A retiring aunt who sent loving notes and insects to her nephew, Gilbert, and her cousins; a shadowy figure listening to the music played in her parlor from the shelter of her bedroom; a shy person who when ill asked that she be diagnosed by a physician while walking through an open doorway—Emily Dickinson has earned a reputation as a reclusive poet disconnected from the social and political worlds of her lifetime. Her cryptic lines and self-imposed isolation have fascinated generations of readers, who often assume that Dickinson's search for meaning was purely internal. Since the publication of her first volume of poems, edited by Colonel Thomas Wentworth Higginson and Mabel Loomis Todd, in 1898, a steady stream of interest in the poet's mysterious life has accompanied her critical elevation. Perhaps it is not surprising that she sparked readers' interest, especially in the 1920's, when the Metaphysical poets, such as John Donne and George Herbert, were coming into vogue as her wit, dense metaphors, and ambiguous phrasing resonated with readers of the period. However, it was not until Thomas Johnson and Theodora Ward published her complete poems in 1955, and three years later published her extant letters, that we could assess fully Dickinson's genius. From the beginning, however, her poetry presented special challenges to the modern editor: as thoroughly as Johnson had preserved the poems for generations of future readers, he regularized Dickinson's stanzas, corrected some archaisms and misspellings, and disregarded many fragmentary lines that appeared to be poems embedded in letters. Partly in response to these concerns and new scholarship discussing Dickinson's "scribal publishing," R. W. Franklin published a new reading edition (1999) and a variorum edition (1998) of her poems; the reading edition makes her poems readily accessible in a format closer to their original intention, while the variorum edition adheres to the manuscripts' phrasing and spelling. These editions have made Dickinson's poems more accessible to the public, but they have not resolved larger questions about the poet's relation to her culture: Why has Emily Dickinson remained such a mysterious figure to generations of readers? Furthermore, what were her views on many of the important cultural and social questions of her day? Her reclusive nature and lack of any external life have led some to conclude that she had little interest in the world outside her home, but recent critics have argued that she was engaged with many of the major theological, political, and social debates of her time. By historicizing and contextualizing her poems and letters within their print culture, we can gain a clearer view of her response to her culture, particularly New England religious life and the Civil War.

New England Spiritual Life

Born in 1830 in Amherst, Massachusetts, Dickinson emerged from the Calvinist tradition and was connected to many of her transcendentalist and romantic contemporaries. Her family heritage included a Puritan forebear, Nathaniel Dickinson, who traveled to America in the Great Migration of 1630, which was led by John Winthrop (Sewall 17). In the six generations before the poet's birth, there is no record of qualities that would suggest a poet's mind. Her forefathers were men of affairs, farmers, and laymen who took an active interest in their church and civic life. Her mother, Emily Norcross Dickinson, also came from a family of farmers (Sewall 76). It is not until her grandfather, Samuel Fowler Dickinson, a lawyer and treasurer of Amherst College, that we see evidence of an investment in higher education and an intellectual life that might prepare us for Dickinson's talent.

As Jane Donahue Eberwein notes, Dickinson was born into the Calvinist Christianity of her era: in 1830, the four Amherst churches traced their origins to the Puritan settlers (68). But though the poet's Puritan background shaped her approach to the world, the social conditions of her generation and her family's status in the Amherst social hierarchy gave her the leeway to question Puritanism's tenets freely. In fact, her entire body of work might be interpreted as a rebellion against the structures and dictates of Puritanism. Writing to Mrs. Joseph Haven in 1859, Dickinson claimed, "I do not respect 'doctrines,'" in particular the Puritan belief in innate depravity and predestination (JL 200). Instead, her Puritan heritage is filtered through a lens of romantic sensibility: much as her father and his generation were concerned with the state of affairs of this world, a preoccupation with acting in accordance with God's will as it is given in the writings of John Cotton and other Puritan divines, Dickinson turned her mind to other interests, ruefully commenting in an 1851 letter to her brother, Austin, who was then away at law school, that "we do not have much poetry, father having made up his mind that its pretty much all real life" (JL 65). Thomas Wentworth Higginson reports in a letter to his wife that Dickinson once said to him, "I find ecstasy in living—the mere sense of living is joy enough" (JL 342a), but her exhilaration was tempered by the realization that the outward events of her life were "too simple and stern to embarrass any" (JL 330).

More important than her choice to live a sheltered life—a choice made not out of theological conviction but for her own comfort—is Dickinson's tendency to observe the world critically, inductively, tentatively. Rather than interpret external events typologically against Old Testament prophecy, as did the Puritans, Dickinson examines the evidence of her senses, as did the romantics and transcendentalists: she emphasizes the process by which we know the world, as implied by the frequent use of verbs such as "suggest," "infer," "believe," and "trust" in her poems. While the Puritan divines frequently mediate between abstraction and sensation, according to Allen Tate, Dickinson's work tests ideals against experience and real life (qtd. in Sewall 22). Furthermore, Dickinson adapted various strands of Puritan thought to her own purposes. Puritanism elevates the renunciation of worldly things as a way to glorify God and save one's soul and encourages its believers to keep careful watch over their spiritual lives through vigilant introspection, and although she did not share Puritanism's theological conviction, Dickinson did absorb its inquisitive habit of mind with respect to her inner life. Rather than keep a diary, like early generations of Puritans, such as Samuel Sewall, or write a narrative spiritual autobiography, as did Jonathan Edwards, Dickinson recorded her moments of spiritual crisis and encounters with the world in her poems. Their frequent shifts in mood, tone, voice, and belief reflect a sensibility common among the Puritans: as Perry Miller notes, the Puritan "lives inwardly a life of incessant fluctuation, ecstatically elated this day, depressed into despair the next" (Miller 221-22; qtd. in Sewall 23). An almanac of moods, her poems and letters register the often extraordinary shifts in emotion and belief that align her with her Puritan ancestors.

Although Dickinson was indebted to her Puritan heritage, her outlook was also shaped by the religious revivals of her era, which were in part shaped by romanticism and sentimentalism and relied on intuition and feeling to access spiritual knowledge. The Calvinist notions of total depravity and predestination, as well as the requisite conversion experience, may have seemed harsh to Dickinson, especially in light of the attitudes the theological movements of her time held toward emotion.

From 1790 to 1840, the Second Great Awakening was one of several successive waves of religious revivalism that spread throughout New England and other parts of the United States. Named for the Great Awakening that had transpired a half century earlier (1730-1755), this movement generated evangelical fervor and spiritual renewal through camp meetings and spurred antebellum America toward such social changes as prison reform, temperance, and the abolition of slavery. Forty years before, the first Great Awakening had divided churches in most Protestant denominations into Old and New Light Christians. Old

Light Christians were liberal and focused on morality rather than on conversion; New Light Christians, in contrast, contended that "sinners could be saved only from the new light of grace by which the Holy Spirit guided those saved by Jesus" (Eberwein 82). New Light Christians insisted on conversion and favored revivals, but they also "gradually modified stern Calvinistic doctrine to accommodate nineteenth-century romantic sensibilities and emerging scientific perspectives" (Eberwein 82). As Barton Levi St. Armand explains, sentimentalism reconfigured Calvinism's process of attaining salvation by substituting "incremental goodness (gradualism) for instantaneous perfection (Pauline crisis conversion)" (89).

During Dickinson's lifetime, this heightened reliance on feeling and intuition evolved into Christian gradualism: the belief that right feeling attained incrementally over a period of years can ensure salvation. A corollary of this belief is that heavenly salvation is part of earthly life. Although some persisted in reading the world typologically for signs of things to come, Dickinson often interpreted spiritual states in terms of the natural world, as can be seen in "'Heaven' has different Signs – to me –" (F 544) when she writes "Sometimes, I think that Noon / Is but a symbol of the Place –." Nature may be only the "symbol" of the heaven that scripture concedes, but there is equal evidence of revelation on earth: the speaker only tentatively approves of reading nature for celestial "Signs," since the religious connotations of the birds' "Victory" and the closing day seem closer to her definition of heaven. The ambiguity of the last line—"Not yet, our eyes can see –"—might hint at her uncertainty about the promise of revelation: not only has the "Superior Grace" not arrived, but, if it were to come, we may not be able to recognize it.

After attending Amherst Academy for her early education, Dickinson was enrolled in Mount Holyoke Female Seminary in South Hadley for a two-term period in September 1847 until July 1848 (Sewall 357-58). During her one year at Mount Holyoke, Dickinson was exposed to progressive evangelical Christianity, and although she was attracted by the idea of professing Christ as her savior, she hardly felt moved to convert. The previous year, she had written a letter to Abiah Root, a childhood friend, in which she recalled a revival meeting "thronged by people old and young" and wondered that "those who sneered loudest at serious things were soonest brought to see their power, and to make Christ their portion" (JL 10), but she also comments that she chose not to attend any meetings during the preceding winter. Under the direction of Mary Lyon, Mount Holyoke sought to prepare young women to do missionary work and to ensure their own salvation by encouraging their Christian conversion. Keenly aware that her spiritual life and future salvation hung in the balance, Dickinson lamented in another letter to Root, "Abbiah, you may be surprised to hear me speak as I do, knowing that I express no interest in the all-important subject, but I am not happy, and I regret that last term, when that golden opportunity was mine, that I did not give up and become a Christian." Of a mutual friend considering converting, who "says she only desires to be good," Dickinson remarked, "How I wish I could say that with sincerity, but I fear I never can" (JL 23). One anecdote of Dickinson's year at Mount Holyoke has Lyon requesting that all students desiring to be Christians should rise, and Dickinson alone remaining seated (Clara Newman Turner, "My Personal Acquaintance with Emily Dickinson," qtd. in Sewall 360 n.17).

St. Armand reasons that her choice not to convert demonstrates Dickinson's connection to the transcendentalists, since "she decided, like Emerson, to be a true child of the Devil rather than a false daughter of Christ" (88). Although it is unclear exactly why she chose not to convert, Eberwein suggests another possibility: that Dickinson recognized that the tranquillity and sweet nature she believed was accentuated among young female converts would lead to a submissive life and marriage within the patriarchal home (77).

Not only did the new religious movements stress emotion and the need for a conversion experience, but scientific research was at the same time undermining doctrinal beliefs and challenging received beliefs about the Bible's authority. Dickinson's studies at Mount Holyoke brought her into contact with scientific thought that questioned received biblical doctrine, for instance Charles Lyell's *Principles of Geology* (1830-1833), which posited that the planet is millions of years old rather than the six thousand suggested by a literal reading of the Old Testament. By Dickinson's time, most believers, except Fundamentalists, had come to accept the biblical story of the world's creation as only metaphorically true.

Dickinson was also familiar with the work of scientists and educators who found a connection between the human and the spiritual by arguing that nature provides evidence of a divine creator. Edward Hitchcock, who served as president of Amherst College (1845-1854) and taught chemistry and botany there, was, in his *Elementary Geology* (1840) and *A Catalogue of Plants Growing Without Cultivation in the Vicinity of Amherst College* (1829), "a pervasive advocate for the compatibility of science with religion; to know God through His works was the thesis woven throughout his teachings and writings" (Lowenberg 57). Hitchcock's presence and formidable reputation in Amherst influenced the young Dickinson, who spoke warmly of his work years later: "When Flowers annually died and I was a child, I used to read Dr Hitchcock's Book on the Flowers of North America. This comforted their Absence—assuring me they lived" (JL 573). The illustration for Hitchcock's chapter "The Resurrections of Spring," from *Religious Lectures on Peculiar Phenomena in the Four Seasons* (1850), drawn by his wife, Orra White Hitchcock, seems aptly to summarize his melding of Christian revelation and nature worship. It depicts a sylvan scene swelling with new life as frogs and tadpoles swim in a pond, a bird stands close to its nest, and a butterfly flits near its cocoon. These images of resurrection might have appealed to Dickinson and underscored her tendency to find solace in nature, even while her scientific studies as a youth were further leading her away from Christian doctrine and toward developing a poet's critical, discerning eye.

Dickinson also absorbed the heady ideas of transcendentalism and romanticism through reading her contemporaries' works. She referred to Henry David Thoreau twice in her letters, and she probably discussed his *Cape Cod* with Susan Gilbert Dickinson, her sister-in-law. She refers to the book in an 1866 letter to Sue, when Sue and Austin were probably vacationing at the seashore: "Was the Sea cordial? Kiss him for Thoreau—" (JL 320). In 1881, after a devastating fire in Amherst, Dickinson wrote to her cousins, Louise and Frances Norcross, about the continual alarms: "The fire-bells are oftener now, almost, than the church-bells. Thoreau would wonder which did the most harm" (JL 691). Perhaps Dickinson had in mind Thoreau's frequent comments in *Walden* about spiritual doctrine that has outlived its usefulness. About Walt Whitman, Dickinson had less to say, although she responds to Higginson's question about reading his work in her second letter to him: "You speak of Mr Whitman—I never read his Book—but was told that he was disgraceful" (JL 261). Her mock fear suggests that she recognizes—and perhaps puns on—his lack of sanctified "grace" and notes his departure from traditional forms of religion in favor of a more transcendent spirituality.

Among her contemporaries, Ralph Waldo Emerson held an important place in Dickinson's constellation of literary influences. The works of Emerson in her family's library included his *Essays: First Series* (1841), *Essays: Second Series* (1844), and *Representative Men* (1850), which she called "a little Granite Book you can lean on" (JL 481); as Jack L. Capps notes, she also read his *Poems,* which she received as a gift from her friend Ben Newton when she was only nineteen (113). In it, she marked with light, parallel lines passages from "The Sphinx," "Each and All," "The Problem," "To Rhea," "The Visit," "The Rhodora," and "Woodnotes I" (Capps 114). These poems may have appealed to her because she felt an affinity for the immersion into nature and the heretical religious stance Emerson displays in them, and her lyrics often reveal that she was inspired by his writings to accept the view that, as expressed in "Nature," "the power to produce this delight does not reside in nature, but in man, or in a harmony of both"

(Emerson 24). Similarly, she locates the meaning of perception not in the object but in the subject's experience, as can be seen in "To hear an Oriole sing" (Fr 402) in the lines "The Fashion of the Ear / Attireth that it hear" (7-8). For Emerson, nature does not embody an objective reality but rather responds to our mood and reflects our perceptions, as he further explains in "Nature": "Nature always wears the colors of the spirit. To a man laboring under calamity, the heat of his own fire hath sadness in it" (29). Similarly, Emerson's view that worship takes place properly in nature and his refutation of doctrine support Dickinson's own views in "Some keep the Sabbath going to Church" (Fr 236), in which she replaces the chorister with a bobolink, a North American bird with a ringed collar and white rump and scapular, and the domed and buttressed cathedral with an orchard. The understated "just" of "Some keep the Sabbath in Surpice – / I just wear my Wings" (5-6) implies not only that Dickinson rejects conventional Christianity but also that she imagines that she has attained salvation on earth without rites. Rather than worship in a church through the mediation of a minister, the speaker has direct access to divinity and finds herself in communion with God throughout her life—she is going to heaven "all along" (12). Although steeped in the progressive Christian evangelicalism of her age, Dickinson shared with the transcendentalists a distrust of doctrine and a similar sense of alienation from her spiritual culture. Ultimately, she found a profound testing ground for those spiritual beliefs in the most cataclysmic event of her time—the Civil War.

Civil War and Print Culture

For Dickinson and her contemporaries, the Civil War underscored the theological and political rifts that had been developing in antebellum America for some time. While several generations of critics have read Dickinson's war lyrics as either personal reflections on her own inner turmoil (as epitomized by what George Frederickson calls "the inner Civil War") or a response to the popular political ideologies that provided theological justification for the war—an early book by Shira Wolosky recounts the poet's introjection of the era's "political theology" into her poems—recent scholars have contended that Dickinson's response to the war is embedded in the antebellum print context of journalism and other poetry about the war.

For those who remained at home during the war, newspapers and magazines defined the war experience, and poets often imbibed the imagery arising from their reports. Arguing that poetry, along with reports on the conflict published in Union newspapers, served to "bind together communities of readers and forge relations between civilians and combatants," critic Eliza Richards claims that "the general consistency of the poetry's ideological message indicates that literate Northerners achieved something resembling a literary consensus, and that poetry served a crucial role in negotiating the crisis of representation, both political and poetic, instigated by the war" ("News" 158). This dynamic can be seen in the genteel Northern magazines of the time, such as *The Atlantic Monthly* and *Harper's Magazine*, which Dickinson read intently. Aside from reports of the war, they contained poems that were meant to "generate popular support for the Union" (Richards, "News" 158). In fact, in the February 1862 issue of *The Atlantic*, Julia Ward Howe's "Battle Hymn of the Republic" appeared prominently on the first page directly below the masthead, signaling the magazine's endorsement of the North's political views. Further, new technologies, such as the telegraph, increased the speed at which reporters' accounts could appear in print and made firsthand accounts of battles more immediate and realistic (Richards, "Correspondent" 147). This immediacy was heightened by the woodcut illustrations of Mathew Brady and Alexander Gardner's famous photographs of the Civil War dead, which were reproduced in *Harper's Illustrated Weekly* and gave readers visual analogues to accompany battlefield reports and lists of the dead.

Partly in response to their own political convictions, some poets had a crisis of conscience about poetry's function during the war. As Richards notes:

A number of poets questioned the role of poetry in wartime. Foregrounding the difference between bloody conflict and its verbal representations, the war raised questions about how properly to write about the experiences of soldiers. This gap was already problematic in journalistic accounts; poets had the complex task of discovering or creating the purpose of art in wartime. ("News" 158-59)

The problem was further complicated by the technological advances, which raised concerns regarding how poets would mediate between direct and indirect forms of experience. In *Battle-Pieces and Aspects of War,* for example, Herman Melville draws on actual newspaper accounts in his long poem "Donelson. (February, 1862)," which purports to compile a series of headlines, reports, and scenes of people reading and hearing news about battles.

A number of Dickinson's poems and letters suggest that for her the Civil War was not a minor disturbance but a major preoccupation. Most intriguingly, her speakers often occupy a position that resists taking a single political perspective, but rather provide an incisive critique of the era's political discourses, and several of the period's technological advances, both in how the war was fought and how it was reported, provide metaphors through which Dickinson questioned the ultimate reasoning by which the war was justified in the North and South.

Although critics have long acknowledged that her military imagery is often suffused in natural landscapes (sunsets, sunrise, crucifixion, wounding, and so on), Dickinson read about political events that might well have instigated her interest in slavery and the Civil War as poetic subjects, and the publication of several of her poems in pro-Union newspapers have led scholars to examine her political views. The 1791 slave uprising in Santo Domingo, for example, which was chronicled in the newspapers at the time of its occurrence, occupied the popular press in Dickinson's time immensely. As Ed Folsom and Kenneth M. Price argue, the words "Santo Domingo," much like the words "Nicaragua" and "Vietnam" today, carried in the mid-nineteenth century a distinct connotation: they reminded readers in the years preceding the Civil War of the bloody slave revolt that might be a harbinger of future dealings with former slaves in America (para. 3). Intriguingly, Dickinson's lyric "Flowers – well, if anybody" (Fr 95), written in 1859, appeared first in the pro-Union newspaper the *Brooklyn Drum Beat* and was reprinted in the *Springfield Republican*, suggesting that Dickinson may have supported the Union cause. Here, she writes that "Butterflies in San Domingo" "Have a system of aesthetics / Far superior to mine!" (13-14). Similarly, in 1863, the poet writes in "I could bring you Jewels" (Fr 726) that she prefers the "little Blaze / Flickering to itself – in the meadow –" to the "Odors from St Domingo" (6-7, 3). Far from showing disinterest in current events, Dickinson appears to have been an avid reader of print accounts of the war.

Like Melville, however, she seems to have felt a disjunction between the accounts of the Civil War and the personal tragedy of its victims, which she mined in her poems and letters. Dickinson's personal, historical connection to the Civil War came through her concern for her friends and family members involved in the war and the war effort. Her father took a leading role in a number of public events supporting the Union: he addressed the faculty and students of Amherst College at a flag raising in April 1861; at a town meeting in early May, he moved to allow selectmen to borrow five thousand dollars to purchase uniforms and care for poor soldiers; and in September, he presided over a ceremony for departing soldiers (Leyda 2: 26, 27, 33). Despite his prominent role in supporting the troops, the family experienced the tragedy of war vicariously. Dickinson's brother, Austin, was subject to the enlistment of soldiers announced by President Abraham Lincoln in 1861, but he paid five hundred dollars for a substitute to take his place (Sewall 536). Although his decision might have prompted a crisis of conscience for the poet, she does not comment on it, even as she shows concern for others who were absent at war. Significantly, newspapers, such as the *Springfield Republican*, which was edited by Dickinson's friend Samuel Bowles, provided her with reports of the battles, including news of those locals who had entered the fray.

In June, 1864, she wrote to Higginson, an active abolitionist and supporter of women's rights who was then the colonel in charge of the first black Civil War regiment:

> I wish to see you more than before I failed – Will you tell me your health?
> I am surprised and anxious, since receiving your note –
>> The only News I know
>> Is Bulletins all day
>> From Immortality.
> Can you render my Pencil?
> The Physician has taken away my Pen.
> I enclose the address from a letter, lest my figures fail – Knowledge of your recovery – would excel my own –
>
> E – Dickinson (JL 290)

Dickinson was in Cambridge, Massachusetts, at the time, receiving treatment for an eye problem, during which time her physician had restricted her reading and writing. Rather than shut herself off from others, however, Dickinson reached out to Higginson. Having read that he was discharged due to an injury, Dickinson asks about his health and offers news of her own. Her comment that she receives "Bulletins all day / From Immortality" might suggest several possibilities. First, she might be complaining that her eye problems prevent her from reading about the war. In fact, since she encloses her address from another letter for Higginson, we might surmise that she feared that her poor eyesight had made her writing illegible. Second, the phrase might evoke the continual reports in newspapers and magazines regarding the myriad fallen soldiers on both Northern and Southern sides (Richards, "News" 165). A third possibility might be that Dickinson accentuates the difficulty of "knowing" the experience of war through the short, journalistic accounts based on information just received before the issue went to press upon which she and others relied. In any case, rather than stress her removal from the war's events, her letter to Higginson underscores her interest in the war's progress and, simultaneously, emphasizes the difficulty of relying on journalism to understand the true experience of another.

Dickinson's historical and personal connection with the Civil War also came through her mourning of Frazar Stearns, a young man of Amherst whose death prompted both Dickinson and her brother, Austin, to meditate on the senselessness of the deaths the war caused. In a letter to her cousins, Frances and Louise Norcross, on New Year's Eve, 1861, she recounts her apprehension for the young enlisted men from Amherst:

> Frazer Stearns is just leaving Annapolis. His father has gone to see him to-day. I hope that ruddy face won't be brought home frozen. Poor little widow's boy, riding to-night in the mad wind, back to the village burying-ground where he never dreamed of sleeping! Ah! the dreamless sleep! (JL 245)

Presciently, Dickinson anticipates Stearns's death on March 14, 1862, in the Battle of Newbern, North Carolina. Not only did Stearns become a central figure for the town's mourning, but he also epitomized for Dickinson the senselessness of war's tragedy. Again writing to her Norcross cousins about Stearns's life and his funeral, she offers them news probably drawn from contemporary newspaper accounts as well as a list of the dead that appeared in the *Springfield Republican* on April 15, 1862: "You have done more for me—'tis least that I can do, to tell you of brave Frazer—'killed at Newbern,' darlings. His big heart shot away by a 'minie ball'" (JL 255). As Faith Barrett explains, Dickinson self-consciously refers to a specific type of bullet, an 1848 invention of Claude Etien Minié that was developed by American weapon manufacturers during the war and that she had also read about in the

Springfield Republican (110). Contrasting Stearns's large-hearted heroism with the small shot that fatally wounded him, she underscores the disjunction between the personal tragedy of the fallen soldiers and the glorified accounts of their deaths. In another letter to Samuel Bowles, she writes:

> Austin is chilled – by Frazer's murder – He says – his Brain keeps saying over "Frazer is killed" – "Frazer is killed," just as Father told it – to Him. Two or three words of lead – that dropped so deep, they keep weighing –
>   Tell Austin – how to get over them! (JL 256)

Although Stearns's death might have particularly resonated with Dickinson because of an unidentified personal loss of her own, the "three words of lead" imply that Stearns's death was mourned by the entire family, much as if they had been wounded themselves (Barrett 110).

In a poem written around this time, "It don't sound so terrible – quite – as it did –" (Fr 384), the speaker describes the shock of loss as she attempts to deal with the psychological trauma by continually "[running] it over – 'Dead', Brain, 'Dead'" (2). These opening lines echo Austin's response to Stearns's death. As Barrett posits, the poem explores the cycle of mourning and repetition's role in encouraging acceptance of loss (111). The phrase "I run it over" implies "the repetitive gestures of ironing or of classroom memorization, an association that is underlined by the first stanza's reference to Latin and 'school.' These lines suggest that powerful emotion can be disciplined—brought 'under rule'—through a numbing repetition that resembles rote pedagogy" (111). In fact, the line "I run it over" also implies railway and carriage accidents (112)—meaningless tragedies that occur every day and were reported in the newspapers Dickinson read—as well as to the finality of a life that is "over." Considering its association with schoolroom learning, the phrase "under rule" might also echo Dickinson's desire to cope with tragedy through writing: because schoolchildren learn to control their handwriting by writing between the lines of lined tablets, this phrase implies that the speaker is similarly trying to keep her emotions from spinning out of control and to overcome her grief by writing her verses. Putting the word "dead" in Latin, as if the act of translation were a trick to disassociate the mind from tragedy, similarly implies that the speaker wishes to distance herself from death. Although she describes literally shifting her angle of vision to gain a different perspective on the tragedy, she acknowledges that thoughts of death will "interrupt" her until she becomes "accustomed" to them. Yet the promise of consolation ultimately seems to evade her: although she may "Put the thought in advance – a Year –" (15), his death still seems like murder. As Barrett argues, the word "Murder" "serves to reframe collective narratives of wartime loss in order to emphasize the individual specificity of the life that has been lost and the individual specificity of the grief felt by the mourners" (112). Placing the poem in the context of theological arguments about the war's necessity makes it apparent that Dickinson feels that the death of the individual in wartime is not sufficiently justified.

Several poems indicate that Dickinson maintained a perspective that may have applied the external events of the war to her inner life, but a more complex and nuanced reading of her poetry suggests that she responded to other issues and current events in a way that emphasizes the difficulty of inhabiting another person's experience of the war. If we consider a final poem, "To fight aloud is very brave –" (Fr 138), we can see that Dickinson might have intervened in discussions about the war, but her perspective complicates rather than simplifies the narratives the North and the South used to justify the war. Probably written in early 1860, this poem underscores Dickinson's awareness of the war effort, but it also emphasizes the difficulty in representing the battle in any meaningful way. The poem seems to argue that the external events of the war are superseded by an inner struggle, but the ambiguous phrasing makes the reason for the battle—as well as who is fighting and who is winning—unclear. Although the speaker elevates the person who might "charge within the bosom / The Cavalry of Wo –"

(3-4), whether the speaker is on the side of the North or South is unclear, since we do not know if those people who "charge" are part of the opposition against the "Cavalry of Wo" or if they join its ranks. Similarly, their sacrifice goes unrecorded, since its events take place internally, where "nations do not see" and "none observe" their ultimate sacrifice with "patriot love" (5, 6, 8). More obviously, Dickinson also does not predict who will win and who will lose the war—unlike those poets publishing in *The Atlantic Monthly* and *Harper's Magazine*, who had early on used theological or moral reasoning to reach a consensus regarding the war's outcome. Rather, Dickinson only tentatively holds out hope that they receive some commendation, as she notes using the collective that "We trust, in plumed procession / For such, the Angels go –" (12-13). Melding the rituals of a nineteenth-century funeral, in which plumes and tassels would often adorn the hearse, with the idea of a heavenly procession, she images a final scene in which the soldiers are deified as they ascend in honor of their sacrifice. Placed in the print context in which she read about the dying soldiers, the phrase "Rank after Rank, with even feet –" (13) also evokes the lines of poetry and the regular meter of the poem, and the "Uniforms of Snow" (14) might signify the blank page onto which Dickinson inscribes her lyrics. Although the poem might be read as a tribute to an unknown soldier, it raises questions about how a solidier's ultimate loss was memorialized publicly and refrains from siding with one political view or another.

Removed from her antebellum print context, uprooted from the theological and political concerns of her era, Dickinson appears to be a rare and original poet who dropped almost fully formed into the literary tradition. Once we situate her writing in its culture and time, however, we can trace her responses to many pressing issues—slavery, race, class, the Civil War, theological debates, science, and her female poet peers. Furthermore, as Ellen Louise Hart and Martha Nell Smith have shown, her sustained correspondence with her sister-in-law, Susan Gilbert, amounted to a "poet's workshop" that allowed her the opportunity to exchange her poems with a sympathetic reader (esp. xi-

xix). Her mystique as a solitary writer developed in part because of her desire for complete intellectual independence and her refusal to cast her verse in terms acceptable to her time's publication standards. "Two Editors of Journals came to my Father's House, this winter—and asked me for my Mind—and when I asked them 'Why,' they said I was penurious—and they, would use it for the World," Dickinson wrote to Higginson in 1862 in her second letter to him (JL 261). In characteristic fashion, she elevates the intellectual qualities of her verses and disparages the terms and conditions to which they would be forced to submit were they to enter into the literary marketplace. Equating her lyrics with nothing less than her "Mind," she shrewdly observes that the journal editors accuse her of stingily holding on to them when their own supposedly charitable intentions would actually net them a tidy profit. "Publication – is the Auction / Of the Mind of Man –," Dickinson writes in another poem, conceding only that "poverty" might make such an act defensible (Fr 788). Rather than submit her poems, she refused. Nevertheless, her decision not to print should not be taken as a personal withdrawal from life or viewed as an abdication of interest in her world. Placed in their antebellum print context, her poems take on new resonances as we discover their connections to important issues of her day.

Works Cited

Barrett, Faith. "'Drums Off the Phantom Battlements': Dickinson's War Poems in Discursive Context." *A Companion to Emily Dickinson*. Ed. Martha Nell Smith and Mary Loeffelholz. Malden, MA: Blackwell, 2008. 107-32.

Capps, Jack L. *Emily Dickinson's Reading, 1836-1886.* Cambridge, MA: Harvard UP, 1966.

Dickinson, Emily. *The Letters of Emily Dickinson.* Ed. Thomas H. Johnson and Theodora Ward. 3 vols. Cambridge, MA: Harvard UP, 1958.

_____. *The Poems of Emily Dickinson: Variorum Edition.* Ed. R. W. Franklin. 3 vols. Cambridge, MA: Belknap Press of Harvard UP, 1998.

Eberwein, Jane Donahue. "'Is Immortality True?': Salvaging Faith in an Age of Upheavals." *A Historical Guide to Emily Dickinson*. Ed. Vivian R. Pollak. New York: Oxford UP, 2004. 67-102.

Emerson, Ralph Waldo. *Selections from Ralph Waldo Emerson: An Organic Anthology*. Ed. Stephen Whicher. Boston: Houghton Mifflin, 1957.

Folsom, Ed, and Kenneth M. Price. "Dickinson, Slavery, and the San Domingo Moment." *The Classroom Electric*. 13 Oct. 2009. http://www.unl.edu/Price/Dickinson/index.html.

Frederickson, George. *The Inner Civil War: Northern Intellectuals and the Crisis of the Union*. New York: Harper & Row, 1965.

Hart, Ellen Louise, and Martha Nell Smith, eds. *Open Me Carefully: Emily Dickinson's Intimate Letters to Susan Huntington Dickinson*. Ashfield, MA: Paris Press, 1998.

Leyda, Jay. *The Years and Hours of Emily Dickinson*. 2 vols. New Haven, CT: Yale UP, 1960.

Lowenberg, Carlton. *Emily Dickinson's Textbooks*. Ed. Territa A. Lowenberg and Carla L. Brown. Berkeley, CA: West Coast Print Center, 1986.

Miller, Perry. *The American Puritans: Their Prose and Poetry*. New York: Doubleday, 1956.

Richards, Eliza. "Correspondent Lines: Poetry, Journalism, and the U.S. Civil War." *ESQ: A Journal of the American Renaissance* 54 (2008): 145-70.

_____. "'How News Feels When Travelling': Dickinson and Civil War Poetry." *A Companion to Emily Dickinson*. Ed. Martha Nell Smith and Mary Loeffelholz. Malden, MA: Blackwell, 2008. 157-79.

St. Armand, Barton Levi. *Emily Dickinson and Her Culture: The Soul's Society*. New York: Cambridge UP, 1984.

Sewall, Richard B. *The Life of Emily Dickinson*. New York: Farrar, Straus and Giroux, 1974.

Tate, Allen. "Emily Dickinson." 1932. *Emily Dickinson: A Collection of Critical Essays*. Ed. Richard B. Sewall. Englewood Cliffs, NJ: Prentice-Hall, 1963.

Wolosky, Shira. *Emily Dickinson: A Voice of War*. New Haven, CT: Yale UP, 1984.

Major Trends in Dickinson Criticism_____

Fred D. White

Providing a trustworthy and ample guide to the 120-year critical legacy surrounding the works of Emily Dickinson, Fred D. White locates a general movement from the "impressionistic and speculative toward the . . . objective and analytic" in critical discussions of Dickinson. Just as early commentators on Dickinson, beginning in the 1890s, sought to connect aspects of the poet's verse with her personal life—"an impulse that persists to this day"—so biographical studies of Dickinson were dominant during the 1920s and 1930s. But beginning in the 1960s, as scholars turned to the critical analysis of Dickinson's work, a new emphasis on the study of Dickinson's artistic development arose, as did assessments of her poetic genius by critics such as Albert Gelpi and David Porter, and around this time topical studies began to appear.

If, during the first half of the twentieth century, scholars had to depend on editions of Dickinson's poetry that heavily edited and "regularized" the "irregularities" of her verse, the publication in 1955 of Thomas Johnson's three-volume variorum edition of Dickinson's poetry "ushered in a new era of Dickinson scholarship" by including the word and phrase variants found in Dickinson's worksheet drafts and by reproducing the irregular grammar and unusual capitalization and punctuation found in her poetry. In the decades since the publication of Johnson's edition, scholars such as Brita Lindberg-Seyersted, Cristanne Miller, and Paul Crumbley have examined the stylistic features of Dickinson's work, with its unusual diction and compressed syntactic structures, its experimental uses of rhyme and meter, and its unconventional punctuation and frequent use of the dash.

Viewed by many scholars as a "major turning point" in Dickinson studies, the publication in 1981 of R. W. Franklin's two-volume holographic reconstruction of Dickinson's poetry, *The Manuscript Books of Emily Dickinson*, led to a wealth of new studies on the sequencing of Dickinson's fascicle poems by scholars such as Sharon Cameron, Dorothy Huff Oberhaus, and Eleanor Elson Heginbotham. Another important trend in Dickinson scholarship is the feminist reassessment of the poet's work by critics such as Suzanne Juhasz, Paula Bennett, and Mary Loeffelholz. In recent years, critics also have increasingly placed Dickinson in her cultural context, arguing that, despite her reclusive behavior, she was deeply engaged in her culture, and scholars have continued to investigate the influence of religion on Dickinson and her poetry. And in yet another recent approach to Dickinson, postmodern critics, such as Marietta Messmer, have called attention to the transgression of genre boundaries in Dickinson's intertwined letters and poems.

Dividing the approaches to Dickinson into three general categories—works-centered, life-centered, and culture-centered—White concludes with a word of caution. "Like filters on a camera," writes White, "literary-critical lenses simultaneously highlight some things and obscure others; no critical approach can embrace everything, nor should it." As White also affirms, however, the existence of such a vast array of approaches to Dickinson offers "testimony to the greatness of Emily Dickinson's transcendent genius."   J.B.B.

As with any major author, the critical legacy of Emily Dickinson is vast and varied. The aim of this survey is to identify the major stages in the 120-year span of critical literature on Dickinson as they move from the impressionistic and speculative toward the more objective and analytic and to highlight the most important contributions associated with each stage. Before beginning the survey, however, it is worth taking into account how the history of the publication of Dickinson's work has affected critics' assessments of her work.

Other than the few poems that were published in her lifetime, Dickinson's work did not reach the public until her first editors, Mabel Loomis Todd and Thomas Wentworth Higginson,[1] collected her poems into three posthumous volumes, which were published in 1890,

1891, and 1896 and titled simply *Poems*. Martha Dickinson Bianchi then published additional volumes of her aunt's poems, beginning with *The Single Hound* in 1914. *Bolts of Melody: New Poems of Emily Dickinson*, edited by Mabel Loomis Todd and her daughter, Millicent Todd Bingham, appeared in 1945.

For the first half of the twentieth century, literary critics had to rely on these incomplete collections, whose editors had substantially altered the original poems, regularizing Dickinson's unorthodox diction, meter, punctuation, and capitalization to make them conform to the expectations of their era's readers. From a marketing perspective these alterations made perfect sense—indeed, the earliest volumes sold extremely well and were reprinted several times apiece—but they prevented scholars from studying the poems as Dickinson wrote them. It was not until 1955, nearly seventy years after the poet's death, that Thomas H. Johnson produced his three-volume variorum edition of all 1,775 poems, which includes the numerous word and phrase variants that commonly appear on Dickinson's so-called worksheet drafts, the pencil-draft manuscripts of poems after 1864 that Dickinson did not transcribe into "fair copies" (always in ink) and bind into fascicles (sewn manuscript gatherings). Twenty-six years later, R. W. Franklin, who had spent decades examining Dickinson's manuscripts, published *The Manuscript Books of Emily Dickinson*, a two-volume holographic reconstruction of the poet's fascicles and unbound "sets," thus returning these poems to their original sequences within Dickinson's original groupings.

Aside from the publication of Johnson's and Franklin's editions, the publication of three other reference tools have had a large impact on Dickinson scholarship. In 1958, shortly after the publication of Johnson's variorum, Dickinson's complete letters were published under the editorship of Johnson and Theodora Ward. Two years later, Jay Leyda's *The Years and Hours of Emily Dickinson* (1960) offered scholars a detailed chronological compilation of the known events of Dickinson's life and has since enabled them to read Dickinson in the context of her immediate historical, sociopolitical, familial, and intellectual milieu. Two other works, S. P. Rosenbaum's *A Concordance to the Poems of Emily Dickinson* (1964) and Cynthia Mackenzie's *Concordance to the Letters of Emily Dickinson* (2000), have greatly aided scholars in locating recurring motifs and themes among the 1,775 poems and 1,049 letters.

Impressionistic Responses to a Very Different Kind of Poetry

The initial criticism of Dickinson's poetry was mainly written by journalists. This important and extensive body of criticism, which appeared mostly as short reviews in newspapers but also as review essays in literary periodicals, has been assembled in a single volume by Willis J. Buckingham: *Emily Dickinson's Reception in the 1890s: A Documentary History* (1989). In his introduction Buckingham notes how, contrary to the widespread assumption that Dickinson's first readers regarded her poetry unfavorably, Dickinson "was published at the moment when the nineteenth century could feel, and take pleasure in, the alien force of her voice"; indeed, many of the reviews published during this period "delighted in her 'strangeness'" (xii). When the first volume of Dickinson's poetry appeared in November 1890, Arlo Bates wrote in the *Boston Sunday Courier*, "There is hardly a line of her work . . . which fails to throw out some gleam of genuine original power, of imagination, and of real emotional thought" (in Buckingham 29). Or consider this passage from a review of the second volume by C. M. Smith, published in the *Dartmouth Literary Monthly*, May 5, 1891:

> The verses all show a faculty for compressing thoughts, and often great thoughts, into small compass: no words are wasted, especially in filling out a line. The line is left incomplete rather than insert a superfluous word. This compactness gives a movement that is rapid and pleasing. (in Buckingham 139)

Some critics from this period, however, attempted to link the poems with what they knew of Dickinson's personal life, which was mostly gleaned from rumors and half-truths—an impulse that persists to this day. "Her wonderful acuteness and her uncompromising naturalism," wrote a *Chicago Tribune* reviewer in December 1891, "are not the effect of culture, but a part of her childhood's unforfeited inheritance. She has a child's ignorance of the world, a child's imagination and love of color" (in Buckingham 270). It would be eighty years before a scholar, John Emerson Todd, entertained the possibility that Dickinson's child's sensibility was one of her several personae: "Her childlike innocence," Todd asserts in *Emily Dickinson's Use of the Persona* (1973), "is often a carefully calculated pose." After all, in hiding behind a child's mask, Dickinson "gains freedom for speaking her mind much more openly than she could otherwise do" (9).

Willis Buckingham, it should be noted, was not the first to anthologize this early Dickinson criticism. In 1964 Caesar R. Blake and Carlton F. Wells published *The Recognition of Emily Dickinson: Selected Criticism Since 1890*, reprinting pieces from 1890-1900 that first appeared in some of the most important periodicals of the time, such as *The Atlantic Monthly, The Nation, Scribner's*, and the London *Times*. The Buckingham collection also includes dozens of reviews and articles from obscure, short-lived periodicals that are today difficult to locate.

During the first two decades of the twentieth century, impressionistic criticism held firm as additional volumes of the poetry were edited and published by Martha Dickinson Bianchi, along with Bianchi's *The Life and Letters of Emily Dickinson* (1924), a mix of Dickinson's correspondence with specious biographical details that did much to stoke the legendary stature of the poet but offered little insight into the poetry. Macgregor Jenkins's charming boyhood recollections, *Emily Dickinson, Friend and Neighbor* (1930), enhanced the poet's legendary allure even further. It was also during this time that Emily Dickinson's poetry began to attract serious scholarly attention.

Early Scholarly Criticism

In 1924 appeared the Modern Library *Selected Poems*, edited by the distinguished poet Conrad Aiken. Aiken's introduction opens with a biographical overview of the poet but warns readers not to leap to conclusions about her alleged "psychic injuries" and encourages them rather to pay more attention to her "remarkable range of metaphysical speculation and ironic introspection" (13).

When Bianchi published another volume of her aunt's poems, *Further Poems of Emily Dickinson*, in 1929, it caught the attention of the philosopher Theodore Spencer, who, in reviewing the collection for the *New England Quarterly* (July 1929), demonstrated Dickinson's closer resemblance to seventeenth-century writers such as Sir Thomas Browne, George Herbert, and John Donne than to her contemporaries such as Henry Wadsworth Longfellow. "There is [in Dickinson] the same development of thought through imagery, the same use of metaphor in a structural, not merely an ornamental, manner, which we associate with metaphysical verse," he concluded (132).

Aiken's and Spencer's essays served as catalysts for the first blossoming of academic criticism that was being shaped by the pioneering formalist critics Allen Tate, R. P. Blackmur, Yvor Winters, and Austin Warren—teacher-scholars who emphasized artistry and literary-historical context over an author's biography. Tate, for example, in his essay "New England Culture and Emily Dickinson" (1932), regards Dickinson's oeuvre as "a poetry of ideas." By situating Dickinson in the Puritan, Calvinist culture of mid-nineteenth-century western Massachusetts, Tate presents her in stark contrast to Emerson, who "discredited more than any other man the Puritan drama of the soul" (156). Indeed, in poem after poem, Dickinson confronts the uncertainties of God's involvement in human affairs, death's unfathomable mystery, and the enigma of immortality and salvation, often with anguished intensity. The passion to fathom these mysteries collides with the impossibility of fathoming them—faith notwithstanding. "We are shown our roots in Nature by examining our differences with Nature; we are renewed by Nature without being delivered into her hands," Tate writes (161). Turning to "Because I could not stop for Death," Tate calls attention to the startling irony of presenting Death, an embodiment of terror, as a gentleman, and even more ironically as the servant of Immortality: "She has presented a typical Christian theme in its final irresolution, without making any final statements about it. There is no solution to the problem; there can be only a presentation of it in the full context of intellect and feeling. . . . We are not told what to think; we are told to look at the situation" (161).

Book-length studies of Dickinson's poetry were slow to come about; meanwhile, biographically oriented works predominated during the 1920s and 1930s (especially 1930, the hundredth anniversary of the poet's birth). After Bianchi's *Life and Letters of Emily Dickinson* came her *Emily Dickinson Face to Face* (1932), Josephine Pollitt's *Emily Dickinson: The Human Background of Her Poetry* (1930), and Genevieve Taggard's *The Life and Mind of Emily Dickinson* (1930), all of which, while engagingly written and providing glimpses into the poet's family life, friendships, and education, are marred by exaggerated and unsubstantiated claims. Pollitt, for example, asserts that the poet returned from her 1855 visit to Washington, D.C., where her father was serving a term in Congress, "in a dreamy state of mind. She had formed a romantic and violent attachment for a man under impossible conditions" (127)—the man in question being the Rev. Charles Wadsworth, about whose purported relationship with the poet so much speculative ink has been spilled.[2]

For these biographers, Emily Dickinson's poetry had to be autobiographical. Then, in 1938, Amherst College professor George Frisbie Whicher published *This Was a Poet: A Critical Biography of Emily Dickinson*. As the subtitle implies, Whicher is more reluctant to connect Dickinson's poetic scenarios to actual events: "We should not expect to find in fervid love poems an exact statement of actual circumstances," he cautions (97). Even Whicher, however, cannot resist reading some of the poems biographically as expressions of unfulfilled love: "A large section of her poetry deals ostensibly with her love for a man whom she could not marry and with the way in which she met the frustration of her hopes" (80), he proclaims. But a paragraph later he catches himself, noting that in other poems Dickinson "described a visit to the ocean which never took place, her own deathbed sensations, and her feelings as she rested in the grave. Were her love poems, like these, figments of the imagination or were they reports in verse of what she had actually experienced?" (81).

It would be another twenty-two years before a predominantly objective analysis of the poet's oeuvre appeared: Charles R. Anderson's *Emily Dickinson's Poetry: Stairway of Surprise* (1960), a study that is both erudite and engagingly written. By devoting separate chapters to the poet's wit, diction, reflections on the problems of perception and the rhythms and processes of nature, and what Dickinson considered to be her "flood subjects," death and immortality, Anderson is able for the first time to produce a richly complex assessment of Dickinson's poetic genius, yet without overlooking their reasonable linkages, via the letters, to Dickinson's personhood. Four other studies of note, which appeared later in the decade, are Clark Griffith's *The Long Shadow: Emily Dickinson's Tragic Poetry* (1964), Albert Gelpi's *Emily Dickinson: The Mind of the Poet* (1965), David Porter's *The Art of Emily Dickinson's Early Poetry* (1966), and William R. Sherwood's *Circumference and Circumstance: Stages in the Mind and Art of Emily Dickinson* (1968). Griffith and Gelpi discuss the poems in the context of Dickinson's intellectual milieu—her intense probing of the relationship between God and humanity, for example, they link to the Calvinist directive, which, in Dickinson's hands, ironically produces rather startlingly un-Calvinist ideas, such as the uncertainty of God's presence or the petulant claim, in the poem beginning "Some keep the Sabbath going to Church –" that the Sabbath can be kept "staying at Home / With a Bobolink for a Chorister / And an Orchard, for a Dome –". Gelpi goes a step further in pointing out Dickinson's foregrounding of the processes of the mind itself, of consciousness, when grappling with these metaphysical subjects. Dickinson, he asserts, "was urgently aware that in the life of consciousness the primary duty was to catch the irrecoverable moment" (102).

Porter and Sherwood, in their respective studies, are concerned with Dickinson's stages of artistic development. Relying on Johnson's chronological ordering of the poems, Sherwood draws connections between motifs in the poems and events or issues in the poet's life (as evidenced in letters). Porter, on the other hand, a formalist critic par excellence, limits his study to the poems written between 1858 and 1861 because of their more certain chronology. A more recent reexamination of Dickinson's development as a poet is Aliki Barnstone's *Changing Rapture: Emily Dickinson's Poetic Development* (2006), in which Barnstone sees the poems as a sustained critique of Dickinson's Calvinist New England milieu.

Topical studies of the poems also began appearing during the 1960s: Thomas W. Ford examines Dickinson's poems about death and dying in *Heaven Beguiles the Tired: Death in the Poetry of Emily Dickinson* (1966); Dolores Dyer Lucas examines the numerous riddle poems in *Emily Dickinson and Riddle* (1969); and Jean McClure Mudge explores Dickinson's poems about domestic space in *Emily Dickinson and the Image of Home* (1975).

Stylistic, Rhetorical, and Manuscript Criticism

Johnson's variorum edition ushered in a new era of Dickinson scholarship when it was published in 1955. For the first time, the poems could be studied in their entirety, in roughly chronological order and, most important, in a format that more or less faithfully reproduced the poems as Dickinson had written them, including the dashes and irregularities in grammar, capitalization, and punctuation—irregularities that the earlier editors had assumed to be a reflection of her lack of proper schooling.

A wealth of stylistic and rhetorical studies proliferated as a result. In

The Voice of the Poet: Aspects of Style in the Poetry of Emily Dickinson (1968), Brita Lindberg-Seyersted meticulously analyzes Dickinson's prosody—her unusual diction, her inventive (and often perplexing) syntactic structures, her experiments with rhyme and meter (especially in the context of hymnody), and her combinations of polysyllabic Latinate with homey, monosyllabic diction. With regard to the last of these, Lindberg-Seyersted sees Dickinson both as an innovator and as part of a long tradition that includes Sir Thomas Browne and John Milton. "The opposition between concrete and abstract nouns," Lindberg-Seyersted explains, "enters into the poetry as a forceful structural pattern" (94).

Extending Lindberg-Seyersted's examination of Dickinson's prosody is Cristanne Miller's *Emily Dickinson: A Poet's Grammar* (1987), which shows how Dickinson's highly compressed syntactic structures yield multiple meanings, in particular meanings that question patriarchal authority and traditional sex roles. For example, "the frequent lack of distinction in her poems between woman and child . . . contribute[s] significantly to the evidence that Dickinson associated femininity with powerlessness and therefore with her need to create independent, disguised sources of power for herself" (167). Miller's study serves as an important link between formalist/textual criticism and feminist criticism; indeed, it should remind us not to make hard-and-fast distinctions between different critical approaches.

Other important examinations of Dickinson's style include Robert Weisbuch's *Emily Dickinson's Poetry* (1975), a study of how Dickinson uses analogy and personae to shape her poetic style; Wendy Barker's *Lunacy of Light: Emily Dickinson and the Experience of Metaphor* (1987), a discussion of Dickinson's pervasive light/darkness imagery and symbolism; Judy Jo Small's *Positive as Sound: Emily Dickinson's Rhyme* (1990), an in-depth analysis of the poet's musical aesthetic and innovative uses of rhyme and meter; Gary Lee Stonum's *The Dickinson Sublime* (1990), a refutation of David Porter's claim, in *Dickinson: The Modern Idiom* (1981), that Dickinson was "a poet without a project"; and Paul Crumbley's *Inflections of the Pen: Dash and Voice in Emily Dickinson* (1997), a fascinating examination of how Dickinson's unconventional punctuation, especially her use of the dash, is central to understanding her "polyvocality."

Closely aligned with stylistic criticism is rhetorical criticism, which focuses on the "macro" elements of composition, such as organization and dramatic technique. Helen McNeil, in her insightful introductory study *Emily Dickinson* (1986), is among the few scholars who reflect on the fact that Dickinson "wrote rhetorically—that is, she used devices which are meant to argue and convince" (7). Her poems, McNeil goes on to explain,

> typically begin with a declaration or definition in the first line and proceed to a metaphorical breaking open of the original premise. . . . The middle of the Dickinson poem is usually a sequence of metaphors, or metaphoric actions. Then the poem veers, often unexpectedly, into surmise, renewed rhetorical inquiry, or an open closure. The dash that ends so many . . . poems is a graphic indication that the debate does not finish with the poem. (11)

For many Dickinson scholars, the 1981 publication of Franklin's *The Manuscript Books of Emily Dickinson* signaled a major turning point in the study of the poet. For the first time, the poems could be studied as unified sequences, not merely isolated lyrics. But unified how? Several manuscript scholars have thus far given different readings. The first to present a theory of the sequencing of Dickinson's fascicle poems are M. L. Rosenthal and Sally M. Gall in *The Modern Poetic Sequence: The Genius of Modern Poetry* (1983). What Rosenthal and Gall see in Dickinson's sequences is interplay, "a process of tensions and counter-tensions in motion, self-contained. . . . At the same time there is an accumulative forward motion from poem to poem" (48-49). For example, the "grim mystery" evoked in the opening poem of Fascicle 15,

The first Day's Night had come –
And grateful that a thing
So terrible – had been endured
I told my Soul to sing –

(1-4)

may be (as implied by later poems in the sequence, such as "'Twas like
A Maelstrom, with a notch" and "I gave myself to Him – ") the death of
a lover or a traumatic rejection of love.

Other scholars have devoted entire monographs to the topic of Dickinson's fascicle sequencing—in particular, Sharon Cameron's *Choosing
Not Choosing: Dickinson's Fascicles* (1992), Dorothy Huff Oberhaus's
Emily Dickinson's Fascicles: Method and Meaning (1995), and Eleanor Elson Heginbotham's *Reading the Fascicles of Emily Dickinson:
Dwelling in Possibilities* (2003). For commentary on the poet's so-
called worksheet drafts (poems written in pencil, many with variant
words and phrases on odd scraps of paper, backs of envelopes, adver-
tising flyers, and the like) see Marta L. Werner's *Emily Dickinson's
Open Folios: Scenes of Reading, Surfaces of Writing* (1995).

Because Emily Dickinson never prepared her poems for publication, scholars have often wondered whether she rejected print because
of how its mechanical limitations reduce orthography to monotype.
Domhnall Mitchell grapples with these concerns in *Measures of Possibility: Emily Dickinson's Manuscripts* (2005). See also Martha Nell
Smith's *Rowing in Eden: Rereading Emily Dickinson* (1992) for an inquiry into the poet's refusal to publish.

Feminist Scholarship

Feminist literary criticism of Dickinson rides on two important assumptions: (1) that a poet's gender inevitably influences her artistry
and (2) that a woman writer, by the very act of writing, of asserting herself, regards social, aesthetic, and spiritual conventions traditionally

assumed to be universalist as masculinist or patriarchal. The feminist critic often merely needs to point to what women writers say that readers have largely overlooked, and this is certainly the case with Emily Dickinson. Her poetry lends itself to feminist readings because Dickinson herself raises feminist issues in her poems.

The principal feminist Dickinson scholar is Suzanne Juhasz. In 1983 she published an edited collection of essays, *Feminist Critics Read Emily Dickinson*, and a monograph, *The Undiscovered Continent: Emily Dickinson and the Space of the Mind*. Traditional criticism, Juhasz explains in her introduction to the former volume, has falsely separated Dickinson the woman from Dickinson the poet. By reuniting the two, feminist critics rethink established notions about the poet's eccentricity or her retreat from life. "From a feminist perspective, Dickinson's life was neither a flight, nor a cop-out, nor a sacrifice, nor a substitution, but a strategy, a creation, for enabling her to become the person she was," Juhasz writes (10). In her monograph she shows how Dickinson regards the mind—the poetic imagination—as the space or landscape on which she plays out her thoughts in ways that would be impossible for her to do in the "real" world because of her gender.

Other important feminist studies include Barbara Antonina Clarke Mossberg's *Emily Dickinson: When a Writer Is a Daughter* (1982), a study of the way Dickinson reenvisions old notions of domesticity and father-daughter and mother-daughter relationships; Paula Bennett's *Emily Dickinson: Woman Poet* (1990), which examines the poet's homoerotic themes; and Suzanne Juhasz, Cristanne Miller, and Martha Nell Smith's *Comic Power in Emily Dickinson* (1993), which calls attention to just how "profoundly humorous" Dickinson's poetry can be—indeed, that her poetry "is throughout imbued with the spirit and form of comedy" (22), as poems such as "We pray – to Heaven – / We prate – of Heaven" and "I'm Nobody! Who are you?" demonstrate.

New Approaches to Dickinson Biography: Psychoanalytic, Medical Perspectives

Works of literature often lend themselves well to psychoanalytic interpretation. After all, the characters we remember best are often the ones whose behavior is enigmatic, erratic, and pathological—think of *King Lear*'s Edmund, just about any character in *Hamlet*, or *Moby Dick*'s Ishmael and Captain Ahab, or of Raskolnikov in Fyodor Dostoevski's *Crime and Punishment*. Authors, too, are frequently targets for psychoanalytic study, as is the case with Emily Dickinson. In 1971 John Cody, a psychiatrist, published *After Great Pain: The Inner Life of Emily Dickinson*. Cody's thesis is provocative: that Emily Dickinson suffered from psychological imbalance and deprivation—a principal cause being her mother, who was incapable of imparting the love that Emily needed. The point, however, as Cody explains, "is that threatening personality disintegration compelled a frantic Emily Dickinson to create poetry—for her a psychosis-deflecting activity" (391).

One other psychologically oriented study of the poet is especially noteworthy: Maryanne M. Garbowsky, in *The House Without the Door* (1989), sees in Dickinson's poetry and letters a woman suffering from agoraphobia, a fear of open spaces. For a feminist psychoanalytic study of Dickinson's work, see Mary Loeffelholz's *Dickinson and the Boundaries of Feminist Theory* (1991).

A few scholars have studied Dickinson's poetry from a medical perspective. James R. Guthrie, for example, in *Emily Dickinson's Vision: Illness and Identity in Her Poetry* (1998), identifies numerous vision-related motifs and links them to the serious eye problems Dickinson suffered throughout her adult life. George Mamunes, in *"So Has a Daisy Vanished": Emily Dickinson and Tuberculosis* (2008), argues that the poet's fear of tuberculosis and other diseases affected both her way of life and her art.

Dickinson in Cultural Context

Because Emily Dickinson was a recluse, it is tempting to think of her as an escapee from society, hiding from the world in the safe haven of her room. After all, in one of her most famous poems she proclaims, "The soul selects her own Society – / Then – shuts the Door –." But Dickinson was very much a part of her culture. Her "shutting the door" enabled her to flourish as an artist, and from the confines of her home she maintained ongoing epistolary communication with friends, neighbors, relatives, and an occasional stranger—enough letters (1,049) to fill three volumes, which scholars estimate to be just a small fraction of her total epistolary output.

Although the earliest academic critics such as Allen Tate recognized Dickinson's close ties with her New England culture, it took until 1984 for a book-length study to appear: Barton Levi St. Armand's *Emily Dickinson and Her Culture: The Soul's Society*. St. Armand examines Dickinson's oeuvre in the context of keepsakes such as portraits of friends, scrapbooks, and letters; rituals associated with death and dying; and images of earthly paradise, for example those depicted in landscape painting.[3] "There is ample evidence from her published letters," St. Armand writes, "that Emily Dickinson . . . kept a scrapbook of clippings from national magazines, local newspapers, and illustrated books, which she used to ornament some of her own manuscripts" (26).

Perhaps the most important cultural influence on Emily Dickinson was religion. In *Dickinson: Strategies of Limitation* (1985), Jane Donahue Eberwein sees Dickinson's poetic project as "an overarching metaphor of quest, spanning the cavernous gap between limitation and boundlessness," and "recogniz[es] this quest as an implicitly religious action" (17). Roger Lundin, in his monograph *Emily Dickinson and the Art of Belief* (1998), sees in the poems Dickinson's "trac[ing] the trajectory of God's decline" and grappling with the notion of God the Father, "questioning not his existence as much as his presence and justice" (4).

Additional studies of Dickinson's explorations of religious themes include James McIntosh's *Nimble Believing: Dickinson and the Unknown* (2000), John Delli Carpini's *Poetry as Prayer: Emily Dickinson* (2002), R. C. Allen's *Emily Dickinson: Accidental Buddhist* (2007), and Patrick J. Keane's *Emily Dickinson's Approving God: Divine Design and the Problem of Suffering* (2008).

For students who wish to gain a clearer understanding of Dickinson's poetry in relationship to other poets and thinkers, several important studies exist. In *The Only Kangaroo Among the Beauty: Emily Dickinson and America* (1979), Karl Keller examines Dickinson's poetry in relation to that of Anne Bradstreet, Edward Taylor, Jonathan Edwards, and her near contemporaries Harriet Beecher Stowe, Nathaniel Hawthorne, Ralph Waldo Emerson, and Walt Whitman. For an in-depth comparison of Dickinson and Whitman, Agnieszka Salska's *Walt Whitman and Emily Dickinson: Poetry of the Central Consciousness* (1985) is especially useful.

Postmodern Literary Criticism

Postmodern critics might be considered metacritics in that they point out the instability of genre conventions and genre boundaries. As such, postmodern Dickinson critics often ask questions like "What makes us so sure that Dickinson wrote poetry?" or "Where does prose end and poetry begin—or are such boundaries wholly arbitrary?" Dickinson postmodernists are also quick to point out that the poet pretty much does their job for them: her letters often possess the compressed, inventive syntax and metaphors of her poems. What is more, she will sometimes present what ostensibly resembles a poem as a letter—a practice that confounded her early editors. As Marietta Messmer states in her monograph *A Vice for Voices: Reading Emily Dickinson's Correspondence* (2001), "The multiple ways in which Dickinson's letters and poems are intertwined both formally and functionally illustrate the extent to which any editorial separation mutilates them both" (22).

Like Marietta Messmer, Virginia Jackson, in *Dickinson's Misery: A Theory of Lyric Reading* (2005), probes our very notions of lyric poetry in the context of Dickinson's oeuvre, arguing that the conventions of print publication have set extreme limits on what constitutes a lyric poem. But since Dickinson did not publish, Jackson claims, her manuscript conventions invite a reassessment of what a lyric can be. Before reading Jackson's study, students may want to consult Sharon Cameron's *Lyric Time: Dickinson and the Limits of Genre* (1979), especially chapter 3, which examines the problem of boundaries, or "What is the relationship between self and other, interior and exterior, literal and figural, past and present, time and timelessness" (91)—questions that Dickinson grapples with in her lyric poetry and that extend our understanding of the possibilities of lyricism.

Conclusion

Presented with such a wealth of critical approaches to Emily Dickinson, it is understandable if students feel overwhelmed. It may be helpful to group these approaches according to three principal emphases:

Works-centered: When it comes to genius, the art is the essence of the life. The whole point of studying a great poet is to gain insight into the poet's artistic techniques.

Life-centered: These are the biographical and psychological approaches. Students of the poet are naturally curious about the relationship between life and art, as Dickinson's poetry is greatly bound up with her personhood. What events in her life, facets of her personality, and interests and passions influenced her art? How like or unlike us was she?

Culture-centered: How shall we compare Emily Dickinson to her contemporaries? What impact, if any, did such events as the Civil War, which coincided with her most productive years, have on her art? To what extent did her religious views influence her, either positively or negatively? How, if at all, did the books and authors she most admired influence her work?

Another point to consider is how these several different critical approaches "resonate" with one another. For example, examination of certain poems through a psychoanalytic lens can generate new insights into Dickinson's prosody, her symbolism. By viewing her poems through a feminist lens, one can generate valuable insights not only into her intense interrogations of romantic love and social customs but into her spiritual experiences as well. Like filters on a camera, literary-critical lenses simultaneously highlight some things and obscure others; no critical approach can embrace everything, nor should it. The fact that so many critical approaches to a single poet are possible is testimony to the greatness of Emily Dickinson's transcendent genius.

Also for beginning students of Emily Dickinson, the following valuable guides and anthologies should prove useful:

Joseph Duchac, *The Poems of Emily Dickinson: An Annotated Guide to Commentary Published in English, 1890-1977* (volume 1); *1978-1989* (volume 2).

Jane Donahue Eberwein, ed., *An Emily Dickinson Encyclopedia* (1998). Entries cover important persons and places as well as topics relating to her poems and letters.

Gudrun Grabher, Roland Hagenbüchle, and Cristanne Miller, eds., *The Emily Dickinson Handbook* (1998). Entries include information on historical background and on Dickinson's manuscripts, letters, and poetic techniques.

Vivian R. Pollak, ed., *A Historical Guide to Emily Dickinson* (2004). The essays situate the poet in her historical and cultural milieu; an illustrated chronology is also included.

Martha Nell Smith and Mary Loeffelholz, eds., *A Companion to Emily Dickinson* (2008). The articles include new insights into the poet's manuscripts, her cultural milieu, and her poetic legacies.

In addition to these, the Emily Dickinson Electronic Archives (www.emilyDickinson.org) is a valuable Internet resource that provides access to documents relating to the Dickinson family, scholarly articles, manuscript reproductions, and bibliographies. Finally, students wishing to study Emily Dickinson's critical reception in greater detail should consult Klaus Lubbers's *Emily Dickinson: The Critical Revolution* (1962) and my own *Approaching Emily Dickinson: Critical Currents and Crosscurrents Since 1960* (2008).

Notes

1. The 1896 volume was edited by Todd alone.
2. For more fact-based speculation on the Wadsworth-Dickinson friendship, see Richard B. Sewall, *The Life of Emily Dickinson* (1974), and Alfred Habegger, *My Wars Are Laid Away in Books: The Life of Emily Dickinson* (2001).
3. For a study of Dickinson's poetry in the context of the visual art, see Judith Farr, *The Passion of Emily Dickinson* (1992).

Works Cited

Aiken, Conrad. "Emily Dickinson." *Emily Dickinson: A Collection of Critical Essays*. Ed. Richard B. Sewall. Englewood Cliffs, NJ: Prentice-Hall. 1963. 9-15. Reprinted from *Dial* 76 (April 1924).

Allen, R. C. *Emily Dickinson: Accidental Buddhist*. Victoria, BC: Trafford, 2007.

Anderson, Charles R. *Emily Dickinson's Poetry: Stairway of Surprise*. New York: Holt, Rinehart and Winston, 1960.

Barker, Wendy. *Lunacy of Light: Emily Dickinson and the Experience of Metaphor*. Carbondale: Southern Illinois UP, 1987.

Barnstone, Aliki. *Changing Rapture: Emily Dickinson's Poetic Development*. Hanover, NH: UP of New England 2006.

Bennett, Paula. *Emily Dickinson: Woman Poet*. Iowa City: U of Iowa P, 1990.

Bianchi, Martha Dickinson. *Emily Dickinson Face to Face*. Boston: Houghton Mifflin, 1932.

_____. *The Life and Letters of Emily Dickinson*. Boston: Houghton Mifflin, 1924.

Blake, Caesar R., and Carlton F. Wells, eds. *The Recognition of Emily Dickinson: Selected Criticism Since 1890*. Ann Arbor: U of Michigan P, 1968.

Buckingham, Willis J., ed. *Emily Dickinson's Reception in the 1890s: A Documentary History*. Pittsburgh: U of Pittsburgh P, 1989.

Cameron, Sharon. *Choosing Not Choosing: Dickinson's Fascicles*. Chicago: U of Chicago P, 1992.

_____. *Lyric Time: Dickinson and the Limits of Genre*. Baltimore: Johns Hopkins UP, 1979.

Cody, John. *After Great Pain: The Inner Life of Emily Dickinson*. Cambridge, MA: Harvard UP, 1971.

Crumbley, Paul. *Inflections of the Pen: Dash and Voice in Emily Dickinson*. Lexington: UP of Kentucky, 1997.

Delli Carpini, John. *Poetry as Prayer: Emily Dickinson*. Boston: Pauline Books & Media, 2002.

Dickinson, Emily. *Further Poems of Emily Dickinson*. Ed. Martha Dickinson Bianchi. Boston: Little, Brown, 1929.

_____. *The Manuscript Books of Emily Dickinson*. Ed. R. W. Franklin. 2 vols. Cambridge, MA: Belknap Press of Harvard UP, 1981.

_____. *Poems: First Series*. Ed. Mabel Loomis Todd and T. W. Higginson. Boston: Roberts Brothers, 1890.

_____. *Poems: Second Series*. Ed. Mabel Loomis Todd and T. W. Higginson. Boston: Roberts Brothers, 1891.

_____. *Poems: Third Series*. Ed. Mabel Loomis Todd. Boston: Roberts Brothers, 1896.

_____. *The Poems of Emily Dickinson*. Ed. R. W. Franklin. 3 vols. Cambridge, MA: Belknap Press of Harvard UP, 1998.

_____. *The Poems of Emily Dickinson*. Ed. Thomas H. Johnson. 3 vols. Cambridge, MA: Belknap Press of Harvard UP, 1955.

_____. *The Single Hound: Poems of a Lifetime*. Ed. Martha Dickinson Bianchi. Boston: Little, Brown, 1914.

Duchac, Joseph. *The Poems of Emily Dickinson: An Annotated Guide to Commentary Published in English, 1890-1977*. New York: G. K. Hall, 1979.

_____. *The Poems of Emily Dickinson: An Annotated Guide to Commentary Published in English, 1978-1989*. Boston: G. K. Hall, 1993.

Eberwein, Jane Donahue. *Dickinson: Strategies of Limitation*. Amherst: U of Massachusetts P, 1985.

_____, ed. *An Emily Dickinson Encyclopedia*. Westport, CT: Greenwood Press, 1998.

Farr, Judith. *The Passion of Emily Dickinson*. Cambridge, MA: Harvard UP, 1992.

Ford, Thomas W. *Heaven Beguiles the Tired: Death in the Poetry of Emily Dickinson*. Tuscaloosa: U of Alabama P, 1966.

Garbowsky, Maryanne M. *The House Without the Door: A Study of Emily Dickinson and the Illness of Agoraphobia*. Rutherford, NJ: Fairleigh Dickinson UP, 1989.

Gelpi, Albert. *Emily Dickinson: The Mind of the Poet*. Cambridge, MA: Harvard UP, 1965.

Grabher, Gudrun, Roland Hagenbüchle, and Cristanne Miller, eds. *The Emily Dickinson Handbook*. Amherst: U of Massachusetts P, 1998.

Griffith, Clark. *The Long Shadow: Emily Dickinson's Tragic Poetry*. Princeton, NJ: Princeton UP, 1964.

Guthrie, James R. *Emily Dickinson's Vision: Illness and Identity in Her Poetry*. Gainesville: UP of Florida, 1998.

Habegger, Alfred. *My Wars Are Laid Away in Books: The Life of Emily Dickinson*. New York: Random House, 2001.

Heginbotham, Eleanor Elson. *Reading the Fascicles of Emily Dickinson: Dwelling in Possibilities*. Columbus: Ohio State UP, 2003.

Jackson, Virginia. *Dickinson's Misery: A Theory of Lyric Reading*. Princeton, NJ: Princeton UP, 2005.

Jenkins, Macgregor. *Emily Dickinson, Friend and Neighbor*. Boston: Little, Brown, 1930.

Juhasz, Suzanne. *The Undiscovered Continent: Emily Dickinson and the Space of the Mind*. Bloomington: Indiana UP, 1983.

_____, ed. *Feminist Critics Read Emily Dickinson*. Bloomington: Indiana UP, 1983.

Juhasz, Suzanne, Cristanne Miller, and Martha Nell Smith. *Comic Power in Emily Dickinson*. Austin: U of Texas P, 1993.

Keane, Patrick J. *Emily Dickinson's Approving God: Divine Design and the Problem of Suffering*. Columbia: U of Missouri P, 2008.

Keller, Karl. *The Only Kangaroo Among the Beauty: Emily Dickinson and America*. Baltimore: Johns Hopkins UP, 1979.

Leyda, Jay. *The Years and Hours of Emily Dickinson*. 2 vols. New Haven, CT: Yale UP, 1960.

Lindberg-Seyersted, Brita. *The Voice of the Poet: Aspects of Style in the Poetry of Emily Dickinson*. Cambridge, MA: Harvard UP, 1968.

Loeffelholz, Mary. *Dickinson and the Boundaries of Feminist Theory*. Urbana: U of Illinois P, 1991.

Lubbers, Klaus. *Emily Dickinson: The Critical Revolution*. Ann Arbor: U of Michigan P, 1962.

Lucas, Dolores Dyer. *Emily Dickinson and Riddle*. De Kalb: Northern Illinois UP, 1969.

Lundin, Roger. *Emily Dickinson and the Art of Belief*. Grand Rapids, MI: Wm. B. Eerdmans, 1998.

McIntosh, James. *Nimble Believing: Dickinson and the Unknown*. Ann Arbor: U of Michigan P, 2000.

Mackenzie, Cynthia. *Concordance to the Letters of Emily Dickinson*. Boulder: UP of Colorado, 2000.

McNeil, Helen. *Emily Dickinson*. New York: Virago, 1986.

Mamunes, George. *"So Has a Daisy Vanished": Emily Dickinson and Tuberculosis*. Jefferson, NC: McFarland, 2008.

Messmer, Marietta. *A Vice for Voices: Reading Emily Dickinson's Correspondence*. Amherst: U of Massachusetts P, 2001.

Miller, Cristanne. *Emily Dickinson: A Poet's Grammar*. Cambridge, MA: Harvard UP, 1987.

Mitchell, Domhnall. *Measures of Possibility: Emily Dickinson's Manuscripts*. Amherst: U of Massachusetts P, 2005.

Mossberg, Barbara Antonina Clarke. *Emily Dickinson: When the Writer Is a Daughter*. Bloomington: Indiana UP, 1982.

Mudge, Jean McClure. *Emily Dickinson and the Image of Home*. Amherst: U of Massachusetts P, 1975.

Oberhaus, Dorothy Huff. *Emily Dickinson's Fascicles: Method & Meaning*. University Park: Pennsylvania State UP, 1995.

Pollak, Vivian R., ed. *A Historical Guide to Emily Dickinson*. New York: Oxford UP, 2004.

Pollitt, Josephine. *Emily Dickinson: The Human Background of Her Poetry*. New York: Harper & Brothers, 1930.

Porter, David T. *The Art of Emily Dickinson's Early Poetry*. Cambridge, MA: Harvard UP, 1966.

_____. *Dickinson: The Modern Idiom*. Cambridge, MA: Harvard UP, 1981.

Rosenbaum, S. P. *A Concordance to the Poems of Emily Dickinson*. Ithaca, NY: Cornell UP, 1964.

Rosenthal, M. L., and Sally M. Gall. *The Modern Poetic Sequence: The Genius of Modern Poetry*. New York: Oxford UP, 1983.

St. Armand, Barton Levi. *Emily Dickinson and Her Culture: The Soul's Society*. New York: Cambridge UP, 1985.

Salska, Agnieszka. *Walt Whitman and Emily Dickinson: Poetry of the Central Consciousness*. Philadelphia: U of Pennsylvania P, 1985.

Sewall, Richard B. *The Life of Emily Dickinson*. New York: Farrar, Straus and Giroux, 1974.

Sherwood, William R. *Circumference and Circumstance: Stages in the Mind and Art of Emily Dickinson*. New York: Columbia UP, 1968.

Small, Judy Jo. *Positive as Sound: Emily Dickinson's Rhyme*. Athens: U of Georgia P, 1990.

Smith, Martha Nell. *Rowing in Eden: Rereading Emily Dickinson*. Austin: U of Texas P, 1992.

Smith, Martha Nell, and Mary Loeffelholz, eds. *A Companion to Emily Dickinson*. Malden, MA: Blackwell, 2008.

Spencer, Theodore. "Concentration and Intensity." *The Recognition of Emily Dickinson: Selected Criticism Since 1890*. Ed. Caesar R. Blake and Carlton F. Wells. Ann Arbor: U of Michigan P, 1968. 131-33. Reprinted from *New England Quarterly* 2 (July 1929).

Stonum, Gary Lee. *The Dickinson Sublime*. Madison: U of Wisconsin P, 1990.

Taggard, Genevieve. *The Life and Mind of Emily Dickinson*. New York: Alfred A. Knopf, 1930.

Tate, Allen. "New England Culture and Emily Dickinson." 1932. *The Recognition of Emily Dickinson: Selected Criticism Since 1890*. Ed. Caesar R. Blake and Carlton F. Wells. Ann Arbor: U of Michigan P, 1968. 153-67.

Todd, John Emerson. *Emily Dickinson's Use of the Persona*. The Hague: Mouton, 1973.

Weisbuch, Robert. *Emily Dickinson's Poetry*. Chicago: U of Chicago P, 1975.

Werner, Marta L. *Emily Dickinson's Open Folios: Scenes of Reading, Surfaces of Writing*. Ann Arbor: U of Michigan P, 1995.

Whicher, George Frisbie. *This Was a Poet: A Critical Biography of Emily Dickinson*. New York: Charles Scribner's Sons, 1938.

White, Fred D. *Approaching Emily Dickinson: Critical Currents and Crosscurrents Since 1960*. Rochester, NY: Camden House, 2008.

Dwelling in Possibility:
An Introduction to Dickinson's Poetics_____

Margaret H. Freeman

Because of the intellectual demands that Dickinson's poetry places on readers, we may be tempted to read her poetry for meaning rather than for feeling. But "to interpret well," in Margaret H. Freeman's view, "we must first experience." In her introductory guide to Dickinson's poetics, Freeman draws on recent studies in "cognitive poetics," which "focuses on the elements of sensory and emotional perception" that can be found in a poem's forms, its repetitions, its meters and rhymes, and its imagery. As we respond to these elements when we read poetry, Freeman explains, "we sense the poet's cognitive processes as we employ our own." Offering an explanation for the oft-described paradox of Dickinson's poetry—that while readers find Dickinson difficult to understand, they also feel emotionally attached to and identify with her—Freeman explains that Dickinson creates this sense of closeness through her intimate discourse and informal style, which draws in readers.

In her readings of two of Dickinson's flower poems—"If *she* had been the Mistletoe" and "I hide myself within my flower"—Freeman uses cognitive poetics to analyze how Dickinson's complex "blending" of flower, poem, and self in these works projects the self from its "initial reality space into another mental space," opening up a "world of possibilities" to the reader in which "things can happen and be made to happen through the agencies of the self." In her analysis of "Opon a Lilac Sea," which offers an example of Dickinson's difficult poetic style, with its characteristic reversals of syntactic elements and dropped words, Freeman shows how attentiveness to the poem's sound patterns aids readers in understanding and experiencing the poem. Finally, in her discussion of "A Bird came down the Walk –," "The Soul has Bandaged moments –," "I dwell in Possibility –," and "Safe in their Alabaster Chambers," Freeman provides insight into the interlocking patterns of Dickinson's symbolic images, in particular those based on the CONTAINER schema (which derives from the bodily experience of physical containment) and the schema of CHANGE (which is rooted in the experience of movement and transformation). While containers can be open or closed—and thus safe or confining places—for Dickinson, as she expresses in her well-known poem "I dwell in Possibility –," life is "above all an open container of expansion and possibility." Demonstrating how Dickinson's structuring metaphorical schemata of CONTAINER and CHANGE "create a dynamic explosion of emotion and feeling" in her verse, Freeman amply shows not only that Dickinson is a poet who has "emotive and explosive resonance" but also that readers need to "experience" her works in order to "understand" them.   J.B.B.

In a letter to his wife in August 1870, Thomas Wentworth Higginson recorded the following comment Emily Dickinson made during their first meeting: "If I read a book [and] it makes my whole body so cold no fire ever can warm me I know *that* is poetry. If I feel physically as if the top of my head were taken off, I know *that* is poetry. These are the only way I know it. Is there any other way" (L342a, Johnson 1965, 473-74).

Dickinson's observation makes a very important point about the nature of poetry and the arts in general. That is, it is not what a work of art means that is important but what a work of art does. As Joseph Conrad notes in his preface to *The Nigger of the Narcissus*:

A work that aspires, however humbly, to the condition of art should carry its justification in every line. And art itself may be defined as a single-minded attempt to render the highest kind of justice to the visible universe, by bringing to light the truth, manifold and one, underlying its every aspect. It is an attempt to find in its forms, in its colors, in its light, in its shadows, in the aspects of matter and in the facts of life, what of each is fundamental, what is enduring and essential—their one illuminating and convincing quality—the very truth of their existence. . . .

. . . All art, therefore, appeals primarily to the senses, and the artistic aim when expressing itself in written words must also make its appeal through the senses, if its highest desire is to reach the secret spring of responsive emotions. . . .

. . . My task which I am trying to achieve is, by the power of the written word to make you hear, to make you feel—it is, before all, to make you *see*. That—and no more, and it is everything.

Because Dickinson's poetry is so challenging, we are tempted immediately to interpret, to read for meaning, rather than to read for feeling, to experience. But to interpret well, we must first experience. By paying close attention to a poem's poetic affects—its forms, rhythms, repetitions, images, and so on, which the writer employs to capture "the very truth of their existence"—we are led, in William Wordsworth's terms, to "see into the life of things."

Literary studies have tended over the course of the modern period to move their focus from (1) the author, at the beginning of the twentieth century, with biographical and historical-philological studies, to (2) the text, in midcentury, with the rise of New Criticism, to (3) the reader, toward the end of the century, with reader response theory and deconstruction. More recently, studies in the cognitive sciences have shown how we need to take all three aspects into consideration to account comprehensively for a literary text. Cognitive poetics, first formulated by Reuven Tsur in the 1980s, focuses on the elements of sensory and emotional perception that can be found in the forms of a poem, in its patterns of sounds, its repetitions, its meters and rhymes, its images. Responding to these elements in our reading, we sense the poet's cognitive processes as we employ our own. This essay highlights some of the features of Dickinson's poetry that enable us to enter her universe of thoughts and feelings, situated as she was in her nineteenth-century world.

Textual Challenges

The fact that Dickinson's poems, with very few exceptions, were not published during her lifetime presents a challenge to her editors. Existing manuscripts include several copies of poems containing variations such as alternate wordings, line breaks, spelling, and punctuation. Even within one manuscript, Dickinson would add variant wordings and not always indicate her preference, forcing editors to decide which version to choose for publication. Further complications arise from determining whether or not a word is capitalized and how to render the differently shaped and positioned markings. Dickinson's early editors smoothed over the difficulties her manuscripts present by regularizing lines, simplifying syntax, adding punctuation, and changing words to make purer rhymes.

In 1955, T. H. Johnson published the first variorum edition, in three volumes. It included copies of all the known manuscripts at the time, and Johnson did his best to represent Dickinson's original wording, though he followed the practice of the early editors in regularizing the lines to conform more closely to hymn meter and end rhymes. Johnson regularized into dashes all markings that were not clearly periods, commas, exclamation points, or question marks. Since Dickinson had given titles to only a few poems, Johnson assigned them numbers (as the early editors had done). With the help of Theodora Ward, he dated the poems according to the handwriting, though he was careful to note in his preface that "all assigned dates are tentative and will always remain so" (lvi). Unfortunately, many readers see the assigned date and assume that the poem was undoubtedly written then.

In 1998, R. W. Franklin published a second variorum edition, revising and correcting Johnson's earlier volumes and placing the various copies of a poem in the order they might have been written. He then numbered the poems according to their earliest appearance, which is why his numbering differs from Johnson's. Franklin added the helpful feature of indicating below the printed copy where the manuscript line breaks occur. For their one-volume reader's editions, Johnson and

Franklin selected one version of a poem according to their own preferences.

This brief overview of the editing of Dickinson's poems is important if only to highlight the perennial and vexing question of what, exactly, constitutes a Dickinson poem. Most Dickinson scholars prefer to consider that the poems represent the fluctuating nature of the poetic process rather than being fixed and unalterable artifacts. For researchers in cognitive poetics, too, it is crucial to consider all extant variants and versions, since they offer a window into Dickinson's mind. The texts represented below are therefore transcribed from the manuscripts, with just one version selected (when more than one exists) to simplify discussion.

A Dickinson Paradox

Experiencing a poem entails responding to its linguistic affects. Cognitive linguists have discovered a close-distant relationship between the ways we communicate and how well we know each other. If we do not know each other very well, we tend to articulate our thoughts and feelings more explicitly than we need to do if we are close to one another. Consider a formal lecture to a general audience as opposed to a conversation between friends: the lecture will likely contain much longer sentences than the friendly conversation. This contrast gives rise to an iconic principle: longer discourse is equated with distance and lack of familiarity, and shorter discourse is equated with closeness and intimacy. This principle explains a paradox of Dickinson's poetry: readers report that although they often find her hard to understand, they nevertheless feel an emotional attachment to and identification with her. Dickinson achieves this sense of closeness because her language is characteristic of intimate discourse. It is colloquial, short, with many gaps and elisions. Take, for example, the following poem, *I've nothing else to bring you know* (Jones Library; F253*A*/J224):[1]

I've nothing Else, to
bring, you know -
So I keep bringing
these -
Just as the Night
keeps fetching stars -
To our familiar eyes.

Maybe - we should'nt
mind them -
Unless they did'nt Come
Then - Maybe it would
puzzle us
To find our way Home!

We are not told if "these" are poems or flowers, or perhaps both; the language is informal, with contractions ("I've") and the familiar "you know." Typical of speech, the poem opens with a main clause, followed by an informal "So." Speech pattern is also reflected in Dickinson's placement of the apostrophe in "should'nt" and "did'nt," not to indicate the elision of the vowel, but to reflect the gap in sound between the [d] and the [n]. Lurking behind the poem, and indicated by the choice of "familiar" in line 7, is the shared understanding expressed in the phrase "familiarity breeds contempt." There's a kind of humorous defensiveness in this poem addressed to Samuel Bowles: "I know that you probably don't take much notice of all these poems I keep sending you, but if I stopped, you'd miss them." The deprecatory "I've nothing Else" strikes a note of humility, counteracted by the wonderful analogy between the night and the poet, the stars and her poems. Just as early human civilizations used the stars as navigational aids, so, Dickinson suggests, it is only through her poems that we can "find our way Home." This phrase suggests seductively that "home" for Bowles is where Dickinson is, as well as suggesting that poetry provides insight into our place in the universe. As we shall see, Dickinson's poems invariably open up into a feeling of expansiveness from simple beginnings.

Self-Identification in Flower and Poem

Another way of experiencing a Dickinson poem is to take account of the cultural context in which it was written. Many of Dickinson's poems, especially her early ones, accompanied gifts of flowers, and some, indeed, can be considered flower-poems in which both flower and poem are fused with the poetic self. Another flirtatious poem she sent to Bowles may have accompanied a rose (*If she had been the mistletoe*, A 648; F60*A*/J44):

> If she had been the Mistletoe
> And I had been the Rose -
> How gay opon your table
> My velvet life to Close -
> Since I am of the Druid -
> And she is of the dew -
> I'll deck Tradition's buttonhole
> And send the Rose to you.

Here Dickinson is identifying herself with the mistletoe, a plant that has sacred and magical powers in Celtic lore and Norse mythology. The "Tradition" is a teasing reference to the Christmas practice of kissing under the mistletoe.[2]

A cognitive analysis shows how the poem is working. Gilles Fauconnier and Mark Turner have developed a theory called "blending" that explains how new meaning is created from old information. The theory involves what Fauconnier calls "mental spaces": temporary dynamic "spaces" we set up in order to imagine all kinds of thoughts that are not part of our current reality space, such as past and future events, hypotheticals, counterfactuals, and negatives. These "spaces" are set up by various "triggers" that create mappings between different spaces, such as past or future tenses and identity relationships. Dickinson's poem begins with a hypothetical counterfactual, "If she had been." In other words, "she" could have been what she is not (and "I" could have been a "Rose" but am not). The poem continues with an elaboration of what might have happened had the speaker been a rose sent to the addressee. The last four lines then reverse this idea by providing the "actual" situation, itself an imaginative tour de force as the speaker identifies herself with the mistletoe and sends the real rose (or perhaps just the poem) to Bowles. The mischievous flirtation arises from the cultural associations of roses with love and mistletoe with kissing. Note that though Dickinson is *sending* a love sign, she is *withholding* her own physical presence, which would be needed for kissing to occur! The identification of the poetic self with the mistletoe suggests that poetry is connected with sacred wisdom, just as the previous poem connected it with heavenly guidance.

Another flower-poem, *I hide myself within my flower* (F80/J903), is even clearer in its blend of flower, poem, and self. Three copies of the poem survive. The earliest imagines the flower being worn on the recipient's breast so that he or she is unknowingly also wearing the poem-self too. The later versions change the image to a more somber and distancing feeling of loneliness as the flower fades. An anecdote by Mary Adèle Allen indicates there may have been another copy sent to her mother as a tiny note (now lost) tucked inside a flower (Allen 76) to her mother. One of the later copies (A 234; F80*B*) reads:

I hide Myself
within My flower,
That fading from
your Vase,
You, unsuspecting,
feel for Me -
Almost a loneliness.

This seemingly simple little poem is in fact a complex blending of feeling and thought. First, an identification trigger creates a mental space mapping between the poet and the poem, since "I" may refer to either or both. The poem may be physically placed inside the flower, and since the self is imaginatively identified with the poem, the self is also contained within the flower. As the flower fades, it produces a feeling of sadness at its departure. But because the self is hidden within the poem within the flower, this feeling becomes one of "loneliness."

Since the recipient of the flower could not feel loneliness for the poem (it does not physically fade), the "Me" of line 6 refers directly to the sender's own self. As I have shown in detail elsewhere, Dickinson's idiosyncratic uses of the -self pronoun have their own grammar (Freeman, "Grounded" 1997). Even though the use of "Myself" in this poem is grammatically regular, many of the -self pronouns in other poems are not. Briefly, we are all grounded in our reality spaces (now, here), from which we project other mental spaces (past, future, distance, and so on). Dickinson uses the -self pronoun when she projects the self from its initial reality space into another mental space so that this projected space becomes a new reality space. In this poem, this cognitive grammar is indicated when "Myself" is projected physically into another "space"— the living flower that resides in the recipient's vase. As we read the poem, we are now "in" that other space. As the flower dies, its recipient experiences a feeling of absence for the poem's speaker, no longer present in that space.

The self-referencing pronoun thus becomes "Me," not "Myself," and refers to the sender, not the poem. Through this use of the -*self* pronoun, Dickinson enables us to experience a world of possibilities, a world in which things can happen and be made to happen through the agencies of the self.

Feeling in Sound and Syntax

From a cognitive point of view, Dickinson's grammar is not irregular. It is idiosyncratic, but it is perfectly consistent within its own grammatical constraints. Understanding the way her grammar works helps the reader understand her poems, and her sound patterns arouse the reader's feelings and emotions. Several of her grammatical principles and sound patterns are discussed here as examples of how one might begin to acquire a greater appreciation of Dickinson's poetics.

Characteristic of Dickinson's poetic style are her reversals of syntactic elements. Although normal English syntax order is subject, verb, object (SVO), she will often put the object before the subject (OSV), as in the line "Bloom I strove to raise" (*On the bleakness of my lot*, H 164; F862*B*/J681), or between subject and verb (SOV) as in "Tell his Arrow sent -" (*Tell as a marksman were forgotten*, A 373; F1148*A*/J1152). In these examples, the agency of the subject indicates which order is the grammatically correct one. Dickinson also shortens her poetic discourse, not only through colloquial elisions of vowels, as we have seen, but also by dropping any words that are not absolutely necessary for comprehension. Consider, for example, the following poem, *Opon a lilac sea* (A 502; F1368*A*/J1337):

Opon a Lilac

Sea

To toss

incessantly

His Plush

Alarm

Who fleeing

from the

Spring

The Spring

avenging fling

To Dooms

of Balm -

The poem has an interesting history. In 1875, Dickinson sent the last seven lines (keeping the same line breaks as in the manuscript copy) as a wedding congratulation to her friend Helen Hunt when she married William S. Jackson in Colorado Springs. Helen sent the note back with a request for an interpretation and then, in her subsequent letter, commented: "Thank you for not being angry with my impudent request for interpretations. I do wish I knew just what 'dooms' you meant, though!"

Many of Dickinson's grammatical and stylistic strategies occur in this short poem. Within one sentence of twenty-three words, Dickinson has created a complex subordinating pattern that can be read in at least two ways. Several readers see Dickinson's syntax as hopelessly scrambled and feel the necessity of unscrambling it in order to make sense.[3] Understanding the poem on its literal level depends on the answer to a simple question: What is the main verb and what the main subject? By having sent just the last seven lines to Jackson, Dickinson encourages us to read "fling" as the main verb and "Spring" as its subject. The structure of these lines is similar to the saying "Whom the gods would destroy, they first make mad" (Latin: *Quem deus vult perdere, dementat prius*). This reading is further encouraged by the fact that, in the printed editions, the word "Alarm" is capitalized and placed on the same line as "His Plush." This has led readers to interpret "Alarm" as a noun and "Plush" as an adjective.

Reading the poem this way, however, creates difficulties in deciding how to place the complement phrases and results in an uneasy and unsatisfactory violation of grammar, something Dickinson may be trusted not to do. If one reads "Alarm" as a noun, "Spring/fling" become the main subject/verb of the sentence. Since "fling" is transitive, its object is the preposed noun phrase "His Plush Alarm." Such a reading makes the phrase "who fleeing from the spring" a relative clause (the spring flings his plush alarm who [is] fleeing from the spring). The problem created by this reading is a syntactic one: how to fit in the line "To toss incessantly." Had the verbal phrase been "tossing," it could have read as an appositive to "His Plush Alarm," and the problem would not exist. But Dickinson did not write this, nor is there any variant to suggest she was unsatisfied with the construction as it stood. "To toss" implies purpose; it is possible to read such purpose as a complement to the main clause—that is, the spring flings his plush alarm to toss incessantly upon a lilac sea. But then what does one do with "to Dooms of Balm"? Even if it were grammatically possible to have two complements in this context, and one could just manage it here, with total disruption of poetic syntactical order (the spring flings his plush alarm to dooms of balm to toss incessantly upon a lilac sea), the effect is to undermine the final line, since "balm" does not connote the turbulent images of "to toss" and "incessantly."

So far, we have repeated the mistake mentioned at the outset: trying to interpret a poem without first experiencing it. Most noticeable in this poem are its sound patterns. Reading the poem aloud makes us conscious of the sound qualities of its consonants and vowels. In English, the pronunciation of consonants occurs in pairs, such as [p/b], [t/d], [s/z]. The only phonetic difference in each pair is whether the consonant is pronounced with the throat valves open (unvoiced) or closed (voiced).[4]

Nonvibrating, unvoiced sounds carry a feeling of sharpness, of tense-ness, whereas vibrating, voiced sounds carry a feeling of continuous-ness, of relaxation. Compare, for example, the opening lines of Wallace Stevens's "Bantams in Pine-Woods,"

> Chieftain Iffucan of Azcan in caftan
> Of tan with henna hackles, halt!

with Alfred, Lord Tennyson's lines from "The Princess,"

> The moan of doves in immemorial elms
> And murmuring of innumerable bees.

The sound of Stevens's lines is staccato, tense, and sharp because of its unvoiced consonants and the open tense vowel [æ]; Tennyson's sound is rounded, unbroken, smooth because of its voiced front rounded vowels.

In Dickinson's poem, the consonant sounds in the first five lines are all unvoiced, unvibrating. It is not until we reach the sixth line, contain-ing just one word, "Alarm," that we get a voiced and vibrating conso-nant in [m]. Both its placement on a separate line and its voiced conso-nant "foregrounds" the word as something special, as does its semantic sense of something we need to take notice of. The five lines that follow are also marked by repetition of the [ing] vibrating sound. The [i] vowel is short, frontal, and tense. Because the voiced [m] consonant in "Alarm" has already been marked, we feel its repetition in the word *from* and the similar voicing of the [v] and [j] sounds in *avenging*. The last two lines lead us to a resolution of the movement toward voicing, as we go to "Dooms / of Balm," where all the consonants after the prep-osition *to* are voiced and the vowels are low and back, with the rhymings on the [m] of the words *dooms* and *balm* and the pure rhyme of *alarm/balm*.

Where does this lead us? The progression from the unvibrating consonants of the first part before "Alarm" to the vibrating consonants after move from feelings of tension and disquietude to feelings of inevitability and calm. The acceleration felt in the first five lines is reinforced by the increase in syllables in the rhyming words "Sea" in line 2 and "incessantly" in line 4, indicating an increase in activity and tension, and by the rhythmic movement of alternation between the voiced [v] and the unvoiced [f] and the voiced [ing] sounds following "Alarm" in the second part before the poem finally settles down to stillness. When we reach the last line, the monosyllabic words give us a feeling of closure, as our lips move together on the [m] of "Dooms" and the [b] and [m] of "Balms." This sense of movement forward suggests that the poem's syntax is not disruptive and discontinuous but rather has a definite, directed momentum.

The syntactic problem, it turns out, arises from the editorial regularizing of Dickinson's original line breaks, which creates the impression that "His Plush Alarm" constitutes a noun phrase. If we follow the manuscript's line break and read "Alarm" as a verb, the syntactical problem is resolved.[5] After the preposed prepositional phrase which begins the sentence, Dickinson employs a subject-object-verb (SOV) order, which, in SVO order, becomes: "To toss incessantly alarm(s) his plush." The last seven lines of the poem are subordinated by means of "who" to the noun phrase "His Plush," which has the effect of maintaining an ongoing movement through the sentence, rather than the rearrangement we were earlier forced to make. We can then read the poem as follows: Our subject, Plush, alarmed by the tossing of the sea (a metaphor for the lilac-scented air), is avenged by Spring flinging it into dooms of balm. The movement of nonvibrating to vibrating sounds also suggests a movement from stasis to activity, from inertness to life.

Although some readers have thought the poem refers to a bee, two other Dickinson poems connect the word *plush* to a caterpillar (*A fuzzy fellow without feet*, H 15, F171*A*/J173; *How soft a caterpillar steps*, A 229, F1523*A*/J1448), and a similar connection here seems probable. Caterpillars are the unwitting victims of air: they can't do anything in their cocoon state except be at the mercy of the wind, wherever it takes them. And until they become butterflies, they certainly cannot partake of lilac blossoms as bees or hummingbirds can. Now "Dooms" takes on new resonance. Spring fatefully flings the caterpillar into summer to become a butterfly who can partake. The avenging image now seems to make more sense, with "Spring," the ultimate agent, avenging the disturbance and unease expressed in the first two verbs, "toss" and "Alarm," by flinging the caterpillar into its metamorphosis as a butterfly. The movement of the sound patterns and the syntax thus iconically simulate the physical movement and transformation of the caterpillar into butterfly.

The wedding congratulation then takes on new dimensions, a more Victorian expression of fulfillment. Dickinson was always sensitive to appropriate words for particular occasions.

Experiencing Dickinson's Poetics

Like sound and structure, images too convey emotional and sensory affects. Metaphor, and figurative language in general, has traditionally been associated with poetry. However, discussions of poetic metaphor have almost always been restricted to isolated examples of metaphorical expressions in individual poems. It was Rebecca Patterson who first noted the interlocking nature of Dickinson's symbolic images, which unify the emotional and experiential affects of her poetry into a cohesive whole. From a cognitive perspective, conceptual metaphors structure much of our thought processes. In *Metaphors We Live By*, published in 1980, George Lakoff and Mark Johnson revolutionized the way we think about metaphor. They have shown that common expressions share what are called "schemata" that organize our mental representations at a more general and abstract level than rich images do. These schemata are based on our bodily experience. For example, as Mark Johnson explains, "our encounter with containment and boundedness is one of the most pervasive features of our bodily experience" (21). Besides the CONTAINER schema, other basic schemata include BALANCE, CHANGE, and PATH.[6]

Schemata structure basic metaphorical expressions that enable us to talk about abstract ideas in terms of embodied experience. So, for example, the metaphor LIFE IS A JOURNEY has a PATH schema, which entails a beginning and an end and various points along the way. Through this schema, we talk about life in terms of new beginnings, detours, obstacles, destinations, and so on. In fact, this metaphorical schema is so pervasive in our everyday thinking that we barely recognize it as metaphorical at all.

If one looks at Dickinson's poetry from this cognitive perspective, one can see metaphorical patterns in her poems based on the CONTAINER schema that reflect the way she experiences her self in the world. Patterson notes that Dickinson associated the time of day, the seasons of the year, and the movement of the sun with the points of the compass:

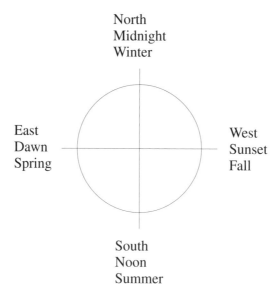

North
Midnight
Winter

East
Dawn
Spring

West
Sunset
Fall

South
Noon
Summer

On these points, Patterson shows, Dickinson hangs her emotional life, expressed through colors, elements (especially jewels), and the lands, countries, and rivers of the geographical world. By relating these images to her emotional responses to the world and others encompassing her, Dickinson unconsciously created the structuring pattern of her poetics. For Dickinson, LIFE IS not so much A JOURNEY "through" time as it is A VOYAGE "in" space. The PATH schema that underlies the JOURNEY metaphor is a linear one, with points along the path. The VOYAGE metaphor, by contrast, is a spatial one. Their etymologies distinguish the two metaphors. Whereas the word *journey* comes from the French word *jour*, which means "day," and denotes literally the distance one can travel in a day (implying beginnings and endings), the word *voyage* comes from the Latin word *via*, which means "path" or "way" and is associated with travel by sea, not land, and focuses rather on the travel itself. Sea imagery, in Dickinson's poems, indicates her adoption of the LIFE IS A VOYAGE IN SPACE metaphor.

Dickinson's sunsets are awash with sea imagery. Take, for example,

A Sloop of
Amber slips
away
Upon an Ether
Sea
(*A sloop of amber slips away*,
A 836; F1599C/J1622)

or

This - is the land - the
Sunset washes -
These are the Banks of
the Yellow Sea
(*This is the land the sunset washes*,
H 110; F297A/J266)

The poem *Opon a lilac sea*, as we have seen, describes air in terms of sea. There are many such examples in other poems like "A soft Sea washed around the House / A Sea of Summer Air" (*A soft sea washed around the house*, A 113; F1199*A*/J1198). This is a conceptual (not linguistic) metaphor because it structures all kinds of entailments.[7] For example, everything that flies will be seen as a sailor: "Bees - by the furlong - / Straits of Blue / Navies of Butterflies - sailed thro' -" (*What would I give to see his face*, H 37; F266*A*/J247) or, speaking of a bird (*A bird came down the* walk, A 85-9/10; F359*B*/J328):

> And he unrolled his feathers
> And rowed him softer
> home -
> Than Oars divide the
> Ocean,
> Too silver for a seam -
> Or Butterflies, off Banks
> of Noon
> Leap, plashless as they
> swim.

Although the poem begins with a PATH schema as the bird "came down the walk," the tone of the poem changes as the bird's eyes "hurried all around." It is noteworthy that in another copy (A 85-9/10), "around" is given as "abroad," thus linking the circular notion of "around" with the idea of movement outward or crossing the sea in "abroad." The bird escapes into the upper reaches of the air, as he "rowed him softer / home -."

The sea imagery marks the difference between Dickinson's LIFE IS A VOYAGE metaphor and the LIFE IS A JOURNEY metaphor. Whereas the JOURNEY metaphor is linear, occurring "through" time, the VOYAGE metaphor is circular and cyclical, occurring "in" space. Images of circles and cycles can be found in many poems, marked by words like *wheels, round, arc, disc,* and *circumference.* And because Dickinson's VOYAGE metaphor is circular, encompassing in nature, it is predicated on and governed by the more general CONTAINER schema.

The CONTAINER schema is directly associated with the emotions. Zoltán Kövecses has shown, for example, how metaphors for anger invoke the CONTAINER schema, as in expressions such as "he flipped his lid" or "she held her feelings in." The prepositions *in* and *out* are linguistic triggers for the CONTAINER schema. Containers may be open or closed, be places of safety or places of confinement. They can be breached or expanded. In *The soul has bandaged moments* (A 85-11/12; F360A/J512), the breaching is one of delirious escape:

> The soul has moments of Escape -
> When bursting all the doors -
> She dances like a Bomb, abroad,
> And swings opon the Hours,
>
> As do the Bee - delirious borne -
> Long Dungeoned from his Rose -
> Touch Liberty - then know no
> more -
> But Noon, and Paradise -

Dickinson expressed her feelings about life to Higginson (recorded in the letter to his wife) as follows: "I find ecstasy in living – the mere sense of living is joy enough." She penned a one-line note to her sister-in-law, Sue: "Oh Matchless Earth – we underrate the chance to dwell in Thee" (HCL, B49, Johnson 1965, 478). Life, for Dickinson, is above all an open container of expansion and possibility. One of her most famous poems, *I dwell in possibility* (H106; *F466A*/J657), expresses the emotions associated with expansion out, with the possibilities afforded by her vocation as a poet described as "a fairer House than Prose -."

The house of possibility expands outward and upward to the "Gambrels of the sky," with the speaker describing her "Occupation" (a pun on where she dwells and what she does) as "The spreading wide my / narrow Hands / To gather Paradise -."

The CONTAINER schema has consequences for Dickinson's view of death. Given a linear metaphor like LIFE IS A JOURNEY, death can be seen either as the end of a PATH or, as in the Calvinist theology of her time, as a point along the way, the gate to the afterlife:

But in a circular universe, where is death?

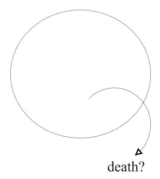

death?

Death is no longer a point on a path but a location out of the circle of life: "Oh for a Disc to the Distance / Between Ourselves / and the Dead!" Dickinson exclaims in one poem (*Under the light yet under*, A 92-3/4; F1068*A*/J949). The notion of dropping out of the circle of life can be seen in two other poems: "She dropt as softly as a star / From out my summer's eve -" (*She went as quiet as the Dew* H 6; F159*A*/J149) and "And I dropped down, and / down - / And hit a World at every / plunge" (*I felt a funeral in my brain*, H 53; F341*A*/J280).

For Dickinson, the CONTAINER schema has two forms: closed and open. Only death can ensure a closed container, one that is static, safe, as in *Doom is the house without the door* (H 42; F710*A*/J475). In life, the CONTAINER is either an open one or one that may be breached under pressure. In either case, the open or breached container provides the environment for the dynamics of movement and transformation to occur, whether it is in the "building of the soul" in *The props assist the house* (H 122; F729*A*/J1142) or the emergence of the butterfly from its cocoon in *My cocoon tightens, colors teaze* (H 189; F1107*A*/J1099). The CONTAINER schema of life, as opposed to that of death, is dynamic, involving movement and transformation, and is therefore associated with the schema of CHANGE. Dickinson's schemata of CONTAINER and CHANGE create a dynamic explosion of emotion and feeling. In the following poem, the difference between life and death is captured in the contrast between the two stanzas (*Safe in their alabaster chambers*, Boston Public Library; F124*F*/J216):

> Safe in their Alabas -
> ter
> Chambers -
> Untouched by Morning -
> And untouched by noon -
> Sleep the meek mem -
> bers of
> the Resurrection -
> Rafter of Satin - and
> Roof of Stone -
>
> Grand go the Years,
> in the Crescent - above
> them -
> Worlds scoop their Arcs -
> And Firmaments - row -

Diadems - drop -
And Doges - surrender -
Soundless as Dots,
On a Disc of Snow.

In the first stanza, the CONTAINER schema of death is "untouched," not affected by the changing cycle of time; in contrast, in the second stanza the years pass in the cyclical sweep of planetary motion. The subtle shifts in the metrical regularities of iambic pentameter and hymn meter and the varied array of partial and unaccented rhymes reflect the CHANGE schema. The echoing partial and unaccented rhymes in "Noon," "Resurrection," and "Stone" contribute toward a sense of containment in the first stanza, with their ending consonant [n], as opposed to the assonantal rhymes "row" and "snow" in the second stanza that are left open. The first stanza, reflecting the closed chamber of death, ends with the words "Roof of Stone"; the second, reflecting the open universe of life, ends with the words "Disc of Snow." Unlike the static position of the dead in their alabaster containers in the first stanza, the CHANGE schema of the second stanza invokes not only change in movement but also transformation as the diadems and doges of the closing lines are subjected to the vicissitudes of mutability.

We have come a long way from the flirtatious and happy examples of the flower-poems to the somber chambers of death. But Dickinson's many voices in her voluminous collection of poems are unified by her poetics, which are marked, as we have seen, by an informal, colloquial style that draws the reader in, her blending of her self with both her poems and her flowers, and, above all, the structuring metaphorical schemata of VOYAGE, CONTAINER, and CHANGE. These are just a few of the many features of Dickinson's poems that show how we need to experience the poems in order to understand them. Thomas Carlisle effectively captures the poet's emotive and explosive resonance in his own poem "Emily Dickinson": Dickinson, he says, is "demure as dynamite."

Acknowledgments

I thank Connie Kirk and Emily Williams for their careful comments on an earlier draft of this essay. I am grateful to the Amherst College Library Archives and the Jones Library for permission to transcribe Dickinson's texts from the manuscripts.

Emily Dickinson texts transcribed and reproduced by permission of the publishers and the Trustees of Amherst College from *The Manuscript Books of Emily Dickinson: A Facsimile Edition*, R. W. Franklin, ed., Cambridge, Mass.: The Belknap Press of Harvard University Press. Copyright © 1981 by the President and Fellows of Harvard College. Copyright ©1951, 1955, 1978, 1979, 1980, by the President and Fellows of Harvard College. Copyright © 1914, 1924, 1929, 1932, 1942, by Martha Dickinson Bianchi.

Notes

1. This poem exists in two manuscript versions. One is housed at the Jones Library in Amherst and was sent to her friend Samuel Bowles, the editor of the *Springfield Republican*. The other appears in one of the booklets Dickinson made (Fascicle 10) and is archived at the Houghton library at Harvard University. The text above is transcribed from the Jones Library manuscript. All transcriptions in this essay are from the manuscript versions ("A" refers to the Amherst College Archives, "H" to the Houghton archives). The other numbering refers to the two major editions: Franklin (F) and Johnson (J).

2. A brief but good introduction to the cultural and historical traditions of the mistletoe may be found in David Beaulieu's article "Kissing Under the Mistletoe."

3. The idea that Dickinson's syntax is frequently "scrambled" can be found in commentaries by scholars such as David Porter and Eric Griffiths.

4. If you hold your hands to the Adam's apple in your throat while pronouncing the pairs above, you will notice a lack of vibration in the first of the pair, while the second creates a vibration.

5. Note that in this reading, "Plush" is no longer an adjective but a noun. Although the *Oxford English Dictionary* records adjectival use of the word *plush* as far back as 1629, its substantive use is more general. Dickinson's use of the term elsewhere in the poetry is always as a noun.

6. In cognitive linguistics, it is customary to indicate conceptual metaphors and schemata by capitalization, to indicate that these are not linguistic expressions but rather abstract conceptualizations that structure the linguistic expressions arising from them.

7. For a more detailed account, see Freeman, "Metaphor Making Meaning."

Works Cited

Allen, Mary Adèle. *Around a Village Green: Sketches of Life in Amherst*. Northampton, MA: Krausher Press, 1939.

Beaulieu, David. "Kissing Under the Mistletoe." About.com:Landscaping. 15 Oct. 2009. http://landscaping.about.com/cs/winterlandscaping1/a/mistletoe.htm.

Carlisle, Thomas John. *Invisible Harvest*. Grand Rapids, MI: Wm. B. Eerdmans, 1987.

Conrad, Joseph. *The Nigger of the Narcissus*. 1897. New York: Doubleday, Page, 1914.

Dickinson, Emily. *The Letters of Emily Dickinson*. Ed. Thomas H. Johnson. 3 vols. Cambridge, MA: Belknap Press of Harvard UP, 1965.

_____. *The Poems of Emily Dickinson Including Variant Readings Critically Compared with all Known Manuscripts*. Ed. Thomas H. Johnson. 3 vols. Cambridge, MA: Belknap Press of Harvard UP, 1955.

_____. *The Poems of Emily Dickinson: Variorum Edition*. Ed. R. W. Franklin. 3 vols. Cambridge, MA: Belknap Press of Harvard UP, 1998.

Fauconnier, Gilles, and Mark Turner. *The Way We Think: Conceptual Blending and the Mind's Hidden Complexities*. New York: Basic Books, 2002.

Freeman, Margaret H. "Grounded Spaces: Deictic Self-Anaphors in the Poetry of Emily Dickinson." *Language and Literature* 61 (1997): 7-28.

_____. "Metaphor Making Meaning: Dickinson's Conceptual Universe." *Journal of Pragmatics* 24.6 (1995): 643-66.

Griffiths, Eric. "The Lavender of the Subjunctive." Rev. of *The Cambridge Grammar of the English Language*, by Rodney Huddleston and Geoffrey K. Pullum. *The Guardian* 13 July 2002.

Johnson, Mark. *The Body in the Mind: The Bodily Basis of Meaning, Imagination, and Reason*. Chicago: U of Chicago P, 1987.

Kövecses, Zoltán. *Metaphor and Emotion: Language, Culture, and Body in Human Feeling*. New York: Cambridge UP, 2000.

Lakoff, George, and Mark Johnson. *Metaphors We Live By*. Chicago: U of Chicago P, 1980.

Patterson, Rebecca. *Emily Dickinson's Imagery*. Ed. Margaret H. Freeman. Amherst: U of Massachusetts P, 1979.

Porter, David. *Dickinson: The Modern Idiom*. Cambridge, MA: Harvard UP, 1981.

Stevens, Wallace. *The Collected Poems of Wallace Stevens*. New York: Alfred A. Knopf, 1961.

Tennyson, Alfred. *The Poems of Alfred, Lord Tennyson: Volume 1, 1830-1856*. London: J. M. Dent & Sons, 1906.

Tsur, Reuven. *Toward a Theory of Cognitive Poetics*. Rev. ed. Amsterdam: North Holland, 2008.

Wordsworth, William. "Lines composed a few miles above Tintern Abbey: On revisiting the banks of the Wye during a tour, July 13, 1798." 1798. *Wordsworth: Poetical Works*. Ed. Thomas Hutchinson and Ernest De Selincourt. London: Oxford UP, 1904. 163-65.

The Conscious Corpse in Browning, Housman, and Dickinson

Matthew J. Bolton

Matthew J. Bolton offers a comparative analysis of the trope of the "conscious corpse" in the poetry of Robert Browning, A. E. Housman, and Emily Dickinson, three poets who responded in their work to the "steady undermining of the pillars of Christian faith" in the nineteenth century. While Browning uses this trope satirically in "The Bishop Orders his Tomb at Saint Praxed's Church" as he depicts Roman Catholicism as a religious practice that is concerned more with material than with spiritual matters, and Housman in *A Shropshire Lad* uses this trope to emphasize life's transience and death's finality, Dickinson, in poems such as "I heard a Fly buzz – when I died –" and "Because I could not stop for Death –," uses the figure of the conscious corpse to explore the "viability of an afterlife in which the body retains its sentience."

To Dickinson, who is preoccupied with the idea of an afterlife "in which consciousness resides with rather than transcends the body," the trope of the conscious corpse may serve "as a means of reconciling faith with doubt." While Dickinson at times, such as in the poem "Going to Heaven!," invokes the traditional Christian idea of heaven, "her more haunting and powerful depictions of the afterlife suggest that the consciousness somehow continues to reside with the body, sleeping or talking within its grave"—an image that suggests the possibility that there may be life after death even if "the Christian promise of Heaven fail[s]to hold true." As "a hedge against the total annihilation of the self," the idea of the conscious corpse is thus a "consolation," since perhaps "any afterlife [is] preferable to nothingness." J.B.B.

Making their way down through the circles of the Inferno, Dante and his guide, Virgil, come to a place where the gorgon Medusa stands watch over a landscape littered with stone sepulchers. Dante describes the sights and sounds of this domain: "Each tomb had its lid loose, pushed to one side, / And from within came forth such fierce laments / That I was sure inside were tortured souls" (78). When Dante inquires about the tombs, Virgil tells him that these are the resting places of heretics who denied that there was an afterlife and therefore sought to "make the soul die when the body dies" (82). The entombment of the heretics is a classic example of the *contrapasso*, an infernal punishment that serves as an ironic reversal of the sins a soul committed in life. On earth, these men denied that there was an afterlife; now, they will spend eternity entombed in their sepulchers. They are conscious corpses, souls who remain trapped in the resting places of their dead bodies. Dante's image of a soul living on in its tomb exerts a powerful hold on the imagination because it speaks to our primal fears and confusions about the relationship between body and mind, life and death, being and nothingness.

The trope of the conscious corpse also figures in major poems by several nineteenth-century British and American poets, including Robert Browning, A. E. Housman, and—most notably—Emily Dickinson. But whereas for Dante the living corpse is associated only with sin and horror, these later poets and their narrators have wider-ranging and more complex responses to the trope. This may be a sign of the changing times, for the nineteenth century witnessed a steady undermining of the pillars of Christian faith. The new social sciences of linguistics, archaeology, and anthropology challenged the inerrancy of the Bible, while the hard sciences of biology and astronomy told a very different story about the creation of the universe than did the Judeo-Christian tradition. Matthew Arnold spoke for his age when he described, in his poem "Dover Beach," "the melancholy, long, withdrawing roar" of the retreating "Sea of Faith" (25, 21). In a more skeptical age than Dante's, the image of the conscious corpse takes on new valences and resonances. Browning uses it satirically, creating a bishop whose belief that he will continue to inhabit his body after death suggests that the Catholic Church is more concerned with material than with spiritual matters. For Housman, an avowed atheist, the conscious corpse is a figure of bittersweet irony that speaks to the transience of life and the irrevocable nature of death. Dickinson, finally, may see the trope of the conscious corpse as a means of reconciling faith with doubt. To lie in one's tomb, physically dead yet still somehow aware of one's identity and surroundings, is to be suspended between the Christian promise of heaven and the skeptic's expectation of nonexistence. Poems such as "I heard a Fly buzz – when I died –" (Fr 591) and "Because I could not stop for Death –" (Fr 479) offer a narrow and compromised afterlife in which the soul continues to reside in the body. Whereas Dante saw this existence as an infernal punishment, for Dickinson and her contemporaries the conscious corpse may be a hedge against the total annihilation of the self.

* * *

The speaker in Robert Browning's 1845 poem "The Bishop Orders his Tomb at Saint Praxed's Church" seems to be unable to accept his own imminent death. Or, to be more exact, he accepts that he will die but believes that he will remain conscious of his body's surroundings after death. It is therefore with great care and deliberation that the bishop communicates his wishes regarding the tomb that will be erected for him in his church. The bishop begins his monologue by invoking Ecclesiastes and claiming that "the world's a dream" (9). Yet his musing gives way to a sudden "And so, about this tomb of mine," and it is the repository of his body rather than the state of his soul that will occupy the remainder of his dying thoughts (15). The bishop is surrounded by his illegitimate sons, to whom he is leaving his possessions and property in exchange for the promise of a well-appointed burial niche. Of course, he does not publicly acknowledge his sexual transgressions; instead, he obfuscates, calling his sons "nephews" and giving vent to his libido in the ornamentation of his tomb. He calls for a rendering of "Pan / ready to twitch the Nymph's last garment off" (60-61). It is strange enough that the bishop would order a pagan rather than a Christian scene to be carved into his monument, and still stranger that it should be one depicting such frank sexuality. Elsewhere, his similes and metaphors reveal his fixation on the human body, as when he calls for "Some lump, ah God, of lapis lazuli, / Big as a Jew's head cut off at the nape, / Blue as a vein o'er the Madonna's breast" (42-44). Both of these grotesque comparisons show the bishop cloaking in religious garb his interest in the body. The "Jew's head" is bodily violence rendered acceptable by its being practiced on the body of an unbeliever, while the "vein o'er the Madonna's breast" is a prurient interest in the female body rendered acceptable by this particular body's belonging to the Virgin Mary. The bishop repeatedly collapses and juxtaposes the sacred with the profane and the soul with the body.

Like a blazon poet, the bishop singles out and catalogs the parts of the human body. Angry at one of his ungrateful sons, for example, he asks: "Will ye ever eat my heart? / Ever your eyes were as a lizard's quick, / They glitter like your mother's for my soul" (103-5). In this rhetorical equivalent of an anatomy lesson, he isolates his own heart, then the eyes of his son, and then those of his former mistress. Incidentally, this is the only time that the bishop mentions having a soul. At another point, he promises his son, "Horses for ye, and brown Greek manuscripts, / And mistresses with great smooth marbly limbs" (74-75). Again he has objectified an element of the female body—the limbs—appraising them with a collector's eye. Moreover, in lumping together horses, manuscripts, and mistresses, the bishop reveals the degree to which his sexual desire is bound up with his avid materialism. He admires only that which is rare and valuable, hence his increasingly more extravagant demands regarding the material out of which his slab will be made: he goes from "basalt" (25) to "antique-black" (54) to "jasper" (68) to "all *lapis*" (102). The tomb, then, is the bishop's last possession, one that will house the body that has been so central to his understanding of life.

The bishop's interest in his tomb betrays his belief about the after-life: he believes that his senses will continue to function after death. The tomb is not just a monument for posterity; it is the couch from which his decaying body will continue to observe the doings of Saint Praxed's. It is therefore important to him that he have a tomb with a view (21):

> One sees the pulpit o' the epistle-side,
> And somewhat of the choir, those silent seats,
> And up into the aery dome where live
> The angels, and a sunbeam's sure to lurk;
>
> (21-24)

And while his late ecclesiastic rival, Gandolf, has snatched the more desirable south corner, the bishop requests to be placed "where I may look at him!" Indeed, the bishop is watching to see "if he leers— / Old Gandolf, at me, from his onion stone" (124-25). The bishop's under-standing of the afterlife extends to include Gandolf, who, like the bishop, will remain conscious after death.

The bishop fears, however, that his sons may be tempted to build him an inexpensive tomb in order to keep his riches for themselves. He is appalled at the idea that they might use a cheap material, saying, "Stone— / Gritstone, a-crumble! Clammy squares which sweat / As if the corpse they keep were oozing through—" (115-17). He ac-cuses his sons of hoping to "revel down my villas while I gasp / Bricked o'er with beggar's mouldy travertine / Which Gandolf from his tomb-top chuckles at!" (65-68). It is a startling image: the bishop believes he will continue to die by degrees, "gasping" in his tomb out of his dismay at the shoddiness of the materials of which it is built. If his tomb is rich and well appointed, then the bishop will be quite con-tent to be dead:

And then how I shall lie through centuries,
And hear the blessed mutter of the mass,
And see God made and eaten all day long,
And feel the steady candle-flame, and taste
Good strong thick stupefying incense-smoke!
(80-84)

The bishop believes he will hear, see, feel, and taste after death. In short, he believes in an afterlife, but one in which the soul continues to inhabit the body. His materialism is such that he cannot conceive of consciousness without corporeality.

The great Victorian art critic and intellectual John Ruskin said of "The Bishop Orders his Tomb," "I know no other piece of modern English, prose or poetry, in which there is so much told, as in these lines, of the Renaissance spirit,—its worldliness, inconsistency, pride, hypocrisy, ignorance of itself, love of art, of luxury, and of good Latin" (in Litzinger and Smalley 197-98). Yet the poem grew out of more than Browning's interest in the Renaissance; it was very much a response to a current, rather than a historic, religious crisis. In submitting the piece to *Hood's Magazine*, Browning wrote, "I picked it out as being a pet of mine, and just the thing for the time—What with the Oxford business, and Camden society and other embroilments" (*Letters* 35-36). Browning is referring to the Oxford Movement, also known as the Tractarian Movement, a push for religious reform spearheaded by a handful of Oxford University professors in the 1830s and 1840s. Theologians such as John Henry Newman and Edward Pusey sought to infuse the Church of England with elements of the older, medieval Mass and of the Catholic tradition. For many Englishmen, the writings of Newman and his peers represented a papist infiltration and betrayal of the church. Some saw the Oxford Movement as a religious fifth column, a group that sought not to reform the Anglican Church but to undermine and replace it. Newman converted to Catholicism in 1845, the same year Browning published "The Bishop Orders his Tomb." In the eyes of his critics, Newman's conversion confirmed that his plan had always been to bring the Church of England under the sway of the Vatican.

The distrust of the Oxford Movement was part and parcel of a larger distrust of Catholicism itself. When Browning published his poem, Catholics had held full rights as citizens in England for only some fifteen years. Though the Catholic Emancipation Movement of the 1820s had repealed the legal restrictions and penalties on English and Irish Catholics, social acceptance of Catholicism was slower to follow. Historian Walter Houghton asserts that through most of the Victorian era, "to enter the Roman Church was literally to exile oneself from English life" (84). This phenomenon is reflected in Victorian literature, in which conversion to Catholicism often figures as a temptation and a threat. In Anthony Trollope's *Barchester Towers* (1857), for example, the Anglican minister Mr. Arabin is said to have flirted with Catholicism as a young man: "His tastes were against him: the ceremonies and pomps of the Church of Rome, their august feasts and solemn fasts invited his imagination and pleased his eye" (189). The Church of Rome is represented here as a religion of grand, but hollow, ceremony. It centers not on faith but on ritual and appeals not to the soul but to the eye.

Browning's bishop should therefore be read as a satirical comment on Catholicism itself. His fixation on his own body and its interment, as well as on the elaborate design of his tomb, may illustrate what Browning perceived as a hollowness at the center of Catholic doctrine and form. At his core, the bishop does not believe in the Christian cosmology: for him, there will be no judgment, heaven, or hell. His soul, such as it is, will stay right where it is, continuing to inhabit his body and the rich tomb that houses it. In Browning's poem, the trope of the conscious corpse is therefore an indictment of a religious practice that centers on external trappings rather than on inner faith.

* * *

In his 1896 collection *A Shropshire Lad*, A. E. Housman uses the trope of the conscious corpse to a very different effect. A classicist and an atheist, Housman dwells on the transience of life and the finality of death. In his poems, there is no consolation of a Christian afterlife, in which the soul leaves the body and ascends to heaven. Instead, consciousness ends when life ends. In "The Immortal Part," for example, it is not the soul but the bones that will live on after death. The speaker imagines his bones asking, "When shall this slough of sense be cast, / This dust of thoughts be laid at last?" (5-6). The bones will live on in the earth after the man's mind and spirit have been extinguished. Aware that he will eventually be annihilated, the speaker resolves to live life fully,

> Before this fire of sense decay,
> This smoke of thought blow clean away,
> And leave with ancient night alone
> The steadfast and enduring bone.
>
> (41-44)

The poem reverses the logic of Christian redemption, in which the soul is immortal and the body perishable. Here it is consciousness that is the most fragile and fleeting part of a person.

Housman often likens death to sleep, for in his cosmology both entail the extinguishment of consciousness. One of the most frequently occurring images in *A Shropshire Lad* is of a person sleeping under the ground. "Reveille," for example, ends with a comparison of death and sleep: "Breath's a ware that will not keep / Up, lad: when the journey's over / There'll be time enough to sleep" (22-24). In "This Time of Year a Twelvemonth Past," to cite another example, a speaker reflects on the fate of his late rival:

Fred keeps the house all kinds of weather,
And clay's the house he keeps;
When Rose and I walk out together
Stock-still lies Fred and sleeps.

(13-16)

Yet a third speaker, a young man courting a woman on the night before he leaves town, invokes the possibility of his own death. In "On Your Midnight Pallet Lying," he pleads with the woman to let him share her bed, so if he should die he will be able to recall that

In a kinder bed I lay,
And the breast the darnel smothers
Rested once upon another's
When it was not clay.

(11-14)

He imagines himself as a corpse that will be able to compare its current bed—the grave—to the "kinder bed" of the young woman. The corpse has become part of the earth again, for its "breast" is now "clay," yet it still retains some measure of consciousness.

Housman's most thorough treatment of the conscious corpse comes in "Is My Team Ploughing?" The poem is a series of exchanges between two friends, one of whom is dead and buried and one of whom is still alive. The dead friend asks about all of the things he has left behind: football, the change of seasons, and his beloved. Finally, he asks about his friend himself:

"Is my friend hearty,
Now I am thin and pine,
And has he found to sleep in
A better bed than mine?"

(25-28)

The young man who is still alive responds with this:

> Yes, lad, I lie easy,
> I lie as lads would choose;
> I cheer a dead man's sweetheart,
> Never ask me whose.
>
> (29-32)

The poem therefore closes with an ironic twist: the living youth reveals that he has been romancing his dead friend's beloved. It is a great comic ending, but it also speaks to a more profound truth: life goes on even though an individual life has ended. It would no doubt pain the dead youth were he to learn that his best friend and his sweetheart have become involved with each other. Yet in Housman's poem, the dead youth has no access to the world he has left behind. He is not a disembodied ghost, flitting about the places he once frequented, nor is he a sanctified soul looking down from Heaven. Even the shades in Homer's underworld have more awareness of the goings-on above the ground than does this dead youth. Neither ghost nor soul nor shade, he is only a buried body and a plaintive voice. One might even read this whole dialogue as originating in the mind of the living friend, who feels some measure of guilt for having taken his dead friend's place.

In Housman's poems, the conscious corpse attests to the suddenness with which life ends and to the finality of the grave. The consciousness of the youth in "Is My Team Ploughing?" lingers like a drawn-out echo of life; it is as if the dead are still too stunned to realize that their lives have ended. One knows, on an intellectual level, that a dead body cannot possibly retain sentience or consciousness. Housman's corpses do, however, even as the corpse itself degrades and turns to clay. Yet nowhere in *A Shropshire Lad* does Housman hold out the possibility that the soul might leave the body; the only afterlife is a solitary buried one. The voice of the buried dead is therefore a literary construct that, ironically, argues against the idea of life after death rather than for it. The buried youth can no more speak or feel than can the bones in "The Immortal Part." It is the living, and not the dead, who have trouble grasping the concept that upon death they will cease to exist at all.

Housman's preoccupation with death may be bound up with his own atheism. Although raised in the Church of England, Housman gradually lost his religious faith, and in his final year at Oxford he declared himself an atheist. He spoke obliquely of this transformation many years later, in 1892, when he delivered his address upon being made a professor at University College London. Housman wrote that "the pursuit of truth in some directions is even injurious to happiness, because it compels us to take leave of delusions which were pleasant while they lasted" (in Graves 82). For him, the afterlife is one such pleasant delusion. Housman's work is therefore both sentimental and unrelenting in its depiction of death. On one hand, the dead are compared to sleepers and their graves to beds, a gentle euphemism that makes death almost an anodyne; yet on the other, Housman is insistent that consciousness itself cannot transcend the body. Many of his most powerful poems center on this gap between the love one bears for the departed and the knowledge one holds that they are gone forever. The conscious corpse therefore bridges the gap between the living and the dead, between the sentimental and the clinical. In Housman, the dead may retain some measure of consciousness only in the minds of the living and in the tissues of a poem.

* * *

Perhaps no poet has more exhaustively explored the image of the conscious corpse than Emily Dickinson. Because she returns to this trope so many times, her treatment of it is more complex and nuanced than those of Browning and Housman. Browning uses the image of the conscious corpse to satirize a Catholicism that devotes itself to outward show, while in Housman the image serves to underscore the sudden but irrevocable nature of death. Only Dickinson seems to be actively considering the viability of an afterlife in which the body retains its sentience. Although at times she invokes an orthodox Christian afterlife (as in poems like "Going to Heaven!"; Fr 128), Dickinson is far more preoccupied with one in which consciousness resides with rather than transcends the body.

On the surface, Dickinson's imagery surrounding death and burial has much in common with that of Housman. Of course, Dickinson wrote and published before Housman: she died in 1886, and her first volume of poetry was brought out in 1890, five years before *A Shropshire Lad*. While it is conceivable that Housman could have read Dickinson before publishing his own volume, there is no evidence that he did so. Any similarities between the two poets are therefore attributable not to influence but to confluence: the two poets arrived independently at some of the same conclusions about the nature of death. Both, for example, liken death to sleep, as in Dickinson's lines "I went to thank her – / But She Slept – / Her Bed – a funnelled Stone –" (206, 1-3). In another short poem, a living speaker wonders about being dead—a sentiment that runs throughout *A Shropshire Lad*: "I Wonder if the Sepulcher / Don't feel a lonesome way –" (Fr 582, 17-18). In a poem Dickinson's early editors titled "Retrospect," it is a dead speaker rather than a living one who speaks of the change of seasons: "'Twas just this time, last year, I died. / I know I heard the Corn, / When I was carried by the Farms –" (Fr 344, 1-3). The corpse that was carried past the farms to the graveyard retained enough of its consciousness to hear the sound of corn in the fields—and retains enough of it now to reflect on the passage of time since his or her burial.

Yet Dickinson goes further in her use of the conscious corpse image than does Housman. Like Browning before him, Housman tends to use this trope to create dramatic irony. In *A Shropshire Lad*, the voice from beyond the grave or the body that retains an awareness of its surroundings is meant to be read as a literary device. Dickinson, in contrast, has less dramatic or narratorial distance from her depictions of a corporeal afterlife. She is after something other than irony: in several of her most famous poems, she asks and tries to answer the most essential metaphysical questions surrounding the death of the body and of the mind. In "I died for Beauty" (Fr 448), for example, a speaker talks about events following on his or her death. He or she is sharing a tomb with another body, and the two speak to each other. The poem ends by marking the slow passage of time: "We talked between the Rooms – / Until the Moss had reached our lips – / And covered up – Our names –" (10-12). This final image quite explicitly collapses the distinctions between the buried bodies, the consciousness that these bodies seem still to contain, and the names engraved on their tombs. To what extent are the lips with which the two speak synonymous with the names and epitaphs that speak for them? Does the consciousness of the dead linger and gradually fade, the way, perhaps, the memory of their life and consciousness gradually fades from the minds of the living? There is a haunting ambiguity about these closing lines, for Dickinson's poem sets up a series of contradictions about the nature of life after death.

"I heard a Fly buzz – when I died –" (Fr 591) likewise centers on a speaker reflecting on his or her own death. In this poem, consciousness survives the body yet does not seem to transcend it. As the speaker is dying, he or she is distracted by the presence of a fly in the death chamber. The precise role that the fly plays is unclear, but in one way or another it distracts from and interferes with the process of dying: "There interposed a Fly – / . . . and then / I could not see to see –" (Fr 591, 12-16). As does "I died for Beauty," the poem closes with a strange and unsettling image. The fly might be read as a reminder of the most physical realities of death: that whatever the state and fate of the soul, the body will become carrion. In this sense, the housefly is a harbinger of the physical decay that is to come. Yet the speaker's fixation on the fly suggests that it somehow compromised the speaker's death—and perhaps his or her afterlife. The fly "interposed" itself "between the light and me." According to Christian doctrine, the soul should leave the body after death to go live in the light of God. Did the fly distract the speaker at a pivotal moment, and did the soul fail to leave the body before the light, the speaker's vision, and his or her chance at salvation fail? Does the fact that the speaker's mind was on earthly rather than spiritual things at the moment of death suggest that the afterlife will also be an earthly one? Dickinson's poems are not riddles to be solved, and there is no one definitive interpretation for a poem like this. In fact, the power of poems such as "I heard a Fly buzz – when I died –" derives from the way in which they seem to be working through the metaphysics of life and death rather than presenting pat answers.

In what is arguably Dickinson's most famous poem, "Because I could not stop for Death –" (Fr 479), a speaker recalls the circumstances of her death. Death arrives in a chariot and takes the speaker away, driving her past the school, the fields, and the setting sun itself. The reader might assume, midway through the poem, that he or she is on the familiar ground of the allegory. Dying, according to the allegorical framework that the first few lines of the poem establishes, is like taking one final journey out of town. Death is not a fearsome figure but a gentleman who "kindly stopped," who "knew no haste," and who possesses "civility." Comparing death to a journey is a fairly common trope. As a point of comparison, take Christina Rossetti's poem "Up-Hill" (1887), in which a speaker asks about the road winding up a hill, the inn perched at the top, and the rooms and companions that will await her at journey's end. The road, one understands, is the road of life, while the welcoming inn is the Christian Heaven. In the prototypical allegory, each concrete object has a symbolic equivalent, such that the poem can function on both the concrete and the allegorical levels. Yet Dickinson is up to something very different, and the reader who has too readily assumed that this carriage ride with death is the stuff of allegory may be surprised by the second half of the poem.

As the chariot reaches its destination, Dickinson's allegorical treatment of death collapses into itself: "We paused before a House that seemed / A Swelling of the Ground – / . . . / The Cornice – in the Ground –" (Fr 479, 13-14,16). If Dickinson were writing in the spirit of Rossetti's "Up-Hill," the "house" would be a gracious mansion full of long-dead friends. Indeed, this is the metaphor Jesus Christ uses to speak of the afterlife when he says, "In my Father's house are many rooms . . . I am going there to prepare a place for you" (John 14:2). The allegory would then be perfectly sound: death is like a charioteer who takes one to a better place. In Dickinson's poem, however, the charioteer delivers the dead narrator not to an allegorical equivalent of heaven but to "a swelling of the ground." In other words, the dignified charioteer simply delivers the narrator to her grave. The concrete and the allegorical lose their meaning, for the personified death brings the narrator to the same destination for which her corpse was bound. In the final stanza of the poem, the narrator indicates that her consciousness has, in fact, continued to abide with her body for "centuries" and will continue to do so for "eternity."

Dickinson's preoccupation with death and the nature of the afterlife may reflect her own struggles with religious faith. In an 1884 letter to her sister, Dickinson asserted that "faith is doubt," a paradoxical creed that manifests itself in so much of her poetry (L912). While she does sometimes write of a traditional Christian vision of Heaven, her more haunting and powerful depictions of the afterlife suggest that the consciousness somehow continues to reside with the body, sleeping or talking within its grave. Perhaps this image splits the difference between faith and doubt, invoking the possibility that there could be life after death even should the Christian promise of Heaven fail to hold true.

That three major nineteenth-century poets used the trope of the conscious corpse in their work speaks to the sea change that Christianity, as well as other religious faiths, suffered during the century. For Dante, writing at a time when Christian faith and doctrine were a nearly monolithic presence in western Europe, the idea of a soul continuing to inhabit its tomb was a horrible one. Only a great sinner would be visited with such an afterlife, for the great promise of Christianity is that the soul will transcend the body after death. For Browning, Housman, and Dickinson, however, the conscious corpse is not an abomination but a consolation. In an age in which Christianity no longer held the assurances it once did, perhaps for them any afterlife was preferable to nothingness.

Works Cited

Arnold, Matthew. "Dover Beach." *The Major Victorian Poets: Tennyson, Browning, Arnold*. Ed. William E. Buckler. New York: Houghton Mifflin, 1973.

Browning, Robert. "The Bishop Orders his Tomb at Saint Praxed's Church." *The Major Victorian Poets: Tennyson, Browning, Arnold*. Ed. William E. Buckler. New York: Houghton Mifflin, 1973.

_____. *New Letters of Robert Browning*. Ed. William Clyde DeVane and Kenneth Leslie Knickerbocker. London: John Murray, 1951.

Dante. *Dante's Inferno: The Indiana Critical Edition*. Trans. and ed. Mark Musa. Bloomington: Indiana UP, 1995.

Dickinson, Emily. *The Letters of Emily Dickinson*. Ed. Thomas H. Johnson and Theodora Ward. 3 vols. 1958. Cambridge, MA: Harvard UP, 1979.

_____. *The Poems of Emily Dickinson*. Ed. R. W. Franklin. Cambridge, MA: Harvard UP, 1999.

Graves, Richard Perceval. *A. E. Housman: The Scholar-Poet*. London: Routledge, 1979.

Houghton, Walter. *The Victorian Frame of Mind, 1830-1870*. New Haven, CT: Yale UP, 1957.

Housman, A. E. *The Poems of A. E. Housman*. Ed. Archie Burnett. New York: Oxford UP, 1998.

Litzinger, Boyd, and Donald Smalley, eds. *Browning: The Critical Heritage*. New York: Routledge, 1968.

Rossetti, Christina. *The Complete Poems*. New York: Penguin, 2001.

Trollope, Anthony. *Barchester Towers*. 1857. New York: Oxford UP, 1953.

CRITICAL
READINGS

Dickinson's Local, Global, and Cosmic Perspectives_____

Jane Donahue Eberwein

Like the first editors of Emily Dickinson's poetry, Mabel Loomis Todd and Thomas Wentworth Higginson, who sought to foreground poems that related the poet to a "familiar world" in order to counter the caricatured view of the poet as a "fragile, otherworldly creature" unaware of the larger world beyond her Amherst home, recent biographers and scholars of Dickinson, as Jane Donahue Eberwein shows, have "convincingly dismantled" the distorted mythic image of Dickinson by "amassing detailed information about her life's circumstances." These include works by Dickinson's major biographers, Richard B. Sewall, who, in his *Life of Emily Dickinson*, offers information on Dickinson's family background, her childhood, her education, her reading, and her friendships, and by Cynthia Griffin Wolff, who, in *Emily Dickinson*, places Dickinson in a social-historical context, including the domestic world of nineteenth-century women. A similar end is sought by Paula Bennett, who, in *Emily Dickinson: Woman Poet*, reads Dickinson in terms of an international nineteenth-century feminine culture as she analyzes the gendered aspects of Dickinson's poetry; by Betsy Erkkila, who, in "Emily Dickinson and Class," argues that Dickinson "'sought to secure the declining status of both her gender and her class through the accumulation of cultural and spiritual capital'"; by Shira Wolosky, who, in *Emily Dickinson: A Voice of War*, argues that Dickinson was deeply engaged in the national and spiritual crisis precipitated by the Civil War; and by Joan Burbick, who, in "'One Unbroken Company': Religion and Emily Dickinson," describes a Dickinson "whose spiritual pilgrimage 'is more relational than individualistic.'"

Dickinson's Amherst culture, as Eberwein concludes, "educated her to ask questions and to settle for nothing less than experiential knowledge of both science and the soul." Indeed, "what Dickinson

---

most derived from her culture was a searching mind—and the resilience not to be overcome by mysteries that eluded religion, science,
and the law. . . . And, for all her awareness of local and global environments, her truest perspective remained more vertical than horizontal, more attuned to speculations on immortality (experienced
even now and promised hereafter) than on Amherst, America, or the
wider world opened by friendships and reading."   J.B.B.

It was probably to counteract readers' anticipated tendencies to cari-
cature Emily Dickinson as some fragile, otherworldly creature that
Mabel Loomis Todd and Thomas Wentworth Higginson introduced
their editions of her poems with an opening group labeled "Life."
Verses gathered under that rubric supposedly differed from those in the
Love, Nature, and Time and Eternity groups by reflecting the poet's
awareness of the world beyond her home and garden. Mrs. Todd had
herself fallen under the spell of the mythic Emily back in 1881 when
she first picked up from Amherst folklore an impression of this "*character* of Amherst," "the climax of all the family oddity," a spectral sto-
rybook figure blessed with a mind said to be "perfectly wonderful" (R.
Sewall, *Life* 216). Finding, however, that many poems created by that
mind bespoke a broad and disciplined education along with sharp observation of the local scene, these first editors attempted to foreground
those that related their poetess to a familiar world.

In the process, they skipped over this minor example of her talent:

What is – "Paradise" –
Who live there –
Are they "Farmers" –
Do they "hoe" –
Do they know that this is "Amherst" –
And that I – am coming – too –
Do they wear "new shoes" – in "Eden" –
Is it always pleasant – there –

Wont they scold us – when we're hungry –
Or tell God – how cross we are –

You are sure there's such a person
As "a Father" – in the sky –
So if I get lost – there – ever –
Or do what the Nurse calls "die" –
I shant walk the "Jasper" – barefoot –
Ransomed folks – wont laugh at me –
Maybe – "Eden" a'nt so lonesome
As New England used to be!

(P215)

Here is one of those poems that—on the surface, anyway—reinforce the image of Emily Dickinson against which most of her editors, biographers, and critics have contended since 1890. Spoken by a pitiful waif, it reflects a child's narrow perspective that constricts attention to home, town, region, and some materially conceived heaven. The speaker is limited by immaturity, anxiety, provinciality, and a reductive imagination. What comes across most strongly here is fear born of deprivation. The child's social class is ambiguous, though reference to "the Nurse" suggests that the speaker comes from a household with servants—more than the hired girls and gardeners known to comfortable Amherst families like the Dickinsons. That she or he classifies potential acquaintances either as farmers or not-farmers, however, suggests experience restricted to an agricultural economy. Perhaps the nurse enters the picture because our speaker is one of those pathetic little invalids so familiar in sentimental fictions of the time. Perhaps, on the other hand, there is a nurse because there are no parents, a conjecture aroused by doubts about the heavenly "Father." In the 1945 *Bolts of Melody* edition of this poem, Todd and her daughter introduced one change in line 9, substituting "homesick" for "hungry" to suggest that the speaker is already lost in the narrow confines of her or his local environment and dreads being similarly outcast for eternity. Poverty and insecurity come to mind in references to hunger as well as to the presence or absence of new shoes. It seems that this speaker has been laughed at by more fortunate children to the point of fearing continued scorn in heaven even though paradise otherwise proffers a welcome escape from New England's humiliations and isolation. If we are to imagine Emily Dickinson as the speaker of this poem, we can find bountiful evidence supporting her mythic self-image as lonely, childlike, timid, and too fragile to withstand the pressures of a world she never understood. This is not the kind of responsive and even controlling intelligence we expect of an artist, even supposing that the reading I have so far provided for this poem is complete and adequate.

Scholars, however, have convincingly dismantled this distorted image of Emily Dickinson as a fugitive in time and space by amassing detailed information about her life's circumstances. Convinced that "what is presently most needed in the study of the life and works of this enigmatic poet, who has been the subject of so much distorting gossip and legend, is the most factual treatment possible," Jay Leyda compiled his chronologically ordered documentary record of her likely range of awareness, listing year by year events in the Dickinson households, Amherst, the United States, and the world as experienced by her family's numerous associates or represented in publications the poet was known to read (the *Springfield Republican, Atlantic Monthly, Harper's*, and *Scribner's* among others) to demonstrate conclusively through *The Years and Hours of Emily Dickinson* that "she wrote more *in time*, that she was much more involved in the conflicts and tensions of her nation and community, than we have thought" (xix-xx). Leyda's documentary record provides abundant factual grounding for biographical, cultural, and critical studies along with inspiration to fill gaps remaining in our knowledge; lately, it has inspired Daniel Lombardo to sketch out in *A Hedge Away: The Other Side of Emily Dickinson's Amherst* a host of brief, entertaining, and sometimes scandalous' narratives opening insight on local events as they impinged on the poet's consciousness.

Both of Dickinson's major biographers, Richard Sewall and Cynthia Griffin Wolff, build upon Leyda's example of coming to know this intensely private poet by gathering information about the many very public figures in her world even while acknowledging that available information about the woman herself makes a less enthralling story than the rumor-enhanced narratives biographers attempt to refute; nor do the facts go far to explain the poems. Sewall responds to this biographical challenge by accepting that, as an artist, Dickinson lived her life metaphorically in ways that call for interpretation. In developing his detailed *Life of Emily Dickinson*, he builds a context for her mystery by focusing attention on whatever can be known: chiefly her Dickinson family background and the distinctive familial rhetoric characteristic of her generation, the "War between the Houses" fomented by her brother's affair with Mabel Todd, information about the poet's childhood and schooling, her reading, and her many friendships. By demonstrating how much she meant in declaring "My friends are my 'estate,'" Sewall assaults impressions of her New England provinciality (9). By heeding the intellectual atmosphere of her home and town, he traces the origins of her metaphors. "She was not reared in a household of lawyers and treasurers for nothing," he observes; "she did not live in a college town for nothing" (10). Also recognizing how much more there is to tell about Emily Dickinson's companions than herself, about her poems' editing history than the circumstances of their creation, Wolff concentrates on placing the poet in an informative social-historical context, finding in her a subtle register of a time of crisis: "She lived in a time and place when God's grandeur still glimmered in the panorama of New England. Yet she never knew the dawning or even the noon of America's heroic age, but only the long shadows of its twilight; and later, she knew the darkness of the merely commercial, instrumental society that was to follow hard upon heroism's end" (*Dickinson* 9). Tracing her central metaphor of Dickinson as "pugilist poet" combating God, Wolff interprets the poetry in terms of her era's intellectual and spiritual currents. More amply than Sewall, she also places the poet within a world of nineteenth-century women, observing the rhythms and pressures of lives spent managing house-holds, nurturing children, and tending the sick—often in the shadows of prominent men.

Other recent studies confirm these biographers' discoveries of Em-ily Dickinson's alert responsiveness to particular circumstances and ambient culture. In *Emily Dickinson's Readings of Men and Books*, Benjamin Lease demonstrates her "passionate involvement with fam-ily, with friends, with a cultural legacy of rebellion against orthodox answers to the religious questions of her time" by foregrounding her friendships with her spiritual counselor, Charles Wadsworth, and liter-ary mentor, Higginson (xii). Paula Bennett, by contrast or complement, shows in *Emily Dickinson: Woman Poet* how "the poet not only lived her entire life 'at home,' but spent her life largely in a circle of women" (14). Like Lease, she focuses on Dickinson's reading—contemporary British women writers, in this case, rather than Shakespeare, the Bible, Watts's hymns, and seventeenth-century devotional writings. This context of an international nineteenth-century feminine culture leads Bennett to discovery of a distinctively gender-grounded poetic (19). Martha Nell Smith's focus in *Rowing in Eden* on the poet's intense re-lationship with her sister-in-law, Sue, represents another attempt to balance already well-documented discussions of Wadsworth, Hig-ginson, Samuel Bowles, and Josiah Gilbert Holland as influences on Dickinson.

Paying close attention to the poet's relationships both with Sue and with their mutual friend Bowles, Judith Farr moves beyond biography in *The Passion of Emily Dickinson* and reads the poetry in its cultural context to reveal Dickinson's "passion to lead a life in and through art—her own and that of others" (viii), specifically art understood in the Ruskinian sense of Victorian high culture. Barton St. Armand shares that concern in *Emily Dickinson and Her Culture*, where he draws analogies between what Higginson identified as his friend's "Poetry of the Portfolio" and popular arts like quilting and scrapbook assemblage practiced by middle-class nineteenth-century American women as well as American folk art and Ruskin's aesthetics (considered in relation to Austin Dickinson's choice of paintings for The Evergreens). Like Karl Keller, whose *The Only Kangaroo Among the Beauty* cleverly links Dickinson to her Puritan literary predecessors and to Robert Frost as well as to authors of her own period (Stowe, Hawthorne, Emerson, Whitman, Boston Bluestockings, and her own literarily ambitious circle of friends), St. Armand finds revealing affinities between Dickinson and the sentimental, aesthetic, and nature writers of her time.

Investigation of Emily Dickinson's environment, then, opens fruitful insight into her poetry's response to specific circumstances of place and time. From the first appearance of her poems, it has been recognized that her rootedness in Amherst, Massachusetts, and particularly in the family household profoundly shaped her imagination. Martha Dickinson Bianchi, her niece, stimulated public curiosity with books that blended family tradition, personal reminiscence, and snatches of correspondence. *Emily Dickinson Face to Face* and *The Life and Letters of Emily Dickinson* provided an idyllic image of Homestead life that tended to generate myths in an attempt to deflect negative attention from Austin and Susan Dickinson's marital discord. Millicent Todd Bingham offered a slightly less self-interested perspective—though necessarily a more distant one—in *Emily Dickinson's Home*, her answer to Bianchi. Among recent scholarly studies, Jean McClure Mudge's *Emily Dickinson and the Image of Home* most fully relates the poet's inner space to the physical designs and contrasting ambiences of her two houses: the Homestead, a brick mansion built by her grandfather, where she was born and spent her first ten years and to which she returned in 1855 to pass her remaining three decades, and the Pleasant Street house of her adolescence and young womanhood—the one Mudge says she associated with "the idyllic possibilities of home" (4). Except for two terms at Mount Holyoke, two extended periods spent in Cambridge to get care for her eyes, a few weeks spent visiting her father in Washington, and some minor youthful excursions, Dickinson lived entirely within the protective confines of "my Father's ground" (L330). By secluding herself in late years and seeing virtually nobody beyond her immediate circle, she freed space and time for creativity while fostering gossip about whatever may have gone on within the Homestead and her brother's home next door.

Grasping for explanations of Emily Dickinson's strange reserve, Higginson was the first to identify her father as key to her psychic formation. He wrote to his wife about his 1870 visit to the Homestead, noting "I saw Mr. Dickinson this morning a little—thin dry & speechless— I saw what her life has been" (L342b). Certainly, her father dominated their patriarchal household, where lofty moral, intellectual, and spiritual standards were imposed on all, habits of stern self-discipline fostered yet a parodic form of merriment generally encouraged, but where gender roles were clearly defined in ways that put pressure on the one son for public success and both daughters for domestic submission.[1] Other studies, notably John Cody's psychobiography, *After Great Pain*, Wolff's *Emily Dickinson*, and Barbara Mossberg's *Emily Dickinson: When a Writer Is a Daughter*, redirect attention to Emily Norcross Dickinson's influence on her daughter, one generally regarded as negative. Mary Elizabeth Kromer Bernhard, however, rebuts this judgment in "Portrait of a Family" by tracing to the poet's maternal family heritage intellectual and civic values generally associated with the Dickinsons and finding the major distinction between the two families to be the Norcrosses' stronger tradition of female education. Other aspects of home life merit study also as stimuli to the poet's imagination. Home obviously provided a wealth of domestic diction as well as the legal and economic vocabularies on which Dickinson drew in her poems—for comic effect sometimes as in "Alone and in a Circumstance" (P1167), linked to religious hope in the manner of Puritan covenant theology in "Mine – by the Right of the White Election!" (P528), or applied to romantic passion as in the poems Joan Burbick examines in "Emily Dickinson and the Economics of Desire."

Given the Dickinsons' intense involvement with their town and its institutions, Amherst may be recognized as a communal extension of household values. Biographical studies necessarily foreground the influence on this poet of growing up in a college town with her father and brother among its most prominent men. Polly Longsworth's pictorial compilation of *The World of Emily Dickinson* now provides a graphic record of the changing local environment that strongly contributed to the world view of this citizen who occasionally even signed herself "Amherst." The town's architectural and spatial features can be documented: its grand homes and mill housing; its churches, college buildings, hat factories, and business blocks; its graveyard behind both the Pleasant Street house and the Homestead meadow; its Common—undeveloped until Austin Dickinson took on the challenge of landscaping; its surrounding hills—Berkshires to the west and Pelhams to the east; and the Connecticut River. So can its sharing in the conservative Congregational culture of New England's historic Connecticut Valley. More important for the formation of Emily Dickinson's mind was the interconnectedness of its domestic, religious, and educational institutions—all of which reinforced a traditional Christian perspective.

A child raised in the habit of family prayer presided over by her father and probably nurtured by her mother in the *New England Primer* (from which Dickinson later snipped engravings for comic messages to Sue) soon came under the church's influence, and Emily Dickinson grew up in a time of special religious excitement. The Second Awakening stretched far beyond Amherst, of course, and is best known for frontier camp meetings and Charles Grandison Finney's spirited revivals. But it was also an occasion of more decorous revivalism in New England's evangelical churches. Among many converts joining Amherst's First Church in 1831, just after the poet's birth, was Emily Norcross Dickinson. Edward Dickinson, although not officially joining the church by proclamation of faith for another twenty years, managed the First Church's business affairs.[2] The whole family attended Sunday worship; and, even though Emily eventually chose to remain home, it is worth noting that the church and the manse were about the last places she ceased to visit as her anxieties about public exposure gradually confined her. She heard a vast amount of preaching over her first thirty years, from guest clergy as well as her own pastors— scripturally centered and often elaborating on doctrines summarized in the *Westminster Catechism*. She also sang hymns at the First Church, with well-known effects on her poetic style and less widely recognized impact on her sense of personal involvement in salvation history. A look at hymnals available to her, *The Sabbath Hymn Book* and *Village Hymns*, demonstrates their systematic theological design and evangelical purpose.[3]

Waves of revivalism touched her town frequently, affecting its Congregational churches, the college, and nearby Mount Holyoke Female Seminary. As an adult, Dickinson came to take a laughing attitude toward these phenomena, but they touched her deeply as a girl. Letters to Abiah Root, the most pious among her early friends, reveal that Emily Dickinson experienced a false conversion as a child that left her with memories "as of a delightful dream, out of which the Evil one bid me wake" (L11). This betrayal of hope also left her skeptical, self-protective, and resistant both to the emotional excitement and social pressure of awakenings. Although expressing hope for her eventual conversion, her letters to Abiah report that she stayed away from revival meetings while watching with fascination how others responded to apparent outpourings of grace. After withstanding still more pressure at Mount Holyoke, however, and witnessing her father's and sister's 1850 conversions, she declared to Jane Humphrey that "I am standing alone in rebellion" (L35). As an adult, she pursued an independent religious quest that has been the subject of considerable scholarly attention.[4] Virginia H. Oliver concludes in *Apocalypse of Green* that Amherst's religious institutions failed to answer Dickinson's persistent questions, leaving her "to make her weary way alone, taking what she could from tradition, science, nature, philosophy, and especially from the Bible, until she outdistanced them all" (45). If the First Church failed to answer Dickinson's questions, it was not because of any conflict with Amherst's educational institutions, all of which strongly supported Congregational orthodoxy. In "The Preparation of a Poet," Rowena Revis Jones shows how the region's elementary textbooks reinforced domestic and ecclesiastical teachings. Benjamin Dudley Emerson's *National Spelling Book*, for example, included biblical passages and exhortations to piety among its lessons, while Noah Webster's *American Spelling Book* featured a Moral Catechism. Webster's other contribution to Emily Dickinson's lifelong education, his *American Dictionary*, provided abundant snatches of poetry to awaken her to nuances of literary language but no doubt also reached her with its painstaking elaborations on words with theological import. Defining one of her favorite nouns, "Glory" for instance, Webster provides three synonyms, a line of natural description from Pope, and an example from 2 Peter with the comment that "in this passage of Peter, the latter word *glory* refers to the visible splendor or bright cloud that overshadowed Christ at his transfiguration. The former word *glory*, though the same in the original, is to be understood in a figurative sense."[5] A temporary resident of Amherst and grandfather of Dickinson's friend Emily Fowler, Webster exerted major force on the community's intellectual life.

Even more influential was Edward Hitchcock, the geologist-theologian who presided over Amherst College during the period Emily Dickinson studied at its affiliated institution, Amherst Academy. Hitchcock's contribution, carefully studied in Wolff's and Sewall's biographies, was to demonstrate how natural revelation discovered through rigorous pursuit of modern science supported scriptural revelation as transmitted through the church. This confident pursuit of scientific knowledge, matched with religious orthodoxy and philosophical conservatism, suffused the curricula by which the poet was educated at Mount

Holyoke as well as the Academy. Carlton Lowenberg's bibliography, *Emily Dickinson's Textbooks*, documents the systematic intellectual formation that prepared her to use various kinds of technical language in apt, imaginative ways. Dickinson's education, which she saluted merrily in a valentine cheer, "Hurrah for Peter Parley!" (P3), opened her eyes to the intricate drama of nature while inspiring her to seek—and question—correspondences between science and God.[6] Growing up in a town known for its collection of prehistoric fossils also nurtured the metonymic tendencies evident in "A science – so the Savans say" (P100); although, as her punctuated reference to "Savans" suggests, her academic background prepared her to doubt authority. Even after leaving Mount Holyoke, Dickinson continued to profit from Amherst's lyceum, reading clubs, bookstore, and private libraries, as Jack Capps's inventory of *Emily Dickinson's Reading* demonstrates.

Yet it would be a mistake to assume that Dickinson's experience was limited to her hometown or that Amherst itself was culturally isolated. As a college community, it drew a constant influx of students from other rural New England towns, of faculty educated elsewhere, and of alumni returning from exotic places. Since Amherst College prepared its graduates for foreign missions, there was a strong global impetus. When Abbie Wood Bliss and her husband left for Syria, where they founded the American College, Dickinson wrote cheerily that "Mr Bliss' *Coronation* takes place tomorrow, at the College church. Charge to the Heathen, by the Pastor! Front seats reserved for Foreign Lands!" but then immediately warned Jane Humphrey, "dont let your duty call you 'far hence'" (L180). Teaching eventually took Jane to Ohio, any-way, and Sue Gilbert to Maryland. Staying in Amherst, Dickinson fret-ted over friends' departures—whether economically necessitated moves or pleasure trips. Those friends, however, became her envoys to the world, bringing back news of distant states, Europe, and Asia.

Proud of the geographic knowledge she absorbed in school and played with in her poems, Dickinson smiled at local provincials who confused Vermont with Asia (L473, L685) but commented to her often-migrant Norcross cousins that "moving to Cambridge seems to me like moving to Westminster Abbey, as hallowed and as unbelieved, or moving to Ephesus with Paul for a next-door neighbor" (L962).[7]

Nonetheless, she lived during the heyday of westward expansion. Even though their father deflected Austin's thoughts of pursuing a career in Michigan or Illinois, other acquaintances made drastic breaks with the East—most notably Charles Wadsworth when he accepted a call from Calvary Church in San Francisco and Helen Hunt Jackson— or "Helen of Colorado" as Dickinson learned to call her. It was also a period when many Americans of Dickinson's social class traveled for prolonged periods in Europe, enriching their historical and cultural perspectives while learning to cope with alien traditions of an aristocratic and still largely Catholic continent. Rather than asking Samuel Bowles about his European observations in the summer of 1862, however, she wrote: "We wish we knew how Amherst looked, in your memory. Smaller than it did, maybe—and yet things swell, by leaving— if big in themselves" (L266). Her apprehensions about travel may be traceable to the loss of her grandfather, Samuel Fowler Dickinson, who died in Ohio exile after ruining himself financially in founding Amherst College. She seems to be thinking of him in "I noticed People disappeared" (P1149), a badly fragmented draft that equates settlement of "Regions wild" with dying, itself for her always "a new Road" (L332). Professor Nathan Fiske, Helen Jackson's father, had departed the Holy Land directly for heaven when both Helen and Emily were young girls, yet Dickinson never forgot President Humphrey's elegy: "From Mount Zion below to Mount Zion above" (L1042). Clinging herself to the security of home, Dickinson availed herself of cultural opportunities from Europe—Jenny Lind's singing and the touring Germania Orchestra as well as English literature—and remained alert to news about freedom fighting in Hungary, British military actions in the Sudan, and the escape of an Egyptian rebel.

She followed public events in her own country also, despite her claim that "The Only News I know / Is Bulletins all Day / From Immortality" (P827), and current scholarship grounds Dickinson almost as strongly in time as in place—if a fruitful distinction can be made, given that the Amherst of her youth clearly reflected the intellectual, moral, and social climate of a particular era. Betsy Erkkila's "Emily Dickinson and Class" stresses the generally ignored fact that Dickinson's formative years came in the Jacksonian era, a time of ferment characterized by a revisionist historian as "an age of materialism and opportunism, reckless speculation and erratic growth, unabashed vulgarity, surprising inequality, whether of condition, opportunity, or status, and a politic, *seeming* deference to the common man by the uncommon men who actually ran things" (Pessen 327). One of those uncommon men was Amherst's Squire Dickinson, who expounded on his ambitions and values in courtship letters to Emily Norcross. Convinced that "we live in a country & in an age when all offices & honors are held out to the deserving, and where the man of merit—the man of untiring energy & perseverance can hardly fail of promotion—& where a man of decision & determination & resolution & energy of character, seldom fails of success," the poet's father tied his personal hopes to community advancement in his resolute quest for power and wealth (Pollak, *Parents* 8). He pursued public service in the electoral realm as a state legislator and Massachusetts representative to the United States Congress while functioning as treasurer to Amherst College, promoting public works from temperance societies to railroad access, and maintaining a prosperous law practice. Erkkila's argument is that, although women were pointedly excluded from the public realm, Emily Dickinson nonetheless profited from her family's social privilege and shared her father's Whig ideology. Seeking "the historical and specifically class formations of Dickinson's life and work" ("Class" 2), Erkkila concludes that the poet "sought to secure the declining status of both her gender and her class through the accumulation of cultural and spiritual capital, what she called 'My Soul's *entire income*'" (17).

Pointing to collegian Emily's nightmare that Amherst's Locofoco postmaster had acquired a lien on the Dickinson rye field (L16) as well as to her dismissive comments about servants, Austin's Irish pupils, and other social inferiors as evidence of the poet's anxiety about aspirant social groups, Erkkila pays less attention to counterevidence of republican spirit. Rather than accepting her father's equation of success with virtue, Dickinson wrote scathingly of someone with "A face devoid of love or grace, / A hateful, hard, successful face" (P1711) and seemed to identify with the cheery robin whose "Dress denotes him socially, / Of Transport's Working Classes" (P1483). Looking at her world from perspectives either of nature or of eternity provided a corrective to Whig ideology while demonstrating her keen-eyed, satiric awareness of her contemporaries' deluded ambitions. "'Tis sweet to know that stocks will stand / When we with Daisies lie," she mocked, "That Commerce will continue – / And Trades as briskly fly –" (P54). From the celestial perspective, status roles had no importance: "Color – Caste – Denomination – / These – are Time's Affair – / Death's diviner Classifying / Does not know they are –" (P970).

There were a number of destabilizing factors in Jacksonian America that prompted anxieties in conservative Connecticut Valley families tracing their ancestry back to the Pilgrim Fathers. Foremost among these was the wave of internal and external immigration that drew small-town New Englanders to the industrial cities, rural youth to western territories, free blacks to the North, and masses of Irish and German immigrants to America. Amherst felt these changes, and so did the Dickinson household. Edward Dickinson's stance was a conservative one, and the few political views his daughter expressed tended to echo his—if only because they often arose in letters to Austin, whose ambitions depended to a great extent on their father's. Despite her personal reclusiveness, Dickinson apparently took some pleasure in acquaintance with the powerful men to whom Edward Dickinson connected her, boasting in a childish letter of knowing Governor Briggs (L18) and threatening in a witty poem to retain Lemuel Shaw, chief justice of the Massachusetts Supreme Judicial Court, in a lawsuit against God himself (P116). On the other hand, she worried

about the burdens public service placed on men she admired and re-
sisted threats to pull her father away from Amherst. When the new
Constitutional-Union party proposed to nominate the Squire for state
office in 1860, she objected to her cousins, "I hear they wish to make
me Lieutenant-Governor's daughter. Were they cats I would pull their
tails, but as they are only patriots, I must forego the bliss" (L225). The
very name of that party, along with its ephemeral nature as one of many
fragments spun off by the exploded Whigs, points to the threat of secession that Edward Dickinson, like Daniel Webster, attempted to
stave off by acquiescence to southern demands.[8] Later, freed from her
father's aspirations, the poet expressed indifference to public affairs in
a letter to Mrs. Holland: "'George Washington was the Father of his
Country' – 'George Who?' / That sums all Politics to me" (L950). Still,
she checked the morning newspapers each day to learn of President
Garfield's condition after his shooting (L721), apparently responding
to this public figure in a humane if not a patriotic way, and referred occasionally to economic scandals and political agitation. Amused by the
posturing of political orators she likened to frogs (P1379), Dickinson
again shifted perspective in a way that both linked the women's sphere
of domestic service to her father's and brother's male sphere of power
and cast both into a kind of comic-cosmic relief when she remarked of
her sister's prodigious energy that "Vinnie is far more hurried than
Presidential Candidates—I trust in more distinguished ways, for *they*
have only the care of the Union, but Vinnie the Universe—" (L667).

Lavinia's formidable industriousness prompted her sister to claim
for her the "patent action" admired in an industrialized, mechanical
age (L194). Dickinson's letters, more than her poems, demonstrate
alert awareness of those technological advances that swelled her countrymen's pride, although her responses to the arrival of the Amherst-
Belchertown railroad reflect a mix of filial delight and discomfort. Letters to Austin adopt a celebratory tone with respect to their father's
achievement in securing the railroad for the town—wishing her
brother home to join in the jubilation and claiming that "I verily be-

lieve we shall fall down and worship the first 'Son of Erin' that comes, and the first sod he turns will be preserved as an emblem of the struggles and victory of our heroic fathers" (L72). Yet among the first loads to arrive was an excursion group of 325 New London visitors, placing heavy burdens of hospitality on Amherst's more realistic if less heroic sisters and mothers (L127). Machinery proved destructive, too, resulting in calamities she read about in newspapers "where railroads meet each other unexpectedly, and gentlemen in factories get their heads cut off quite informally" (L133). Railroads, moreover, promoted westward expansion that threatened her region. It was mainly in an ironic spirit, obviously, that Emily Dickinson claimed enthusiasm for what her contemporaries hailed as progress. In her 1850 prose valentine, she parodied familiar rhetoric:

But the world is sleeping in ignorance and error, sir, and we must be crowing cocks, and singing larks, and a rising sun to awake her; or else we'll pull society up to the roots, and plant it in a different place. We'll build Alms-houses, and transcendental State prisons, and scaffolds—we will blow out the sun, and the moon, and encourage invention. Alpha shall kiss Omega—we will ride up the hill of glory—Hallelujah, all hail! (L34)

That skeptical attitude held for reformism in general and for social causes enlisting women in particular. Though declaring admiration for Elizabeth Fry and Florence Nightingale in an apology to Bowles for mocking at women (L223), she remarked drolly to Jane Humphrey a decade earlier about the sewing society she avoided in their hometown, noting wryly that "all the poor will be helped—the cold warmed—the warm cooled—the hungry fed—the thirsty attended to—the ragged clothed—and this suffering—tumbled down world will be helped to it's feet again—which will be quite pleasant to all" (L30). When solicited for a literary contribution to help some charitable cause, she claimed to have burned the letter "requesting me to aid the world by my chirrup more" (L380).

Dickinson's spirited contempt for "Soft – Cherubic Creatures" among the "Gentlewomen" she observed (P401) should not blind us, however, to ways in which she drew strength from a network of female friends and the sentimental women's culture of her time. Paula Bennett argues persuasively that the poet willingly submerged herself in the feminine sphere of home and garden and that "her presentation of herself as 'poetess' (a woman poet) was, therefore, a good deal more than simply a role she played in order to keep from playing others" (*Woman Poet* 13). She found intellectual, artistic, and psychological support in women's writings also. Dickinson's relationship to the distinctively female literary culture of her time, chiefly British, is the subject of Sandra Gilbert and Susan Gubar's groundbreaking *Madwoman in the Attic*, while Joanne Dobson examines in *Dickinson and the Strategies of Reticence* how this poet carried to an extreme the restrictions placed by Jacksonian-Victorian culture on American poetesses. In "'One Unbroken Company': Religion and Emily Dickinson," Joan Burbick discloses a Dickinson whose spiritual pilgrimage "is more relational than individualistic" by placing her within the context of a sentimental religious culture that significantly altered the emphasis and tone of evangelical Calvinism (63). Beth Maclay Doriani, in *Emily Dickinson, Daughter of Prophecy*, links Dickinson to a deeply rooted New England tradition of female prophecy that combined in antebellum America with transcendentalist oratory, evangelical preaching, and the Bible's wisdom literature to provide the poet with both a culturally sanctioned rhetoric and the courage to employ that rhetoric in her unorthodox expression of spiritual searching.

Countering the hoary supposition that Dickinson's seclusion in the 1860s and intensive engagement with both her poems and her eyes precluded her taking an interest in the Civil War, Shira Wolosky demonstrates in *Emily Dickinson: A Voice of War* that she shared in the national political and moral crisis in a way that severely challenged her faith. Arguing that Dickinson's poetry "can be seen as profoundly engaged in problems of the external world and aggressively so," Wolosky places her at "a point of intersection of literary, cultural, and metaphysical concerns" exacerbated by national conflict that found expression in the "disjunctions and discontinuities" of her writing (xiii, xviii). Particularly compelling questions brought to the forefront were those prompted by massive, incomprehensible human suffering that challenged belief in God's providential justice. St. Armand brings the war's theological impact home to Amherst in analyzing that community's response to the 1863 battle death of Frazar Stearns, the valiant, spiritually searching, but unconverted son of Amherst College's president and friend of Austin Dickinson. How could Amherst—or evangelical Christians more generally—rationalize "the loss of an entire generation of young risen who in sacrificing their lives on the altar of their country, simultaneously condemned themselves to eternal hellfire and damnation, all for the lack of a public profession of religion" (*Culture* 103)? St. Armand traces to that quandary the triumph of the Brother-Christ of a sentimental love religion like Dickinson's over the Father-God of traditional Calvinism. Lease (*Readings*) shows how the Civil War affected Dickinson through her vicarious sharing in transformations it brought to lives of her two mentors, Wadsworth and Higginson, prompting her lament to the latter (then colonel of a black regiment) that "I did not deem that Planetary forces annulled—but suffered an Exchange of Territory, or World—" (L280).

Such evidence of complexity and contradiction in Dickinson's experience compels a rereading of "What is – 'Paradise' –" (P215). It should be obvious by now that the speaker is a persona, perhaps voicing some latent child within this sophisticated and knowledgeable poet but hardly articulating her full mind. Like many poems in which Dickinson adopts a child's persona, this one should be read ironically as her means of raising subversive thoughts. This speaker naively grasps at literal interpretations of promises held out by teachers, pastors, and the Bible, much as the speaker of poem 460 construes the scriptural promise that saints will "thirst no more" in heaven to mean that "The Wells have Buckets to them there." Dickinson often travestied such literalism, seeing how it entrapped imaginations in images introduced at the earliest stages of religious formation. "Is Heaven a Place – a Sky – a Tree?" she demanded, then answered her own question: "Location's narrow way is for Ourselves – / Unto the Dead / There's no Geography – // But State – Endowal – Focus –" (P489). What we realize in following the trail of her child-persona's anxious inquiries in poem 215 is how unheavenly he or she finds pious Amherst and how negative a view of eternity New England Calvinism projects. Moreover, quotation marks around key words communicate the writer's doubts about language's ability to represent truth, not just about "Paradise" and "Eden" that might be considered examples of religious myth but even about here-and-now seeming realities like "Amherst" and its economy. The poem offers nothing but questions—perhaps fortunately, since answers might prove so devastating to the faith society was attempting to transmit to its children, including Emily Dickinson.

On the other hand, that Amherst culture also educated her to ask questions and to settle for nothing less than experiential knowledge of both science and the soul, and the question to which she devoted her energies was the same one we recognize behind the little waif's queries. "Is immortality true?" That was what Dickinson apparently asked the Reverend Washington Gladden when staggered by deaths and alarmed about Judge Lord's stroke (L752a). In writing to a Congregational minister, locally educated at Williams College but known for receptivity to newer kinds of biblical criticism, she turned to someone who might help her resolve doubts exacerbated by intellectual currents of her day that threatened the science-religion bond she had been educated to search out. By this last decade of her life, she wondered who could provide authoritative solace: "Are you certain there is another life?" she asked Charles Clark after his brother's death. "When overwhelmed to know, I fear that few are sure" (L827). Dickinson's response to the crumbling religious and scientific orthodoxies of her youth is the subject of Oliver's *Apocalypse of Green*, which examines how intra- and intersectarian strife disrupted New England churches while "scientific discoveries, which at first seemed benign and often supportive of religion, quietly became treacherous and life-threatening to cherished theological beliefs" (17). Chief among these threats, obviously, were Darwin's findings about evolutionary natural selection that challenged the familiar Genesis narrative. Equally alarming was the Higher Criticism of the Bible, which employed historical methods to display the mythic aspects of Scripture. Dickinson, who confessed once that "sermons on unbelief ever did attract me" (L176), confronted many challenges to her faith—challenges that reached her from her reading, certainly, but also from directly observed changes in Amherst.

When Emily Dickinson was born in 1830, Amherst had two churches, both Congregational. When she died in 1886, it claimed a third Congregational church, an Episcopal one, and even a Roman Catholic parish. While successive statements of communal belief from the 1834 *Articles of Faith and Government* through the 1880 *Manual of the First Congregational Church* showed Amherst's First Church maintaining its basic doctrinal core, they revealed heightened awareness of community with other churches and gradual softening of requirements for admission so that, had she desired full membership, Dickinson might easily have qualified for admission to the Lord's Supper even without experiential evidence of conversion.[9] Although the Dickinsons' church remained solidly Trinitarian, their Norcross cousins in the Boston area were Unitarians.[10] Dickinson chose a Presbyterian minister as her spiritual confidant and a Unitarian one as her literary guide. Amherst College, founded to prepare Congregational clergymen, numbered among its most distinguished alumni Austin's friend Bishop Frederick Dan Huntington. Another Episcopalian leader among the town's summer residents was E. Winchester Donald, rector of Boston's Trinity Church. The new Massachusetts Agricultural College had no connection to any church.

An 1859 Christmas letter reflects the diversity of spiritual influences bearing down on Emily Dickinson (L213). Thanking Mary

Bowles for Theodore Parker's *The Two Christmas Celebrations*, she writes, "I never read before what Mr Parker wrote. I heard that he was 'poison.' Then I like poison very well." But her apparent openness to transcendentalist assaults on New England orthodoxy clashes with her next statement, which is an amused report about Austin's staying home from church to read and Sue's asking how to spell "Puseyite." Evidently the younger Dickinsons were somehow balancing Congregationalism, transcendentalism, and the Oxford movement—and finding the play of mind invigorating. Other influences to which she was exposed through Wadsworth, Higginson, and even Hitchcock included the Christian spiritualism to which Lease devotes a chapter. Choices in the religious realm seemed as various—and even more life-threatening—than medical options that befuddled her neighbor: "'Mrs Skeeter' is very feeble," Emily told Austin, "'cant bear Allopathic treatment, cant have Homeopathic'—dont want Hydropathic—Oh what a pickle she is in—should'nt think she would deign to *live*—it is so decidedly vulgar!" (L82). Yet she laughed as wryly at "The Fop – the Carp – the Atheist," all those who refused to credit evidence for immortality she discovered everywhere (P1380). Dickinson's typical stance in her letters was a brave one, holding herself open to Charles Darwin, George Eliot, and similar influences that her cautious mother dismissed as "very improper" (L650). Nonetheless, she held to the central promises of Scripture, even if—in sophisticated society— "no one credits Noah" and "No Moses there can be" (P403, P597). "Better an ignis fatuus / Than no illume at all," she reasoned, in a world left unprotected by scholarship's amputation of God's right hand (P1551).

Finally, what Dickinson most derived from her culture was a searching mind—and the resilience not to be overcome by mysteries that eluded religion, science, and the law. "Why the Thief ingredient accompanies all Sweetness Darwin does not tell us," she remarked to Mrs. Holland; "Each expiring Secret leaves an Heir, distracting still" (L359). Living in an era of expiring secrets, the period Wolff describes as that of "the fading of transcendence from the world" (*Dickinson* 10), Dickinson exposed herself courageously to conflicting, disruptive currents of thought and responded with a mind firmly educated to demand experiential evidence in all areas and an imagination that found metonymic suggestiveness in fragmentary observations and metaphoric illuminations even in darkening light. And, for all her awareness of local and global environments, her truest perspective remained more vertical than horizontal, more attuned to speculations on immortality (experienced even now and promised hereafter) than on Amherst, America, or the wider world opened by friendships and reading.

From *The Emily Dickinson Handbook*, edited by Gudrun Grabher, Roland Hagenbüchle, and Cristanne Miller (1998): 27-43. Copyright © 1998 by The University of Massachusetts Press. Reprinted with permission of The University of Massachusetts Press.

Notes

Where there is no specific mention of a text source, reference is to the Johnson editions of the *Poems* (cited as P) and the *Letters* (cited as L). Franklin's edition of the poems is cited with fascicle or set number as F, followed by the page number(s).

1. Vivian Pollak's edition of their courtship letters in *A Poet's Parents* revealingly discloses assumptions both Edward Dickinson and Emily Norcross brought to their marriage. Pollak expands upon implications of this "family romance" in *Dickinson: The Anxiety of Gender*.

2. The Reverend Aaron M. Colton reminisced in *The Old Meeting House* about being interviewed by Edward Dickinson (and meeting his young family) while a candidate to fill the Amherst pulpit. As Colton served the First Church from 1840 to 1853, his memoirs offer valuable insight into the solid doctrinal substance but genial tone that apparently characterized Emily Dickinson's acculturation into the church.

3. Although not focused on Dickinson, Mary De Jong's "'With my burden I begin'" provides rich insight into the effect of hymn singing on the spiritual development of nineteenth-century women churchgoers.

4. In the concluding chapters of *Dickinson: Strategies of Limitation* and in several articles, I have attempted to do more justice to this topic than is possible here.

5. I rely here on Dickinson's beloved lexicon, the 1844 two-volume edition she used as an adult, while recognizing that she probably also had access at school, in college, and in friends' homes to other versions of this widely used reference that was first published in 1828.

6. See Fred D. White's essay "'Sweet Skepticism of the Heart': Science in the Poetry of Emily Dickinson" for a listing of major scientific and technical developments of the 1830s and 1840s.

7. The best discussion of Dickinson's geographic vocabulary is Rebecca Patterson's essay "Emily Dickinson's Geography" (chap. 6 in *Imagery*).

8. In *Touching Liberty*, Karen Sanchez-Eppler explores Dickinson's antipolitical response to contemporary agitations for freedom, considering "what has happened when a concern with the corporeality of identity that appears political and public in the writings of feminist-abolitionists, Whitman, and Jacobs is fashioned by Dickinson into a poetic, ahistorical and ontological dilemma" (106).

9. Sister Regina Siegfried draws upon dissertation research on the doctrinal odyssey of the First Church in her "Bibliographic Essay."

10. See Jones, "A Taste for 'Poison,'" for illuminating insights into the denominational interplay in the poet's environment.

Works Cited

Bennett, Paula. *Emily Dickinson: Woman Poet*. Iowa City: University of Iowa Press, 1990.

Bernhard, Mary Elizabeth Kromer. "Portrait of a Family: Emily Dickinson's Norcross Connection." *New England Quarterly* 60 (1987): 363-81.

Bingham, Millicent Todd, ed. *Emily Dickinson's Home: Letters of Edward Dickinson and His Family*. New York: Harper, 1955.

Burbick, Joan. "Emily Dickinson and the Economics of Desire." *American Literature* 58 (1986): 361-78.

_____. "'One Unbroken Company': Religion and Emily Dickinson." *New England Quarterly* 53 (1980): 62-75.

Capps, Jack L. *Emily Dickinson's Reading, 1836-1886*. Cambridge: Harvard University Press, 1966.

Cody, John. *After Great Pain: The Inner Life of Emily Dickinson*. Cambridge: Harvard University Press, 1971.

Colton, A. M. *The Old Meeting House and Vacation Papers, Humorous and Other*. New York: Worthington, 1890.

De Jong, Mary. "'With my burden I begin': The (Im)personal 'I' of Nineteenth-Century Hymnody." *Studies in Puritan American Spirituality* 4 (1993): 185-223.

Dickinson, Emily. *The Letters of Emily Dickinson*. Ed. Thomas H. Johnson and Theodora Ward. 3 vols. Cambridge: Harvard University Press, 1958.

_____. *The Poems of Emily Dickinson*. Ed. Thomas H. Johnson. 3 vols. Cambridge: Harvard University Press, 1955.

Dobson, Joanne. *Dickinson and the Strategies of Reticence: The Woman Writer in Nineteenth-Century America*. Bloomington: Indiana University Press, 1989.

Doriani, Beth Maclay. *Emily Dickinson, Daughter of Prophecy*. Amherst: University of Massachusetts Press, 1996.

Eberwein, Jane Donahue. *Dickinson: Strategies of Limitation.* Amherst: University of Massachusetts Press, 1985.

Erkkila, Betsy. "Emily Dickinson and Class." *American Literary History* 4 (1992): 1-27.

Farr, Judith [Banzer]. *The Passion of Emily Dickinson.* Cambridge: Harvard University Press, 1992.

Gilbert, Sandra M., and Susan Gubar. *The Madwoman in the Attic: The Woman Writer and the Nineteenth-Century Literary Imagination.* New Haven: Yale University Press, 1979.

Jones, Rowena Revis. "The Preparation of a Poet: Puritan Directions in Emily Dickinson's Education." *Studies in the American Renaissance* (1982): 285-324.

_____. "A Taste For 'Poison': Dickinson's Departure from Orthodoxy." *EDJ* 2.1 (1993): 47-64.

Lease, Benjamin. *Emily Dickinson's Readings of Men and Books: Sacred Soundings.* New York: St. Martin's 1990.

Leyda, Jay. *The Years and Hours of Emily Dickinson.* 2 vols. New Haven: Yale University Press, 1960.

Lombardo, Daniel. *A Hedge Away: The Other Side of Emily Dickinson's Amherst.* Northampton: Daily Hampshire Gazette, 1997.

Longsworth, Polly. *The World of Emily Dickinson.* New York: Norton, 1990.

Lowenberg, Carlton. *Emily Dickinson's Textbooks.* Berkeley: West Coast Print Center, 1986.

Mossberg, Barbara Antonina Clarke. *Emily Dickinson: When a Writer Is a Daughter.* Bloomington: Indiana University Press, 1982.

Mudge, Jean McClure. *Emily Dickinson and the Image of Home.* Amherst: University of Massachusetts Press, 1975.

Oliver, Virginia H. *Apocalypse of Green: A Study of Emily Dickinson's Eschatology.* New York: Lang, 1989.

Patterson, Rebecca. *Emily Dickinson's Imagery.* Ed. Margaret H. Freeman. Amherst: University of Massachusetts Press, 1979.

Pessen, Edward. *Jacksonian America: Society, Personality, and Politics.* Rev. ed. Homewood, Ill.: Dorsey, 1978.

Pollak, Vivian R. *Dickinson: The Anxiety of Gender.* Ithaca: Cornell University Press, 1984.

_____, ed. *A Poet's Parents: The Courtship Letters of Emily Norcross and Edward Dickinson.* Chapel Hill: University of North Carolina Press, 1988.

St. Armand, Barton Levi. *Emily Dickinson and Her Culture: The Soul's Society.* Cambridge: Cambridge University Press, 1984.

Sanchez-Eppler, Karen. *Touching Liberty: Abolition, Feminism, and the Politics of the Body.* Berkeley: University of California Press, 1993.

Sewall, Richard B. *The Life of Emily Dickinson.* 2 vols. New York: Farrar, Straus and Giroux, 1974.

Siegfried, Regina. "Bibliographic Essay: Selected Criticism for Emily Dickinson's Religious Background." *Dickinson Studies* 52.2 (1984): 32-53.

Smith, Martha Nell. *Rowing in Eden: Rereading Emily Dickinson.* Austin: University of Texas Press, 1992.

Webster, Noah. *An American Dictionary of the English Language.* 2 vols. New York: Converse, 1828; Amherst, 1844.

White, Fred D. "'Sweet Skepticism of the Heart': Science in the Poetry of Emily Dickinson." *College Literature* 19 (1992): 121-28.

Wolff, Cynthia Griffin. *Emily Dickinson.* New York: Knopf, 1986.

Wolosky, Shira. *Emily Dickinson: A Voice of War.* New Haven: Yale University Press, 1984.

Further Reading

Conforti, Joseph A. *Jonathan Edwards, Religious Tradition, and American Culture.* Chapel Hill: University of North Carolina Press, 1995.

Douglas, Ann. *The Feminization of American Culture.* New York: Knopf, 1977.

Epstein, Barbara Leslie. *The Politics of Domesticity: Women, Evangelism, and Temperance in Nineteenth-Century America.* Middletown, Conn.: Wesleyan University Press, 1981.

McLoughlin, William G. *Revivals, Awakenings, and Reform: An Essay on Religion and Social Change in America, 1607-1977.* Chicago: University of Chicago Press, 1978.

Smith-Rosenberg, Carroll. *Disorderly Conduct: Visions of Gender in Victorian America.* New York: Knopf, 1985.

Welter, Barbara. *Dimity Convictions: The American Woman in the Nineteenth Century.* Athens: Ohio University Press, 1976.

Emily Dickinson Thinking _____

Helen Vendler

Commentators have long found evidence in Dickinson's work for "thinking in poetry." While scholars, in assessing the style of Dickinson's thinking, have focused on the "grammatical, syntactical, and metaphorical idiosyncrasies" of her verse, what Helen Vendler finds "equally intrinsic" to Dickinson's style of thinking is her invention of ways to plot temporality in her verse. In earlier poems, such as "I like to see it lap the Miles –" and "The Heart asks Pleasure – first –," Vendler finds evidence of what she calls Dickinson's "chromatic form" of thinking: that is, the plotting of events in a chronological succession with the aim of offering "a complete coverage of temporal experience from beginning to end." But if in "I like to see it lap the Miles –" Dickinson offers serial incidents of the train journey from sunrise to sunset when the journey is complete, the *and then*'s of the cheerful train journey turn into the inflexible and horrifying *and then*'s of the torturer's chamber in the chromatic seriality of "The Heart asks Pleasure – first –."

"The great crisis in Dickinson's work," according to Vendler, occurs when the poet's "instinctive practice of chromatic advance encounters an unavoidable discontinuity, a fissure," which leads Dickinson to recount in her poetry the "fracture of all serene or predictable forms of serial plot." For example, in "I felt a Cleaving in my Mind –," Dickinson acknowledges her inability to assemble thoughts sequentially: "The thought behind, I strove to join / Unto the thought before – / But Sequence ravelled out of Sound – / Like Balls – upon a Floor –"; in "I felt a Funeral, in my Brain," madness "leads to great unforeseen plunges which are the opposite of ritually controlled chromatic motion towards an anticipatable end"; and in "After great pain, a formal feeling comes –" chromatic advance is replaced with a kind of "repetitive circling" as "The Feet, mechanical, go round." While chromatic sequence retains a "strong hold" on her poetic imagination, Dickinson, in her postcatastrophe thinking, is also attracted to "'philosophi-cal' tenseless thinking" in which experience is weighed "in the scales of an hypothesized eternity" and in which the poet's "melodrama of imagining her own posthumous state fades . . . in favor of looking on things from 'God's' vantage point, from which life and death are seen under the rubric of timeless moral vision." Yet Dickinson's "impulse toward the philosophical, as an escape from the serial, wrestles al-ways, in her later work, with an empirical recognition of change."

Offering a view of Dickinson as thinker in a series of close readings of well-known poems, Vendler argues that readers can deduce Dick-inson's thinking by the way she structures time, as she "first 'ar-ranges' time serially (from beginning to end) and chromatically (not-ing each step), then begins, instructed by catastrophe, to rearrange temporal structures and even to abandon them." For Vendler, "Each new cast of the imagination represents a form of thinking—the sort of thinking poets do—which leaves its secret trace."   J.B.B.

It is natural that Emily Dickinson should come to mind when one re-flects on the evidence for thinking in poetry. Her work has been called metaphysical, philosophical, theological. Vocabularies have been in-vented to describe her style of thinking—its cryptic ellipses, its com-pression, its enigmatic subjects, its absent centers, and its abstractions. These qualities indeed are her "carbonates"—the residue of the fire that preceded them: "Ashes denote that Fire was" [1097; 1865].[1] But equally intrinsic to her verse is Dickinson's invention of structures that mimic the structure of life as she at any moment conceives it. By those structures she channels our reactions, adjusts our pace to hers, and molds our thinking after her own. Any detailed assertions about her work must be partial ones in view of the almost 1800 poems she com-posed. Nonetheless, I believe there is something to be said about her thinking as she invents ways to plot temporality.[2]

The larger ideas in Dickinson are not recondite ones: She satirizes received religious thought, while retaining its metaphysical dimension and much of its compensatory solace; she continues the European lyric tradition of an erotic adoration coming to grief; and she dwells much on nature's appearances, death's certainty, and an uncertain immortality. If it is not Dickinson's themes that determine her style of thinking, what does? Her well-described grammatical, syntactical, and metaphorical idiosyncrasies certainly play an important role in conveying her style of thought to us, but to understand her imaginative thinking we also need to perceive how, in her poems, over time, she altered "normal" temporal organization. I take for granted the usual critical account, derived from the poetry, of Dickinson's emotional crises, in which a soul of intense sensitivity, hoping to find stability in religion or love, is brought to grief by some unidentifiable calamity, sometimes represented as an inner death, which leads almost to madness. After each such crisis, she experiences a long aftermath[3] marked by new traumas, punctuated by forms of denial, stoicism, and regressive idealization. I will be paying particular attention to how Dickinson orders the inner structure of her poems to represent the way such life-events reshape a person's conception of serial existence itself.

Dickinson's original and "natural" style of thinking about serial plot—by which I mean a plot of events in chronological succession—aimed at a temporal exhaustiveness: Her poems unscrolled, like her sun, "a ribbon at a time," and wished to project, by displaying one "ribbon" after another, a complete coverage of temporal experience from beginning to end. Her early poems tend to believe not only that all roads have an end, but also that "all roads" have "A 'Clearing' at the end," as she says in the 1859 poem "My Wheel is in the dark" [61]. En route to the dénouement at the clearing, the poem strings out experience phase by phase, aspiring to leave no gaps in event or perception before arriving at the end of the sequence. The 1861 poem "I'll tell you how the Sun rose –" [204] generates four such "ribbons," each characteristically possessing a strong active verb:

The Steeples swam in Amethyst!
The news like squirrels ran!

The hills untied their Bonnets!
The Bobolinks begun!

Dickinson paid out her successive ribbons of such verbs again in her 1862 poem on the locomotive: "I like to see it lap the Miles / And lick the Valleys up," [383].[4] Because the train is said to complain "In horrid – hooting stanza" we can see this early exercise as an *ars poetica*: "I like to see it do X and Y . . . And then . . . And then . . . Then . . . And . . . Then." The poet's work of thinking fills up with serial incidents the extended journey of the train, just as it had filled up the rising of the sun with serial "ribbons." In each case, the impression is given that all of the manifest phenomena have been noted, since the rising of the sun is followed in the poem by its setting, and the beginning of the train's journey is completed when it stops "At its own stable door."

I adopt the term "chromatic" from musicology to express Dickinson's need to sound, in her serial plots, *every* note in a scale—black and white, step and half-step. Her compulsion to a chromatic form of thinking is what Dickinson herself called, in an early poem, "Notching the fall of the even sun" ["Bound – a trouble –"; 240; 1861].[5] Although the poet in fact makes up the "slots" she fills, the early poems wish to obscure that constructive invention, and to appear merely transcriptive. If the train stops at tanks, goes around mountains, peers in shanties, crawls between the cliffs of a quarry and chases itself downhill, we are meant to believe that the narrator saw the shanties and the quarry; the mountains and the tanks. If, by contrast, we suspected the poem were being "made up," we would worry that it might be prolonged forever in other landscapes, new stops. Anxious because time is infinitely divisible, Dickinson attempts to master that fact by pretending the train has only a limited number of places to pass before it stops, and the sun only a number of phenomena to exhibit before it has exhausted its "ribbons" of rising. Once you have pointed out the effect of the dawn on the steeples, the squirrels, the hills, and the bobolinks, you have finished, and appeased your anxiety.

Dickinson's chromatic scale, which aims to exhaust each possibility within seriality, bares the hidden anxiety behind its construction when the leisurely and widely separated *and then*'s of the jaunty train turn into the immediately successive, grim, and inflexible *and then*'s of the torturer's chamber. We find, in "The Heart asks Pleasure – first –" of 1863, the same "notched" chromatic thinking, the structure of inch-by-inch ribbon-unrolling and slot-filling. Now, however, the consciousness that had earlier seemed so reassuring turns into a horror of time's infinite divisibility; matched by a terror of a loss of control over its termination. This road has no clearing at the end:

> The Heart asks Pleasure – first –
> And then – excuse from Pain –
> And then – those little Anodynes
> That deaden suffering –
>
> And then – to go to sleep –
> And then – if it should be
> The will of its Inquisitor
> The privilege to die –
>
> [588; 1863]

This little poem imitates, in its chromatic seriality, the ratcheting of the wheel on which the victim is stretched. Once the single clause *The Heart asks* generates the rest of the poem, we find no bustling quantum of active verbs (as in the poems of sunrise and train-journey) propelling the *and then*'s. In the first stanza, the objects of the Heart's asking are nouns: *Pleasure, excuse, Anodynes*—boons that might be obtained from a benevolent superior. In the second stanza, the objects of the Heart's asking are inactive verbs of state: *to go to sleep; to die*. As the positive goods requested in the first stanza, and even the forms of unconsciousness implored in the second, are refused, the poem spreads its syntax out, abandoning its peremptory terseness for a pitiful grovelling. How boldly the Heart had asked "Pleasure – first –"; how reduced it has become, as it begs that there be a last stage to this process.[6] Thought is unable to control the chromatic scale here in the way it could when Dickinson expected the ribboned sun to set predictably, or the train to stop at its stable door; instead Fate holds the power to determine the unknown end. The poet's ability to think up a plot, she sees, now contends with Fate's own plotting; and peaceful slot-filling seriality is the casualty of this recognition.

In other Dickinson poems, thought loses not only mastery of sequence but also cognitive dominion. Perceptions simply crowd too thick and fast to be arranged in a single chromatic series. In an 1863 poem on the sunset, Dickinson suppresses the regular progressions we have seen in sunrise, train, and torture. Now so many candidates for inclusion in the sequence present themselves at once that the emotional result of their profusion is not mastery, but ignorance:

> An ignorance a Sunset
> Confer upon the Eye –
> Of Territory – Color –
> Circumference – Decay –
>
> Its Amber Revelation
> Exhilarate – Debase –
> Omnipotence inspection
> Of Our inferior face –
>
> And when the solemn features
> Confirm – in Victory –
> We start – as if detected
> In Immortality –
>
> [669; 1863]

The opening and closure here resemble those of the poems earlier cited: We begin at the beginning of the sunset, and we end with the Victory and Immortality associated with the end of life. But the chromatic middle is troubled; too many categories apply for individual exhaustiveness of treatment. Territory? Color? Circumference? Decay? Where to begin? Each material object named by Dickinson implies that there should be within it a temporal unfolding: The spread of the sunset over the *territory varies*; the *colors* change as the sunset progresses; the sunset's *circumference* in the heavens mutates, its beauty takes time to *decay*. Furthermore, in this poem, the emotional "slots" to be filled exhibit the same multiplicity as the material ones of the first stanza: Should one express one's *exhilaration* at the spectacle or one's feeling of being *debased* in comparison to its glory? Her incompetence to match the revelation with words generates in the poet the postlapsarian shame of God's *inspection*, from which one hides one's *inferior* face as did Adam and Eve in the garden. Although the religious dose of this sunset poem attempts resolution in the old vein of "setting" or "stopping" via the word "confirm," the failure to exhaust the chromatic scale here remains a frustrated, even guilty one, scattered and confused both descriptively and emotionally. The world of "Omnipotence" is less predictable, even, than that of an earthly Inquisitor, and the tremor of ignorance, with its "as if," shakes the confidence of the closure in Immortality.

In sacrificing the neatness of the serial *and then*, in multiplying material and emotional slots beyond the possibility of filling them, in making ignorance the revelation of the sunset, Dickinson shows that, far from forsaking her chromaticism, she is letting it lead her in unforeseen directions. It remains the first resort of her mind when she begins to think. Even when, as in "He scanned it – Staggered –", she allows the attempt at full serial comprehension to lead first to blindness and then to suicide, she stays determinedly on the rails of a chromatic and serial inquiry, seamlessly connecting a beginning to a middle and an end. Here, however, the active verbs are chiefly not material, but epistemological (*scan, caught at a sense, groped*):

He scanned it – Staggered –
Dropped the Loop
To Past or Period –
Caught helpless at a sense as if
His Mind were going blind –

Groped up, to see if God were there –
Groped backward at Himself
Caressed a Trigger absently
And wandered out of Life –

[994; 1865]

To the man in despair, the slots of description are wholly unfillable:
Scan as he will, catch at sense though he may, grope his way to God
though he try, retreat to self though he does, he can make no sense of
the world before him, past or present. Without time, which he has
"dropped," there can be no intelligible construction of sequence. His
last friend is the trigger that frees him from his unintelligible serial existence and lets him, at last, "wander" to no destination.

It is clear from "He scanned it –" that this method of thinking, in
which it is hoped that systematic inquiry—asking or groping in chromatic sequence—will eventually "solve" the emotional crisis and
bring closure, has become bankrupt for Dickinson.[7] She has come to
think (as she later puts it) that "Capacity to terminate / Is a specific
Grace –" [1238; 1871], and when it is denied her, she will, metaphorically speaking, caress a trigger—that is, represent herself as already
dead, or quasi-dead.

The great crisis in Dickinson's work arrives when her instinctive
practice of chromatic advance encounters an unavoidable discontinuity, a fissure. This is the lesson, so to speak, that anyone wedded to
chromaticism was bound to learn. Over the years, Dickinson writes
many poems recounting fracture of all serene or predictable forms
of serial plot. The poem in which "Sequence" is explicitly mentioned

is the 1864 poem called "I felt a Cleaving in my Mind –". The mind, she acknowledges, no longer obeys the will that wishes to assemble thoughts in a seamless continuum (as notes are assembled in music):

> The thought behind, I strove to join
> Unto the thought before –
> But Sequence ravelled out of Sound –
> Like Balls – upon a Floor – [8]
>
> [867; 1864]

As sound ceases to display a meaningful sequence of tones, so thought unspools itself out of reach.

Poems written earlier than "I felt a Cleaving in my Mind –" cannot quite consent to the unravelling of sequence. The best-known of these is the 1862 "I felt a Funeral in my Brain," written in a posthumous voice. It ought to find a terminus to its sequence, because it retells the break as the speaker's funeral; and it is psychologically still wedded (as "I felt a Cleaving in my Mind –" is not) to the structural form of exhaustive sequence and dénouement. Yet it shows its bewilderment about terminal experience by constructing two alternate endings to its narrative, neither of which is the expected burial that "ought" to follow a funeral. In the first ending, the speaker is imagined as leading a solitary "wrecked" life, coffined but conscious; but in the second, unable to maintain the stasis and stability of that sepulchral survival, her Reason cracks, and she plummets through the firmament, colliding with one plane of existence after another, until consciousness is wholly abolished:

> I felt a Funeral, in my Brain,
> And Mourners to and fro
> Kept treading – treading – till it seemed
> That Sense was breaking through –

And when they all were seated,
A Service, like a Drum –
Kept beating – beating – till I thought
My mind was going numb –

And then I heard them lift a Box
And creak across my Soul
With those same Boots of Lead, again,
Then space – began to toll,

As all the Heavens were a Bell,
And Being, but an ear,
And I, and Silence, some strange Race
Wrecked, solitary, here –

And then a Plank in Reason, broke,
And I dropped down, and down –
And hit a World, at every plunge,
And finished knowing – then –

[340; 1862][9]

Ritual procession, the most solemn representation of chromatic order, is enacted here in the successive phases of the funeral: the entrance
of the mourners, the church service, the exit of the mourners with the
coffin, and the tolling of the funeral knell. Yet the serial advance suggested by these sequential phases is countered by the stasis implied in
the repetitions within the phases: "treading – treading – / . . . beating –
beating – / . . . those same Boots of Lead, again, / space – began to toll, /
. . . I dropped down, and down – / And hit a World, at every plunge."
These tormenting repetitions of obsessive thinking, which persists
through the break in Reason, are formally abolished only by the unconsciousness consequent on the traumatic falls. The speaker's collapse

reveals that although ritual and other such exhaustive orderings have in the past kept existence intelligible for her, this rupture defeats ritual. Desolation is figured as the absence of sequential motion in a final, wrecked "here"; madness leads to great unforeseen plunges which are the opposite of ritually controlled chromatic motion towards an anticipatable end. The last destination is not a knowable place but a time: a "then" unavailable to consciousness.

The unconsciousness to which Dickinson resorts in bringing "I Felt a Funeral" to some kind of *terminus ad quem* cannot be a satisfactory end for an inquisitive mind which must return, even after crisis, to some sort of apprehension: "No Drug for Consciousness – can be –" ["Severer Service of myself"; 887; 1864]. But since nothing further can possibly happen, something has to happen to sequence itself, something that can replace its suspenseful *and then*'s. In the 1862 poem "After great pain, a formal feeling comes –" Dickinson imagines a structure which is still one of sequence, but this sequence, though serial, is not linear: The speaker's feet enact a repetitive circularity made meaningless by her apathy. Because of her emotional deadness, the speaker's actions are linked not by the progressive *and then* but by the futile *or*:

After great pain, a formal feeling comes –
The Nerves sit ceremonious, like Tombs –
The stiff Heart questions 'was it He, that bore,'
And 'Yesterday, or Centuries before'?

The Feet, mechanical, go round –
A Wooden way
Of Ground, or Air, or Ought –
Regardless Grown,
A Quartz contentment, like a stone –

This is the Hour of Lead –
Remembered, if outlived,
As Freezing persons, recollect the Snow –
First – Chill – then Stupor – then the letting go –
[372; 1862]

The speaker of "After great pain" is not, in fact, dead. It is only "the glittering retinue of Nerves" ["Severer Service of myself"] that has become "like Tombs –" In aftermath, the speaker feels uncertain not only about identity ("Was it He? [or *I*] that bore") but about time (Did it happen "Yesterday; *or* Centuries before?"). A monumental "posthumous" present tense reigns in lieu of sequence: "The Nerves *sit ceremonious*, like *Tombs*." Chromatic advance has vanished in favor of repetitive circling, a new form of unavailing ritual: "The Feet, mechanical, go *round*." Some parts of the body have already undergone *rigor mortis*: Flesh has become unchanging *wood*, and the formerly pulsing heart is *stiff*. The feet are indifferent ("regardless") concerning the character of the floor they mechanically tread: The floor could be named terrestrial "Ground" *or* ethereal "Air" *or* moral "Ought" / "Aught." The emotions experience "A Quartz contentment, like a stone –."[10] Quartz, a vitreous crystal, is the birthstone, so to speak, of this poem. Insofar as the "formal feeling" can be described, it is like a stone in its immobility, but it is not amorphous; it is tensely rigid; its self-interlocking crystal-lattice goes nowhere.

The metrical irregularity of the second stanza of "After great pain" marks, I believe, Dickinson's sensing of the difference between chromatic *advance* (marked by the *and then* of true sequence) and the faux-chromatic *repetition* of aftermath, in which one still moves step by step, with every second of existence marked, but only in an incrementally traced circle—a prisoner's circuit that leads nowhere. In the final simile of "After great pain," Dickinson relents and slips into sequence (*then . . . then*); but, like the speaker of "I felt a Funeral, in my Brain," the "Freezing persons" are lapsing into unconsciousness instead of attaining a conclusive *terminus ad quem*.[11] The ambiguous "outliving" of snow-death—if one attains it—is involuntary.

It might seem that no worse fate could befall thinking than to "finish knowing" or concede to a "letting go" of consciousness. There is a worse mode of mental life, though, and that is to "continue knowing," but in a horrible new way. This conception demands a poetic structure that does not end in a final state, whether of static "wreck" or of obliteration of consciousness in "letting go." Thus in "The first Day's Night had come –", the soul, after surviving a rupture imagined as "a thing so terrible" that it goes unnamed, stoically begins to mend her "snapt" strings so as to sing again. A new development then occurs, as a second "horror" arrives (with a characteristically sequential *and then*):

> And then – a Day as huge
> As Yesterdays in pairs,
> Unrolled its horror in my face –
> Until it blocked my eyes –
>
> My Brain – begun to laugh –
> I mumbled – like a fool –
> And tho' 'tis Years ago – that Day –
> My Brain keeps giggling – still.
>
> [423; 1862]

A Brain that "keeps giggling – still" would be grateful to have been allowed to "finish knowing" or to "let go," but instead finds itself being tortured by a new form of consciousness, in which intelligible sequence has been replaced by mere vibration, without even the steps of the circular sequence of "After great pain." "Giggling" is a noise without articulation, a cry wrenched out of its proper grief. A form of thought because it issues from the "Brain," it has despaired of comprehension. Hysteria as a form of thought—the incessant oscillation Dickinson names "giggling"—must eventually undo sequence, the mark of rationality and advancing life.

* * *

For the rest of her life, Dickinson alternates between a posthumousness that obliterates all, and one that allows some form of continuing life. She is fertile in thinking up ways to write in a voice of one who died and yet include chromatic sequence, to the point of running her cinema backward, even into the grave. Frightened of imagining the immobile future of the corpse, she imagines—in a macabre imitation of the steps of creation—resurrecting the dead person, giving it "motion" backward into life:

> Oh give it motion – deck it sweet
> With Artery and Vein –
> Upon its fastened Lips lay words –
> Affiance it again
> To that Pink stranger we call Dust –
> Acquainted more with that
> Than with this horizontal one
> That will not lift its Hat –
>   [1550; 1881]

This late poem shows what a strong hold chromatic sequence retained on Dickinson's imagination; she would rather run it backward in fantasy than lose it altogether.[12]

In spite of such evasions, death—being "Gathered into the Earth, / And out of story –" [1398; 1876]—makes sequence meaningless. The only structure suitable to an existence in which one has "Dropped the Loop / to Past or Period –" is the invariant present tense adumbrated in "After great pain"; and it is to this form, once she has abrogated seriality, that Dickinson turns more and more. But present tenses are many, and commentators have not always distinguished among them. The present tense of stasis can be seen not only in the part of "After great pain" preceding the coda, but also in "The Bone that has no Marrow," in which a "finished Creature" exists in the arid present of two verbs, *is* and *has*, relieved only by a trapped future-tense query which attempts to find a *terminus ad quem* by alluding to the figure of Nicodemus (who asked Jesus whether a man can be born again):

> The Bone that has no Marrow,
> What Ultimate for that?
> It is not fit for Table
> For Beggar or for Cat –
>
> A Bone has obligations –
> A Being has the same –
> A Marrowless Assembly
> Is culpabler than shame –
>
> But how shall finished Creatures
> A function fresh obtain?
> Old Nicodemus' Phantom
> Confronting us again!
>
> $\qquad\qquad$ [1218; 1871]

The intrinsic hopelessness of this "plot" to change the present life is summed up and dismissed in the alliterative sequence "Finished . . . function fresh . . . Phantom!" Nicodemus' question, so serious in the Vaughan that Dickinson knew,[13] appears here as part of a folk tale not entirely dismissible, but not redemptive. The existence of *has* and *is* will go on without end.

But dearer to Dickinson's post-catastrophe thinking than the present tense of arid routine is the philosophical present tense (an "eternal" present, and therefore not a true tense), which appears in axioms and definitions. The poet's attraction to abstraction produces a notable group of poems. How is this "philosophical" tenseless thinking related to the chromatic thinking which was so compulsive for Dickinson that she imagined chromaticism as the essential mechanism of nature (see not only the sunrise poem, but also such fundamental poems as "Crumbling is not an instant's Act" [1010; 1865])? It is useful, in assessing the relation of untensed to chronological thinking, to compare two poems, one tensed and one untensed, that employ the same metaphor—that of a person whose eyes have been put out (an image Dickinson may have drawn from her own increasing eye-trouble, or from *King Lear*, or both).

The tensed poem, "Before I got my eye put out," shows Dickinson struggling with the post-rupture reduction of multiple time-zones to the crucial two: Before and After. The poet, speaking from a single "now," looks before and after. She purports to be willing to refuse the glories of seeing, even if they were to be regranted, in order to remain perpetually safe from the known power of the burning sun:

> Before I got my eye put out –
> I liked as well to see
> As other creatures, that have eyes –
> And know no other way –
>
> But were it mid to me, Today,
> That I might have the Sky
> For mine, I tell you that my Heart
> Would split, for size of me –
>
> The Meadows mine –
> The Mountains – mine –
> All Forests – Stintless stars –
> As much of noon, as I could take –
> Between my finite eyes –

The Motions of the Dipping Birds –
The Lightning's jointed Road –
For mine – to look at when I liked,
The news would strike me dead –

So safer – guess – with just my soul
Upon the window pane
Where other creatures put their eyes –
Incautious – of the Sun –

[336; 1862]

The tenses are jumbled here because chromatic sequence has been abrogated by the maiming event: When one disaster looms larger than everything else, all other moments must be crowded into the bare two categories, "Before" and "After," rather than appear in the *and then*'s of
even sequencing. Written serially, the poem would begin with the pastoral idyll of "Before," pass through Catastrophe, and arrive at the
present averred preference for blindness. But in her intent to make the
emotional climax determine the sequencing of the poem (since it generated the poem), Dickinson now puts the middle first. Catastrophe
takes pride of place, occupying the first line of the poem. And the closing stanza does not end with the victim's own fate; rather, it prophesies
the same fate of a host of other "incautious" creatures, creating a sequence infinitely repeatable in identical shape. The uniqueness of one
is subsumed under the iterative stasis of catastrophe.

When Dickinson later "rewrites" this poem, it is no longer tensed: It
has turned into a "philosophical" poem, a definition of "Renunciation"
in which the speaker no longer asserts that it was the Sun, to which she
had incautiously exposed herself, that put her eyes out. Rather, it is
she who has put out her own eyes, at sunrise, so that the glory of the
earthly sun would not blind her to the glory of its Creator. The Christian apocalypse—the uncovered vision of revelation—provides her
with a metaphor for erotic renunciation:

Renunciation – is a piercing Virtue –
The letting go
A Presence – for an Expectation –
Not now –
The putting out of Eyes –
Just Sunrise –
Lest Day –
Day's Great Progenitor –
Outvie
Renunciation – is the Choosing
Against itself –
Itself to justify
Unto itself –
When larger function –
Make that appear –
Smaller – that Covered Vision – Here –
[782; 1863]

Dickinson surrounds the central event of self-blinding with many implied tenses: There was the brief moment of sunrise, then the moment
when the speaker (spurred on by that "piercing" virtue, Renunciation)
put out her eyes to eschew day; there had been a smaller "covered Vision" here, before the self-mutilation, but there will be a larger, apoca-
lyptic (uncovered) Vision hereafter. Yet all of these moments—tensed
in "Before I got my eye put out"—have now been crowded into a single definitional "now" and "here." Dickinson turns the events into gerunds ("The letting go / A Presence," "The putting out of Eyes," "the
Choosing") and appends—to end the suspense—a final clause justify-
ing the gerunds: We do all these things "when larger function make that
covered Vision here appear smaller." The definitional frame and the
"eternal" present tense of philosophical utterance support the apodictic
certainty of Dickinson's propositions.

But, we must ask, why does Dickinson, so intent on compression, proffer in this poem a *double* definition of Renunciation, giving the poem the formal structure of reprise? She has written—if we regularize the poem—two eight-line stanzas, of which the first formulates a complete definition of Renunciation in the first-order terms of the natural: Sunrise, eyes, and their Great Progenitor (a Miltonic version of God). Why, then, to this metaphorical definition employing (if changing) the metaphor of mutilation borrowed from "Before I got my eye put out," does Dickinson feel she must add a second stanza, which defines Renunciation in the second-order religious diction of choice, justification, and Vision? The second stanza cancels out Nature (sun, eyes) in favor of an almost mathematical formulation of renunciatory choice: "Renunciation is the [self's] choosing against itself to justify itself unto itself." The word that belongs to neither natural nor biblical discourse is "function"—a word more scientific, more algebraic,[14] than we might have expected in this context had we not seen the strict mathematics of the self, which is allied (via the word "function") with the larger mathematics of the universe.

The splitting of the self—by which the voluntary self chooses against its erotic self in order to justify its existential self to its spiritual self (or so I unfold the phrases)—is conveyed in a dry analysis of moral anguish, which stems from the belief in a "larger function" that the speaker must respect. Devoting the second stanza to the abstract function of choice, rather than to the earlier metaphorical drama of self-mutilation, shows Dickinson's ultimate allegiance, in moral questions, to the most skeletal form of thought. And the revision here of the metaphor of mutilation borrowed from "Before I got my eye put out"—revealing that her blindness was self-inflicted rather than imposed upon her—reflects her habitual interrogation of formulas she has previously relied on.[15] The previous poem's victim has been replaced by a deliberate moral agent; Gothic melodrama has been replaced by minimalist analysis; and two forms of tensed narration have been replaced in "Renunciation" by the tenseless absolutes of confirmed decision. As Dickinson comes to realize the extent to which she has willed her own deprivation, she investigates further and further the paradox by which, for her, the desired object ceases to be compelling once it is obtained. In consequence, her verse becomes less narrative, less overtly sequential, and more philosophical. The involuntary stasis of the "giggling" brain has been superseded: Now the brain, in a voluntary and philosophical stasis, weighs experience in the scales of an hypothesized eternity. Dickinson's melodrama of imagining her own posthumous state fades (thought it never disappears) in favor of looking on things from "God's" vantage point, from which life and death are seen under the rubric of timeless moral vision.[16]

There is a falling off in Dickinson's verse in the later years of her life, a regression, sometimes, to earlier and easier formulations. Yet she continues to perfect, in addition to her poems of a philosophic present, the gnomic mixture of tenses into a single complex formation clustered around a catastrophe, as in a single-quatrain poem about having said a normal goodbye to a person who, shortly afterward, died. Paraphrased, this poem would read, "How infinite would the encounter be if we suspected—as we cannot ever do—that that recent casual interview would be marked, afterwards, as the last time we were to see that person." Dickinson ironically indulges in tense-play and mood-play on the verb *to be*, the verb of existence no sooner invoked than extinguished— *Were it to be*; *would be*; *was*:

> Were it to be the last
> How infinite would be
> What we did not suspect was marked
> Our final interview.
>
> [1165; 1870][17]

Moments such as these, which focus on life's unavoidable contingency, render nugatory the confident tenseless definitions so attractive to Dickinson. No axioms can describe a moment of remorse such as that enacted by this little multi-modal quatrain. Dickinson's impulse toward the philosophical, as an escape from the serial, wrestles always, in her later work, with an empirical recognition of change. On the one hand, we hear of the final superiority of the Platonic forms of thought:

> For Pattern is the mind bestowed
> That imitating her
> Our most ignoble services
> Exhibit worthier –
> > ["Who goes to dine must take
> > his Feast"; 1219; 1871]

And on the other hand, we hear of the final superiority of sequential discovery, always capable of overthrowing our axioms even before we can enunciate them:

> Experiment escorts us last –
> His pungent company
> Will not allow an Axiom
> An Opportunity –
> > [1181; 1870]

By glancing "behind" Dickinson's thematic material to the way she structures time, we can deduce her thinking, as she first "arranges" time serially (from beginning to end) and chromatically (noting each step), then begins, instructed by catastrophe, to rearrange temporal structures and even to abandon them. Each new cast of the imagination represents a form of thinking—the sort of thinking poets do—which leaves its secret trace.

From *Parnassus: Poetry in Review* 26, no. 1 (2001): 34-56. Copyright © 2001 by Poetry in Review Foundation. Reprinted with permission of Helen Vendler.

Notes

1. I cite Dickinson's poems by first line, number, and date from *The Poems of Emily Dickinson, Variorum Edition*, ed. R. W. Franklin (Harvard University Press 1998), 3 vols. However, I silently substitute *its* for Dickinson's characteristic misspelling *it's*, and *upon* for Dickinson's *opon*, both retained by Franklin. I do not find any compelling reason, given my purposes here, to refer to the groupings of Dickinson's poems as "fascicles" and "sets."

2. All of Dickinson's critics have had something to say about her structuring of time. The most insightful account in this respect remains that of Sharon Cameron in *Lyric Time: Dickinson and the Limits of Genre* (The Johns Hopkins University Press 1979). Although Cameron calls attention to some of the restructurings of time in Dickinson, she does so to further a theoretical claim: that lyric can really tolerate only a single tense, the present. Her aim is to conflate the poems to this model; my aim is to distinguish them from each other in their revision of temporal structures.

3. The word "aftermath," used by David Porter in *Dickinson: The Modern Idiom* (Harvard University Press 1981), 12, and initially proposed in his 1974 article "The Crucial Experience in Emily Dickinson's Poetry" (*ESQ: A Journal of the American Renaissance* 20), 281, has been widely adopted in criticism, because it covers both the poems that adopt a posthumous voice and others, such as "After great Pain," which do not.

4. Here, the verbs are, successively, *lap*, *lick*, *stop*, *feet*, *step*, *peer*, *pare*, *crawl*, *chase*, and *neigh*, before coming to an end at *stop*.

5. The whole poem "Bound – a trouble –" is significant for my argument, since in it Dickinson states her conviction that life is bearable only if one is told that suffering (measured out, as her dashes show, drop by bleeding drop, in a chromaticism heading toward exsanguination) eventually will come to an end. She imagines counting off the time till its end (the setting sun) by "notching" it moment by moment, as on a primitive calendar-stick:

> Bound – a trouble –
> And lives can bear it!
> Limit – how deep a bleeding go!
> So – many – drops – of vital scarlet –
> Deal with the soul
> As with algebra!
> Tell it the Ages – top a cypher –
> And it will ache – contented – on –
> Sing – at its pain – as any Workman –
> Notching the fall of the even sun!
>   [240A; 1861]

To "deal with the soul / As with Algebra" is, for Dickinson, to arrange it in a continuous line such as that found on a graph in which time is plotted against some other variable, such as drops of blood.

---

6. Other inch-by-inch chromaticisms strive for pure motion not only by omitting the *and then*'s but also by including multiple implied sequences, as in "The Love a Child can show – below –", in which the poet remarks of temporality:

'Tis this – invites – appalls – endows –
Flits – glimmers – proves – dissolves –
Returns – suggests – convicts – enchants –
Then – flings in Paradise!
                        [285; 1862-63]

Rearranged in their four individual serial groups, these lines will read:

invites— appalls
endows—flits
glimmers—proves—dissolves
returns—suggests—convicts—enchants—then—flings in Paradise

The three initial "disappointing" sequences are nonetheless "regular" in their temporally-logical inceptions and closures, whether expressed in binary (beginning and end) or ternary (beginning, middle, and end) form. The final sequence, one of resurrection of the past (when that which has dissolved "returns") is followed by the happy ending, by which the final "clearing in the road" is Paradise. As in this case, Dickinson will often reduce plot—while maintaining its chromaticism—to two or three essential "steps": "Born – Bridalled – Shrouded – / In a Day –" ["Tide divine – is mine!" 194; 1861]. The point is still exhaustiveness—the idea is to omit no *indispensable* step in the process, even if one has reduced the number of steps to the crucial ones alone.

7. Are there, then, no chromatic poems of seriality after 1863? Yes, there are; but they have mostly become epistemologically innocuous, by the suppression of analogy to human experience, which must end in death or bafflement. Because sequence has no inner consequence for harmless natural phenomena, such as the rain, active verbs can return in a delightful set of "ribbons," in, e.g., the 1872 poem "Like Rain it sounded":

That was indeed the Rain –
It filled the Wells, it pleased the Pools
It warbled in the Road –
It pulled the spigot from the Hills
And let the Flood abroad –
                        [1245; 1872]

Dickinson shrinks from imagining the destruction of human beings in the rainfall, and presses thought to leap to another plane rather than follow out to deluge the sequence it has initiated. Thus when she makes the rain cease, Dickinson resorts to the analogy of Elijah's translation from the earthly plane to a heavenly one:

It loosened acres, lifted seas
The sites of Centres stirred
Then like Elijah rode away
Upon a Wheel of Cloud –

And in the poem that immediately follows in Franklin's edition, while thunder and lightning destroy forests (but not habitations or human beings) on the earthly plane, the dead, in their graves, are, like Elijah, immune to the disasters of sequence:

The Thunder crumbled like a stuff
How good to be in Tombs
Where Nature's Temper cannot reach
Nor missile ever comes.
[1246; 1872]

8. Cameron reads "out of Sound" as meaning "out of hearing." This is tenable, but does not account for the irruption of sound into a hitherto soundless poem. Nor do balls of yarn go "out of Sound" when they fall to the floor. Somewhere, I believe, Dickinson is thinking of the sequence of sound in music when she generates this line. A manuscript variant offers a more logical remark to make of falling balls of yarn: They go not "out of Sound" but "out of Reach." Another revealing variant exists for ll. 1-2:

The Disk behind, I strove to join
Unto the Dust before.

The metaphors make clear the spherical beauty of the early "formed" thought and the organic incoherence of the next thought, which disintegrates into dust that cannot be "joined" to the circlet of former thoughts.

9. To "finish knowing" seems to me unambiguous; once one is reduced to numbness of mind, silence, and only one organ ("Being, but an Ear"), there is nowhere to go but the obliteration of consciousness. Some commentators have wanted to believe that the speaker may, now that she has finished "knowing," have other possibilities. I cannot see any room for such possibilities after the "funeral."

10. This line puzzles Cameron, who finds it "redundant": "The stanza's final line boldly flaunts its own redundancy. 'A Quartz contentment' is 'like a stone –' because quartz is stone." Rather, quartz is a vitreous crystal, as Dickinson would have known from her scientific reading if not from her lexicon.

11. Cameron, unlike other commentators, reads the final simile as a return to feeling: "The 'letting go' is not a letting go of life, is not death, but is rather the more colloquial 'letting go' of feeling, an unleashing of the ability to experience it again" (169). I find this improbable: The freezing persons are on their way to being frozen. The fact that they are part of a simile of survival does not mean that their recollection is one of survival. Rather, they recollect the last phase before unconsciousness, before their consciousness lapses altogether.

12. If Dickinson cannot preserve serial temporality after death, she hopes to pre-

serve at least motion, and this leads to her imagining a burial in the "tumultuous" sea (the "swinging sea" in one manuscript variant), in which the stiff sitting of "After great pain" could not possibly occur:

> Fortitude incarnate
> Here is laid away
> In the swift Partitions
> Of the awful Sea –
>
> . . .
> Edifice of Ocean
> Thy tumultuous Rooms
> Suit me at a venture
> Better than the Tombs
> [1255; 1872]

13. See Jack Lee Capps, *Emily Dickinson's Reading, 1836-1886* (Harvard University Press 1966).

14. See Dickinson's comment on the "algebra" of emotion in "Bound – a trouble –", quoted in note 5.

15. Dickinson's serio-comic recipe for self-revision can be found in "These are the Nights that Beetles love":

> A Bomb upon the Ceiling
> Is an improving thing –
> It keeps the nerves progressive
> Conjecture flourishing –
> [1150; 1868]

16. It even seems to Dickinson, at times, that the dead are the truly alive ones, and we the dead, as in "Of nearness to her sundered Things":

> As we – it were – that perished –
> Themselves – had just remained till we rejoin them –
> And 'twas they, and not ourself
> That mourned –
> [337; 1862]

17. Written to her aunt Catherine, whose son Henry died on February 17, 1870.

Trying to Think with Emily Dickinson_____

Jed Deppman

Portraying Emily Dickinson "not as a mystic but as a serious thinker" whose verse can be read as a "thoughtful production of, and reaction to, extreme states of being," Jed Deppman examines how Dickinson viewed the activity of thinking and how the process of writing poetry helped her think. In her poems, thought is often presented as "rapid, uncontrollable, and self-contesting," and it is "associated with power, extreme inner experience, fantasy, madness, pleasure, logic, suffering, and risk." A postmodern Lockean-Kantian artist who refused "to accept or reject the powerful explanatory discourses of her time" and who mixed and extended "contemporary religious, literary, scientific, and other vocabularies along with their metaphysical presuppositions," Dickinson attempted to "present the unpresentable" or to "render palpable the absence of the unpresentable" in her verse as she used poetry to stretch and expand the limits of her mind.

Describing Dickinson's poems as "negotiated transcriptions of difficult thoughts," Deppman focuses particular attention on a distinctive group of poems, which he calls Dickinson's "try-to-think" poems. "Precisely sequenced, if difficult, thought experiments," try-to-think poems aim to "force the mind to do something extremely difficult" and "invite readers to (try to) repeat their steps and monitor the results." Offering a close reading of "I tried to think a lonelier Thing," Deppman states that the purpose of the poem is "not to invent or define an extreme experience but to deal with it once it arrives, to knead it, battle it, alter it, realize it, or just survive it through thought." In this try-to-think poem, "the basic communicability of the poem's try," according to Deppman, "hinges on the reader's willingness to identify with and follow a process of despairing thought well beyond where thinking usually wants to go." While Dickinson invites her readers to join in and repeat her "thinking about and beyond thinking" in her try-to-think poems, in "I tried to think a lonelier Thing" we join with her thought experiment "only at the risk of experiencing a loneliness we cannot sound."   J.B.B.

Why not an 'eleventh hour' in the life of the *mind* as well as such an one in the life of the *soul*—greyhaired sinners are saved—simple maids may be *wise*, who knoweth?

—Emily to her brother Austin, 1851 (L44)

With every increase in the degree of consciousness, and in proportion to that increase, the intensity of despair increases: the more consciousness, the more intense the despair.

—Søren Kierkegaard, *Sickness unto Death*, 175

In 1870, during their first meeting, Emily Dickinson told Thomas Wentworth Higginson that "If I read a book [and] it makes my whole body so cold no fire ever can warm me I know *that* is poetry. If I feel physically as if the top of my head were taken off, I know *that* is poetry. These are the only way I know it" (L342a). A few such memorable remarks about how poetry makes one feel, along with hundreds of lyrics celebrating ecstasy, awe, and exhilaration, have naturally led readers to privilege emotional and physical responses to her poems as well. If we throw in those poems' famous opacity, we can understand why many have concluded that Dickinson's affective force does not always depend on clarity of thought or even intelligibility. Margaret Peterson has argued that Dickinson's most "impassioned poems" can "become a series of ecstatic assertions, an abandonment to excess verging on mental unbalance" (500). While I agree that emotions and other language-defying topics are at the heart of many Dickinson poems, in what follows I will argue the opposite case and portray her not as a mystic but as a serious thinker. In my view she provides far fewer "ecstatic assertions" than careful sequences of ideas and images, not so much "abandonment to excess" as thoughtful production of, and reaction to, extreme states of being. My goal is to show both how important the category of thought was for Dickinson and how committed she was to certain projects of thinking. In so doing, I hope to provide a starting point for further exploration of how Dickinson conceived of the activity of thinking, how she imagined the relationship between thought and poetry and, ultimately, how writing poetry helped her think.

Dickinson wrote too much about thinking to catalogue exhaustively, but a few observations will help chart the territory. Thought, in her poems, is often represented as rapid, uncontrollable, and self-contesting; it is associated with power, extreme inner experience, fantasy, madness, pleasure, logic, suffering, and risk. While every poem represents thought on some level, many also thematize it and reflect precise attitudes. Some are celebratory: "Best Things dwell out of Sight / The Pearl – the Just – Our Thought" (Fr1012) and others cautionary: "If wrecked upon the Shoal of Thought / How is it with the Sea? / The only Vessel that is shunned / Is safe – Simplicity –" (Fr1503). One group draws attention to the problems involved in expressing thought or clothing it in language: "Your thoughts dont have words every day / They come a single time / Like signal esoteric sips / Of the communion Wine" (Fr1476). An analytical cluster considers the mind's basic powers, size, and shape: "The Brain – is wider than the Sky –" (Fr598); "The Brain has Corridors – surpassing / Material place –" (Fr407) and a related set describes thought's wildness and weirdness: "The Brain, within it's Groove / Runs evenly – and true – / But let a Splinter swerve – / 'Twere easier for You – // To put a Current back – When Floods have slit the Hills –" (Fr563). Others posit thought as sufficient, or almost, to provide happiness: "It's thoughts – and just One Heart – / And Old Sunshine – about – / Make frugal – Ones – Content –" (Fr362); "To make a prairie it takes a clover and one bee, / One clover, and a bee, / And revery. / The revery alone will do, / If bees are few" (Fr1779). This list could easily include more categories and be analyzed at greater length, but it is already clear that Dickinson saw thought under many lights and through many lenses.

Thought was a consistent as well as kaleidoscopic topic. According to the Rosenbaum *Concordance to the Poems*, which is based on the 1955 Johnson edition, Dickinson's poems include the verb "feel" 39 times, "felt" 35; "feels" 16, and "feeling" 8. By contrast, "thought" occurs a total of 69 times, "think" 43, and "thinking" 6. "Know" occurs a staggering 230 times, "knew" 80, and "knows" 31, putting this verb in a virtual tie with "do" (170), "did" (150) and "does" (45) for fourth most common verb after "to be," "to be able," and "to have." The form "knowing" also occurs 13 times, and "unknown" 34. If we look at the classic distinction between mind and body, we find "mind" used 79 times (usually as a noun), "minds" 9, "brain" 26, and forms of "consciousness" 40. "Body" occurs only 10 times and "bodies" 1. Partial and decontextualized as such statistics are, they nonetheless make it tempting to cut the Gordian knot and declare that Dickinson's poetry is much more about thought than feeling. At the very least, they remind us how much thought was on Dickinson's mind as she wrote.

Where did Dickinson acquire her thoughts on thought? The question is too vast to answer in full. Cynthia Griffin Wolff calls her an "artist of the age of transition," and cogently argues that her "self-imposed labor was to question God's authority and to free language from the tyranny of His definitions; thus the diction of her poetry is in the process of revising transcendent implication and pulling away from it even as the speaker addresses herself to God" (429). The Dickinson "mark of modernism," David Porter similarly says, is the mind "explosive with signifying power but disinherited from transcendent knowledge" (7). To this joint portrait of a post-transcendental Dickinson I would add that her self-imposed labors and disinheritance can be understood as postmodern. In the ways she refused either to accept or reject the powerful explanatory discourses of her time, for example, we can recognize the attitude Jean-François Lyotard finds definitive of postmodernism: incredulity toward metanarratives. And in the many ways she chose not choosing (as Sharon Cameron puts it) and became aware of herself as a site of vocal and intellectual conflict, torn or traversed by competing language games (in the Wittgensteinian and Lyotardian sense of rule-based usages), and ultimately developed a variorum poetics (as Marjorie Perloff puts it) she can legitimately be taken as a postmodern artist *avant la lettre*.[1] It would be possible to distinguish further among the various strains and strengths of Dickinson's postmodernism, but the spectrum of her attitudes on thinking emerges mainly from a specific cultural condition: the tension between the Lockean empiricist premises that saturated her schoolbooks and the Kantian themes of apprehending the supersensible that circulated throughout Transcendentalism. In the play of irreconcilable differences between these systems, one can glimpse the origin of many of Dickinson's stances on the nature and powers of the human mind.

To read Dickinson as a postmodern thinker and writer is, on the one hand, to explore the ways postmodern theory makes visible important aspects of her work, and, on the other, to see how her poetry exemplifies and illuminates central postmodern predicaments. We shed light on both problems when we see Dickinson as a Derridean *bricoleuse*, mixing and radically extending contemporary religious, literary, scientific, and other vocabularies along with their metaphysical presuppositions.[2] "We have a very fine school," wrote Dickinson to Abiah Root in 1845, "There are 63 scholars. I have four studies. They are Mental Philosophy, Geology, Latin, and Botany. How large they sound, don't they?" (L6). If she later chose the tropological power of poetry to pursue her tries at thinking, it is precisely because she was neither committed to nor trapped in any systematic, disciplinary patterns of thought. Of course there are differences: Dickinson played more seriously, engaged more sharply with her culture's vocabularies, and had more all-around faith in the agency of the writer than does your average postmodern. And despite occasional comic effects, Dickinson's mixing was rarely just a playful or idiosyncratic patchwork of cultural fragments. What should not get lost in a celebration of Dickinson as *bricoleuse* is the engineering depth and variety with which she employed specific language games of critical thought.

As I have suggested, one of these has clear Kantian contours. While Dickinson did not read Kant, she did share his basic attitude toward the self-contesting mind and, especially, toward the links between specific kinds and sequences of thoughts and the experiences of beauty and the sublime.[3] Indeed, many Dickinson poems make use of a key scene in the *Critique of Judgment*, precisely the one Lyotard parlays into a description of the postmodern condition. It is the scene in the theater of the mind where reason conceives of something conceivable but hard to represent (e.g. infinity, death, the very large, the very small) and demands an image adequate to it, which the faculty of imagination tries but fails to provide. The mind repeatedly tries but fails to satisfy its own demand, and from this amplifying situation emerge the inner experiences that define the Kantian sublime.[4]

Many of Dickinson's poems can be read as resourceful, even desperate attempts to supply imagery for the thoughts and experiences that most defy the imagination. Trying to present the unpresentable or, failing that, to render palpable the absence of the unpresentable, they take up Lyotard's later neo-Kantian gauntlet: "it must be clear" he says, calling on would-be postmodern artists, "that it is our business not to supply reality but to invent allusions to the conceivable which cannot be presented" (*Postmodern* 81). I would suggest that Dickinson does precisely that to a degree that other poets do not and that her lifelong commitment to difficult projects of thinking has early origins. The following extract from an 1846 letter to Abiah Root shows Dickinson relentlessly trying to think something for which no adequate image exists: her own death.

Does not Eternity appear dreadful to you. I often get thinking of it and it seems so dark to me that I almost wish there was no Eternity. To think that we must forever live and never cease to be. It seems as if Death which all so dread because it launches us upon an unknown world would be a relief to so endless a state of existence. I dont know why it is but it does not seem to me that I shall ever cease to live on earth – I cannot imagine with the farthest stretch of my imagination my own death scene – It does not seem to me that I shall ever close my eyes in death. I cannot realize that the grave will be my last home – that friends will weep over my coffin and that my name will be mentioned, as one who has ceased to be among the haunts of the living, and it will be wondered where my disembodied spirit has flown. I cannot realize that the friends I have seen pass from my sight in the prime of their days like dew before the sun will not again walk the streets and act their parts in the great drama of life, nor can I realize that when I again meet them it will be in another & a far different world from this. (L10)

Written less than two months after she had turned fifteen, this early letter carries *in nuce* many of Dickinson's mature traits, not least of which are tenacity and the will to force the mind beyond its human limits. As Lyotard puts it: "The obligation to which the imagination is subjected by reason does not only leave the imagination terrified, but gives it the courage to force its barriers and attempt a 'presentation of the infinite'" (*Lessons* 151). Dickinson obviously has this courage: she cannot think death or Eternity, cannot present them adequately to herself, but she cannot not think them either, and as she struggles with this predicament she reveals a mind that seems almost willing to turn to clichés—friends passing "like dew before the sun"—but is in fact relentless and uncompromising: "I cannot imagine . . . I cannot realize . . . I cannot realize . . . nor can I realize . . . ." Her mind repeatedly stretches, fails, realizes it fails, regroups, rewords, and reaches its limit again. In increasingly figural language, she describes each new failure without ever arbitrarily changing the subject or leaping into the safety of a platitude or a faith.

What is not yet joined to this coiling and uncoiling mental activity is an associated and analyzed emotional experience; here she does not worry over the ways the very try of thought is affecting her as she is thinking and rethinking, and does not explicitly reach or address Kant's point that what is sublime is "not so much the object, as our own state of mind in the estimation of it" (94).[5] She just keeps trying to think, or rather, to realize; this recurring verb is the best one she has for expressing a complex desire to imagine fully and translate understandingly something unpresentable into conscious life. In this case, the difference Dickinson intends between not realizing and realizing is the difference between understanding conceptually but superficially that one is going to die and understanding viscerally and profoundly that one is going to *die*. It is obviously hard for anyone at any age to realize that difference; again, the lyric may have been the richest language game she knew for such difficult projects of thought. To elucidate this idea, it will help to highlight certain elements from the only professional correspondence she ever carried out.

As literary history has recorded in italics, on April 15, 1862 Dickinson responded to Thomas Wentworth Higginson's *Atlantic Monthly* essay "Letter to a Young Contributor" by writing him to ask: "Are you too deeply occupied to say if my Verse is alive?" (L260). This question was abrupt but not as cryptic as it now sounds. She was asking what he thought of four poems: "Safe in their Alabaster Chambers" (Fr124); "The nearest Dream recedes – unrealized –" (Fr304B); "We play at Paste" (Fr282); and "I'll tell you how the Sun rose –" (Fr204). Each of these uses playful imagery to present cosmic or existential settings and questions. The only one not featuring children prominently is "Safe in their Alabaster Chambers" (Fr124), and it displays "meek" members of the resurrection "Safe[ly]" sleeping.

Beneath these poems' placid surfaces, the gears of metaphors are grinding. The whirring "ee" and "r" sounds cycling through the first line of "The nearest Dream recedes – unrealized –" aurally enact the poem's superimposed narratives of frustration: a boy chasing a bee and a mind reaching for heaven. All four poems mobilize contrasting or parallel perspectives (children/adult; alive/dead; unaware/aware) and these multiple frames make the poems richly open to interpretation. Dickinson's alive-or-dead question thus draws attention to a depth of thought that might be missed when a professional critic first encounters the work of a new poet. Indeed, on second look it is not easy to intuit all the thinking that went into "gem tactics," "steadfast honey," and the poems that carry them.

Dickinson justified her question by adducing not only the poems but the reason she could not answer it: "The Mind is so near itself – it cannot see, distinctly – and I have none to ask –" (L260). When the mind encounters itself, reads its own writing, or thinks about its own thinking, it is so self-obtruding that it casts a shadow on its own light.[6] This is the real reason Dickinson wrote to Higginson, and her next three questions in this letter, asking whether he thought the verse "breathed," whether she had made "the mistake," and whether he would tell her "what is true" all follow from the same epistemological predicament (L260).[7]

It is an acute problem for Dickinson because, as becomes abundantly clear in the rest of the correspondence with Higginson (72 letters extant from 1862-1886), she generally thought of writing as thought and, more specifically, as thought's psychotherapeutic response to troubling emotion. She tells him that she writes because she had "a terror" she could "tell to none – and so I sing, as the Boy does by the Burying Ground – because I am afraid" (L261). Later she explains that when "a sudden light on Orchards, or a new fashion in the wind troubled my attention – I felt a palsy, here – the Verses just relieve –" (L265). Dickinson rarely writes about writing in terms of spirit, creativity, formal or stylistic choices, historical period, influences, audience, literary movement, experimentation, appropriateness of theme, or any of the technical difficulties of shaping and sharing one's experience in literary language. This silence is one reason critics have had difficulty pinpointing Dickinson's ideas about her poetic composition; another is that she prized equally two things which have long been hard to reconcile in writing: mental lucidity and intense emotional experience. More than anything, she seems startled by the way Higginson answered her second letter with comments on form: her "gait spasmodic," her style "uncontrolled" (L265).

Shouldn't he have said what he thought of her thinking? Or at least explained why "uncontrolled" and "spasmodic" were inappropriate modes for a poet who had, she hoped, "told it clear" (L265)? He is the one who in the "Letter to a Young Contributor" had introduced the two-step compositional metaphor of thought first, language second. "Labor . . . not in thought alone," he had exhorted potential poets, "but in utterance; clothe and reclothe your grand conception twenty times, until you find some phrase that with its grandeur shall be lucid also." In her letters, Dickinson eschews the inflationary rhetoric of "grand conceptions," and phrases "with grandeur," and worries very little about whether she has managed in her poems to think something interesting, true, or otherwise worthy. On that topic she makes very few self-deprecating remarks, but she does wonder whether she has made plain the distinctions that she herself sees. "While my thought is undressed – I can make the distinction, but when I put them in the Gown – they look alike, and numb" (L261). This response domesticates the writing process and privileges the thinking over the clothing: to put "undressed" thought "in the Gown" is much less pretentious than to "clothe and reclothe" a "grand conception."[8]

Sometimes poetry was something she did rather than made. Casting herself as a sailor and Higginson as one of her tools, a compass, she wrote: "If I might bring you what I do – not so frequent to trouble you – and ask you if I told it clear – 'twould be control, to me – The Sailor cannot see the North – but knows the Needle can –" (L265). She also reported to him that "Two Editors of Journals came to my Father's House, this winter – and asked me for my Mind – and when I asked them 'Why,' they said I was penurious – and they, would use it for the World – I could not weigh myself – Myself –" (L261). Again, as these last two comments and many poems suggest, her recurring quandary is that her mind may not satisfy its own demands or understand itself or its products. The "Ignorance out of sight" she clarified later that summer of 1862, "is my Preceptor's charge –" (L271).

Despite being anxiogenic, thought is a constant and valued theme in the correspondence. Along with Dickinson's disdainful complaint to him about how her own "Mother does not care for thought" (L261), perhaps the most famous remark comes in a question reported by Higginson to his wife: "How do most people live without any thoughts. There are many people in the world (you must have noticed them in the street). How do they live. How do they get strength to put on their clothes in the morning" (L342a). For Dickinson this was a serious question. Later, she exclaims: "How luscious is the dripping of February eaves! It makes our thinking Pink –" (L450). And she repeatedly refers to Higginson's writing as thought, too: "I had read 'Childhood,'" she tells him, referring to his essay by that name, "with compunction that thought so fair – fall on foreign eyes –" (L449). She opens one letter with the comment that "Your thought is so serious and captivating, that it leaves one stronger and weaker too, the Fine of Delight" (L458)[9] and comments in another: "I recently found two Papers of your's that were unknown to me, and wondered anew at your withdrawing Thought so sought by others" (L488). She flattered him with the conceit that she had "thought that being a Poem one's self precluded the writing Poems, but perceive the Mistake. It seemed like going Home, to see your beautiful thought once more, now so long forbade it –" (L413). She then summed up their shared faith in the primacy of thought with this rhetorical question: "Is it Intellect that the Patriot means when he speaks of his 'Native Land'?" (L413).

Perhaps most impressively, in the spring of 1876 Dickinson wrote to Higginson after reading two anonymous essays in *Scribner's Monthly*, "I inferred your touch in the Papers on Lowell and Emerson – It is delicate that each Mind is itself, like a distinct Bird –" (L457).[10] She had caught him out! In a twenty-four-year relationship marked by Dickinson's decorous diffidence, this confident interpretation of her friend's mental signature stands as remarkable proof of their intellectual kinship and her sensitive perspicacity. And finally, in the last month of her life, Dickinson wrote to tell him: "I have been very ill, Dear friend, since November, bereft of Book and Thought, by the doctor's reproof, but begin to roam in my Room now –" (L1042). She knew he would understand how important "Book and Thought" were to her.

It must be noted that this was not a one-way relationship. Higginson, for his part, also spoke of writing as thought and clearly understood and appreciated the way thinking and solitude were essential to Dickinson's life and work.[11] At one point he tells this "dear friend" that he sometimes takes out her letters and verses and when he feels their "strange power" it is hard to write to her (L330a). She enshrouds herself in such a "fiery mist," he explains, that he feels "timid lest what I *write* [he italicizes *write* to suggest that he could do better face-to-face] should be badly aimed & miss that fine edge of thought which you bear" (L330a). He continues:

> It is hard [for me] to understand how you can live s[o alo]ne, with thoughts of such a [quali]ty coming up in you & even the companionship of your dog withdrawn. Yet it isolates one anywhere to think beyond a certain point or have such luminous flashes as come to you—so perhaps the place does not make much difference. (L330a)

Higginson was one of the first readers to be nicked by Dickinson's "fine edge of thought" and overwhelmed by her thinking "beyond a certain point," with "such luminous flashes." Nonetheless, it is clear that these cordial yet intimate correspondents understood each other very well, not least because so much of their conversation was about thought and literary writing understood as thought.[12] Emphasizing these elements of their dialogue not only brings into view a thinking Dickinson but also encourages us to recognize and interpret her poems as negotiated transcriptions of difficult thoughts.

One group of poems brings these negotiations especially to the fore. The express purpose of what I will call Dickinson's "try-to-think" poems is to force the mind to do something extremely difficult. The project often entails satisfying reason's unsatisfiable demand for a complete image, narrative, or understanding of a certain idea or experience.

While much lyric poetry can generally be said to think through and express thought and trauma, I nonetheless find Dickinson's try-to-think poems distinctive.

In them, the try is usually serious, the goal explicitly stated, and the emphasis squarely on the willful movements of thought. The speaker in these poems usually tests and tries to transform her own mind using a wide variety of tools, and the resourcefulness of her consciousness makes virtually every poetic element interpretable as contributing to the overriding try. The 1882 "Of Death I try to think like this" (Fr1588) is exemplary for the way its thinking is written into the poem's fabric; deputized and fused in the try's service is a wide array of signifying strata including words, moods, figural elaborations, dashes, spaces, sound patterns, narratives, memories, and allusions.[13] "The nearest Dream recedes – unrealized –" (Fr304B) is also a try-to-think poem, one of a group trying to think immortality and eternity. With each word, mark, sound, image, and idea pressured so heavily, these open-minded poems reward close reading and can be understood as especially concentrated doses of *bricolage*.

In the way they stage the mind attempting to satisfy or improve itself, try-to-think poems sometimes also have a try-to-*believe* quality. In the 1863 "I think To Live – may be a Bliss," the word "may" should be emphasized in the first line; then the whole first stanza sets the terms for another thought-defying thinking:

> I think To Live – may be a Bliss
> To those who dare to try –
> Beyond my limit – to conceive –
> My lip – to testify –
>
> (Fr757)

In the rest of the poem, the speaker tries to become, through the power of self-persuasive and self-transforming thought, one of the hypothesized "those" who live blissfully because they "dare to try" to conceive beyond her limit. Lastly, as these brief examples suggest, try-to-think poems are precisely sequenced, if difficult, thought experiments. They invite readers to (try to) repeat their steps and monitor the results.

The 1863 "I tried to think a lonelier Thing" (Fr570) exhibits all of these features. It is not the only poem in which Dickinson tried to understand that unique exposure of the self to infinity and emptiness that she often called loneliness, but it is certainly a difficult one.[14] "Wherever Emily Dickinson's mental processes may have led," Albert Gelpi has written, "they began with an intolerable sense of emptiness which drove her to project as concrete evidence of her incompleteness the loss of childhood, father, mother, lover" (69). But this poem treats a case so extreme that it cannot be pinned on any specific loss:

> I tried to think a lonelier Thing
> Than any I had seen –
> Some Polar Expiation – An Omen in the Bone
> Of Death's tremendous nearness –
>
> I probed Retrieveless things
> My Duplicate – to borrow –
> A Haggard comfort springs
>
> From the belief that Somewhere –
> Within the Clutch of Thought –
> There dwells one other Creature
> Of Heavenly Love – forgot –
>
> I plucked at our Partition –
> As One should pry the Walls –
> Between Himself – and Horror's Twin –
> Within Opposing Cells –

I almost strove to clasp his Hand,

Such Luxury – it grew –

That as Myself – could pity Him –

Perhaps he – pitied me –

(Fr570)

One understands why the 1890s editions of her poetry all passed this poem over, as did every edition until *Bolts of Melody* in 1945.[15] Despite its advertised attentiveness to the movements of thinking, it is hard to know how to interpret even its most basic mental gesture of trying to think. Is it, as the bold opening line suggests, a proactive, virtuoso attempt to conceptualize an extreme human possibility? Or is it, as I have come to think, a more reactive attempt to use language, argument, and other mental tools to deal with the painful conditions into which the poet has been thrown? I think the main purpose of this poem and many others is not to invent or define an extreme experience but to deal with it once it arrives, to knead it, battle it, alter it, realize it, or just survive it through thought.[16]

"I tried to think a lonelier Thing" poses a second problem: it does not give what it seems to promise—namely a full story of how and what "I tried to think." Although it begins in the reassuring past tense and makes us anticipate resolution and critical distance, we are finally deprived of those things. As usual, there is no synthetic dialectical finish to this uncompromising and uncomfortable poem, no final stanza beginning, say, 'Then loneliness despaired of me / and vanished into noon.' This poem that begins so actively with a try ends in a stop-motion picture, a paralytic image of almost striving in which action is arrested.

What is still moving, of course, is thinking, which is represented not as patient, observant, analytical, meditative, or argumentative but as creative, tenacious, and desperately involved. The poem begins with a rapid series of thoughts (lines 1-6), then slows with a tangential, almost conversational remark (lines 7-11), then ends with two evenly-paced, narrative stanzas (lines 12-19). Yet while the fast-slow-medium pacing rhythmically suggests a resolution, the intellectual and emotional atmosphere is volatile throughout. Among other things, the speaker, trying to think, reaches for a lexical toolbox brimming with nervous vocabulary: "tried to think," "probed," "borrow," "Haggard comfort," "Clutch," "plucked," "pry," "almost strove," "clasp," "Perhaps." That is not a family of overconfident words.

What exactly does thought do as it tries to think? The first line represents an attempt to will or define loneliness into the category of thing, a hypostasizing gesture Dickinson uses to enable linguistic access to otherwise unspeakable loneliness, roughly on the model of the assertive but mysterious "'Hope' is the thing with feathers –" (Fr314). The speaker then tries to find a clearer name for the "Thing" being thought, and we see right away both how important indexing can be in a serious try of thought and how defiant this particular lonely feeling is to nominative language. The question is not only how to communicate this unprecedented loneliness, but what to call it. Constrained by reason to present it in an image, the mind generates two quiddities (lines 3-4), two tries, that is, at something more precise than the vague "Thing." The first is "Some Polar Expiation" and the second, "An Omen in the Bone / of Death's tremendous nearness."[17] These two molecules of intellection, so different yet suggestive—"drained" or "strangely abstracted" as David Porter would say—initially suspend the try of thought in doubtful parataxis.

How are they related, and how do they help the speaker think? First, "Some Polar Expiation" shows her mind leaping to a traditional kind of lonely undertaking, a cleansing process of soul-searching in which one divides, objectifies, despises, and ultimately rejects some part of one's self.[18] This is not only more precise than thinking of a lonely thing, it is more purposeful, religious, moral, conventional, and self-directed, all of which suggests that specific cultural forces are pressuring the try of thought. Were it not for the frigid adjective "Polar," the idea of performing an expiation or atonement might actually seem consolatory, a painful but useful work. But by punning on polar expedition and exploration, the speaker emphasizes the unforgiving, epic, arctic, limits-of-the-civilized-and-natural-world connotations of the enterprise.[19] "Polar Expiation" thus expresses something like the feeling of being radically and painfully removed from one's natural surroundings, culture, and self.

The second vision of the loneliest thing, complementing, improving upon or replacing the first, is no longer retrospective and inward-looking but anticipatory: an "Omen in the Bone / Of Death's tremendous nearness –." This portent is felt rather than witnessed or imagined; suddenly death seems tremendously near in time (the speaker's own death feels nigh) as well as space (another dead soul or spirit is there, nearby). These feelings are self-alienating, too, but no longer illustrating. One does not willfully create omens for oneself in the way one examines, analyzes, and repents one's past acts; the omen of death "in the Bone" is received unexpectedly, from without, and remains to be interpreted.

The unlike options of expiation and omen might suggest that the poem is essentially playful, a game of how much loneliness would a lonely woman think if a lonely woman could think loneliness. Yet the care with which those two metaphorical clauses were chosen makes me think instead that the try of thought they represent is dead serious. Even the reaching motion of the mind is made evident by non-specific articles: "*Some* Polar Expiation," "*An* Omen in the Bone" (italics mine). The calculating, self-repudiating transformations of expiation mutate, and yet equate—emotionally if not conceptually—to the imminent, incalculable, dispersive loneliness of the self facing death. Shifts and equations like these make paraphrasing difficult, but one might speculate that thought is attracted to the way these two brief phrases amount to a basic binary set of loneliness-generating possibilities: the idea-glimpses of being coldly removed from one's past self (through expiation) or from one's present and future self (in death.) So while on the one hand these phrases are semantic placeholders, self-consciously inadequate way-stations pointing to the unreachable summit of a nascent thought, a thought one can only try to think, on the other hand they hypostasize the most self-annihilating thoughts and feelings.

However brilliantly or succinctly one manages to bring a painful emotion into language, one does not, for all that, palliate it, and that is what the speaker tries to do with the next gesture of thought. Having put forth unstable but generative concepts and imagery, the speaker then proceeds, quite unexpectedly, to reach into the world of the dead for a kindred spirit: "I probed Retrieveless things / My Duplicate – to borrow –." Since her duplicate qualifies only on the basis of also being "Of Heavenly Love – forgot –," the core idea is that somebody already dead has been, like her, rejected by God. This makes it clear for the first time that the "lonelier" idea/feeling she is trying to think is derived not just from an acute awareness of her death but also, and especially, from her catastrophically alienated ontological status. The idea that a rare and special loneliness was reserved for God's forgotten was a recurring thought for Dickinson. It is clearly expressed, for example, in this commiserating 1850 letter to Abiah Root:

> *You* have stood by the grave before; I have walked there sweet summer evenings and read the names on the stones, and wondered who would come and give me the same memorial; but I never have laid my friends there, and forgot that they too must die; this is my first affliction, and indeed 'tis hard to bear it. To those bereaved so often that home is no more here, and whose communion with friends is had only in prayers, there must be much to hope for, but when the unreconciled spirit has nothing left but God, that spirit is lone indeed. I don't think there will be any sunshine, or any singing-birds in the spring that's coming. (L39)[20]

In "I tried to think a lonelier Thing," the technique of borrowing one's "duplicate," or imagining a fellow "unreconciled spirit," is meant to mitigate the unique loneliness of the non-believer. The chief interest of this mental replication seems to be that it creates *ex nihilo* the smallest possible unit of imagined community. A self thinking of another absent and possibly imaginary self, a copy-self or twin ontological orphan, has at least that chance of relationality with another, of existence outside the self.

Such a mental leap is not a full statement of method, but it is constructive. It serves as the founding premise for the rest of the try at thinking, and from it, somehow, a "Haggard comfort springs." This announcement interrupts the past-tense narration of what the speaker has felt and announces instead a general law, one that moves the poem into the thinking present and perhaps universalizes it. (Of course, in order to feel included and therefore relieved by the "Haggard comfort," a reader must also be "of Heavenly Love – forgot –.") Yet the precise claim given lawlike properties is not easy to see:

> A Haggard comfort springs
>
> From the belief that Somewhere –
> Within the Clutch of Thought –
> There dwells one other Creature
> Of Heavenly Love – forgot –

The difficulty is that the phrase "Within the Clutch of Thought" is precariously ambiguous. It means reachable by thought, just within the power of thought, or else composed solely of thought, purely imaginary. The undecidability is important and one can easily make the poem pivot upon it: since one cannot know that one's duplicate "dwells" somewhere, one must (try to) take it on faith. This is the difference between a recognizably Romantic misery-loves-company logic and a more desperately lonely awareness that one is completely fabricating one's source of comfort.[21]

Negotiating those two possibilities, the last two stanzas of the poem are an uneasy endgame. They relate the speaker's two attempts to do something on the basis of the preceding sequence of thoughts, beginning with "I plucked at our Partition." To understand this plucking, we must see that this "Partition" is the invisible, enigmatic, and absolute line separating the speaker from the imagined duplicate: the line between life and death.[22] And, crucially, it is "our" rather than 'the' "Partition." The collective pronoun reveals the inventive force of the speaker's thought, for it signals that her mind is not turning back from the infinitesimal sense of community it has captured or created. A we has been formed, a communion of souls however imaginary or weak, and the "Partition" they share is thus both bridge and barrier between a live, thinking, trying consciousness and a hypothesized dead twin.

The poem is clearly trying to realize, in the Dickinsonian sense discussed above, a terrifyingly solipsistic condition. We are made aware of the impossibility of reaching across the partition by the physical and visual activity of "pluck[ing]" at it. Like other Dickinson images of awkward, unnatural responses to intolerable conditions, it is extremely disconcerting. One thinks of the desperate bird in "Of course I prayed" (Fr581) stamping her foot "on the Air" in protest to God's indifference. To feel something of the futility registered by the simile "As One should pry the Walls – / Between Himself – and Horror's Twin –," one need merely picture oneself thinking of one's own dead "duplicate" and plucking in the air (as opposed to more hopeful possible gestures like extending a hand). It is no less unnerving if plucking at the partition is taken as a metaphor for movements of the mind; on the contrary, it would then join the series of probing retrieveless things and borrowing one's duplicate to form a trio of mental procedures desperate enough to be a symptomatology of unfathomable, sickening loneliness. Indeed, the basic communicability of the poem's try hinges on the reader's willingness to identify with and follow a process of despairing thought well beyond where thinking usually wants to go. While many readers may refuse, not recognizing or believing in this extreme loneliness, those who have come to trust Dickinson may go deeply into the experiment.

The result is a chilling scene reminiscent of Beckett's *Godot*: two God-forsaken souls in opposing cells, one alive and one imaginary and/or dead. The last stanza narrates the way the live one, the speaker, comes to accept being part of a carceral community stripped to its atomic minimum:

> I almost strove to clasp his Hand,
> Such Luxury – it grew –
> That as Myself – could pity Him –
> Perhaps he – pitied me –

The mirroring twins are connected only by a fantasy of mutual pity, but somehow this self-consciously pathetic vision results in a feeling of "Such Luxury –." It turns out that it was the purpose of the original try of thought to produce this mental drama of a virtual community and make it credibly intelligible as a consolatory grace earned by thought alone. The feeling of luxury, the awe on this human trinket, would thus grow out of the confidence produced by the experimental force of thought itself; in fact, rereading the poem I hear the implied but elided phrase "to think" in the middle of this last stanza: "Such Luxury – it grew [– *to think*] / That as Myself – could pity Him –." That is what I think the poem is saying and the poet is thinking. Or rather, trying to think, for despite the past tense this is surely a fragile state and a momentary victory: how long can meditating on one's dead duplicate continue to console? Will it not ultimately reinforce one's intolerable loneliness and return it to the intolerable and ineffable status it had before the valiant attempt at thought?

In this as in every other try-to-think poem, we do not know if Dickinson succeeded or even thought she succeeded in thinking what she tried to think. We know only that these were poems in which she tried to help or save herself by representing her own efforts to help or save herself. Such trying poetry invites us to join and repeat her thinking about and beyond thinking, but in the case of "I tried to think a lonelier

Thing," we join, paradoxically, only at the risk of experiencing a lone-liness we cannot sound.

Notes

1. See Cameron, *Choosing Not Choosing*; Wittgenstein, *Philosophical Investigations*; Lyotard, *The Postmodern Condition*; Perloff, "Emily Dickinson and the Theory Canon."

2. For Derrida's analysis of Lévi-Strauss's *bricolage*, see "Structure, Sign, and Play in the Discourse of the Human Sciences."

3. Critics have not explored the links between Kant and Dickinson in great depth. See Gelpi (124-5) and the articles by Frederick Morey and myself.

4. The beautiful occurs when a satisfying image *is* found and harmony reigns throughout the mind's faculties. For the fullest discussion to date of the ways Dickinson's poetry responds to and reinvigorates the Romantic sublime, see Gary Lee Stonum's *The Dickinson Sublime*.

5. Many theoretical approaches and vocabularies can be used to describe Dickinson's mental activity. Because I wish to emphasize the movements and processes of thought, I prefer in this essay to draw upon the language developed by Stonum in *The Dickinson Sublime* on the basis of the philosophical, literary, and aesthetic traditions of the sublime. In *The Undiscovered Continent*, Suzanne Juhasz has also written compellingly of "dimensional" and "conceptual" terminologies in Dickinson.

6. The mind's self-elusiveness was a common issue in Dickinson's many text-books of mental philosophy. The difficulty often described is that the mind cannot treat itself as an object of science. In the Thomas Brown volume in her library, for example, we read that analyzing "is not less [necessary] in mind, than in matter; nor, when nature exhibits all her wonders to us, in one case, in objects that are separate from us, and for-eign; and, in the other, in the intimate phenomena of our own consciousness, can we justly think, that it is of *ourselves* we know the most. On the contrary, strange as it may seem, it is of her *distant* operations, that our knowledge is least imperfect; and we have far less acquaintance with the sway which she exercises in our own mind, than with that by which she guides the course of the most remote planet, in spaces beyond us, which we rather *calculate* than *conceive*" (Brown's italics; 108). For Upham, similarly, the problem is that we cannot "see the mind, nor is it an object . . . of sense. Nor, on the other hand, is the notion of mind a direct object of the memory, or of reasoning, or of imagination" (125). Lawrence Buell has recently brought new attention to Emerson's perhaps more famous epistemological wrestling with the problem of "double con-sciousness" (204ff.).

7. "Should you think it breathed" means: is my thought now living on its own,

apart from me? Does it make sense to others? "If I make the mistake" means: have I included or omitted sounds, words, rhymes, ideas, or something else that is keeping my thought from living on its own and becoming fully intelligible? And when Dickinson asks Higginson for "what is true" she wants him to give his unadorned opinion.

8. When she says "*they* look alike and numb," Dickinson switches naturally but oddly from the singular to the plural form: "while *my thought* is undressed, I can make the distinction, but when I put *them* in the gown" (my italics). Thought thus exhibits a kind of cell division, moving from single (when abstract and unwritten) to plural (when materialized in writing).

9. Here "Fine" means the price or penalty of delight.

10. Johnson explains that Dickinson "correctly guessed that Higginson wrote the unsigned review of Lowell's *Among My Books: Second Series* for the March 1876 issue of *Scribner's Monthly*. . . . The review of Emerson's *Letters and Social Aims* in the April issue, likewise unsigned, may be Higginson's but has not been so identified" (L457, Note). The Emerson review reads very much like Higginson to me.

11. Dickinson's family also understood how much she valued thought. Lavinia undoubtedly expressed the general sentiment when she wrote: "As for Emily, she was not withdrawn or exclusive really. She was always watching for the rewarding person to come but she was a very busy person herself. She had to think—she was the only one of us who had that to do. Father believed; and mother loved; and Austin had Amherst; and I had the family to keep track of" (Bingham 413-4).

12. She asked him during his visit: "Is it oblivion or absorption when things pass from our minds?" and then, in the next letter, asked him "to forgive me for all the ignorance I had" (L342b, L352).

13. For a close reading of this poem, see my "Dickinson, Death, and the Sublime."

14. In another poem, pure thought has the power to produce a vastly enriching kind of loneliness: "There is another Loneliness / That many die without – / Not want of friend occasions it / Or circumstance of Lot // But nature, sometimes, sometimes thought / And whoso it befall / Is richer than could be revealed / By mortal numeral –" (Fr1138).

15. "I tried to think a lonelier Thing" (Fr570) appears in fascicle 25 between the poems "A precious – mouldering pleasure – 'tis –" (Fr569) and "Two Butterflies went out at Noon –" (Fr571). These last two were first published in 1890 and 1891, respectively.

16. Dickinson's letters are also peppered with comments and études on loneliness. In a December 1854 letter to Susan Gilbert Dickinson, she wrestled with the difficulty of expressing extreme loneliness in words, ultimately nominating visual art as the superior medium: "Susie – it is a little thing to say how lone it is – anyone can do it, but to wear the loneness next your heart for weeks, when you sleep, and when you wake, ever missing something, *this*, all cannot say, and it baffles me. I would paint a portrait which would bring the tears, had I canvass for it, and the scene should be – *solitude*, and the figures – solitude – and the lights and shades, each a solitude. I could fill a chamber with landscapes so lone, men should pause and weep there; then haste grateful home, for a loved one left" (L176).

17. "Expiation" is one of the loneliest words in Dickinson's lexicon. This poem has the only recorded use in any poem or letter.

18. I disagree with Paul Muldoon's argument that this poem involves a commentary on the Civil War, that there is "no doubt that a strand" of this poem "refers to that 'Horror' involving 'Polar' opposites, North and South, between whom there falls a 'Partition'" (24).

19. The series of expeditions to the Arctic funded by Lady Franklin in search of her husband Sir John Franklin were much in the news in the 1850s; Dickinson read an April 1851 *Harper's* article on the subject (see Muldoon 13-18). She never forgot these events; in an 1885 letter she joked to her nephew Ned: "How favorable that something is missing besides Sir John Franklin!" (L1000).

20. The letter refers to the death of Leonard Humphrey on 13 November 1850.

21. Goethe's Werther is a good example of a Romantic who is lonely but consolable by others: "Sometimes I say to myself: 'Your destiny is unique; call the others fortunate—no one has been so tormented as you.' Then I read an ancient poet, and it seems to me as though I look into my own heart. I have so much to endure! Oh, were there other men before me as miserable as I!" (119).

22. Dickinson uses the singular form of the word "partition" only twice in poems, never in letters. In both cases it unambiguously means this barrier/bridge between the living and the dead. See "In falling Timbers buried –" (Fr447).

Works Cited

The following abbreviations are used to refer to the writings of Emily Dickinson:

Fr   *The Poems of Emily Dickinson.* ed. R. W. Franklin. 3 vols. Cambridge, MA: Harvard UP, 1998. Citation by poem number.

L   *The Letters of Emily Dickinson.* ed. Thomas H. Johnson and Theodora Ward. 3 vols. Cambridge, MA: Harvard UP, 1958. Citation by letter number.

Bingham, Millicent Todd. *Emily Dickinson's Home: Letters of Edward Dickinson and His Family.* New York: Harper & Brothers, 1955.

Brown, Thomas. *Lectures on the Philosophy of the Human Mind.* 2 vols. Hallowell: Masters, Smith & Co., 1848.

Buell, Lawrence. *Emerson.* Cambridge, MA: Harvard UP, 2003.

Cameron, Sharon. *Choosing Not Choosing: Dickinson's Fascicles.* Chicago: U of Chicago P, 1992.

Deppman, Jed. "Dickinson, Death, and the Sublime." *The Emily Dickinson Journal.* 9:1 (2000): 1-20.

_____. "'I could not have defined the change': Rereading Dickinson's Definition Poetry." *The Emily Dickinson Journal.* 11:1 (2002): 49-80.

Derrida, Jacques. "Structure, Sign, and Play in the Discourse of the Human Sciences." *Writing and Difference.* Trans. Alan Bass. Chicago: U of Chicago P. 1978. 278-293.

Gelpi, Albert. *Emily Dickinson: The Mind of the Poet.* Cambridge, MA: Harvard UP: 1965.

Goethe, Johann Wolfgang von. *The Sorrows of Young Werther.* New York: Random House, 1990.

Higginson, Thomas Wentworth. "Letter to a Young Contributor." *The Atlantic Monthly: A Magazine of Literature, Art, and Politics.* Vol. 9. #14. April, 1862. 26-36; 401-411.

Juhasz, Suzanne. *The Undiscovered Continent: Emily Dickinson and the Space of the Mind.* Bloomington: Indiana University Press, 1983.

Kant, Immanuel. *Critique of Judgment.* J. H. Bernard, trans. New York: Macmillan, 1951.

Kierkegaard, Søren. *Fear and Trembling and The Sickness unto Death.* Trans. Walter Lowrie. New York: Doubleday & Co., 1954.

Lyotard, Jean-François. *Lessons on the Analytic of the Sublime.* Elizabeth Rottenberg, trans. Palo Alto: Stanford UP, 1994.

_____. *The Postmodern Condition.* Geoff Bennington and Brian Massumi, trans. Minneapolis: U of Minnesota P, 1984.

Morey, Frederick L., "Dickinson-Kant: The First Critique." *Dickinson Studies* 60 (December 1986): 1-70.

_____. "Dickinson-Kant: Part II." *Dickinson Studies* 64 (December 1987): 3-30.

_____. "Dickinson-Kant: Part III." *Dickinson Studies* 67 (December 1988): 3-60.

Muldoon, Paul. "Polar Expeditions: 'I tried to think a lonelier Thing' by Emily Dickinson. *New England Review.* 24: 2 (2003): 6-24.

Perloff, Marjorie. "Emily Dickinson and the Theory Canon." http://epc.buffalo.edu/authors/perloff/articles/Dickinson.html.

Peterson, Margaret. *American Women Writers: A Critical Reference Guide from Colonial Times to the Present. Volume I: A to E.* Ed. Lina Mainiero. New York: Frederick Ungar Publishing Co., Inc. 1979.

Porter, David. *Dickinson: The Modern Idiom.* Cambridge, MA: Harvard UP, 1981.

Rosenbaum, S. P., *A Concordance to the Poems of Emily Dickinson.* Ithaca, NY: Cornell UP, 1964.

Stonum, Gary Lee. *The Dickinson Sublime.* Madison: Wisconsin UP, 1990.

Upham, Thomas C. *Elements of Mental Philosophy.* New York: Harper and Brothers, 1842.

Watts, Isaac. *Improvement of the Mind.* New York: A. S. Barnes & Co. 1849.

Wittgenstein, Ludwig. *Philosophical Investigations.* G. E. M. Anscombe, trans. Oxford: Blackwell, 1958.

Wolff, Cynthia Griffin. *Emily Dickinson.* New York: Knopf, 1986.

The Ample Word:
Immanence and Authority
in Dickinson's Poetry_____

Joanne Feit Diehl

While Dickinson's poetics has sometimes been described as "austere," Joanne Feit Diehl argues instead that "the proliferation of
tropes and richness of figurative language" in Dickinson's work "constitute a realm of verbal amplitude, yet an amplitude that she regards
with ambivalence." A poet who places value on power, which is poet-
ically expressed through her "rhetoric of immanence and authority,"
Dickinson constructs "a voice of magisterial presence" in her verse
and casts her reader "in the position of entering a consciousness that
everywhere inhabits the world." But even as Dickinson's poems "display a magisterial power," they call it into question, revealing Dickinson's ambivalence toward the linguistic powers she claims. If in a
poem such as "It would never be Common – more – I said –" the
speaker, through language, achieves an experience of blissful immanence as she transforms the world through her verbal powers, her experience of immanence proves transient. "Ostensibly, immanence, or
the power to create it," writes Diehl, "is precarious, indeed fleeting."
And yet, "the poem itself as performative act reaffirms the poet's
claim to her supposedly lost verbal power, for in its very recounting of
that loss, it recreates the proliferation of language that reinscribes its
presence." Finding in Dickinson's "obsessive return to the mysteries
of death and immortality" a desire for "cognitive mastery" and a "determination to wrest knowledge from the unknowable," Diehl finds
the presumption of an "outrageous authority" in a single line from
Dickinson's poem "'Tis so appalling – it exhilarates –." By saying that
"Looking at Death, is Dying –," Dickinson "posits the power of language to overcome the distinctions we must inevitably draw when
we refer to human experience." If, as Dickinson "makes her boldest
forays into the world beyond the self and the world within," she is ac-

companied by "anxiety, hesitation, doubt," hers nevertheless is "an audacious poetics that pushes language to the very edge of meaning and, at times, beyond" as the "immanence and authority manifested in Dickinson's poetry bespeak a will to power second to none in the history of Romanticism."   J.B.B.

Writing to her sister-in-law, Dickinson urges Sue to:

Cherish Power – dear –
Remember that stands in the Bible between the Kingdom and the Glory, because it is wilder than either of them. (L583)

The value Dickinson places here on power manifests itself throughout her poems in a rhetoric of immanence and authority. Thus I begin my discussion by examining these terms. I then go on to look at four instances from the poems that illustrate the verbal strategies by which Dickinson establishes her foundational relation to the world and interrogate their character. Throughout I maintain that a consideration of "immanence" and "authority" allows us not only to note how Dickinson constructs a voice of magisterial presence but to observe as well the anxieties that surround her poetics of consciousness. Although Dickinson's poetics has at times been viewed as austere, through another lens, the proliferation of tropes and richness of figurative language constitute a realm of verbal amplitude, yet an amplitude that she regards with ambivalence.

First, definitions: "Immanence" can refer both to that within the mind and to a consciousness indwelling in the world, thus referring to a condition omnipresent yet wholly within. This dual definition characterizes the quality of the uncanny that pervades Dickinson's poetry, a phenomenon that casts the reader in the position of entering a consciousness that everywhere inhabits the world. Through such assertion of the ubiquity of authorial presence, Dickinson establishes the reader's extreme dependence upon poetic subjectivity. The *Oxford En-*

glish Dictionary tells us that "immanent" can be applied to the Deity regarded as permanently pervading and sustaining the universe. By associating the immanent with her own poetic presence, Dickinson substitutes her voice for orthodox, godlike power.

Similarly, Dickinson's understanding of "authority" carries a dualistic meaning, for her poems display a magisterial power as they simultaneously call it into question.[1] Moreover, they attest to the poet's role both as active agent and observing witness. Among its entries, the *Oxford English Dictionary* defines "authority" as the "weight of testimony" and, indeed, it is in this sense that the poems provide first-person accounts that testify to the singular cast of Dickinson's imagination. Yet this authority does not remain unchallenged as Dickinson questions the implications it holds for the experiential self. To speak authoritatively may exact too great a price because it potentially arouses in the poet an awareness of the dangers such an assertion of primacy over experience holds for the authorial psyche. Conflicts relating to identification with the sources of her own power lie at the heart of Dickinson's ambivalence toward it. Thus "authority" signifies both a salutary accomplishment and a phenomenon to be viewed with ambivalence.

I turn now to four poems to illustrate how Dickinson conveys such a sense of immanence and concomitant authority and, secondly, to suggest the rhetorical means by which she interrogates the origins of these linguistic powers. If elsewhere I have claimed that Dickinson creates a counter-aesthetics based, in part, upon psychosexual difference, I want here explicitly to examine the poetic language that testifies to that difference (26-43). I begin by invoking a phrase from Paul de Man, which he uses in an utterly different context, to suggest that Dickinson's poems articulate "a phenomenology of consciousness as a constitutive act." My first example of such an act comes from that especially productive year, 1862.

There came a Day – at Summer's full –
Entirely for me –
I thought that such were for the Saints –
Where Resurrections – be –

The Sun – as common – went abroad –
The Flowers – accustomed – blew –
As if no Soul the Solstice passed –
That maketh all things new.

The time was scarce profaned – by speech –
The symbol of a word
Was needless – as at Sacrament –
The Wardrobe – of Our Lord –

Each was to each – the sealed church –
Permitted to commune – this time –
Lest we too awkward – show –
At "Supper of the Lamb."

The hours slid fast – as hours will –
Clutched tight – by greedy hands –
So – faces on two Decks – look back –
Bound to opposing Lands –

And so – when all the time had failed –
Without external sound –
Each – bound the other's Crucifix –
We gave no other bond –

Sufficient troth – that we shall rise –
Deposed – at length – the Grave –
To that New Marriage –
Justified – through Calvaries of Love!

(Fr325)

In its recollected evocation of a moment of high crisis, "There came a Day – at Summer's full –" exemplifies those poems where Dickinson graphically presents the lineaments of a crucial occasion in which the identities of the principals and the literal circumstances that surround the crisis remain obscured—what Robert Weisbuch has called poems of the "omitted center."[2] Such poems establish not only an uncanny relation to their subject but to their readers as well for, although the poems may gesture toward intimacy with their audience through a purported act of disclosure, they simultaneously erase all circumstantial facts from view. Cristanne Miller notes how such an inherently paradoxical form of poetic communication, such an innately conflictual speech act, results in "the confiding but non-informative voice of Dickinson's poems" (10).[3] I would emphasize, moreover, that "There came a Day –" and others like it not only place the reader in a vexed relation to the text, but that such poems, because of their referential opacity, direct readerly attention away from an attempt to discern "realistic" facts and invite us to focus instead upon the psychodynamics enacted by the poem. Freed from the conventional burdens of representation, "There came a Day – at Summer's full –" unnames self and other, evacuates circumstantial details, and proceeds by a mode of symbolic discourse. The poem opens with the speaker's stating her exclusive proprietorship over the event to follow: "There came a Day – at Summer's full – / Entirely for me –." She then states what has proven to be, after the fact, a false supposition: that such a day would be reserved only for the religiously sanctified, for "Saints." By negating this false premise, by an act of rhetorical indirection, the poem establishes the exceptionality of its spiritual occasion, which continues to be identified by an overturning of assumption. The apparent ordinariness of the weather belies the significance of the event that is about to transpire: "The Sun – as common – went abroad – / The Flowers – accustomed – blew –." The full import of the occasion is presented in a negative conditional construction: "As if no Soul the Solstice passed – / That maketh all things new." What then transpires is so sacred that speech would only seem profanation. Denied access to the utterances of the actors, we must rely upon the speaker's metaphoric characterization of them: "Each was to each – the sealed church –"—separate, sacred edifices granted a special dispensation to "commune," because of doubt that they would appear "too awkward"—ill suited (unprepared?) if such communication were to take place at the Last Supper. Having heard not a word spoken by the principals themselves, our attention is directed, as at the poem's opening, toward time: "The hours slid fast – as hours will – / Clutched tight – by greedy hands –." Such urgency to stop time testifies to the desperation of those who would prolong it. This categorical statement about how time works when experienced subjectively is immediately troped upon: "So – faces on two Decks – look back – / Bound to opposing Lands –." This trope serves a dual purpose: first, it graphically underscores the ferocity of desire doomed to separation through a synecdoche upon a personification ("So – faces on two Decks – look back –")—the same figurative technique that governs the preceding line, "by greedy hands." Secondly, the simile functions as a transition that returns us to the poem's main plot, "And so – when all the time had failed – / Without external sound – / Each – bound the other's Crucifix – / We gave no other bond –." Note Dickinson's characteristic irony: "failed" meaning that both human time has run out and that the lovers have entered a realm beyond it. By binding each other's crucifix, the lovers have made a commitment to a reunion beyond the Grave, "justified" "through Calvaries of Love!" Thus, at the poem's close, the exchange of religious faith suffices to assure a marriage after death earned through Christ's sacrifice. The poem takes as its subject nothing less than the sanctification of two lives, an exchange of eternal commitment; yet how little we learn about either party outside the force of their mutual devotion. The poem operates through a series of tropological displacements, the discourse of the temporal, and the strategy of withheld language. By deploying such deflective verbal techniques, Dickinson assumes control over readerly interpretation, directing us away from our more conventional heuristic habits to focus instead upon the speaker's subjectivity and the symbolic. Although "There came a Day – at Summer's full –" portrays a pledge enacted between two persons, the poem is right to declare in its opening lines that the day of crisis belongs entirely to the speaker. Not only is it her voice that we hear, but even more significantly, the rhetoric through which that voice speaks functions both prescriptively and proscriptively, as it draws us away from the literal into a series of figural displacements that work to control our relation to the text. Dickinson appropriates crisis by maintaining a double relation to it, both as observer and as experiential subject. The power of trope grants Dickinson an enabling authority.

Elsewhere verbal mastery may itself become the subject of its own tragic occasion as language spreads its transformative powers through the world only to be brutally, mysteriously subsumed. Consider "It would never be Common – more – I said –" (Fr388), which opens with such astonishing bravado. Without identifying the origins of her newfound power to affect universal change, the speaker simply announces, "Difference – had begun –." Infused with a joy whose source is unknown and never revealed, the speaker undergoes a transformation that manifests itself in explicitly physical ways. Note, moreover, that in describing these corporeal changes, Dickinson employs diction associated with language:

> I'd so much joy – I told it – Red –
> Opon my simple Cheek –
> I felt it publish – in my eye –
> 'Twas needless – any speak –
>
> I walked – as wings – my body bore –
> The feet – I former used –
> Unnecessary – now to me –
> As boots – would be – to Birds –

> I put my pleasure all abroad –
> I dealt a word of Gold
> To every Creature – that I met –
> And Dowered – all the World –

"I told it," "I felt it publish," "I dealt a word of Gold." Endowed with bliss, the speaker transforms the world through her word. Language expands as the speaker puts her "pleasure all abroad," as her consciousness pervades everything beyond the self. Language is the means by which the speaker achieves what, in another context, the Marxist critic Georg Lukács names "self-immanence."[4] Yet the experience of blissful immanence suddenly shrinks, as inexplicably as it had begun. Here, immanence, if not illusory, proves transitory, a loss Dickinson describes in fairy-tale-like images of "Goblin," "Palaces," and "beggared." Perhaps, the fantastic character of these images itself constitutes a verbal defense against the full experience of that loss.

> When – suddenly – my Riches shrank –
> A Goblin – drank my Dew –
> My Palaces – dropped tenantless –
> Myself – was beggared – too –

In a futile attempt to hold on to her receding powers, the speaker clutches "at sounds" (again a vocal image) and gropes at "shapes" (might these be the very tropes that constitute the poem?) only to feel "the Wilderness roll back / Along [her] Golden lines –," lines that serve not only as a geographical marker but surely as the now effaced lines of poetry as well. The voice that recounts this fairy tale of failed metamorphosis speaks from a position of destitution:

> The Sackcloth – hangs opon the nail –
> The Frock I used to wear –
> But where my moment of Brocade –
> My – drop – of India?

The sackcloth of the mourner, of the present self, is at hand, as is the frock worn by the recollected younger self, but what has been lost is the rich fabric of a fleeting transformation, the single drop of India, the far-distant exotic. Ostensibly, immanence, or the power to create it, is precarious, indeed fleeting. Yet, on another level, the poem itself as performative act reaffirms the poet's claim to her supposedly lost verbal power, for in its very recounting of that loss, it recreates the proliferation of language that reinscribes its presence. Such an ironic turn on a loss that through its articulation cancels itself out while leaving the trace of its always endangering presence can be understood as a manifestation of a self-reflexive consciousness that knows that the only way for the poet to triumph over time and silence is through a further reinscription of her language-making powers.

Yet such powers are not themselves without risk for Dickinson. In another poem from 1862, the "supposed person," who, Dickinson said, spoke in her poems, willfully abjures the vocation of the artist. "I would not paint – a picture –," "I would not talk, like Cornets –," "Nor would I be a Poet –" (Fr348)—this last should give us pause, for we need to inquire what the speaker would choose instead and the reasons for that choice. The last stanza reads:

> Nor would I be a Poet –
> It's finer – Own the Ear –
> Enamored – impotent – content –
> The License to revere,
> A privilege so awful
> What would the Dower be,
> Had I the Art to stun myself
> With Bolts – of Melody!

To "Own the Ear – / Enamored – impotent – content –" itself contains its own hesitation, for it registers in its middle term, "impotent," the price of such a position. If we read the dash between "content" and the line that follows, "The License to revere," as a link between the two lines rather than a pause between them, then to be the one who listens to the poet is to be she who would be content to revere his freedom as well as his authority. To attain such a license constitutes a privilege that would be "awful" in the two ways that are typically invoked in Dickinson's associations with language: awful here meaning "full of awe" and "terrible." Such an awful and implicitly awesome privilege could only be acquired at great cost. We recall here the "dower" of "It would never be Common," invoked when Dickinson alludes to her moment of ecstatic amplitude when she "Dowered – all the World –." Here, in "I would not paint – a picture –," not only would the expense be great if she were to assume the identity of the poet but the nature of that identity would itself pose a potentially lethal danger:

> What would the Dower be,
> Had I the Art to stun myself
> With Bolts – of Melody!

If, as we learn from other Dickinson poems, the cost exacted by conventional marriage is exorbitant, so, too, is the price exacted if one were to become a bride of oneself. Here a submerged erotic, possibly autoerotic, charge appears. Indeed, to stun oneself with "Bolts – of Melody" may refer not only to the force of poetic power but also to an imagined masturbatory act, which, however ravishing, might exact the too high price of self-censure. To be a poet, therefore, would be to practice an "art" so powerful that it would "stun" its creative source. The poem's speaker explicitly abjures the very identity she manifests by writing the poem; thus the poem serves as ironic testimony to the poet's awareness of the dangers she runs by practicing her craft, by writing the very poem that we are reading, by dowering the world with an eroticized poetics. This irony resembles the irony of "It would never be Common – more – I said –," for in both cases the continued production of language overrides the negative vision of an avowed linguistic power that has been or must be sacrificed.

If Dickinson's poems couple eros and poetics in a will to power that is shadowed by ambivalence, this desire also manifests itself in that other great confrontation, between consciousness and death. Dickinson's obsessive return to the mysteries of death and immortality, her "Flood subject" (L319), as she called it, betrays a yearning for cognitive mastery over the delimitations of mortality. One line of a single poem from Dickinson's prolific canon on the subject illustrates the sweeping ambition that fuels her determination to wrest knowledge from the unknowable. In "'Tis so appalling – it exhilarates –" (Fr341), Dickinson makes an especially bold move: with a rhetorical gesture of apparent simplicity, she elides the difference between life and death by asserting that "Looking at Death, is Dying –," an assertion of faith in the power of observation to obliterate the boundary between life and death. Dickinson carries out her teleological imperative in an attempt to resolve the origins of human doubt before the threat of the unknown. The poem claims that through an act of empathic witnessing, the speaker can acquire knowledge that is inherently unknowable by any mortal. Pushing past the distinction between observation and experience, raising this distinction to the level of a final challenge, the poem asserts that one can supersede the limitation of human knowledge by assuming through imaginative projection the identity of the dying individual who is being observed by the speaker. Thus, in the presence of the dying, one can erase the distinction between viewer and viewed by translating empathic witnessing into speech. To assert that to view and to be viewed in life's final moments are identical presumes an outrageous authority. In its very articulation, "Looking at Death, is Dying –" posits the power of language to overcome the distinctions we must inevitably draw when we refer to human experience. Implicit is a concept of language as allusive, as separable from epistemological limitation. While we might wonder at such audacity, we cannot help but admire the courage of a poet who would make such a claim for the linguistic imagination.

The extremes to which Dickinson will go in her quest for an adequate mode of expression find their origins in her self-perceived crisis. No longer able to rely upon a fluent relation between writerly self and natural world, Dickinson strives to invent an alternative rhetoric of representation. Responding to the realization that the world will no longer suffice as a ground for figuration, that "The Stars are old that stood for me – / The West a little worn –" (Fr1242), Dickinson consequently makes it her business to disestablish, deconstruct the imagistic coherence of the naturalizing Sublime. This displacement proliferates throughout the poems as Dickinson experiments with grammar, with the dash, and with figuration itself. Through these techniques of dislocation, Dickinson makes her boldest forays into the world beyond the self and the world within. Anxiety, hesitation, doubt—all accompany Dickinson on her quest to ascertain the strength of the isolate imagination, her quest to discover what will suffice, if not prevail, against the forces of time, death, and silence.

The immanence and authority manifested in Dickinson's poetry bespeak a will to power second to none in the history of Romanticism. Hers is an audacious poetics that pushes language to the very edge of meaning and, at times, beyond.[5] Whatever hermeneutic opacity we encounter in her poetry is balanced by an intense figurative energy that works in the service of a formidable revisionist poetics. By investing the world with her consciousness, by achieving the illusion of immanence and the authority of rhetorical control, Dickinson converts her singularity into a vast, originary strength.

From *The Emily Dickinson Journal* 14, no. 2 (2005): 1-11. Copyright © 2005 by The Johns Hopkins University Press. Reprinted with permission of The Johns Hopkins University Press.

Notes

1. For an explicitly literary historical and linguistic analysis of the origins of Dickinson's verbal authority, see Bryan C. Short's "Emily Dickinson and the Origins of Language," wherein Short asserts that "the origins of Dickinson's verbal authority depend, in part, on her use of pronouns and other refined—that is thought to be late developing—aspects of language, including the abstractions discussed by David Porter (25-36), to give her voice its extraordinary ability to appropriate and critique masculine forms of authority, as in the second stanza of 'Behind Me – dips Eternity –' (Fr743), where repeated pronouns and abstract nouns and verbs create an effect of lofty ironic detachment:

> 'Tis Kingdoms – afterward – they say –
> In perfect – pauseless Monarchy –
> Whose Prince – is Son of none –
> Himself – Himself diversify –
> In Duplicate divine –

The passage shows Dickinson at her most sophisticated, modern, authoritative and adult. Her understanding of how language works is closer to Pope than to Emerson" (112).

2. Both Jay Leyda, in *The Years and Hours of Emily Dickinson*, and Robert Weisbuch, in *Emily Dickinson's Poetry*, discuss the usefulness of this term. Leyda notes that "a major device of Emily Dickinson's writing, both in her poems and in her letters, was what might be called the 'omitted center.' The riddle, the circumstance too well known to be repeated to the initiate, the deliberate skirting of the obvious—this was the means she used to increase the privacy of her communication; it has also increased our problem in piercing that privacy" (xxi).

3. See Cristanne Miller, *Emily Dickinson: A Poet's Grammar*, 10.

4. See Paul de Man, *Blindness and Insight: Essays in the Rhetoric of Contemporary Criticism* quoting Georg Lukács, *The Theory of the Novel*, 42-43.

5. Short also asserts that Dickinson learned from various linguistic sources: "Dickinson's art, as a result of her eclectic, at times backward-looking education, occupies the pinnacle of a long and fruitful intellectual tradition. Not until the emergence of modernism in the twentieth century will a rhetoric, a theory of linguistic power and its application, offer a comparably comprehensive and sophisticated alternative to that in which Dickinson was schooled. Consideration of the origins of language permits us to see her as a master of rather than escapee from the history she bent to her extraordinary poetic purposes" (115).

Works Cited

The following abbreviations are used for reference to the writings of Emily Dickinson:

Fr   *The Poems of Emily Dickinson*. ed. R. W. Franklin. 3 vols.
      Cambridge, MA: Harvard UP, 1998. Citation by poem number.
L   *The Letters of Emily Dickinson*. ed. Thomas H. Johnson and
      Theodora Ward. 3 vols. Cambridge, MA: Harvard UP, 1958.
      Citation by letter number.

de Man, Paul. *Blindness and Insight: Essays in the Rhetoric of Contemporary Criticism*. New York: Oxford UP, 1971.

Diehl, Joanne Feit. *Women Poets and the American Sublime*. Bloomington: Indiana UP, 1990.

Felman, Shoshana, and Dori Laub. *Testimony: Crises of Witnessing In Literature, Psychoanalysis and History*. New York: Routledge, 1992.

Leyda, Jay. *The Years and Hours of Emily Dickinson*. North Haven: Archon Books, 1970.

Miller, Cristanne. *Emily Dickinson: A Poet's Grammar*. Cambridge, MA: Harvard UP, 1987.

Short, Bryan C. "Emily Dickinson and the Origins of Language." *The Emily Dickinson Journal* 9.2 (1999): 109-119.

Weisbuch, Robert. *Emily Dickinson's Poetry*. Chicago: U of Chicago Press, 1975.

The Irresistible Lure of Repetition and Dickinson's Poetics of Analogy

Suzanne Juhasz

Suzanne Juhasz provides an analysis of the "centrality of analogy" to Dickinson's poetics, which is evident in Dickinson's "habit of repeating, in the service of some kind of definition, the same idea or experience, but always analogously." In relating Dickinson's analogical structure to the psychodynamic process of the repetition compulsion described by Hans Loewald, Juhasz explains that unlike "passive repetition," which is a duplication or reproduction of events, "active repetition" is understood as "creation, using the same elements of the original, constantly destroying or breaking it down and reforming it, so that its new form is, in fact, an analogue."

Juhasz finds a telling illustration of the process of re-creative repetition in the poem "It was not Death, for I stood up." In using a series of analogies in the poem to describe an unnamed psychic state or experience—"It was not Death"; "It was not Night"; "It was not Frost . . . Nor Fire"—Dickinson is not "playing riddle games with her reader" but instead is "remembering an unidentified 'it' that requires the aid of analogic language to be remembered." Indeed, as Dickinson offers a "compulsively repetitive and full set of analogues" to describe her unnamed experience, "analogies analogize analogies, so that the experience becomes all that can be said about it." For Dickinson, there is a "satisfaction or pleasure that comes from repetition itself" in the creative process of making analogic language. "That the analogies compound one another rather than fit neatly, that the definitions never quite dovetail, is the point. The mastery, and pleasure, comes from the repetition, that is not only re-creation but transformation." Thus in Dickinson's poetics of analogy, "analogy is repetition with a difference. Telling it again and again but in the process recreating it is at the crux of her artistic endeavor."   J.B.B.

Recent attention to the materiality of Dickinson's writing has made even clearer the centrality of analogy to her poetics. If analogy in the semantic structure of language is the evocation and representation of partial similarity between like features of two things, so, too, are the formal structures of many of her poems. Stanzas exist in appositional or analogous relation to one another, as do lines and also phrases. Her habitual use of the dash is particularly conducive to this structure. When we observe the materiality of her writing, we see how some of her habits of composition, especially her use of variant words but also an inclination to use the same sets of words more than once in different contexts, expand upon the work of analogy.[1]

Here I am using the concept of analogy to refer particularly to her habit of repeating, in the service of some kind of definition, the same idea or experience, but always analogously. The variant words in a poem may be viewed as analogues for one another in much the same way as the stanzas of a poem are analogues, in much the same way that a phrase such as "It was as if" will introduce an analogue, and then another one, and then another one: each phrase or image referring back both to the phrase that precedes it and to the original impetus for the analogue. Sometimes the original referent is never named (for example, Fr14, "As if I asked a common alms –"), sometimes its identity is complicatedly ambiguous (for example, Fr576, "The difference between Despair / And Fear . . ."), and sometimes, as in a poem that apparently functions as a definition for some concept or idea—eternity, despair, death—the analogical structure itself denies any literalness to the definition that has been advanced and ends, or does not end, really, by giving the reader the sense that definition is not conclusive but ongoing (for example, Fr720, "As if the Sea should part," which stops with the line, "Eternity – is Those –"). You can surely add many more poems to the list. Robert Weisbuch has noted how often the boundary of a Dickinson poem is neither scene nor situation but the movement of analogy. "Dickinson gives us a pattern in several carpets and then makes the carpet vanish" (16).

This figurative hocus pocus is a sign of her poetic genius, but it is also indicative of her poetic purposes. It is the act of making the words, words that tend to work analogically, that seems finally to be the most important gesture and not the arriving at a definitive endpoint. In fact, the overall structure of her oeuvre, the defining, or analogizing, or staking out the circumference (which might be her own word for the procedure) of a specific set of experiences—love, death, spirituality, for example—over and over again, is further indication of the process to which I have been pointing. In this paper I want to advance some ideas about Dickinson's writing process by relating it to the psychodynamic process of repetition. The irresistible compulsion to repeat, in forms of repetition that are re-creative, even transformative, seems to me to be the underlying impulse for the forms of writing in which she indulged.

The compulsion to repeat is a phenomenon that sits at the basis of Freudian psychoanalytic theory, as Freud noticed how certain elements of a past conflict are consistently reproduced in present activity. The repressed seeks to return in the present, whether in the form of dreams, symptoms, or "acting-out." These forms of behavior can be characterized as irresistible, write Laplanche and Pontalis, having that "compulsive character which is the mark of all that emanates from the unconscious" (78, 79). The repetition compulsion is usually invoked to discuss the systematic structuring of pain and the methodological disavowal of pleasure. In "Anxiety and Instinctual Life" Freud, noting our instinctive efforts to "reveal an effort to restore an earlier state of things," explains that "the forgotten and repressed experiences of childhood are reproduced during the work of analysis in dreams and reactions . . . although their revival runs counter to the interest of the pleasure principle" (106).

Using a slightly different slant, the contemporary psychoanalyst Edgar Levenson connects repetition with neurosis, linking the painful scenarios that people tend to orchestrate again and again to a mechanism of protection:

Patients' infamous resistance to change, the repetition compulsion, may be due—not so much to the hegemony of fantasy, not to the limitations imposed by developmental deficit—but rather, to the need of the patient to recreate, over and over again, a psychologically "safe" milieu. "Safe" may sound like an odd formulation for the distressed lives most patients lead; but, as the psychoanalytic saw has it, whatever the patient does, it is a lot better than something else! A neurosis is a compromise solution. (241)

These descriptions of repetition, whether in their evocation of pain or of safety, don't seem to have very much to do with the adventurous and expansive nature of Dickinson's analogues. What is significant about them, however, as a place to begin, is that they point to the compulsion to repeat unconscious conflicts, wishes, and experiences that is due primarily to their having remained under repression. The repressed seeks to return, to find "expression," if you will, in everyday and ongoing life. In the way that Dickinson persistently uses poetry to evoke a frequently unnamed referent, an "it" that she tries to identify in her versions of "as if," we can see how language becomes her particular medium for manifesting unconscious memories, as Hans Loewald puts it in his essay, "Some Considerations on Repetition and Repetition Compulsion."

Repetition and remembering are aspects of one another, Loewald says, for remembering, a mental act, is a kind of repetition, and repetition in the form of action or behavior and affect is another kind of remembering (88). In poems such as "As if I asked a common alms –" or "It was not Death, for I stood up," Dickinson is remembering an unidentified "it" that requires the aid of analogic language to be remembered—not because she is playing riddle games with her reader but because the "it" is probably not consciously known to her. "Your thoughts don't have words every day," she writes in a poem to which I will return later in this paper.

Yet remembering/repetition in language, in poetry, occurs in a space that is neither that of thought nor of action and behavior. Here Loewald's concept of passive and active repetition becomes important. For

Loewald, there is a distinction to be made between passive repetition, or reproduction—events "suffered again even if 'arranged' by the individual that undergoes them,"[2] and active repetition, when they can be "taken over in the ego's organizing activity and made again into something new—a re-creation of something old as against a duplication of it." "In such re-creation," he continues, " the old is mastered, where mastery does not mean elimination of it but dissolution, and reconstruction out of the elements of destruction" (89-90).

Here is where and how analogy fits in and indeed, becomes crucial. Repetition here is understood not as duplication but creation, using the same elements of the original, constantly destroying or breaking it down and reforming it, so that its new form is, in fact, an analogue. Loewald goes on to point to the processes of psychoanalysis, and especially the working through of the transference, as the place where this re-creation most effectively transpires. But Dickinson's poetry is surely an example of another medium especially conducive to this same process.

For example, in a poem like "It was not Death, for I stood up," a long series of analogies works to describe a state of the mind, or an experience, that is circled by the process of circumference but never named. (The final word, "Despair," may be a significant hint about the experience, but since it itself occurs within an analogy—to "Chaos"—which is prefaced by a dash, the poem does not actually identify Despair as its subject.)

> It was not Death, for I stood up,
> And all the Dead, lie down –
> It was not Night, for all the Bells
> Put out their Tongues, for Noon.
>
> It was not Frost, for on my Flesh
> I felt Siroccos – crawl –
> Nor Fire – for just my marble feet
> Could keep a Chancel, cool –

And yet, it tasted, like them all,
The Figures I have seen
Set orderly, for Burial,
Reminded me, of mine –

As if my life were shaven,
And fitted to a frame,
And could not breathe without a key,
And 'twas like Midnight, some –

When everything that ticked – has stopped –
And space stares – all around –
Or Grisly frosts – first Autumn morns,
Repeal the Beating Ground –

But most like Chaos – Stopless – cool –
Without a Chance, or spar –
Or even a Report of Land –
To justify – Despair.

(Fr355)

I do not wish to perform a reading of this poem so much as to expli-
cate its analogical structure in order to demonstrate how re-creative
(poetic) repetition occurs. The poem begins, as I have been saying,
with a "missing" referent. It refers to an "it" that exists somewhere
else, outside, beyond the poem. We could understand that place as the
unconscious, the "it" as something that has been experienced but not
named, that Dickinson needs to remember/repeat. The poem begins
with an attempt at identification which is already not literal, for its
route is through the negative: it was not death; it was not night; it was
not frost; it was not fire. The terms death and frost already function
analogically—i.e., there must be something about these states that is

like the "it" for the poet to consider and then discard them in their greater dissimilarity. The explanation is further complicated by a use of metaphors that are consistently and deliberately contradictory. It wasn't frost (cold) because she was, to translate, warm; it wasn't fire (hot) because she was, to translate, cold. In the course of the negatives she circumnavigates a frightening, dreadful positive: standing on marble feet, hot winds crawling on her skin, mid-day bells mocking her.

And yet, as she concludes this section of the poem, a simile is demanded; for all the dissimilarity that she has described, there is indeed likeness. To explain this she switches the sensory register from bodily feelings to taste and then to sight. What she produces is a synechdochal and intensely metaphorical description of the "it," making it vitally, powerfully sensory, yet she concludes that her feeling is that of no-feeling, as if she were a corpse. Paradox is the ultimate configuration of the "it"—the experience that she must insistently tell.

But she is not finished; she must begin again. This time with analogy/ simile: as if. We can count three of them: "As if my life were shaven," "And 'twas like Midnight, some –," "But most – like Chaos –." Each is followed by an elaborated metaphor replete with personification: "And could not breathe without a key"; "And space stares – all around," for example. These metaphoric scenarios create image after image of a place or experience of no feeling horrific in its sensory intensity. The final such image—and analogy, and metaphor—resorts once again to negation in order to create a presence that is an absence: "Stopless;" "Without a Chance, or spar – / Or even a Report of Land –." Images are evoked only to be denied: no chance, no spar, no report. At the same time, through the very range of phenomena invoked, physical (spar), abstract (report), conceptual (chaos, chance), all aspects of experience are brought into play in the speaker's attempts to explain where, what she is.

The final line is the most dramatic—and the most confusing. "It" is most like chaos, which (what which? "Chaos," or "it"?—the dashes make it impossible to delineate: either, or both?) is stopless and cool; most like because there is no chance, spar, or report that, if they existed, would be able to "justify – Despair." Why would these signs, if present, justify despair? And what is present, then, if even despair cannot be justified? Despair is a condition of no hope; what is beyond that? Death? But "It was not Death . . . ."

We are left, at the last, with a compulsively repetitive and full set of analogues describing a condition and with nothing literal that can fix or name it. We do not know what it is, but we are amply provided with images for what it feels like. Exactly in the manner of Loewald's concept of repetition as re-creation, the poet compulsively repeats the evocation of her experience but never as duplication. Each time a new analogy, comprised of new metaphors, is invented to describe it, so that the result is a composite portrait made from the elements of the original, constantly broken down and reformed. Analogies analogize analogies, so that the experience becomes all that can be said about it.

The purpose of repetition as re-creation, says Loewald, is "mastery," meaning that the person comes to understand that her memories and acts are her own and in the process of doing so generates new organizations out of something old (94). "To acknowledge, recognize, and understand one's unconscious as one's own means to move from a position of passivity in relation to it to a position where active care of it becomes possible, where it becomes a task worthy of pursuit to make one's business those needs and wishes, fantasies, conflicts . . . and defenses that have been passively experienced and reproduced" (95-96). So far so good. There is certainly an aspect of this kind of mastery in a poem like "It was not death," because the frightening psychic state of a deadening lack of vitality, control, etc. (whatever, whenever that is or was) achieves a life of its own, another or different life, by way of the linguistic remembering/repeating that the poem accomplishes. The reality that is language intercedes on behalf of that other reality, recorded and suspended in the unconscious.

And yet there seems to be more to it, and that "more" has to do with the compulsive quality of these repetitions, the lure—irresistible, it appears—of repetition itself. For Dickinson this kind of repetition seems less a desire to re-experience the trauma or even to keep to familiar albeit painful experience as it is for the satisfaction or pleasure that comes from repetition itself, which for her is the creation in language of experience that is not and never can be the experience in everyday life, be it unconscious or conscious. Hence the excessive nature of her signifiers, often without a signified in sight. Analogy piled upon analogy, words inadequate in the singular, so often needing to be multiplied into variants. That the analogies compound one another rather than fit neatly, that the definitions never quite dovetail, is the point. The mastery, and pleasure, comes from the repetition, that is not only re-creation but transformation.

Witness two poems that Dickinson wrote about the language-making process, stanzas that are not as contradictory as they may at first seem to be.

> Your thoughts dont have words every day
> They come a single time
> Like signal esoteric sips
> Of the communion Wine
> Which while you taste so native seems
> So easy so to be
> You cannot comprehend it's price –
> Not it's infrequency
>
> (Fr1476)

Her reference to the gap between thought and word seems to place thought in an intermediate realm between event and language and also to imply that thoughts can be signals from both the unconscious and the conscious mind. The words that sometimes come can be likened to sips of the communion (or "sacramental," in a variant) wine, a reference that points to their sacred and even transformational power, as well as to their ability to substantiate, or give body to, the wordless messages inside us, even as the wine and wafer of communion do for

Jesus Christ. (This poem seems in many ways a variant, or analogue, of Fr1775, "A word made Flesh is seldom.") But there is much more here of interest about the process of word making. The words that are like sips are "signal" and "esoteric": "signal" coming very close to signifier in its connotations, "esoteric" giving them a private or code-like quality. Not literal, perhaps—literal being not the point.

But when language transpires, the experience of it is "native," "adjacent," "easy," "kindred," "fully," "ample," "intimate," "free," "affable," "affluent," "gracious" (a veritable excess of variants!), the very opposite in many ways of the esotericism, price (or "worth"), and infrequency (or "stint," or "divinity") of the act, or gift, of language. The tasting of the word/wine seems to be the reading experience, an experience of singleness, infrequency, esotericism, price, and worth the writing. This poems tells us that procuring the special word for that sea of wordless signifieds in which we swim is a difficult process (infrequent, esoteric, demanding a price, etc.) which however almost magically releases a bounty of excess so pleasurable that it is quite another experience altogether from either the wordless thoughts or the writing act that works to release signified into signifier.

Yet another poem (or variant) on this subject is Fr1689, which initially seems to take the opposite tack but concludes by again reinforcing our sense of the importance of the process, the act of making analogic language:

> To tell the Beauty would decrease
> To state the spell demean
> There is a syllableless Sea
> Of which it is the sign
> My will endeavors for it's word
> And fails, but entertains
> A Rapture as of Legacies –
> Of introspective mines –
> (Fr1689)

"Decrease," "demean"—this poem begins by suggesting that the words that do come, rather than being intimate or bounteous or affable, are actually reductive in relation to the originary, "syllableless" event (that Beauty, that Spell). Indeed, Dickinson is very clear here about the necessary gap between signifier and signified. And yet in the second half of the poem she seems to valorize the very process of search that must always end in seeming failure. It produces a "Rapture," she calls it, that is of "Legacies," of "introspective mines." These analogies, each one of these words—"legacy," "introspective," "mine"—evoke a sense of the unconscious, of the repressed, and of its potential for return. The "Rapture" to which she refers can be likened to the irresistible lure and pleasure of the repetition itself.

It is Loewald who uses the phrase "transformative repetition." At this point in his essay he is speaking about society as institution, of the importance of using the past not as a rule to follow but as a prototype. He affirms the prototypical importance of the past but sees how such a prototype "exists to be creatively transformed in the act of repetition, not to be imitated or reproduced . . . nor to be eliminated" (98). I think his words can apply to people, as well—for example, to Dickinson, and to her poetics of analogy. From her very love of language and her submission to its lure comes her creation of a world of linguistic experience that is neither imitation nor elimination of the well of psychic experience inside her, the source of her need and her art. Analogy is repetition with a difference. Telling it again and again but in the process recreating it is at the crux of her artistic endeavor. Of course that process is an aspect of her personal self, produced from needs and desires that stimulate her urge to taste those signal esoteric sips, to experience the irresistible "Rapture" that is language.

From *The Emily Dickinson Journal* 9, no. 2 (2000): 23-31. Copyright © 2000 by The Johns Hopkins University Press. Reprinted with permission of The Johns Hopkins University Press.

Notes

1. See my essay, "Materiality and the Poet," in *The Emily Dickinson Handbook*.
2. See Freud, p. 21.

Works Cited

Unless otherwise indicated the following abbreviations are used for reference to the writings of Emily Dickinson:

Fr   *The Poems of Emily Dickinson*. Ed. R. W. Franklin. 3 vols. Cambridge, MA: Harvard UP, 1998. Citation by poem number.

J   *The Poems of Emily Dickinson*. Ed. Thomas H. Johnson. 3 vols. Cambridge, MA: Harvard UP, 1955. Citation by poem number.

L   *The Letters of Emily Dickinson*. Ed. Thomas H. Johnson and Theodora Ward. 3 vols. Cambridge, MA: Harvard UP, 1958. Citation by letter number.

Freud, Sigmund. "Anxiety and Instinctual Life." *New Introductory Lectures on Psychoanalysis*. Trans. and ed. James Strachey. New York: W.W. Norton, 1963, 81-11.

Juhasz, Suzanne. "Materiality and the Poet." *The Emily Dickinson Handbook*. Ed. Gudrun Grabher, Roland Hagenbüchle, and Cristanne Miller. Amherst: U Mass P, 1998, 427-440.

Laplanche, J., and J. B. Pontalis. *The Language of Psycho-Analysis*. New York: W.W. Norton, 1973.

Levenson, Edgar. "Character, Personality, and Change." *The Purloined Self: Interpersonal Perspectives in Psychoanalysis*. New York: William Alanson White Institute, 1991, 175-184.

Loewald, Hans. "Some Considerations on Repetition and Repetition Compulsion." *Papers on Psychoanalysis*. New Haven: Yale UP, 1980, 87-102.

Weisbuch, Robert. *Emily Dickinson's Poetry*. Chicago: U of Chicago P, 1975.

Emily Dickinson:
Reclusion Against Itself_____

Shira Wolosky

Calling Emily Dickinson's famous withdrawal from the world "the riveting central counterevent of her life," Shira Wolosky argues that Dickinson's representation of reclusion in her work should be viewed "in terms of traditions of withdrawal from the world and of her resistance to them." Dickinson's reclusion grows out of her disapproval of a world that she finds "unpredictable, violent, and terrifying." But if, "in continuity with the Platonist and Christian traditions of reclusion," Dickinson finds the world deeply flawed, she does not seclude herself "in hope of a redemption experienced as an inner state transcending the external world"; instead, "her reclusion is closer to despair— or better, to defiance of the world that makes her retreat necessary. There is defiant defense: to protect herself as much as possible from the grave disorder that surrounds her. And there is defiant attack: to protest, to pummel, to punish nature and nature's God for the seductive yet ultimately undesirable reality for which he is responsible."

For Dickinson, the "image of reclusion," as Wolosky observes, is often "a scene of tremendous conflict," and her "verses zigzag between efforts to find her place within traditions of reclusion and her dogged refusal to do so." For example, while Dickinson's poem "Renunciation – is a piercing Virtue –" seems to offer "almost a creedal declaration and definition of reclusion," it also, Wolosky remarks, "proves to be utterly conflicted, retractive, and torn about renunciation"; in a similar way, the poem that begins "A Prison gets to be a friend –" ends with profound misgivings by showing that interiority is imprisoning, not liberating. In her "most exuberant" reclusion poem—"I dwell in Possibility –"—Dickinson exchanges religious reclusion for aesthetic reclusion and finds in limitation "various kinds of possibility." Yet her experience largely remains one of "discontinuity, rupture, antithesis, and counterclaim between experiential and metaphysical realms." Indeed, in Dickinson's works, "the conflicts that divide her—female vs. male, this world vs. the next, interiority vs. exteriority, experience vs. redemption—find neither resolution nor the promise of it in her reclusion, but only persistent reenactment." J.B.B.

> Renunciation – is the Choosing
> Against Itself –
>
> (J 745)

Emily Dickinson's reclusion, the riveting central counterevent of her life, is so obtrusive as to block even itself from view. Her reclusion verges on occlusion, both with regard to its causes in her life and, more problematically, to its meaning in Dickinson's work. Early accounts assume some romantic crash, for which there has however been essentially no evidence. Nor would mere brokenheartedness, whether hetero- or homosexual, go very far in accounting for the literature Dickinson wrote. Her reclusion, as represented in her work, should instead be seen in terms of traditions of withdrawal from the world and of her resistance to them. In many ways, her reclusion represents a quite original stance, in critical relation to (rather than containment within) the meanings of reclusion that come before her. Dickinson's reclusion marks a shift, subtle and yet extreme, in the history of reclusion and its significance—a shift extending past her own retreat retrospectively to the tradition itself. The particularities of her reclusion suggest how any act or event and its terms may mean differently within different historical distributions.

Dickinson's poetry provides a record of her responses to a world she found at times alluring but of which she ultimately disapproved as deeply flawed and indeed alarming. It is not, however, disapproval of reality that makes Dickinson's reclusion thoroughly original. Disapproval had been, after all, the motive for withdrawal from the world since the earliest eremitic and monastic regimens. But hers is not a reclusion attesting to interiority as a superior resource of meaning. Rather, Dickinson in reclusion protests the lack of design in the external world of phenomena and events, where she holds that intelligibility should (but does not) reside.

Born in 1830 in Amherst, Massachusetts, Dickinson seems to have passed an ordinary girlhood in a prominent town family. At around the age of twenty-eight in the year 1858, however, she began to display distinctive behavior: declining to go out; dressing in white; speaking to visitors from behind screens and stairwells or from other rooms; refusing to address the envelopes of her correspondence, from letters and myriad condolence notes to messages for her sister-in-law next door. And of course Dickinson began to write intensively, and also to not publish, poems which she only circulated in private letters or sewed into small fascicle booklets (found by her sister Lavinia on Dickinson's death in 1886). That this retreat coincided with hostilities leading to the American Civil War—as did her great outburst of poetic production—I have discussed elsewhere.[1] The war's relevance here is not only, or is perhaps (in a special sense) precisely, historical. Dickinson's reclusion was born in reaction against a world manifesting itself as unpredictable, violent, and terrifying. She had suspected that the world was defective for some time. Her early letters track her irreconcilable anguish over schoolfriends' deaths. But the war, one should imagine, seemed a final and overwhelming evidence that the world was indeed a badly conducted place.

In the history of thought, this conclusion was hardly news. St. Augustine, for example, surveying the fall of Rome, had long since provided ample terms for suspecting the City of Man. The human world displayed itself as at best a scene of trial, at worst a punishment that, if properly regarded, could act also as purgation. Plato (in his worst moods) and Neoplatonists, notably Plotinus, understood the cosmos itself as an ascending ladder of introspection; and the Desert Fathers of Christendom followed their lead. Augustine, along roughly the same path, turned inward and upward (inward *as* upward) toward the City of

God. As he wrote of God in the *Confessions*: "You were more inward than the most inward place of my heart and loftier than the highest above me."[2] The metaphysical realm was no longer to be reached by the philosophical route, since Augustine believed in redemption through unearned grace.[3] But Augustine still required detachment from the world of flesh in favor of an inward realm metaphorically "above" it. Conducted with greater or lesser distaste, greater or lesser suspicion, greater or lesser regret, detachment pledges itself to a spirituality facing inward and heavenward. The motives of detachment may be more or less orthodox (unification and deification being major portals into heresy for, among others, Meister Eckhart and Jacob Boehme); but the goal is always a better world than that of matter, time, multiplicity, and change.

This is a tradition Dickinson breaks with and breaks open. Interior spiritual ascents and exits are not the directions, claims, or maps of Dickinson's seclusion (despite efforts to read her in such terms and despite specific poems that lend themselves to such readings). Hers is not withdrawal from the world to an interiority detached from it as an antidote, substitute, or consolation. In continuity with the Platonist and Christian traditions of reclusion, Dickinson too sees the phenomenal world as wanting. Yet her reaction is not the traditional one. She does not accept, or seek, an interior realm as resolution or sign or path or promise of redemption. Indeed she is critical of the dualist representation of the world as a temporal materiality separated, in an unbridgeable and shrill manner, from unchanging, incorporeal essence, spirit, and truth. Her retreat does not fulfill but, rather, condemns this division; she condemns also the consequent abandonment of the temporal world for any dimension removed from it, facing away from time toward an escapist eternity. Certainly she sees the flaws of the world, which appears to her as a scene with promise, though frighteningly ill managed. She is not moved, however, to substitute for the experience of this defective world an experience renouncing external events and terms. Instead she is filled with rage at having to retreat from a world so compromised. Her stance is one of frustration and blame, directed not least at a divine power who could have established creation, she is sure, in a more just, more harmonious, less violent and lethal manner. She has no desire to split the world apart into a quicksand phenomenal realm and a stable mountain of eternity. Rather she wishes an integrated experience in the reality she knows: an experience of both fact and meaning, body and spirit, phenomena and (phenomena *as*) intelligibility.

Nor does her retreat signify renunciation of a lesser realm for a higher aesthetic one. Art is not for Dickinson separate and self-constituting, redemptive within its own terms. Writing does not, on the whole, provide for her a secure enclosure, nor represent one. Her poems become the setting for Dickinson's anguished and angry recognition that human reality is chaotic and that, as Nietzsche was shortly to proclaim, no intelligible principle can be detected in it. Yet the failure of intelligibility does not lead her, as it does him, to dismiss its possibility and seek some immanent force, such as the will to power, to replace it. Nor is her position like his straight condemnation of the category of eternity itself. Dickinson's central problem is not the notion of immortality and divine values as such, but rather their location. What infuriates, terrifies, and frustrates her is the lack of stability and security, justice, and redemptive love within the world she knows. Dickinson recluses herself not in hope of a redemption experienced as an inner state transcending the external world. Her reclusion is closer to despair—or better, to defiance of the world that makes her retreat necessary. There is defiant defense: to protect herself as much as possible from the grave disorder that surrounds her. And there is defiant attack: to protest, to pummel, to punish nature and nature's God for the seductive yet ultimately undesirable reality for which he is responsible. God remains a central figure in Dickinson's verse, as both protagonist and antagonist, infuriatingly unwilling or unable fully to take his proper role. Dickinson addresses God—repeatedly—in longing and yearning that he prove to be who and what is always said of him. She addresses him in disappointment and distress that his praises seem mere rumor, contradicted by the chaos that does, yes, attest a cause. Hers is an argument from design where, however, the design defaults, leaving her furious at the designer. In terms of the tradition, Dickinson does not experience the dark night of the soul, doubting its own worthiness, as St. John of the Cross described it. Nor does she experience T. S. Eliot's dark night, doubting the reality of God until vision is renewed and healing granted. Dickinson does not doubt God's existence. She instead questions his ways, which seem to her unjustifiable. She examines the wedded plight between theodicy and mysticism, where retreat into spirit is offered as a remedy to the world's suffering, and rejects it. She will not accept any solution to the world's disorder that is removed from the world. That strategy seems to her either a category mistake—an answer that fails to address the problem—or frank betrayal of the care, love, and design that God supposedly represents.

This is not to say that Dickinson has no qualms. Her verses zigzag between efforts to find her place within traditions of reclusion and her dogged refusal to do so. She refuses because consolation would gainsay her own experience of the world and her understanding of what would be required to make it make sense. Splitting off inner from outer, spiritual meaning from tangible history, is to her ultimately a manifestation of the problem of disorder and not its solution. But there are moments in the poems when Dickinson attempts this traditional solution, casting her own reclusion in its pattern. This tradition she knew first hand through, at the very least, Thomas à Kempis's *Imitation of Christ*, her 1857 copy of which is in Harvard's Houghton Library. Richard Sewall concludes that Dickinson found in it a positive model for "renouncing the world, bearing the burden, shouldering the Cross— that is, the simple, stern life of the dedicated religious"; but Dickinson's relation to the *Imitation* is complex and critical.[4] Poems such as the one Sewall cites—"To put this World down, like a Bundle . . . Trodden with straight renunciation" (J 527)—may reflect a mood, or explore one, or register a response to or commentary on the *Imitation* itself.[5] What Thomas à Kempis offers is a severe and uncompromising opposition between this world and the next, with reclusion a way of living in this world as if already dead to it.[6] As he writes in his first chapter: "This is supreme wisdom—to despise the world, and draw daily nearer the kingdom of heaven." Or again: those "who strove to follow in the footsteps of Christ . . . hated their lives in this world, that they might keep them to life eternal." The Spirit "speaks within them," teaching them "to despise earthly things and to love heavenly; to forsake this world, and to long for heaven." Yet again: "Learn now to die to the world, that you may begin to live with Christ. Learn now to despise all earthly things, that you may go freely to Christ."[7] Just so, Dickinson writes:

> Through the strait pass of suffering
> The Martyrs – even – trod
> Their feet – upon Temptation –
> Their faces – upon God –
>
> (J 792)

The martyrs' feet stand in the world (the world figured as temptation), but the face turns away from and in opposition against the world, to God.

For Dickinson does grasp Thomas's vision of the world as "swiftly passing away," where "all things are transitory, all things are passing, and yourself with them." Hence Thomas urges "that you do not cling to them, lest you become entangled and perish with them."[8] Indeed, the alternatives to religion can seem to her as unsatisfactory as they do to Thomas—and for her also the world without God is fearful. This terror is reflected in her reclusion. And yet neither can she abandon her sense that heaven too is awry, and she is led repeatedly on this account to disputation, dismay, and often disguised assault. Even when she writes poems as if she retreats into private devotion, her attempts at traditional piety mostly conceal pitfalls:

The Soul should always stand ajar
That if the Heaven inquire
He will not be obliged to wait
Or shy of troubling Her

Depart, before the Host have slid
The Bolt unto the Door –
To search for the accomplished Guest
Her Visitor, no more –

(J 1055)

"Desire to be familiar only with God and his angels," Thomas à Kempis writes, "and do not seek the acquaintance of men"—"the further the soul withdraws from all the tumult of the world, the nearer she draws to her Maker. For God with His holy angels will draw near to him who withdraws himself from his friends and acquaintances."[9] This poem opens in apparent agreement, as if embracing the inner sanctum. Reclused at home, the Soul stands ever ready for divine visitation. As so often in Dickinson, however, the grammar of declaration proves delusive. This poem is written under the sign of the conditional: "That if the Heaven inquire" (does "That" point to and underscore "if")? Moreover, although the Soul may be dedicated in her waiting, the compliment is not returned by the "accomplished Guest." Even if he were to come calling, this Guest would not wait: "Before the Host have slid / The Bolt," the divine Visitor is gone.

There is as well a shift in person here that has for Dickinson large resonance. The "Soul" is gendered female; but her role as "Host" is gendered male. Indeed, the line "He will not be obliged to wait" is itself ambiguous as to whether it is the Soul or Heaven who is left waiting. Another reclusion poem intensifies this gender ambiguity:

The Soul that hath a Guest
Doth seldom go abroad –
Diviner Crowd at Home –
Obliterate the need –

And Courtesy forbid
A Host's departure when
Upon Himself be visiting
The Emperor of Men –

(J 674)

The Soul awaits at home, as anyone hosting a Guest would do. "Diviner Crowd" is ambiguous. It could describe a wonderful group of visitors, or one properly divine, as is suggested in the last line ("The Emperor of Men"). Yet the transition from stanza to stanza, although taking the form of analogical argument, is hypothetical and conditional. The first stanza spells out the etiquette of hosting, not the actuality; while the second stanza is again under the sign of conditionality, in the trickier form of "when," which however is here equivalent to *if*. Finally, the Soul is clearly marked as male in gender: as Host "Himself" (not "Herself"). Only a himself, not a herself, can be visited by God.

Dickinson's work offers a rich field of investigation into the implications of gender in projecting relationships with God. "The Emperor of Men" is obviously male. What of the Soul waiting to receive him? Dickinson repeatedly explores the ways in which relationship with God varies with gender. The approach to the divine that reclusion hopes to enact works one way, Dickinson suggests, when both God and worshipper are male; another way, when the worshipper is female. The former allows a kind of identification that is not possible for the latter. Not only grammatical identity but social and of course sexual roles alter as images for (and indeed paths of relation to) God. While metaphysical terms define for her any ultimate account or justification of social and historical life, gender remains a central category of her metaphysical imagination and complaints. The poem "What Soft – Cherubic Creatures – / These Gentlewomen are –" (J 401) registers disdain for the emergent domestic lady whose own reclusion Dickinson's at once echoes and exposes. In "Title Divine – is mine," Dickinson moves immediately from claiming the Title Divine as her own (with no doubt an implication that she has titled her untitled poem divinely) to making this qualification: "The Wife – without the Sign!" (J 1072). To be, as she goes on to say, "Empress of Calvary!"—removed from the world, in other words—is still to be associated with divinity, though at one remove. "Title Divine" suggests direct claim to identity; but "wife" is a derived and mediated status. Dickinson's work includes a series of "wife" poems (often with the word in quotation marks) in which the meanings of the term are contested not only in social terms (and of course Dickinson never was a wife) but in religious ones. The social terms are continuous with—both reflecting and constructing—the religious history of wifehood as a particular image of devotion to God.

Dickinson's own consciousness of this tradition is clearly attested in "Only a Shrine":

>Only a Shrine, but Mine –
>I made the Taper shine –
>Madonna dim, to whom all Feet may come,
>Regard a Nun –
>
>Thou knowest every Woe –
>Needless to tell thee – so –
>But can'st thou do
>The Grace next to it – heal?
>That looks a harder skill to us –
>Still – just as easy, if it by thy Will
>To thee – Grant me –
>Thou knowest, though, so Why tell thee?
>   (J 918)

Yvor Winters famously remarked that Dickinson's plight would have been resolved if she could only have been born Catholic.[10] The appeal to Catholic terms, however, resolves nothing in this text. Dickinson only acknowledges the obvious: that a woman recluse dressed in white inevitably brings to mind the figure of the Nun. But the obvious in Dickinson tends to be obscuring. She imaginarily lights her taper to the Madonna, appealing to Mary as mediating figure and channel of grace. Yet here, as in the Host poem (J 674), where God does not visit, the Madonna does not answer. Genuine healing looks "a harder skill" than knowing woe and, even if—Dickinson's ubiquitous conditional—the Madonna should grant healing (assuming she exists), the poem ends not in grant or even in appeal, but in interruption and self-silencing.[11]

Most Dickinsonian approaches are to God as clearly male, though the poems vary in their human gendering. The erotic plays its full part in her poetry, as it does in the tradition; and reclusion can be figured, as traditionally it was for women, as marriage. For Dickinson, however, marriage is a contestable state (although poems such as "Mine by the Right of the White Election" [J 528] fulfill the traditional schema). As a trope for reclusion, marriage no longer signals devotion and contact with the divine as against the world, but now a sequestering from world *and God*, both of which have become severely compromised. There can still be an erotics of interplay, but less as flirtation than retaliation:

> We shun it ere it comes,
> Afraid of Joy,
> Then sue it to delay
> And lest it fly,
> Beguile it more and more –
> May not this be
> Old Suitor Heaven,
> Like our dismay at thee?
>
> (J 1580)

In this poem of ambivalence, Dickinson discloses her basic structure of evasion.[12] She desires yet fears desire, and especially its disappointment. Courtship is proposed as one image for this evasive desiring—that is, courtship never consummated. Yet the pivotal figure emerges in the end as religious. It is God who is model courtier, and it is his opaque unavailability that grounds the disappointment as well as her own reciprocal behavior. For he, she suspects, is himself a recluse. Her reclusion thus becomes an image and enactment not of access to the divine but its impasse. God is not forthcoming to her, nor she to him. Withdrawal becomes withholding—a very strange rendering of divine reflection: reflected not as love but as love's betrayal or failure.

One of Dickinson's complaints, then, is that the promise of spirituality is not fulfilled. Reclusion is a defensive measure. "The Missing All – prevented Me / From missing minor Things" (J 985)—the verse is succinct but also aggressive, a site from which to launch her indignation at divine failure. Not only has redemption failed to take place but its very structure and nature are failures: this is the sense of her earliest letters, where she examines her own resistance to conversion during the height of the Second Great Awakening. She feels that stark opposition between the human and divine worlds presents a harsh and unjust choice. "I have perfect confidence in God and his promises," she writes in one early letter: "and yet I know not why, I feel that the world holds a predominant place in my affections" (L 13). Later, she writes: "I wonder often how the love of Christ is done—when that below holds so" (L 262). Later still, she is still bolder: "Is God love's Adversary?" (L 792). Thomas à Kempis might warn to "keep yourself free from all worldly entanglement . . . the soul that loves God regards as worthless all things other than God."[13] But Dickinson can counter:

> The worthlessness of Earthly things
> The Ditty is that Nature Sings –
> And then – enforces their delight
> Till Synods are inordinate –
>
> (J 1373)

The concluding clever pun against ordination turns this warning of worthlessness into a contrary endorsement of nature's delights. Similarly art, in the form of music, is "Earth's corroboration," summoning us "to something upper wooing us / But not to our Creator" (J 1480).

As to those aspects of the world—of "Earthly things"—that she did find unacceptable, the metaphysical construction of transcendence seems to her to fail to address them. Her work affords many poems of metaphysical critique. In one of these, she writes:

> Their Height in Heaven comforts not –
> Their Glory – nought to me –
> 'Twas best imperfect – as it was –
> I'm finite – I can't see
>
> (J 696)

From her finite position, she cannot "see" the "Glory" of heavenly reward, which therefore "comforts not." For her, the "imperfect" is best, the world she inhabits—or would be best, if it only were not so subject to change, time, and extinction. The only eternal power of which she has direct evidence is that of death itself. "Thou only camest to mankind / To rend it with Good night –" (J 1552). This is a God who gives only to "take away The Loved" (J 882). Her prayers, then, take strange turns:

Some Wretched creature, savior take
Who would exult to die
And leave for thy sweet mercy's sake
Another Hour to me
                                (J 1111)

Heaven emerges not as salvation, but as a competitor, draining meaning from our world and failing to provide any satisfactory other:

No Other can reduce
Our mortal Consequence
Like the Remembering it be nought
A Period from hence
But Contemplation for
Contemporaneous Nought
Our Single Competition
Jehovah's Estimate.
                                (J 982)

The perspective of the other world reduces this world to nought. Far from elevating our experience and endowing it with value, the idea of transcendence serves instead (as Nietzsche too would insist) to empty it. Urged by Christian tradition to assess her own "Contemporaneous" experience as nought, Dickinson comes instead to the view that "Jehovah's Estimate" of this world is in competition against her own. What God offers is irrelevant and ultimately reductive, not redemptive, of earthly life:

When we have ceased to care
The Gift is given
For which we gave the Earth
And mortgaged Heaven
But so declined in worth
'Tis ignominy now
To look upon –

(J 1706)

This world, as a price to pay (Dickinson's uses of economic imagery are acerbic) for heaven, is a swindle. And having to give up the earth as mortgage to heaven finally reduces the value of heaven itself. Yet for Dickinson, this world, alone, is not enough. Without eternity, "not any Face cohere – Unless concealed in thee" (J 1499). Death without recourse renders all around us "The spectre of solidities / Whose substances are sand" (J 1107). "Without this – there is nought," she writes; and although in this poem it is never clear whether her "this" refers to the present world or the one beyond, the poem argues that neither can be complete without the other: "I could not care to – gain / A lesser than the Whole." And yet, the two domains remain mutually exclusive. In the end, she can only wish "a way might be / My Heart to subdivide" (J 655).[14]

It is this image of division that, perhaps more than any other, governs Dickinson's figures of reclusion:

Renunciation – is a piercing Virtue –
The letting go
A Presence for an Expectation –
Not now –
The putting out of Eyes –
Just Sunrise –
Lest Day –
Day's Great Progenitor –
Outvie

Renunciation – is the Choosing
Against itself –
Itself to justify
Unto itself –
When larger function –
Make that appear –
Smaller – that Covered Vision – Here –

(J 745)

The most remarkable thing about this poem is the way it seems almost a creedal declaration and definition of reclusion yet proves to be utterly conflicted, retractive, and torn about renunciation—about what renunciation of the world does and does not obtain. Especially confusing are the terms of measure. The first stanza follows tradition in proposing blindness to the external world as the price paid for spiritual vision. As Thomas à Kempis writes, "Strive to withdraw your heart from the love of visible things, and direct your affections to things invisible." Invisibility in turn is a sign of interiority: the saints "cling to God in their innermost hearts." "The Kingdom of God is within you," therefore "forsake this sorry world. . . . learn to turn from worldly things and give yourself to spiritual things, and you will see the Kingdom of God come within you." For "blessed are the eyes that are closed to outward things but are open to inward things."[15] So Dickinson too enjoins "The letting go" of immediate, presumably concrete "Presence," in "Expectation" of an invisible but superior world (and as proleptic participation in it). "The putting out of Eyes" will block out the visible "Day" of the external world, lest it "outvie" the interior vision of "Day's Great Progenitor."

To say this act of renunciation and reclusion is painful, a "Choosing against itself" requiring sacrifice and the severing of attachments, is not an argument against renunciation but a defining element of it. Reclusion (in Thomas à Kempis's words) is to "count all earthly things as dung" and to "renounce" one's "own will for the will of God."[16]

Less clear, as Dickinson's poem proceeds, is what in the end is to be gained by renunciation. "Larger" and "Smaller" are the key terms here, figured as a paradoxical exchange between what seems greater—the world—but is really smaller than the spiritual life, which demands that one give up the world. Yet in the second stanza, "greater" and "lesser" do not quite line up with the terms proposed in the first one, a confusion further confounded by unclear references for the deictic "that." Is "larger function" the exterior world of "Day," whose lure is registered in the very threat to "outvie" its "Great Progenitor?"—is the grammatical order of the second stanza parallel in sequence to that of the first? Or is it "Day's Great Progenitor" that is "larger"?—in which case, the exterior world might only "appear" smaller, as an illusion or result of mismeasuring. Or again, does the "Covered Vision" refer to "Expectation" (that is, to what is yet to come)? But how then can the "Covered Vision" be "Here" and thus recall the "Presence" of this world? Above all, if everything is clear in the poem's terms of exchange, why is it so hard to tell which is which? Renunciation is a choosing against itself in the traditional sense of the human will's self-denial in subjection to God's. But it is also a choosing against renunciation itself, whose justifications the poem at once represents and overturns.

This sort of obfuscation generally structures Dickinson's reclusion poems. "A Prison gets to be a friend," she declares elsewhere. Yet if the speaker comes to feel "a Kinsmanship" between the prison walls' "Ponderous face / And Ours," she does so at best as a concession:

> We learn to know the Planks
> That answer to Our feet –
> So miserable a sound – at first –
> Nor ever now – so sweet –

What the poem does trace is ever stricter and narrowing circles:

As plashing in the Pools –
When Memory was a Boy –
But a Demurer Circuit –
A Geometric Joy –

The Posture of the Key
That interrupt the Day
To Our Endeavor – Not so real
The Cheek of Liberty –

As this Phantasm Steel –
Whose features – Day and Night –
Are present to us – as Our Own –
And as escapeless – quite –

The narrow Round – the Stint –
The slow exchange of Hope –
For something passiver – Content
Too steep for looking up –

The Liberty we knew
Avoided – like a Dream –
Too wide for any Night but Heaven –
If That – indeed – redeem –

(J 652)

Richard Lovelace, in "To Althea from Prison," claims "Stone walls do not a prison make," but here they do, in an elaborate reflective figure in which prison becomes a mirror of the self. "Phantasm Steel" reflects "features . . . as Our Own." And this reflection is "escapeless." Interiority is not free from its circumstances, but severely circumscribed by them. And the retreat into utter selfhood becomes self-reflection as trap. Dickinson's circle imagery rejects Emerson's, with his vision of ever expanding selfhood, each new version outstripping and indeed abandoning the one before. Here is contraction, not expansion. The self itself proves a narrow circle indeed. On the other hand (or is it the same one?), the poem goes against the circle imagery of tradition, where, from Plotinus through Dionysius, from Augustine through Thomas à Kempis, the journey upward is one of interior contraction. Yet here interiority remains, or rather increasingly becomes, a "Demurer circuit," more constrictive from an earlier freedom imaged "As plashing in the Pools – / When Memory was a Boy." Is boyhood an image meant to oppose girlhood? Is Dickinson's prison her female body? In any case, its space contracts rather than expands through time, a "narrow Round." Interiority is not larger, but smaller.

The poem's ending with "Liberty" points Dickinson's reclusion poems in yet another direction. One way the question of reclusion recurs through philosophical history is as a debate between the active and the contemplative life. Beginning in Plato's cave with the reluctance to return from sunlight to shadows—and formulated explicitly in Aristotle's *Nicomachean Ethics*, book 10—philosophical answers to the question of what constitutes the good life are sharply divided. Many favor exclusive theoretical contemplation (as fulfilling the most distinctive and hence highest human faculty, reason); others prefer more inclusive notions of the person, and more inclusive notions of happiness, that authorize participation in public life.[17] Dickinson seems extreme in her choice of the contemplative model. But interiority becomes for her a prison, not a liberation. The promised conversion of interiority to expansion is not accomplished. This poem, "A Prison gets to be a friend," thus concludes with profound misgiving. Rather than offering blissful contemplation of an inner world, the poem seems to bear witness to a problematic outer one. Written in 1862, the poem concludes with "Liberty"—an absolutely pivotal term around which the Civil War revolved, defined in contrasting ways in South and North: liberty to own slaves, as against their claim to freedom.[18] The still per-

sonified "Cheek of Liberty" seems "Not so real" as the prison's reflective "Phantasm Steel." In the last stanza, liberty itself seems threatening—a motive for retreat to prison in the first place. For, if unbounded,
liberty is "Too wide for any Night but Heaven." Extent becomes overwhelming, formless, without direction, and hence needing rescue by
heaven. Yet heaven in turn is figured ominously as "Night." In its
opposition to the world, heaven is moreover experienced as impris-
onment. Withdrawn, the poet remains uncertain of future redemption, and unredeemed in the present. "Content," or contentment, is
indistinguishable from resignation or despair. The appeal to heaven is
so costly—its cost, the "slow exchange of Hope / For something
passiver"—that it consumes the promise of redemption it is meant to
invoke.

Dickinson's perhaps most exuberant reclusion poem is:

I dwell in Possibility –
A fairer House than Prose –
More numerous of Windows –
Superior – for Doors –

Of Chambers as the Cedars –
Impregnable of Eye –
And for an Everlasting Roof
The Gambrels of the Sky –

Of Visitors – the fairest –
For Occupation – This –
The spreading wide my narrow Hands
To gather Paradise –

(J 657)

Dickinson has reshuffled her terms. Religious reclusion seems pretty thoroughly exchanged for an aesthetic one.[19] "Possibility" becomes, in contrast to "Prose," a figure for poetry. And in contrast to "Expectation" in the "Renunciation" poem, here the promise and expansion of "Possibility"—though possibility by definition is not immediately possessed—penetrate immediate experience as present delight: "Of Visitors – the fairest," as she goes on to say. Yet the aesthetic experience, in displacing the religious one, incorporates its terms. The second stanza alludes to "Cedars," the pillars of the Jerusalem Temple, and claims an "Everlasting Roof," suggesting not only a church but the afterworld itself. The third stanza's "Visitors" similarly appear to displace or incorporate divine visitation, as also with "The Soul that stands Ajar." This time, the waiting was not vain. As to "Occupation," might the word suggest the Protestant notion of calling? As a calling from God, worldly work acquires religious meaning, thus healing the breach between contemplative, reclusive interiority and active pursuits in the external world. As another poem attests, "The Province of the Saved / Should be the Art – To save" (J 539). The "Art – To save" is an activity in the external world through which it is possible for "narrow Hands / To gather Paradise."

It is interesting nonetheless to note that, in "I dwell in Possibility," the imagery affirms or at least adopts reclusion. The poet is still situated in a "House," where she remains. This house figuration structures the exterior world. Even the "Sky" is represented as "Gambrels," a feature of New England roofing. And the Cedar "Chambers" remain "Impregnable of Eye." Does imagination, like spirit, belong to the invisible and not visible world? "Paradise" itself, whether aesthetic or religious or reflective of an emotional state, is still received, and framed if not measured, by "narrow Hands." *Hands*, as a trope for writing, reaffirms the poem's opening poetic gesture. Reclusion then becomes an image for a human condition that, even without renouncing its possible domains, remains inevitably limited. Yet this limitation may attest various kinds of possibility, ones not requiring the exchange or radical sacrifice or even conversion of one to obtain the other. In another poem situated in the home, Dickinson writes that "Some keep the Sabbath going to Church, / I keep it by staying at Home," where "Instead of going to Heaven at last / I'm going there all along." Or again, in a rehandling of the imagery of guest and host, Dickinson writes: "The Infinite a sudden Guest / Has been assumed to be – / But how can that stupendous come / Which never went away?" (J 1309). The human world, like the home here, can become an image for greater domains, rather than the price paid for them. Here continuity between worlds, between experience and meaning, seems possible; whereas in the reclusive tradition, the discontinuity between world and God means that one must choose between them.

These lines and images may suggest a Dickinsonian resolution, worked through the image of reclusion that is so often for her a scene of tremendous conflict. Dickinson's experience remains on the whole, however, one of discontinuity, rupture, antithesis, and counterclaim between experiential and metaphysical realms—conflicts internalized in her life and work. Reclusion remains a piercing venture. The poet is torn by self-division, by mutually exclusive and hence agonizing choices, expressed in conflictual imagery and complex accusation:

> I took my Power in my Hand
> And went against the World
> 'Twas not so much as David had
> But I was twice as bold –
>
> I aimed my Pebble – but Myself
> Was all the one that fell –
> Was it Goliath – was too large –
> Or was myself – too small?
>
> (J 540)

"Hand" may again evoke writing. Taking power in her hand may contest norms of her time: women were assigned to domestic and not public spaces. In one sense, reclusion is simply another name for domesticity. But the speaker's "Power" is directed "against the World," an opposition and alienation that bespeaks displacement from or within every realm accessible to her. David, although a poet like herself, is male, publicly active, authorized by God; he can hardly serve to authorize her. A biblical hero cannot be her model; nor can she represent God, nor be secure in (or of) his presence in her world. Yet neither is her reclusion a retreat; she goes out with power in hand. In this alienated and conflicted state, Dickinson, when she strikes at "Goliath," can defeat only herself. The conflicts that divide her—female vs. male, this world vs. the next, interiority vs. exteriority, experience vs. redemption—find neither resolution nor the promise of it in her reclusion, but only persistent reenactment.

Notes

1. Shira Wolosky, *Emily Dickinson: A Voice of War* (New Haven, CT: Yale University Press, 1984); "Poetry and Public Discourse, 1820-1910," in *Nineteenth-Century Poetry 1800-1910*, vol. 4 of *The Cambridge History of American Literature*, ed. Sacvan Bercovitch (New York: Cambridge University Press, 2004). The question of Dickinson's not-publishing has of course attracted much notice. It seems clear to me that she could have published easily if she had so chosen. Among her close acquaintance were prominent publishers such as Samuel Bowles, editor of the *Springfield Republican*; and Helen Hunt Jackson asked her repeatedly to allow publication of her poems, even anonymously.

2. See, for example, Andrew Louth, *The Origins of the Christian Mystical Tradition from Plato to Denys* (Oxford: Clarendon, 1981), 37-41.

3. For the role of grace in Augustinian philosophy, see Étienne Gilson, *The Christian Philosophy of St. Augustine*, trans. L. E. M. Lynch (London: Gollancz, 1961).

4. There is a second copy of 1876 in the Beinecke Library at Yale, presented to Dickinson by Susan Gilbert Dickinson for Christmas; but the earlier copy, which was Sue's, was shared between them. See Richard Sewall, *The Life of Emily Dickinson*, 2 vols. (New York: Farrar, Straus, and Giroux, 1974), 2:688, 692.

5. The poems are cited and numbered according to *The Poems of Emily Dickinson*, ed. Thomas Johnson (Cambridge, MA: Harvard University Press, 1955).

6. Since this is an essay on Dickinson, not Thomas à Kempis, it will be convenient to write as if Thomas were the sole author of the *Imitation of Christ*.

7. Thomas à Kempis, *The Imitation of Christ* (New York: Penguin, 1979), 28, 46 (citing John 12:25), 97, 59.

8. Thomas à Kempis, *Imitation*, 28, 68.

9. Thomas à Kempis, *Imitation*, 35, 52.

10. Yvor Winters makes this cranky remark in *In Defense of Reason: Primitivism and Decadence* (New York: Swallow Press, 1947).

11. Cf. J 648: "Mine to supplicate Madonna – / If Madonna be / Could behold so far a Creature – / Christ – omitted – Me –."

12. For a fine discussion of ambivalence in this poem, see Joanne Feit Diehl, *Dickinson and the Romantic Imagination* (Princeton, NJ: Princeton University Press, 1981), 19. Ambivalence is widely and well discussed in Dickinson criticism, as for example in Suzanne Juhasz, "Reading Dickinson Doubly," *Women's Studies* 16 (1989): 217-22.

13. Thomas à Kempis, *Imitation*, 73. Dickinson's early letters in particular can be lively, as for example L 30: "The path of duty looks very ugly indeed, and the place where I want to go more amiable . . . it is so much easier to do wrong than right, so much pleasanter to be evil than good, I wonder that good angels weep, and bad ones sing songs." I should resist mentioning that these Dickinson letters appeared recently in a circular warning students against irreverent literature.

14. For a fuller discussion of Dickinson's metaphysical critique and its dilemmas, see Wolosky, "Metaphysical Revolt," in *Emily Dickinson*, 99-135.

15. Thomas à Kempis, *Imitation*, 28, 67, 91.

16. Thomas à Kempis, *Imitation*, 32.

17. For an extensive discussion of Aristotle's division between active and contemplative happiness, see William Ross Hardie, *Aristotle's Ethical Theory* (Oxford: Clarendon, 1968). See also Anthony Kenny, *The Aristotelian Ethics* (Oxford: Clarendon, 1978), and Amélie Oksenberg Rorty, ed., *Essays on Aristotle's Ethics* (Berkeley: University of California Press, 1980), esp. Rorty, "The Place of Contemplation in Aristotle's *Nicomachean Ethics*," 377-94.

18. The central meanings of *liberty* are discussed in, for example, James McPherson, *Battle Cry of Freedom* (New York: Oxford University Press, 1988). For the uses of the word in Dickinson, see Cristanne Miller, "Pondering 'Liberty': Emily Dickinson and the Civil War," in *American Vistas and Beyond: A Festschrift for Roland Hagenbüchle*, ed. Marietta Messmer and Josef Raab (Trier, Germany: Wissenschaftlicher Verlag Trier, 2002), 45-64; and Shira Wolosky, "Public and Private in Dickinson's War Poetry," in *A Historical Guide to Emily Dickinson*, ed. Vivian Pollak (New York: Oxford University Press, 2004), 103-32.

19. Just as a footnote one might point out that Thomas à Kempis writes of the "vanity to love things that so swiftly pass away, and not to hasten onwards to that place where everlasting joy abides" (*Imitation*, 28). He also urges the reader to "Commune with your own heart, and in your chamber, and be still" (citing Ps. 4:4 and Isa. 26:20).

The Back Story:
The Christian Narrative and Modernism in Emily Dickinson's Poems _____

Nancy Mayer

Nancy Mayer finds something modern in the "peculiar urgency" of the "sketchy stories" intimated rather than told in Dickinson's poems. "The poems," remarks Mayer, "retain their freshness because the work the reader has to do just to orient herself feels modern, as does the shock of originality in the diction and the associative rather than narrative structure that dominates the poems in spite of the half-told stories." Yet if the associative structure and indirection of Dickinson's poetry anticipate twentieth-century modernism, Dickinson, in her "metaphysical engagement," is also "very much a poet of her time."

Dickinson, who famously wrote that "Immortality" was her "flood subject," repeatedly engages with Christian teleology and the narrative of the resurrection of souls both to "contemplate human mortality and to complicate the very notion of narrative." If in the Christian narrative resurrection is the climactic event in which humans are freed from death, Dickinson uses the Christian story of salvation "to imagine what would be lost, including our defining limitations, if she believed unequivocally that death could be undone." For example, in "Before I got my eye put out –," Dickinson "accedes to the narrative of salvation" only to find it "heartrendingly empty"; indeed, "the perspective from beyond the grave, which Dickinson insists on fleshing out in all its lifeless immutability, serves only to make what has been and will be lost more unbearably dear." As she expresses both astonishment and anger at the fact of death, she also questions how death can be accepted "by conscious beings who must themselves die and watch others die."

Comparing Dickinson to two poets who are also actively engaged in their poetry with questions of death and transcendence—Dickinson's nineteenth-century contemporary Walt Whitman and the twentieth-

and twenty-first-century poet Charles Wright—Mayer finds a sense of intimacy and urgency in Dickinson's "horrified surprise" at the fact of death, which is not found in Whitman or Wright. Thus Dickinson still matters to contemporary readers, in Mayer's view, for "each of us must live defined by a body that is destined to decay and an identity constructed of narratives we tell; and each of us has intimations that the consciousness we inhabit is too large for that framework." By acknowledging these facts of life and taking them personally, Dickinson "writes from a place where each of us stands alone on common ground."   J.B.B.

There is a peculiar urgency in the sketchy stories that Emily Dickinson's poems intimate rather than tell. The suggestion of narrative seems to inspire us to take these poems personally, the way we commonly tell stories to make things matter or to show what's at stake, but in a Dickinson poem we seem to have arrived in the midst of the telling, so we are left with a remnant of incident and a strong aftershock of emotion, but no marks of ownership.[1] Her intimacy is not the intimacy of the confessional poet but is located instead somewhere under the reader's skin. The poems retain their freshness because the work the reader has to do just to orient herself feels modern, as does the shock of originality in the diction and the associative rather than narrative structure that dominates the poems in spite of the half-told stories.[2]

But for all her immediacy, Dickinson is also very much a poet of her time. She comes embracing and dragging the full weight of the metaphysical paraphernalia that endlessly fascinated mid-nineteenth century New England but can smell a little musty in the twenty-first. For Dickinson, metaphysical engagement, which in her case is serious and deep, is steeped in a widely shared Christian (and specifically American Protestant) narrative of the resurrection of souls.[3] Dickinson engages tirelessly with "Immortality," the possibility, commonly accepted not just by her family and neighbors but by most of the intellectuals of her day, that there is another always-pending form of human life that will follow and transform the trajectory of embodied lives that end in death. I don't know whether Dickinson believed consistently in this teleology, but certainly she carried it with her, although it was often more disturbing than comforting to her implacable imagination.[4] ("Does not eternity appear dreadful to you?" a young Emily Dickinson writes to a pious friend; "It seems that Death . . . would be a relief to so endless a state of existence" [L10].) As a poet, Dickinson does not so much question received ideas of an afterlife as use them. In this essay, I am not interested in defining Dickinson's theological position on immortality. Given the contradictory evidence her poems provide—some of them disavowing any conceivable life after death, and some of them resting secure in a comfortable nineteenth-century depiction of heaven—that seems impossible in any case. Instead, I am interested in how she uses available ideas and images of an afterlife to contemplate human mortality and to complicate the very notion of narrative.

Dickinson's way with a story and particularly her way with the Christian resurrection narrative both epitomizes her historical moment in American poetry and keeps her fresh.[5] The back story that allows Christians a reprieve from the given teleology of human lives allows Dickinson to acknowledge our common inability really to grasp the fact of our own mortality. It allows her to do what she does with story fragments in her personal poems: to examine the emotional aftermath of a narrative and to make it matter, not in relation to the writer's biography, but as something both interior and shared. The sketchiness of the poems' "plots," along with Dickinson's habit of beginning her poems either in the midst of the action or after the fact, places the emphasis on emotional response and on reflection rather than event. To better understand the link between Dickinson's use of narrative and her obsession with teleology, I will be reading Dickinson alongside two poets, one of whom, Walt Whitman, is her contemporary, and the other, Charles Wright, who is ours. Each of them shares her thematic concerns with what might be called (as a variation on Charles Wright's term "negative spirituality") "negative transcendence," by which I mean a sense of unease with the limits of consciousness and mortality rather than the certainty that they will be overcome.

The nineteenth-century American poet who, like Dickinson, engages with questions of death and transcendence (rather than figuring forth convictions) and engages at the level of poetic structure is Walt Whitman. The more vulnerable version of the poet presented in the third, 1860, edition of *Leaves of Grass* shares some of Dickinson's astonishment at the fact and finality and intimacy of death.[6] (In "Scented Herbage of My Breast" from "Calamus," for instance, death becomes "the real reality" that "will one day perhaps take control of all"; in "A Word out of the Sea," the young apprentice poet learns the word death, "And again Death—ever Death, Death, Death" [277].) But here, in order to bring Dickinson's way with narrative into relief by contrast, I concentrate on the earlier Whitman, the voice of "Song of Myself," where Whitman's narratives fragment or succeed each other dizzyingly, and where the assurance that "Death is different from what we suppose and luckier" arises from experiencing the goodness of embodied life on earth ("Song" section 6).[7]

In a recent essay, Helen Vendler writes, "Modern poets (of all languages) have been forced to invent a new language for extinction, one depending neither on the organic naturalness of death, as in Whitman, nor on the remnants of Christian theology, as in Dickinson" ("'A Powerful, Strong Torrent'" 66). This states precisely the metaphysical context that separates nineteenth-century poets from those of the twentieth and twenty-first centuries. Of course there remain serious Christian poets, but they cannot assume that there is an audience who takes Christian eschatology for granted. I am arguing that, as Dickinson employs it, the Christian narrative, rather than offering her a reliable reprieve, highlights our common inability either to come to terms with death or to imagine an alternative. While Whitman's Zen-like acceptance of death is attractive, Dickinson's capacity for horrified surprise in response to even the most "natural" of deaths creates a certain emotional affinity with readers living in an age when mass extinction could conceivably become complete.

Charles Wright is one living poet who shares Dickinson's uneasy assumption that transcendence—the possibility of transcending the limits of embodiment and particularity—is an idea to be reckoned with, although, like Dickinson, he retains a wary agnosticism. Mark Jarman says that "Charles Wright writes about the empirical world as if transcendental metaphysics were possible" (25). Similarly, although we cannot know what Dickinson believed (or whether she subscribed to any system of metaphysical ideas stable enough to be called "beliefs"), she wrote *as if* eternal life were a possibility to be reckoned with. Nevertheless, for all her strangeness, she is grounded in and loyal to the empirical world, an attitude which her affinity to narrative reflects. In an interview with Thomas Gardner, Wright contrasts the associative organization characteristic of the modern lyric poem (and of his poems) to his observation that in Dickinson's poems there is "a little narrative going on most of the time" (105), although he notices that the narratives seem to dissolve in the telling: "[S]he would tell a story without telling a story" (96). He finds himself influenced by Dickinson's indirection, but closest to her in what he calls the "content" of his poems (by which he means ideas, not subject matter). They have in common "a negative spirituality," in which (in her case) "God is defined by what he isn't, what isn't available to her" (96, 98). Wright's own version of "spirituality" does not require a definition of God, and he distances himself from Dickinson in matters of belief and locates that distance in the historical space between them: "She believed in the idea of God much more than I do" (101).

I am less sure than Wright is about what Dickinson believed; I am interested instead in what she assumed and used. When she wrote that "Immortality" was her "flood subject" (L319), I am supposing that by "flood subject" she means something like what Wright meant by "content," a theme or overarching idea (perhaps overwhelming is the better term, given her metaphor). We must suppose, as Wright does, that she begins with the Christian (specifically, the nineteenth-century American Protestant) version of immortality, a story that makes resurrection the climactic event. In the rest of that story, displaced souls are freed from the constraints and the coherence of a life in time. It is a narrative, therefore, that proposes to free us from narrative. This desire to free oneself from the constraints of time—from decay, therefore, and the threat of death, and also from anticipation and reminiscence, which lose the present moment—is common to many forms of religious thought and to lyric poetry, especially to the American poetry that has turned away from narrative and toward more associative structures in the twentieth and twenty-first centuries. Dickinson's poems also reflect that desire, but the Christian narrative that is indelible in her poems requires different terms of engagement. Dickinson uses the omnipresent back story of salvation to imagine what would be lost, including our defining limitations, if she believed unequivocally that death could be undone. She also, more indirectly, considers a commonplace end run around mortality by writing poetry that is, as she put it, "alive" (L260). The strategy she employs is to tell and untell her story in the same breath, to remind us that the teleology that defines a single human life is inexorable but, if only because we can and seemingly must contemplate the possibility of transcending it, it is never the whole story. The Dickinson poem that begins "Before I got my eye put out –" employs one of her most basic strategies for un-telling a story; it plunges us into the disorienting middle of the thing. One way of reading it is as one of those poems narrated by a speaker who has died (got her "I" put out, a dreadful pun) and found that the afterlife comes up short of the bliss of seeing the world through the mechanism of embodied sight.

> Before I got my eye put out –
> I liked as well to see
> As other creatures, that have eyes –
> And know no other way –

But were it told to me, Today,
That I might have the Sky
For mine, I tell you that my Heart
Would split, for size of me –

The Meadows – mine –
The Mountains – mine –
All Forests – Stintless stars –
As much of noon, as I could take –
Between my finite eyes –

The Motions of the Dipping Birds –
The Morning's Amber Road –
For mine – to look at when I liked,
The news would strike me dead –

So safer – guess – with just my soul
Opon the window pane
Where other creatures put their eyes –
Incautious – of the Sun –

                              (Fr336)

The poem makes its argument in the Whitman-like celebration of
earthly life at its center. The mode of argument is a hymn to ordinary
visual experience. With high irony the speaker finds the afterlife safer
than earthly life because disembodiment protects her from dying
of joy, which would happen if she were restored to life on earth with
her eyes fully opened by the loss of it. After the background of the
first stanza (where the speaker says, in effect, "This is what I used
to be: a creature untutored by loss"), the narrative is all conditional—
announcement, event, description, and supposed, destructive result.
The speaker's focus is back toward earthly life—back toward what

would happen if she were to return to fully embodied consciousness from her present state, in which memory and some diminished kind of knowing remain cruelly intact. Dickinson accedes to the narrative of salvation, but, in submitting it to poetic scrutiny, she finds it heartrendingly empty. Although the sense Dickinson emphasizes is vision, which affords the early Emerson his easy access to transcendence, the sensibility in her poem rebukes even his momentary triumph over the limitations of ordinary embodied life.[8] Dickinson's poem serves as a reminder that Emerson's triumph comes through the body, that it depends on the fragile intricacy of the living eye.

Walt Whitman doesn't share Dickinson's sense of physical vulnerability, but he, too, implicitly rebukes Emerson's "transparent eyeball" perspective when he insistently plants his speakers where she does, in embodied life. Section five of Whitman's "Song of Myself" begins not by refusing merely the specific consolations of the resurrection narrative or those of the Emersonian sublime; instead it undermines the whole hierarchy of soul over body that underlies them both. The section begins: "I believe in you my soul, the other I am must not abase itself to you, / And you must not be abased to the other." For at least the early Whitman of "Song of Myself," transcendence is a full-body experience, and the soul, instead of displacing the body after death, embraces it in the midst of life:

> I mind how once we lay such a transparent summer morning,
> How you settled your head athwart my hips and gently
>   turn'd over upon me;
> And parted the shirt from my bosom-bone; and plunged your
>   tongue to my bare-stript heart,
> And reach'd till you felt my beard, and reach'd till you held
>   my feet.
>
>   ("Song" section 5)

The plot begins with seduction. The "other" self, the ego enmeshed in the body, invites the soul, which Whitman in an earlier section names "the Me myself" ("Song" section 4), to this union on the grass, where no poetry is allowed. ("No words, not music or rhyme I want, not custom or lecture, not even the best / Only the lull I like, the hum of your valvèd voice.") Instead of words, the soul accompanies what sounds like sex but isn't, quite, with an om-like hum.

It is within the passive, embodied self that the rudimentary plot moves forward. Something happens, did happen, to mark the occasion. There is an influx of knowledge:

> Swiftly arose and spread around me the peace and
>   knowledge that pass all the argument of the earth,
> And I know that the hand of God is the promise of my own,
> And I know that the spirit of God is the brother of my own,
> And that all the men ever born are my brothers and the
>   women my sisters and lovers,
> And that a kelson of the creation is love,
> And limitless are leaves stiff or drooping in the fields,
> And brown ants in the little wells beneath them,
> And mossy scabs of the worm fence, heap'd stones, elder,
>   mullein and poke-weed.
>
> ("Song" section 4)

Knowledge allows and requires the dismantling of hierarchy—God becomes a brother, all human beings are brothers and sisters as well, and the minutiae of the familiar visible world become invaluable treasures. The climactic word in the poem is not God but poke-weed. The image the poem conjures is of the newly integrated self, at the center of a circular web on which God, stones, and human beings are randomly and democratically arranged for the central eye's loving and ultimately wordless inspection. Love makes unadorned present-tense naming—Whitman's famous lists—the only language fit for the occasion, but, because the fecundity of the given world is limitless, naming too will be defeated. Rather than a narrative arc, the motion of the poem is circular, from the wordless melding with the soul, to the recognition of others, to the happy silence of the speaking self, exhausted by the richness of the world.

In contrast, Dickinson's resurrected self insists on speaking: "mine," she says, and then she says it again. This is not just an anxious self reclaiming the physical world; it's a realization of what it takes to be in relationship to the objects of that world. For Dickinson, it takes re-identifying oneself as separate and vulnerable, as mortal. It takes remembering what she has to lose and then remembering that she will lose it. The perspective from beyond the grave, which Dickinson insists on fleshing out in all its lifeless immutability, serves only to make what has been and will be lost more unbearably dear. Although she can observe with the reawakened intensity of Whitman's soul-infused speaker, she does not get lost in the moment; she is required to see the story through to imagining the possibility of a self severed from the world, sentenced to an empty security where nothing more can happen.

Whitman does, in section six of "Song of Myself," draw conclusions about eschatology, but, although "Song of Myself" is filled with stories, he does not imagine himself into an afterlife, as Dickinson does in "Before I got my eye put out –." Instead he constructs an argument with imagery both observed and imagined serving as his empirical evidence that "to die is different from what anyone supposed, and luckier." His evidence is the fecund tendency of the living world, as he observes it. There is, Whitman asserts, a general triumph of life over death at work and observable:

> The smallest sprout shows there really is no death,
> And if ever there was it led forward life, and does
>   not wait at the end to arrest it,
> And ceased the moment life appear'd.

All goes onward and outward, nothing collapses,

And to die is different from what anyone

supposed, and luckier.

("Song" section 6)

The argument depends on a leap from a personal response to a commonplace observation—surprise at the tenacity of plant life—to an undefined and unprovable universal claim. (What would count as "something" collapsing? A species? A star? A mind?) In order to be convincing, the consolation Whitman offers depends on his characteristic pleased astonishment at embodied life. It is as if the unlikeliness of the facts of life were alone a guarantee that further miracles are inevitable, as if some force at the heart of the universe must be as thrilled with the triumph of life on earth as Whitman himself is and therefore as unwilling as he would be to halt its future development. The other qualification for finding this "argument" consoling is a willingness to be consoled with the survival of life and perhaps some form of consciousness without an investment in the personal ego. Whitman sometimes flirts with somewhat vague notions of re-incarnation, but the early Whitman, in particular, is quite casual about the survival of memory or identity.[9]

As "Before I got my eye put out –" illustrates, Dickinson, like Whitman, begins from a position of enchantment with the living earth. Her astonishment, though, is reserved for the fact of death. This astonishment and its portrayal underlies the teleology of most of her narratives, even the barest, and depends on a perspective that is insistently, even militantly, trained on individual lives and fates.

Apparently with no surprise

To any happy Flower

The Frost beheads it at it's play –

In accidental power –

The blonde Assassin passes on –
The Sun proceeds unmoved
To measure off another Day
For an Approving God –

                (Fr1668)

Like Whitman, Dickinson uses plant life as an emblem of all lives, and especially human lives, but while Whitman's "single sprout" is important because of what it has in common with all living things, Dickinson's flower, although it may be "any happy Flower," is important because of its irreplaceable singularity. In other words, her rhetorical move is precisely the opposite of Whitman's. Where he naturalizes human deaths by merging them into the deaths of plants that renew themselves each spring, Dickinson reminds us that, like human bodies and minds, *particular* flowers will not reappear. No matter how fecund the plant, each flower's disappearance properly calls for mourning, its murder for indignation. Although the flower "Apparently" belongs to and accedes to the system that murders it ("at it's play," suggesting that this acceptance may be a form of childish innocence or ignorance), the speaker clearly does not. In fact, the real story here is the loneliness of the human speaker, who seems to be the only being with the ability to see a moral implication, to expect something other than indifference from the universe. She is also the only one with access to the anger that makes the story meaningful. It will be her story too, except that, for her and other human beings, when death cuts off a loved one or threatens oneself, surprise is apparent, no matter how many times we've heard this story before. Dickinson's flower is as common as Whitman's blade of grass, but that is only cause for greater indignation: how can the facts of life and death be accepted by conscious beings who must themselves die and watch others die?

Dickinson returns to this theme over and over, sometimes in poems where the graceful, unconscious lives and deaths of plants are contrasted to human suffering and fear, and sometimes in narratives that sketch fierce mourning or stark terror, both unmitigated by promises of salvation. In other Dickinson poems, though, eschatology is a more dimly lit backdrop that influences not so much the content of the poem as the way it works. In "How the old Mountains drip with Sunset" (Fr327), the narrative is simply a series of discrete events that trace the onset of evening from sunset to nightfall. An implied chronology structures the poem, but it is linguistically overripe, with vivid, sometimes eccentric imagery conjured by verbal agility rather than observation. The poet's hand is everywhere visible, pulling things in and shaping them up. The trajectory is inevitable, but the poem counters that vertical pull with close attention to *how* the story unfolds in unconnected moments and how the poet recreates with her own self-consciously present language the sense of time slowed by a thick overlay of sensory experience.

> How the old Mountains drip with Sunset
> How the Hemlocks burn –
> How the Dun Brake is draped in Cinder
> By the Wizard Sun –

In this first stanza, the imagery is economical; much of the effect on the reader is produced by sound—all those *n*'s, the predominance of one-syllable words, the cleverly buried near-rhymes. Rather than evoking a sunset with visual clues, the poet confesses her failure: "How" is an exclamation that begs off full description. What we get instead is a stanza impelled forward not by incident but by echo and distortion, just as in watching a sunset, we move through time by color and glow; everything and nothing changes.

In the second stanza, although the sound effects remain, the focus is on metaphor.

How the old Steeples hand the Scarlet
Till the Ball is full –
Have I the lip of the Flamingo
That I dare to tell?

The elaborate and fanciful image—the sun as a ball of yarn, the stee-ples as spindles that hold the unwinding skein—is too elaborate, really, to bring a sunset to mind. The reader has to work for it—the sun grows larger, like the ball of yarn, as it nears the earth; the yarn must be cirrus clouds, reddened in the glow. What is most prominent is the speaker, persistent, alive, and outrageous. She's embroidering the stitching that's holding this together, so that the poem emphasizes the process of how a poet conveys an impalpable event that unfolds over time—how to compress presence and transformation, sensory experience and the lan-guage that abstracts it, into a single, startled breath. It's the hurried effort the reading requires, making that connection without stopping to think, that creates the little pop of startled recognition, the effect of familiar, gaudy colors in the sky. And then there's the faux-humble signature— the lipped flamingo—to remind us who's behind all of this—an ab-surdly conspicuous figure, claiming to be unqualified to say it.

The last stanza of the narrative (but not of the poem) is the one whose non-visual imagery elicited David Porter's attention in the 1981 monograph *Dickinson: The Modern Idiom*. The book title signals Por-ter's overriding concern, that Dickinson's poetry unwittingly antici-pates all that he disapproves of in what he calls "terminal modernism" (292).[10] Porter writes:

> Dickinson's poems do not invoke a full world. Instead, they are the vast
> hoard of a traveler's snapshots without itinerary of the trip or a map show-
> ing the destination. The momentariness, the language flashes, signal the
> unique qualities in the Dickinson idiom that, for all its arresting power and
> audacity, render it a hazard for later poets. (293)

While I take strong issue with Porter's overriding assumption that Dickinson's poems were the unintentional result of an ignorance of poetic tradition and a reliance on instinct over intellect, the comparison to snapshots taken on a trip without a map seems perfect (except that I am insisting that she always held the destination in her mind).[11] The charge that Dickinson does not "invoke a full world" is, however, based not just on the disjointedness of the poems, but on Dickinson's fondness for this kind of non-visual imagery:

> How it is Night – in Nest and Kennel –
> And where was the Wood –
> Just a Dome of Abyss is Bowing
> Into Solitude –
>
> (Fr327)

It is the "Dome of Abyss" that inspires Porter's mixture of admiration and wariness for Dickinson's portrait of "not only a preverbal but a preconscious sensation" of *"an absence felt as a presence"* (32). The stanza begins, once again, with "How," as in, "How will I tell this story?" The event—night usurps what was only recently bright daylight—is an established fact in the first line, and then the poem backs up, and the woods disappear as we watch. Inevitably, the reader does create an image to make sense of the stanza. For me the "Dome of Abyss" is a kind of palimpsest: first the dome of the sky (which is itself more a conceptual image than a visual one, especially where forests obscure the horizon), then the sense of that dome—that sense of structure—is blotted out. And then the nothingness that remains bows down, becomes in some way an action, the act of "Bowing" (the verb is capitalized so that it carries a hint of noun), which obliterates the more accessible chaos of the "Wood."

The content of the back story here is, of course, death (again) and who bears witness. The story recurs endlessly, but it also ends, finally and completely, with an erasure that comes from outside and above, in which the very framework of things, Whitman's kelson of the creation, becomes an action ("Bowing") and in that becoming obliterates the known world—both time and place. The poem's final stanza takes us back into time, into history, but it tells the story of the defeat of artistic attempts to preserve and reframe these moments:

> These are the Visions flitted Guido –
> Titian – never told –
> Domenichino dropped his pencil –
> Paralyzed, with Gold –

Of course, the defeated artists here are visual artists, whose works are static and framed. Dickinson's poem, on the other hand, comes to life in the breath and mind of each new reader; its obscurities require active and conscious co-creation every time it is read. In significant ways, Dickinson's speaker, like the painters, also "never told"; instead she makes the reader do the work of collaborating or even originating from her hints.[12] While the onset of "Night" in the poem does the standard work of reminding the reader of the onset of death, Dickinson's verse becomes a new live thing in the reader's active mind, a kind of modest, recurring, and still mortal resurrection for the poem and for the impersonal but utterly distinctive voice of the poet.

Dickinson's expectations for the reader anticipate those of twentieth-century poetry, as Porter dolefully observed. "How the old Mountains drip with Sunset," where the narrative really is a back story—at once too banal for telling and, as the speaker claims, impossible to capture—is a particularly good anticipation of the associative structure of modern poetry. The sequence is held together with nothing more than happenstance—this and then this, then this; in keeping with the essential mystery of this light show, there isn't any causal connection that matters to the observer between the separate sensations. The speaker turns her attention to different objects as the poem progresses, so we don't even get the progress of evening in one particular place; it's a traveling light show. In keeping with this narrative disjointedness, the figurative language shifts abruptly from visual to aural to abstract references, and the speaker is uninhibited in piling up wildly disparate images.

Stylistic effects like these anticipate and, as Thomas Gardner notes, directly influence Charles Wright. Gardner finds strong traces of "There's a certain Slant of light" (Fr320) in this first stanza from Charles Wright's "Yard Journal," but in its combination of thematic ambition, fixed attention on the passage of time in a domestic outdoor setting, and mysterious and abundant imagery, it also recalls the poem above.

> —Mist in the trees and soiled water and grass cuttings splotch
> The driveway,
>   afternoon starting to bulk up in the west
> A couple of hours down the road:
> Strange how the light hubs out and wheels
>   concentrically back and forth
> After a rain, as though the seen world
> Quavered inside a water bead
>   swung from a grass blade:
> The past is never the past:
>   it lies like a tongue
> We walk down into the moist mouth of the future, where new teeth
> Nod like new stars around us,
> And winds that itch us, and plague our ears,
>   sound curiously like the old songs.
>   (3)

Wright shares with Dickinson the technique of seeming to pick up whatever is at hand or comes to mind (workbasket with red yarn or grass blade with water drop) and making it apt; a haphazard interior world enlarges into general significance without losing its strangeness.

The world inside the raindrop suspended in the grass is convincing because the image (one's visible surroundings reduced and distorted in reflection) is both familiar and unimaginable (placing us along with "the seen world" inside the raindrop); but it also works because it is a recognition of our collective and essential ignorance of where and what we are. It posits the possibility of an unknowable outside, which might be a definition of Dickinson's afterlife. The stanza also offers the possibility of replacing this precarious exclusion with an enveloping, toothed darkness, which might, not too fancifully, be read as a portrait of Dickinson's God.

Wright's allusion, though, is not to Dickinson and not to God, but to Dante's Satan, whose teeth, encased in three separate heads, joined "at the crown" (canto 34, 44), eternally grip and gnaw the betrayers Judas Iscariot and Brutus and Cassius. Likening the teeth to stars recalls the last lines of *The Inferno*, where the stars show the way out of hell and toward heaven: "Through a round aperture I saw appear // Some of the beautiful things that Heaven bears, / Where we came forth, and once more saw the stars" (canto 34, 138-40). This conflation of the teleologies of Heaven and Hell (stars or teeth) reflects Wright's interest in memory and repetition, the spiraling journey into the underworld rather than its function as a final destination or result. Richard Tillinghast calls Wright's Dante "a Buddhist's Dante" (195), and clearly there is something in the relationship to time and in the poet's ambivalent relationship to the material world that turns consciously to the East. Mark Jarman notes that it is "the combination of Christian and Zen views of the nature of reality that makes him speak of the immanent in terms of the transcendent" (27). In a complicated equation, "Yard Journal" demonstrates how transforming visual images into verbal imagery renders them transcendent, that is, both free of the limitations of place and time and redolent of an inarticulate, overarching meaning:

—Exclusion's the secret: what's missing is what appears
Most visible to the eye:
> The more luminous anything is
The more it subtracts what's around it,
Peeling away the burnt skin of the world
> making the unseen seen:
Body by new body they all rise into the light
Tactile and still damp,
That rhododendron and dogwood tree, that spruce,
An architecture of absence,
> a landscape whose words
Are imprints, dissolving images after the eyelids close:
I take them away to keep them there—
> That hedgehorn, for instance, that stalk . . .

> (4-5)

Whether the poet's words are a preservative like photographs—
"imprints"—or what must be peeled away is not clear. The trick is in
finding and keeping fresh the sense of an unreachable something—
something that is as raw as what lies behind "the burnt skin of the
world." The phenomenal world is backlit by the luminous real. Each
"new body" must "rise into the light," and can become a transcendent
reality only behind the eyes of each observer.

Helen Vendler acknowledges Wright's preoccupation with "what is
not there [in sensory experience] but makes its presence felt" (29), but
she distinguishes his explorations from true mysticism because of his
devotion to language, which mysticism, finally, defeats. She herself
gestures toward the spiraling concentric circles of *The Inferno* as she
marks the stopping point in the poet's journey inward toward immate-
riality:

Wright's poetry reproduces the circling and deepening concentration that
aims at either obliteration or transcendence, blankness or mysticism. But

---

Wright stops short of either polarity because he remains bound to the materiality and temporal rhythm of language, whereas both Eastern nothingness and Western transcendence at their utmost point, renounce as meaningless both materiality and time. (30)

This is an observation that could also be made of Dickinson's poetry, as, for instance, she supplants the Word (the one "in the beginning" that "was God") that is meant to end all words with poetry, a "word made Flesh" (Fr1715), and the communion bread (Christ's "Flesh") with text. Her complaint against the comforts offered by Christ is that even a God who was "'Made Flesh and dwelt among us'" lacks the "condescension" of language, which provides not just spiritual sustenance, but nourishment suited "To our specific strength –," that is, to individual experience in the material world and to individual psyches instead of souls. Dickinson's "word made Flesh" is, by virtue of its rarified nature and intimacy, characteristically lyric rather than narrative. It implies and engenders present-tense experience rather than recounting a fully realized story that makes spectators of its readers. This poem itself does not sketch a story, but it intimates a teleology: "A word that breathes distinctly / Has not the power to die." The whole poem is a debate about the preservative value of language versus Christian redemption; like Wright, Dickinson sees a mystical Presence as necessarily lethal to language. This opens once again the question of how Dickinson's insistence on an implied teleology for human life influences the way she approaches the same intimations of transcendence that haunt *Zone Journals*.

Helen Vendler recognizes the "the unseen" that continues to haunt Charles Wright and other modernist poets and calls it, "what is not there but makes its presence felt—eternity, death, transcendence, extension, rhythm: the unseen can go by many names" (29). For Dickinson, though, while each of these terms describes something that matters, they are emphatically not interchangeable, and those that matter most have to do with teleology—what remains or doesn't. Dickinson, like the transcendentalists (or perhaps more like Charles Wright in her persistent agnosticism), subscribes to a distinctly "haunted" version of experience, but the kind of momentary transcendence of the quotidian that Whitman or Emerson or even Thoreau describes doesn't speak to her fundamental questions. The following poem reads like a transcendentalist manifesto, but, where "filaments" of the divine only need to gesture toward sublimity for transcendentalists, in this poem there is a teleology, although, characteristically, it is notably negligent of human interest.

> The Love a Life can show Below
> Is but a filament, I know,
> Of that diviner thing
> That faints opon the face of Noon –
> And smites the Tinder in the Sun –
> And hinders Gabriel's Wing –
>
> 'Tis this – in Music – hints and sways –
> And far abroad on Summer days –
> Distills uncertain pain –
> 'Tis this enamors in the East –
> And tints the Transit in the West
> With harrowing Iodine –
>
> 'Tis this – invites – appalls – endows –
> Flits – glimmers – proves – dissolves –
> Returns – suggests – convicts – enchants –
> Then – flings in Paradise –
>
> (Fr285)

The first verse sounds like catechism, something learned and dutifully recited. This is the most metaphysical of the verses, with the "diviner thing" responsible for both earthly time and the timing of the Apocalypse. The second stanza is more earthbound, and closer to Wright's sense of some possibly painful reality within or behind the sensual world. Dickinson's language, though, is more abstract than Wright's. Except for the final image of the colors of sunset as "harrowing Iodine," the expressive work of the stanza is done exclusively by verbs. The verbs themselves do not even sketch narrative action, although the last three lines invoke narrative enclosure, both in the boundaries of dawn and sunset, and in the implied boundary of death (which the "diviner thing" colors with pain or fear). The stanza's dominant emotions are teasing uncertainty, longing (the "uncertain pain" that is "distilled"—a characteristic Dickinson verb—by beauty in nature and/or by maturity itself, living a given life to an age of reflection), and, finally, fear and beauty co-mingled in the face of death's inevitability. The only trajectory here is the trace of a life ending in death, and all of the verbs are the actions of a mysterious "thing" that demonstrates "Love" by grafting these emotions onto passive human natures.

In the last stanza—remarkably, nothing but verbs until the final verb phrase—the process of abstraction accelerates, with the material world and the "diviner thing" both reduced to a single blur of activity. With the exception of "Flits," "glimmers," "dissolves," and "returns," all of the verbs are transitive; all describe actions done to the conscious subjects who live their lives "Below." (And the last two of these four verbs are ambiguous; they could be transitive. Human subjects—including the speaker and reader, of course—could be both "dissolved" and "returned," if we take resurrection as a given possibility.) Although there are small sequences within the order of the verbs, most of which tend to undo previous actions ("glimmers – proves – dissolves – returns –"), they do not imply a narrative. Sequence and purpose are reserved for the last four words, which begin with the first sequential claim, "Then – flings in Paradise –." This teleology, a landing in "Paradise" propelled by "Love," seems to reach for a certainty Wright would never claim. But the verbs carry the poem, and the action sounds more like discarding a rind than protecting a cherished being. And if

"Paradise" resembles the place where the speaker who had her eye put out landed, it's more an exile than a reward. The point seems to be the helplessness of human subjects to change or even to discern the arc of their stories.

In spite of the two poets' common claim to the attitude that Wright names "negative spirituality," the experience of reading *Zone Journals* is quite different from the experience of reading Dickinson's spare lyrics, and that difference reflects, I think, not just different techniques but different contexts: Christian teleology versus a series of discrete moments that might loop back into something like reincarnation or endless, disorienting repetition. The interior openness of a Dickinson poem—the dashes, the associative leaps, multiple variants of specific words—is contained within lyrics that are physically compressed. The reader is made to feel disorientation but also, always, the limitation of the short poem. The stopping point is always definite and visible. In contrast, reading *Zone Journals* is more like Wright's description of retracing one's steps endlessly into a spot-lit familiar strangeness. Although the revelations accumulate, there is no clear end in sight; instead there is evanescence. There is a dreamy, disquieting quality to the *Journals*, but there is a less intimate and personal risk than in Dickinson's strongest poems. Dickinson's insistence on irrecoverable loss positions her speakers and her readers where we must find ourselves, within a life circumscribed by time; her affinity for passive constructions with the speaker as object rather than actor ("Before I got my eye put out –") reminds us of the fundamental powerlessness of persons so situated. It is not that she resists ideas of the afterlife, but that she attempts actually to imagine what any notion of "after" might be. Sometimes as in the famous post-mortem poems (notably, for instance, in "I heard a Fly buzz – when I died –" [Fr591]), she can only imagine imagination failing, since imagination, like the rest of our mental equipment, is attuned to the time-bound creatures we are. But even where she concedes the possibility of some sort of restoration, the question of how fundamentally individuals would need to change for an existence of "Costumeless Consciousness" (Fr1486) can only be answered with a loss of the familiar and well-loved.[13]

Dickinson's obsession with death and with Christian eschatology's attempt to re-write that ending is central to her poetry.[14] It accounts, I think, for the sense of urgency and engagement in her poems. It positions a vulnerable personal presence not at the center of the visible and invisible universe, as in "Song of Myself," and not from the vantage point that sees Wright's world-containing droplet of water from both inside and out, but within a fragile, mortal, and painfully sentient body and a beloved world destined to darken and disappear. Repeated encounters with the absurd, intractable solidity of those boundaries keep her fear and indignation fresh. But the question naturally arises: how are modern readers to take seriously all of this furious wrestling with an outmoded set of premises? Dickinson's preoccupation with a received theology that was already losing its universality as a premise as she wrote would render irrelevant any current poet who hoped to matter to an audience not limited to Christian believers. And yet Dickinson continues to matter—to poets unconcerned with metaphysics as well as to readers.

I submit that Dickinson matters not in spite of, but in terms of her insistence on grappling with the Christian resurrection narrative and with the God behind it, the personification, in many of her poems, of an indifferent universe. Modern readers need not participate in the theological interrogations that occupy the poems in order to find themselves exactly in the place where Dickinson's speakers stand: within bodies and lives that do not fully contain any of us, but hold us. The trick to her immediacy is the way she gets to places that are intimate but held in common, and the route to those places is not through specific or idiosyncratic narratives, which are inevitably exclusive, but beginning from somewhere in the middle of things moving outward toward our inevitable limitations. The inescapable narrative arc, of course, begins at birth and ends in death, but she needs the alternative of the Christian resurrection narrative, not just because that was the alternative available to her, but also because it is a narrative that recuperates (and therefore acknowledges the importance of) individual histories and egos and attempts to make them retrospectively meaningful. Modernism and contemporary poetry in general have made a valiant effort to remain free of the blinding limitations imposed by either of these competing narratives, which do, in fact, hamper our sense of the present moment and the unframed and haphazard mental lives we experience. Nevertheless, each of us must live defined by a body that is destined to decay and an identity constructed of narratives we tell; and each of us has intimations that the consciousness we inhabit is too large for that framework. Dickinson manages to acknowledge both of those facts of life and to take them personally. She writes from a place where each of us stands alone on common ground.

From *The Emily Dickinson Journal* 17, no. 2 (2008): 1-23. Copyright © 2008 by The Johns Hopkins University Press. Reprinted with permission of The Johns Hopkins University Press.

Notes

1. Familiar examples of emotions generated by partial or sketchy narratives in Dickinson's poems include the following: "That after Horror – that 'twas *us* –" (Fr243) for a danger narrowly averted; "The Nerves sit ceremonious, like Tombs –" (Fr372) for the aftershock of loss; "that forcing, in my breath – / As staples – driven through" (Fr292) for heartbreak stirred by memories of an absent lover or beloved; "And then an awful leisure was / Belief to regulate –" (Fr1100) after witnessing a death. In each example, the story is too vague to identify, but the emotion seems familiar and valid to the reader.

2. I use the terms modern and modernism loosely to describe poetry from the twentieth century onward that continues the Romantic project of rejecting both utilitarian materialism and religious tradition in favor of "claims that artists could articulate dynamic energies of spirit which cannot be rendered within any mode of representation committed to appearances" (Altieri 793). Charles Altieri finds a fundamental distinction between Romanticism and modernism in Romanticism's need "to harmonize mind and nature" and modernism's need "to exacerbate the differences between productive mind and passive nature in the hope that the spirit would be enabled to appreciate its own energies and the needs they generate." It is the implied faith in the integrity of what Altieri calls "productive mind" that both links Dickinson to and distinguishes her from the modernists (793). While, as Suzanne Juhasz has demonstrated, Dickinson

treats the mind as a place of refuge, she also remembers that the "brain" (her preferred term) is always vulnerable to the depredations of nature and of time.

3. For more on Dickinson's specific affiliations with the various branches of American Protestantism available to her, see Jane Donahue Eberwein's useful tour of the religious landscape of Dickinson's Amherst in "Dickinson's Local, Global, and Cosmic Perspectives." Karl Keller made an earlier, more speculative case for Dickinson's lingering affiliations to American Puritanism in *The Only Kangaroo Among the Beauty*. In *Emily Dickinson and Her Culture*, Barton Levi St. Armand traced the influence of both Victorian America's (Protestant) sentimental religious culture and an earlier, highly imaginative and grotesque folk tradition on the diction, imagery, and genre (especially parodies of hymns and psalms) in Dickinson's treatment of religious subjects. Most recently and completely, James McIntosh's *Nimble Believing* considers not only the influence of "religiously conservative schools and churches in Amherst and South Hadley" that were important in Dickinson's upbringing, but also her affinity with the "fluid consciousness and uncertainty" that characterize the trajectories of Emerson and those who followed, each of whom was grounded in one or more strains of American Protestantism (3-4, 14-30).

4. In *Dickinson: Strategies of Limitation*, Eberwein notes that for Dickinson, "Death presented itself as a barrier, a closed door; but she insisted on trying the lock in any way she could to discover whether she could trust the Christian promise of eternal and intensified life" (199). Eberwein emphasizes that, although Dickinson frequently rebels against the distance between any imagined immortality afforded those who have died and the imaginations of the living who mourn them, uncertainty exhilarated her and informed her writing. On the whole, Eberwein stresses the transformative possibilities of life after death in Dickinson's poems and letters. McIntosh sees a movement toward increased acceptance of death and optimism about what comes after in the late letters and poems, when the reality of her own death is closer:

> Late in her life especially, Dickinson meditated on "the Extension of Consciousness after Death." Since such a prospect is necessarily uncertain, it brings a new uncertainty to some of Dickinson's late writings that gives them in turn a new kind of expressiveness. In these particular writings her lifelong dialectic between her intuitive faith and her quarrel with Calvinism subsides into the background. She is neither so infatuated with the "Eden always eligible" in earthly life nor so angry with a Calvinist God who causes death. (71)

The three poems I examine at length in this essay are each dated 1862 by R. W. Franklin, although "Apparently with no surprise" (Fr1668) is a bitter little poem from 1884, two years before her death, which may simply serve to re-iterate the point made by both authors that uncertainty remained a necessity to this poet's imagination right up to the end of her life.

5. McIntosh makes the case for the value of Dickinson's poems as serious philosophical poetry for modern readers. While acknowledging the Christian tradition as a source of Dickinson's concepts of immortality and eternity, Gudrun Grabher places Dickinson's related interest in the nature of time and consciousness into a larger con-

text, referring to a variety of disciplines, traditions, and thinkers, including Aristotle, St. Augustine, Kant, Lévinas, and Stephen Hawking. Grabher notes that Dickinson's "eternity or immortality" emphasizes "the *absence* of time" and that she "uses precisely those signifiers of the absence of time as a means of approaching the concept of time" (260), an argument that emphasizes the use Dickinson makes of these concepts rather than her beliefs.

6. Roy Harvey Pearce makes a case for the primacy of the 1860 edition, which he sees as a continuation of the two earlier (1855 and 1856) editions, but which contrasts to them chiefly in its insistence on things as they are, its requirement that the ego "must come to realize the limits of its own humanity" (69). M. Jimmie Killingsworth, in reading the "Calamus" sequence of 1860, links the longing for death in "Scented Herbage" to the longing to "release the self into love" and the "confessional impulse" whereby "the poet gives himself to his readers" (122). In both instances, there is a new element of human risk for the speaker.

7. The quoted passages and section numbers included here are from the 1891-92 edition of "Song of Myself" for the convenience of the reader. The 1855 edition included neither section numbers nor clear section breaks to delineate what became, beginning with the 1871 edition, discrete poems, numbered as they are here. The title "Song of Myself" first appeared in 1881. The sequence was untitled in 1855 and called "Walt Whitman" in 1860.

8. The illustrative passage is the famous one from *Nature*:

> I become a transparent eyeball; I am nothing; I see all; the currents of the Universal Being circulate through me; I am part or particle of God. The name of the nearest friend sounds then foreign and accidental: to be brothers, to be acquaintances, master or servant, is then a trifle and a disturbance. I am the lover of uncontained and immortal beauty. (10)

9. For Pearce, in the 1860 edition of *Leaves of Grass* in particular, "The humanism is painful, because one of the crucial elements (centering on 'death' as a 'clew' in 'A Word Out of the Sea') is an acknowledgement of all-too-human limitations and constraints" (79-80). Pearce thus emphasizes Whitman's acknowledgement of death as a terminal limitation, although he believes that the later "prophetic" Whitman softened this "realist" position. Making no distinction as to the different editions of the poem on the issue of life after death, Harold Aspiz declares, "Whitman firmly embraced some form of future life." This view is supported by lines like these from "Song of Myself": "And as to you Life I reckon you are the leavings of many deaths, / (No doubt I have died myself ten thousand times before)" (section 49). However, Aspiz notes that "although he appears convinced that he will continue as a distinct entity in some future state, he cannot define what that state may be like or what the relation may be between his mortal, material self and any future manifestation of himself" (25). Each of these critics, then, albeit in contrasting ways, notices either inconsistency or vagueness in Whitman's statements on life after death. Even David Kuebrich, who sees Whitman as a prophet of self-styled religion based loosely on Protestantism and who declares that there is "abundant evidence of Whitman's belief in personal immortality" (113), notes

that "the more complex poems . . . make no explicit affirmations but instead try to move the reader's soul to an existential realization of this article of Whitman's faith" (115).

10. In his introduction, Porter distinguishes Dickinson's baleful influence from "the commonly observed richness and ambiguity of high modernist art." The trait that most distinguishes Dickinson's poetry—which leads to what Porter calls "terminal modernism"—from high modernism is "its simultaneously incoherent and fierce imagination." According to Porter, this dangerously uncontrolled power shows itself in poetry that is both "disinherited from transcendent knowledge" and disconnected from "broad fields of ordinary experience" (7). The first charge, about the disconnect from "transcendent knowledge," recalls Helen Vendler's distinction (quoted above) between modern poets and Whitman, who naturalized death, and Dickinson, who clung to the remnants of Christian theology, though in Vendler's analysis the inaccessibility of "transcendent knowledge" is a defining mark of modernism.

Charles Altieri similarly makes a certain distancing from the empirical world not a fault of modernism gone astray but a defining principle of modernist poetics: "First 'realization' had to replace description, so that instead of copying the external world the work could render it an image insisting on its own distinctive form of reality." Altieri's second "fundamental principle" of modernist poetics is the development of "collage techniques" (793). As a result of the turn away from narrative and discursive reasoning, "it becomes the spaces between images that offer the audience its access to the mode of spirit defined by the work" (798). This sounds like a description of precisely the poetic technique that Porter decries in Dickinson: "Dickinson's language produces a strange discourse that is full of gaps and shadows and brilliant glints of light. It pulled poetic art away from prose and into chaos" (7).

Since Porter does see Dickinson's influence in strains of modernist and especially postmodernist poetry of which he disapproves, the distinction here may be more aesthetic than historical. While I see Dickinson's distinction from modernism to be primarily theological and a product of her time, I am, like Porter, arguing for what could be a conservative aesthetic—that is, I believe that Christian teleology gave Dickinson a focus for a more interesting and thorough agnosticism than is available to those who can no longer lay claim to the Christian redemption narrative.

11. There have been other objections to Porter's claim that Dickinson's poetry is brilliant in its effects but lacking in intention or control. The most specific and complete is Gary Lee Stonum's *The Dickinson Sublime*, which locates the intentionality in Dickinson's poems in her habit of imagining herself as reader, aware of and seeking to tap "the affects of power" in "the circuit of author and audience" (15). More recently, Jed Deppman grants the proto-post-modern intimations that Porter discerns, but he reads Dickinson's indirection as deeply intentional, anticipating Lyotard's re-working of Kant's mathematical sublime: "Many of Dickinson's poems can be read as resourceful, even desperate, attempts to supply imagery for the thoughts and experiences that most defy the imagination" (87).

12. The unusual level of participation required of Dickinson's readers is central to both Stonum's argument and Cristanne Miller's stylistic analysis in *Emily Dickinson: A Poet's Grammar*. According to Stonum, "Dickinson imagined that the reader should

play as prominent a part as the author. What the author has created thus initiates at best a richly productive process of response" (47). Miller demonstrates with a close analysis of specific poems how characteristic strategies such as compression require the reader's full engagement. Thus, for example, the poem "Essential Oils – are wrung –" (Fr772),"provides the bones of minimal thought which we must flesh into personal statement and idea by creating the connective, explanatory links for ourselves" (27).

13. Besides "Those not live yet" (which portrays "Costumeless Consciousness" as an unimaginable but desirable state [Fr1486]), a very partial sampling of poems that concern themselves with imagining life inside a mind unbounded by time includes "This World is not conclusion" (Fr373), "This Consciousness that is aware" (with the unforgettable figure of identity as the unshakeable "single Hound" that attends the dying Soul [Fr817]), "Their Hight in Heaven " (Fr725), "The Soul's Superior instants" (Fr630), "The going from a world we know" (Fr1662), and the strikingly strange "No Crowd that has occurred" in which the long dead awaken in a general resurrection but instead of celebrating a joyous reunion each "separate Consciousness" remains "August – Absorbed – Numb –" (Fr653). For me, Dickinson's quintessential attempt to imagine and articulate the state of a mind stripped of the defining limitations of time and space is the series of negations, the disjunction of time, and final sigh that releases our hold on history in "Great Streets of silence led away":

> Great Streets of silence led away
> To Neighborhoods of Pause –
> Here was no Notice – no Dissent
> No Universe – no Laws –
>
> By Clocks, 'Twas Morning, and for Night
> The Bells at Distance called –
> But Epoch had no basis here
> For Period exhaled.
>
> (Fr1166)

14. Many critics have, of course, written about Dickinson's varied representations of and attitudes toward the afterlife. Most influential to the development of my argument have been Robert Weisbuch's *Emily Dickinson's Poetry*, Sharon Cameron's *Lyric Time*, and especially Suzanne Juhasz's chapter "Costumeless Consciousness" in *The Undiscovered Continent*.

Works Cited

The following abbreviations are used to refer to the writings of Emily Dickinson:

Fr   *The Poems of Emily Dickinson.* ed. R. W. Franklin. 3 vols. Cambridge, MA: Harvard UP, 1998. Citation by poem number.

L   *The Letters of Emily Dickinson.* ed. Thomas H. Johnson and Theodora Ward. 3 vols. Cambridge, MA: Harvard UP, 1958. Citation by letter number.

Alighieri, Dante. *The Inferno of Dante.* Trans. Robert Pinsky. New York: Noonday/ Farrar, Straus and Giroux, 1994.

Altieri, Charles. "Modernism and Postmodernism." *The New Princeton Encyclopedia of Poetry and Poetics.* Ed. Alex Preminger and T. V. F. Bogan. Princeton, NJ: Princeton UP, 1993. 792-96.

Aspiz, Harold. *So Long! Walt Whitman's Poetry of Death.* Tuscaloosa: U of Alabama P, 2004.

Cameron, Sharon. *Lyric Time: Dickinson and the Limits of Genre.* Baltimore, MD: Johns Hopkins UP, 1979.

Deppman, Jed. "Trying to Think with Emily Dickinson." *The Emily Dickinson Journal* 14.1 (2005): 84-103.

Eberwein, Jane Donahue. *Dickinson: Strategies of Limitation.* Amherst: U of Massachusetts P, 1985.

_____. "Dickinson's Local, Global, and Cosmic Perspectives." *The Emily Dickinson Handbook.* Eds. Gudrun Grabher, Roland Hagenbüchle, and Cristanne Miller. Amherst: U of Massachusetts P, 1998. 27-43.

Emerson, Ralph Waldo. *Emerson: Essays and Lectures.* Ed. Joel Porte. New York: Library of America, 1983. 5-49.

Gardner, Thomas. "Restructured and Restrung: Charles Wright's *Zone Journals.*" *A Door Ajar: Contemporary Writers and Emily Dickinson.* New York: Oxford UP, 2006. 70-94.

Giannelli, Adam, ed. *High Lonesome: On the Poetry of Charles Wright.* Oberlin, OH: Oberlin College P, 2006.

Grabher, Gudrun. "'Forever – is Composed – of Nows': Emily Dickinson's Conception of Time." *A Companion to Emily Dickinson.* Ed. Martha Nell Smith and Mary Loeffelholz. Malden, MA: Blackwell, 2008. 258-68.

Jarman, Mark. "*from* 'The Pragmatic Imagination and the Secret of Poetry.'" *Gettysburg Review* 1.4 (1988): 647-60. Rpt. in Giannelli. 25-29.

Juhasz, Suzanne. *The Undiscovered Continent: Emily Dickinson and the Space of the Mind.* Bloomington: Indiana UP, 1983.

Keller, Karl. *The Only Kangaroo Among the Beauty: Emily Dickinson and America.* Baltimore, MD: Johns Hopkins UP, 1979.

Killingsworth, M. Jimmie. *Whitman's Poetry of the Body: Sexuality, Politics and the Text.* Chapel Hill: U of North Carolina P, 1989.

Kuebrich, David. *Minor Prophecy: Walt Whitman's New American Religion.* Bloomington: Indiana UP, 1989.

McIntosh, James. *Nimble Believing: Dickinson and the Unknown*. Ann Arbor: U of Michigan P, 2000.

Miller, Cristanne. *Emily Dickinson: A Poet's Grammar*. Cambridge, MA: Harvard UP, 1987.

Pearce, Roy Harvey. "Whitman Justified: The Poet in 1860." *Modern Critical Views: Walt Whitman*. Ed. Harold Bloom. New York: Chelsea House, 1985. 65-86.

Porter, David. *Dickinson: The Modern Idiom*. Cambridge, MA: Harvard UP, 1981.

St. Armand, Barton Levi. *Emily Dickinson and Her Culture: The Soul's Society*. Cambridge, MA: Cambridge UP, 1984.

Stonum, Gary Lee. *The Dickinson Sublime*. Madison: U of Wisconsin P, 1990.

Tillinghast, Richard. "An Elegist's New England, A Buddhist's Dante." Rev. of *Old and New Poems* by Donald Hall and *Ten Thousand Things* by Charles Wright. *New York Times* 22 Feb. 1991. Rpt. in *The Point Where All Things Meet: Essays on Charles Wright*. Ed. Tom Andrews. New York: Oberlin College P, 1995. 195-98.

Vendler, Helen. "'A Powerful, Strong Torrent.'" Rev. of *Sea Change* by Jorie Graham. *New York Review of Books* 12 June, 2008: 64-67.

_____. "Travels in Time." Rev. of *Zone Journals* by Charles Wright. *New Republic* 18 Jan. 1988: 34-36. Rpt. in Giannelli. 29-35.

Weisbuch, Robert. *Emily Dickinson's Poetry*. Chicago: U of Chicago P, 1975.

Whitman, Walt. *Leaves of Grass*. Boston: Thayer & Eldridge, 1860. *The Walt Whitman Archive*. Ed. Ed Folsom and Kenneth M. Price. July, 2008. CDRH, U of Nebraska-Lincoln. 1 Sept. 2008. http://www.whitmanarchive.org/published/LG/1860/whole.html.

_____. "Song of Myself." *Leaves of Grass*. 1891-92. *Walt Whitman: Complete Poetry and Collected Prose*. Ed. Justin Kaplan. New York: Library of America, 1982. 188-247.

Wright, Charles. "Interview with Charles Wright." *A Door Ajar: Contemporary Writers And Emily Dickinson*. Thomas Gardner. 95-108.

_____. *Zone Journals*. New York: Farrar, Straus and Giroux, 1988.

Dickinson's Death-Haunted Earthly Paradise

Patrick J. Keane

Patrick J. Keane draws on Dickinson's letters and poems, including "'Nature' is what we see –," "Going to Heaven!," "Some keep the Sabbath going to Church –," and "The Fact that Earth is Heaven –," in his discussion of the poet's "death-haunted earthly paradise." In Dickinson's Romantic vision of the natural world as a "fusion of nature and heaven," Keane explains, her earthly paradise is "all the more beautiful because it is under the shadow of death." Keane finds parallels to the "nature worship" of Wordsworth, Keats, and Emerson in Dickinson's "God immanent rather than transcendent" earthly paradise, which leads to her "audacious, even blasphemous preference for the tangible things of this earth, to be cherished above thoughts of an otherworldly heaven, an abstract place offensive to our nature."

The "problem" for Dickinson, according to Keane, "is that this earth, however 'matchless,' is *not* free of frost and death, so often almost indistinguishable in Dickinson," who, in a dominant motif, links the "fading and freezing-by-frost of her flowers" to the "death of those she cannot waken." Thus Dickinson's "cherishing of a heavenlike earth is sometimes connected with the pain inflicted from above"—from heaven's "marauding Hand," which seems "both a grim reaper and a cruel leveler." And for Dickinson, "if the 'Heavenly Father' who presides over this beautiful but doomed world really *is* 'an Approving God,'" she "seems to care less for him and for a posthumous, perhaps empty heaven than for this earthly paradise—the perishable beauty that must die, everything she wishes *could* 'transcend the "frost" of death.'"   J.B.B.

Emily Dickinson's "awareness" of sure obliteration is reflected in both poems and letters, many of the latter not only accompanied by poems but occasionally themselves poetic. A number of such letters written in the 1850s contextualize the human implications of the death-by-frost of the Flower in "Apparently with no surprise." They also provide examples of Romantic natural supernaturalism. In a letter to Elizabeth Holland, written in August 1856, the human/floral analogy is explicit, with a fortunate exception: "I'm so glad you are not a blossom, for those in my garden fade, and then 'a reaper whose name is Death' has come to get a few to help him make a bouquet for himself." The preceding paragraph assumes the analogy and claims this earth would be Paradise enough were it not for frost and that Grim Reaper. Poet Jack Spicer is hardly alone in remarking how often Dickinson's letters are "experiments in a heightened prose combined with poetry."[1] The passage just referred to begins in modified ballad meter: "If roses had not faded, and frosts had never come and one had not fallen here and there whom I could not awaken, there were no need of other Heaven than the one below, and if God had been here this summer, and seen the things that *I* have seen—I guess he would think His Paradise superfluous" (*L* 329).

The relatively open-minded Christianity of Elizabeth Holland and her husband may have freed Dickinson to confide such thoughts. A few years later, she would put this fusion of nature and heaven, of the physical and spiritual senses, into poetry. What we see, hear, and know is nature: a harmonious heaven whose simplicity is superior to our supposed wisdom:

> "Nature" is what we see –
> The Hill – the Afternoon –
> Squirrel – Eclipse – the Bumble bee –
> Nay – Nature is Heaven –
> Nature is what we hear –
> The Bobolink – the Sea –
> Thunder – the Cricket –
> Nay – Nature is Harmony –
> Nature is what we know –

Yet have no art to say –
So impotent Our Wisdom is
To her Simplicity.

(668)

Dickinson's Romantic vision of an Earthly Paradise, its minute particulars as cherished as its sublime manifestations and all the more beautiful because it is under the shadow of death, is reminiscent of Wordsworth, before he froze over, and of Dickinson's beloved Keats, who never froze over. Keats told a religiously conservative friend that his own "favorite Speculation" was that "we shall enjoy ourselves hereafter by having what we called happiness on Earth repeated in a finer tone, and so repeated."[2] In one of the most beautiful passages ever written by Emily Brontë, Catherine Earnshaw's daughter (the second "Cathy" in *Wuthering Heights*) describes *her* "most perfect idea of heaven's happiness." She would be "rocking" at the heart of the natural world, "in a rustling green tree, with a west wind blowing, and bright, white clouds flitting rapidly above; and not only larks, but throstles, and blackbirds, and linnets, and cuckoos pouring out music on every side, . . . grass undulating in waves to the breeze; and woods and sounding water, and the whole world awake and wild with joy. . . . I wanted all to sparkle and dance, in a golden jubilee."[3]

Such passages explain Dickinson's reverence of "gigantic Emily Brontë" (*L* 721), one of whose poems, a favorite of Emily Dickinson's, was appropriately read at her funeral service. Wonderful as it is, Brontë's description of a naturalized "heaven" or "paradise"—a world in motion, *natura naturans*, in which the speaker actively and joyfully engages in her surroundings is both Keatsian and Wordsworthian. The final gathering (waves, breeze, woods, water, the whole world awake and joyous), especially Cathy's wanting "all to sparkle and dance, in a golden jubilee," unmistakably recalls Wordsworth's (and Dorothy's) "host of golden daffodils, / Beside the lake, beneath the trees, / Fluttering and dancing in the breeze." Those flowers, which outdo "the sparkling waves in glee," comprise "a jocund company" in whose presence a "poet could not but be gay," a joy recalled whenever "They flash upon that inward eye / Which is the bliss of solitude; / And then my heart with pleasure fills, / And dances with the daffodils."[4]

* * *

Had God, like that flower girl Ophelia, "seen the things that I have seen" this summer, Dickinson surmises, he would "think His Paradise superfluous." Emerson claimed that the only thing "certain" about a possible heaven was that it must "tally with what was best in nature, . . . must not be inferior in tone, . . . agreeing with flowers, with tides, and the rising and setting of autumnal stars." "Melodious poets" will be inspired "when once the penetrating key-note of nature and spirit is sounded,—the earth-beat, sea-beat, heart beat, which makes the tune to which the sun rolls, and the globule of blood, and the sap of trees." Like Keats's "a finer tone," Emerson's "not . . . inferior in tone," and his emphasis on keynote, melodiousness, and tune, echoes a text familiar to both Keats and Emerson: Wordsworth's *Excursion* and the Solitary's reference (in book 2) to "Music in a finer tone." Even the later Wordsworth, tamed down and religiously orthodox, never entirely ceased to be a lover "of all that we behold / From this green earth," a poet who found his "Paradise, and groves / Elysian"—provided the human intellect was "wedded to this goodly universe / In love and holy passion"— to be a "simple produce of the common day." Even in revising from a more conservative perspective his account of his early enthusiasm for the French Revolution, he never recanted the desire initially expressed to exercise his skill, "Not in Utopia" or some other ideal place, "Heaven knows where! / But in the very world, which is the world / Of all of us,—the place where, in the end, / We find our happiness, or not at all!"[5]

"Oh Matchless Earth," Emily Dickinson exclaimed in a one-sentence letter, "We underrate the chance to dwell in Thee" (*L* 478). She was borrowing from the "Prologue" to Wordsworth's *Peter Bell*. Having sailed into the heavens in his little boat in the shape of a crescent moon, and described the constellations and planets, the speaker asks rhetorically, "What are they to that tiny grain, / That little Earth of ours?" And so he descends: "Then back to Earth, the dear green Earth . . . See! There she is, the matchless Earth!"[6] Dickinson herself might be "glad" that others believed they were, in the opening exclamation of her early poem, "Going to Heaven!" But, for herself,

> I'm glad I don't believe it
> For it would stop my breath –
> And I'd like to look a little more
> At such a curious Earth!
>
> (79)

There is yet another parallel to Emily Dickinson's thought that "Nature is Heaven," or that heaven would be superfluous, if only our earthly paradise were free of frost and death. In a passage familiar to Wordsworth, Keats, Emerson, *and* Dickinson, Milton's archangel Raphael offers a speculative analogy. Explaining to Adam the mysteries of celestial warfare by likening spiritual to corporeal forms, he adds: "Though what if Earth / Be but the shadow of Heaven, and things therein / Each to the other like, more than on earth is thought?" Apparently reversing Raphael's "therein," Dickinson locates love "*Here*in" and concludes this 1852 letter to "Dear Susie" by taking literally the angel's rhetorical but intriguing question: "But *that* was Heaven—*this* is but Earth, Earth so *like* to heaven that I would hesitate should the true one call away."[7]

In a jocoserious, life-affirming poem looking back to Romantic and Emersonian "nature worship" and ahead to the Wallace Stevens of "Sunday Morning," Dickinson rejects religious ritual, a formal "church," and an otherworldly heaven in favor of an earthly paradise, a God immanent rather than transcendent, and salvation as a daily process rather than a static end state:

> Some keep the Sabbath going to Church –
> I keep it, staying at Home –
> With a Bobolink for a Chorister –
> And an Orchard for a Dome –
>
> Some keep the Sabbath in Surplice –
> I just wear my Wings –
> And instead of rolling the Bell, for Church,
> Our little Sexton – sings.
>
> God preaches, a noted Clergyman –
> And the sermon is never long,
> So instead of getting to Heaven, at last –
> I'm going, all along.
>
> (324)

In an 1863 letter to T. W. Higginson, in which she describes herself as "not reared to prayer," Dickinson pronounces "the 'Supernatural' . . . only the Natural, disclosed" (*L* 423-24). In a poem written that year or the year before (Johnson dates it 1862, Franklin 1863), dawn and noon seem symbols of what she *calls* "Heaven." The skepticism implicit in the setting of *Heaven* in quotation marks seems confirmed in the final two stanzas:

> The Rapture of a finished Day –
> Returning to the West –
> All these – remind us of the place
> That Men call "Paradise" –

Itself be fairer – we suppose –
But how Ourself, shall be
Adorned, for a Superior Grace –
Not yet, our eyes can see –
(575)

In two letters of 1873, Dickinson subverts Paul's text ("For this corruptible must put on incorruption, and this mortal must put on immortality") about the dead being raised and changed as a consequence of Christ's Resurrection (1 Cor. 15:52-53). In the first letter (April 1873), she pronounces the novelist George Eliot (revealed by the *Springfield Republican* in 1859 to be a woman, Marian Evans) a "mortal" who "has already put on immortality," adding that "the mysteries of human nature surpass the 'mysteries of redemption,' for the infinite we only suppose, while we see the finite" (*L* 506). Later that year, in a letter to Elizabeth Holland, she notes that her sister Lavinia, just back from a visit to the Hollands, had said her hosts "dwell in paradise." Emily declares: "I have never believed the latter to be a supernatural site"; instead, "Eden, always eligible," is present in the intimacy of "Meadows" and the noonday "Sun." If, as Blake said, "Everything that lives is holy," it is a this-worldly truth of which believers like her sister and father are cheated: "While the Clergyman tells Father and Vinnie that 'this Corruptible shall put on Incorruption'—it has already done so and they go defrauded" (*L* 508).

Paul, the perpetrator of the "fraud," insists, most dramatically in 1 Corinthians 15, that the resurrection of Jesus heralds the imminent coming of the imperishable Kingdom of God in which pain and suffering will be no more and death will be swallowed up in victory (1 Cor. 15:54-55). For Emily Dickinson, paradise remains an earthly rather than a "supernatural site." In a notably legalistic affirmation of earth, included in an 1877 letter to a lawyer, her increasingly skeptical brother Austin, she goes even further:

The Fact that Earth is Heaven –
Whether Heaven is Heaven or not
If not an Affidavit
Of that specific Spot
Not only must confirm us
That it is not for us
But that it would affront us
To dwell in such a place –

(1408)

Wallace Stevens, who imagines his female persona asking if she shall not "find in comforts of the sun," in any "balm or beauty of the earth / Things to be cherished like the thought of heaven?" insists elsewhere that "poetry / Exceeding music must take the place / Of empty heaven and its hymns"; that we must live in "a physical world," the very air "swarming" with the "metaphysical changes that occur, / Merely in living as and where we live."[8] Stevens seems to be recalling Wordsworth, Emerson, and Nietzsche; he might as well have been thinking of Emily Dickinson and her audacious, even blasphemous preference for the tangible things of this earth, to be cherished above thoughts of an otherworldly heaven, an abstract place offensive to our nature. Dickinson never accepted the Death of God, which is the Nietzschean premise for Zarathustra's imperative that, instead, we must love, and remain faithful to, the earth. Still, when she was only fifteen, Emily confided in her friend Abiah Root that the main reason she was "continually putting off becoming a Christian," despite the "aching void in my heart," was her inability to conceive of an existence beyond this earth as anything but horrible: "Does not Eternity appear dreadful to you? . . . it seems so dark to me that I almost wish there was no Eternity" (*L* 27, 28). Two years later she told Abby that, while she regretted that she did not seize a past opportunity to "give up and become a Christian," she won't: "it is hard for me to give up the world" (*L* 67).

The problem, of course, is that this earth, however "matchless," is *not* free of frost and death, so often almost indistinguishable in Dickinson. The invasive force in her Earthly Paradise was less the worm than the frost. The link between the fading and freezing-by-frost of her flowers on the one hand, and the death of those she cannot waken on the other, becomes a dominant motif. Her cherishing of a heavenlike earth is sometimes connected with the pain inflicted from above. In one poem, while noting the "firmest proof" of "Heaven above," she significantly adds, "Except for its marauding Hand / It had been heaven below" (1205). In another letter to Elizabeth Holland and her husband, heaven's "marauding Hand" seems both a grim reaper and a cruel leveler. Writing during autumn 1858, when an epidemic of typhoid fever had struck Amherst, she cries out, not in concluding but in opening the letter: "Good-night! I can't stay any longer in a world of death. Austin is ill of fever. I buried my garden last week—our man, Dick, lost a little girl through scarlet fever. . . . Ah! Democratic Death! Grasping the proudest zinnia from my purple garden,—then deep to his bosom calling the serf's child" (*L* 341).

This letter has become controversial. The admittedly jarring reference to the "*serf's* child," which happens to be not only "politically" but factually incorrect, has been described as insensitive, shocking, an indication of casual snobbishness at best and class-conscious callousness at worst, compounded by her "equating 'the serf's child' with her frost-killed flowers."[9] We may be reminded of Virginia Woolf's Clarissa Dalloway, who imagines people saying of her, "she cared much more for her roses than for" such human but distant "victims of cruelty and injustice" as those who perished in the Armenian genocide. But the best response, it seems to me, is that by Judith Farr. After acknowledging the "insensitivity it projects," she reminds us that "Austin's [serious] illness and the coming of winter are also equated" in the letter. She then makes her central point, one I have been making all along in regard to "Apparently with no surprise," and make again in the Appendix, discussing Derek Mahon's humanizing of a colony of neglected mushrooms in an extraordinarily empathetic poem expressing precisely what Farr calls the "communion and equality of all living forms":

> To begin with, it is simply the case that Emily Dickinson loved flowers quite as much and as if they were human; her implicit comparison was . . . not intended to diminish the "little girl," as she is rather tenderly called. . . . With the cadences of Ecclesiastes and the Elizabethans always vivid in her ear, it was only natural that Dickinson should express the communion and equality of all living forms in death. Indeed, her letter's zinnia and child commingling in Death's grasp calls up such lines as *Cymbeline*'s "Golden Lads, and Girles all must, / As Chimney-sweepers come to dust." . . . Not snobbery, but the power of the aesthetic impulse to which she was subject is chiefly manifested in Dickinson's much-discussed letter.[10]

I would add only that Dickinson's equation, not limited to the influence of Ecclesiastes and Shakespeare, also had Romantic auspices: Between Death's "grasp" on a proud flower in her royally purple garden and the death of the little child of a servant there is no more gap than we find in "Threnody," Emerson's elegy for *his* little boy, Waldo. Also a victim of scarlet fever, dead at the age of five, that "hyacinthine boy" and "budding man" was never to blossom, though his father prepares for him, in the conclusion of the elegy, an appropriate heaven: not "adamant . . . stark and cold," but a rather Wordsworthian or Keatsian "nest of bending reeds, / Flowering grass and scented weeds" ("Threnody," lines 15, 26, 272-75).

A less discussed but similar letter to Elizabeth Holland, whose child had suffered a crippling injury, is, as we have seen, mentioned, and dismissed, by Charles Anderson in connection with "Apparently with no surprise." Dickinson had commented that "to assault so minute a creature seems to me malign, unworthy of Nature—but the frost is no respecter of persons." In other letters, starting in the 1850s, Dickinson assumes this floral/frost/human analogue, making explicit what is implicit in "Apparently with no surprise": namely, her pervasive connection of flowers and frost with human life and death—and, at times, a vision of transcendence for believers, the hope of spiritual resurrection.

Even when "the frost has been severe," killing off flowers and plants that try in vain "to shield them from the chilly north-east wind," there can be an imperishable garden. I am quoting from a touching letter of October 1851, anticipating the arrival of Austin. She had "tried to delay the frosts," detaining the "fading flowers" until he came. But the flowers, like the poor "bewildered" flies trying to warm themselves in the kitchen, "do not understand that there are no summer mornings remaining to them and to me." But no matter the effect on her flowers and plants of the severe frost brought by the "chilly north-east wind," she can offer her brother "another" garden impervious to frost.

The theme kindles her prose into poetry, minus the line breaks (in fact, this portion of the letter is printed by Johnson as a poem, his number 2). She offers a bright, ever-green garden, "where not a frost has been, in its unfading flowers I hear the bright bee hum; prithee, my Brother, into *my* garden come!" (*L* 149). As Judith Farr remarks, such a garden—which "could never exist, except in metaphor"—is "the garden of herself: her imagination, her love, each of which, she says, will outlast time." As much as any poem in her canon, this early letter-poem, probably written when Dickinson was twenty-one, "discloses the rapt identification she made between herself, her creativity, and her flowers." The passage describing her brighter garden "instinctively focuses on the garden of her mind, with its loving thoughts that transcend the 'frost' of death."[11]

In a remarkably similar letter, written a third of a century later, there is, at least for her beloved brother, an autumnal harbinger of a spiritual as well as a natural spring to come. In this late letter of autumn 1884, the same year she wrote "Apparently with no surprise," she tells a family friend, Maria Whitney:

Changelessness is Nature's change. The plants went into camp last night, their tender armor insufficient for the crafty nights.

That is one of the parting acts of the year, and has an emerald pathos—and Austin hangs bouquets of corn in the piazza's ceiling, also an omen, for Austin believes.

The golden bowl breaks soundlessly, but it will not be whole again till another year. (*L* 848)

Anthropomorphizing (as in the 1851 letter, where the flowers try to shield "them[selves]" from the autumn wind), she presents the "tender armor" of her plants as inadequate to protect them against the autumnal frost. So, alert to their needs, she brings them indoors, into the "camp" of her conservatory. She ends by quoting the admonition from Ecclesiastes, that we are to remember God *before* the body disintegrates, before "the silver cord be loosed or the golden bowl be broken" (12:6). But Emily differentiates herself from her brother Austin, a closet skeptic who, for the purposes of this letter, "believes"—has faith, that is, not only in the seasonal rebirth of corn from seeds but also in the spiritual resurrection of the body. His sister confines her hope to a *natural* spring; *her* "golden bowl" will "not be whole again till another year."

Two of her most beautiful, and most Keatsian, poems mark her major seasonal transition, from summer to autumn. In "As imperceptibly as Grief," summer has "lapsed away," a beloved season that can't quite be accused of "Perfidy" since she was always a "Guest, that would be gone." The poem ends with summer having "made her light escape / Into the Beautiful," a Platonic realm beyond us, leaving behind only the cherished memory (1540). In "Further in Summer than the Birds," which has been described as "her finest poem on the theme of the year going down to death and the relation of this to a belief in immortality,"[12] Dickinson employs liturgical language to commemorate, as in Keats's "To Autumn," the insects' dirge for the dying year. "Pathetic from the Grass," that "minor Nation celebrates / Its unobtrusive Mass," the barely noticeable requiem nevertheless "Enlarging Loneliness."

The music of the crickets, coming later in summer than the song of the birds, is a "spectral Canticle." Their hymn typifies—in the transition from summer to autumn, with "August burning low"—the winter sleep to come, a "Repose" perhaps implying eternal rest on another level. In the final stanza, Christian and Hebraic vocabulary yields to pagan. At this moment of seasonal transition, there is, "as yet," no "Furrow on the Glow" of sunlit, burning August, "Yet a Druidic difference / Enhances Nature now" (1068).

That final religious image, whether we take the Druidic reference as stressing primarily the sacrificial or the animistic element in Celtic nature worship, powerfully reinforces Dickinson's *own* reverence for Nature, its beauty enriched and intensified less, perhaps, by what Anderson calls a "belief in immortality" than—again, as in the ode "To Autumn"—by time's evanescence and the pathos of mutability, the deeply moving contrast between seasonal return and human transience. That transience extends to all animal life. This poem, written in late 1865 or early 1866, was enclosed in a laconic January 1866 note to Higginson, with whom she had not corresponded for eighteen months. Referring to her beloved dog and constant companion, Emily Dickinson restricted herself to a single statement, and a wry question, less pleading than ironic, perhaps bitter: "Carlo died. . . . Would you instruct me now?" (*L* 449).

* * *

Though of course haunted by the thought of immortality, Dickinson was also dubious. In an 1858 letter to Samuel Bowles, she adopts an ironic, pretension-mocking tone. Distinguishing between nature and "us," she at once anticipates and deflates modern "species chauvinism," wondering, tongue in cheek, how it is that we mere humans, described by her pastor as a "worm," should also be the very species singled out for a majestic and special end, a resurrection allegedly obviating any need for mourning, including mourning the death of what would seem to be paradise enough for us: summer with its cherished fields, its bumblebees and birds:

Summer stopped since you were here. Nobody noticed her—that is, no men and women. Doubtless, the fields are rent by petite anguish, and "mourners go about" [Eccles. 12:5] the Woods. But this is not for us. Business enough indeed, our stately Resurrection! A special Courtesy, I judge, from what the Clergy say! To the "natural man," Bumblebees would seem an improvement, and a spicing of Birds, but far be it from me, to impugn such majestic tastes! Our pastor says we are a "Worm." How is that reconciled? "Vain, sinful Worm" is possibly of another species. (*L* 338-39)

By this time, the 1730s thunderings of Jonathan Edwards against the moral ills of New England's sinners in the hands of an angry God had lost some of their resonance, even in Calvinist Amherst. But in his debasement of man as a "worm," Dickinson's pastor may (the trope is hardly restricted to Edwards) have been echoing the great Puritan's description of man as "a little, wretched, despicable creature; a worm, a mere nothing, and less than nothing; a vile insect that has risen up in contempt against the majesty of Heaven and earth." Edwards himself—whose "Martial Hand" of "Conscience" threatens "wincing" sinners with hellfire, the "Phosphorus of God" (1598)—was echoing Bildad, the second of Job's false comforters. From the outset, he had advised the innocent sufferer to abase himself. In his final discourse, Bildad wonders if it is even *possible* for man to "be righteous before God." To this fear-instilling God of "dominion," even the moon and stars are unclean; "how much less man, that is a worm? and the son of man, which is a worm!"[13] How is that abject status reconcilable with our potential for "stately resurrection"?

Man's biblical genesis itself seemed to put that glorious end in doubt, even before the Fall. Prior to ejecting guilty Adam and Eve from Eden, the "Lord God" tells them, "dust thou art, and unto dust shalt thou return" (Gen 3:19). For Hamlet, man is "the paragon of animals . . . , how like a god," and yet, to him, "what is this quintessence of dust?" (2.2.305-7). Wordsworth, in the opening book of *The Prelude*, "reconciles" the contradiction between "discordant elements." In the 1805 version, the passage had begun, "The mind of man is framed even like the breath / And harmony of music" (1.351-53). The 1850 version reflects the poet's movement from celebrations of the human *mind* to triumphs of the deathless *spirit* over its abject origin: "*Dust* as we are, the *immortal Spirit* grows / Like harmony in music" (1.340-41; italics added).

Emily Dickinson can engage this tension in the grand tradition, observing that "Death is a Dialogue between / The Spirit and the Dust," with Spirit triumphant, "Just laying off for evidence / An Overcoat of Clay" (976). But she takes a different tack in a couplet-poem she opens by ironically addressing God as "Heavenly Father":

> "Heavenly Father" – take to thee
> The supreme iniquity
> Fashioned by thy candid Hand
> In a moment contraband –
> Though to trust us – seem to us
> More respectful – "We are Dust" –
> We apologize to thee
> For thine own Duplicity –
>
> > (1461)

So much for Bildad-like groveling! Like the image of the *worm*, that of *dust* reflects the Calvinist estimate of human worthlessness. But here the "worm" turns, with the "sinful" creature finding fault with the Creator. Despite his seeming straightforwardness, God committed a dubious act (an inconsistency emphasized by the alliterated *candid* and *contraband*). In fashioning us as he did, he set up, between dust and immortal spirit, not so much a creative tension as a radical contradiction. He thus stands accused of double-dealing, and any "apology" we make to so duplicitous a God will be less an acknowledgment of our own guilt, or a seeking of pardon, than a self-justifying defense—an *apologia* in the form of *j'accuse* directed against a divine adversary. That vindictive God himself supplied the right word. "For I the Lord thy God am a jealous God, visiting the *iniquity* of the fathers upon the children" (Exod. 20:5). Dickinson, who often relishes the role of lawyer for the plaintiff when it comes to amassing evidence against God's providence, has the children of Dust visit the charge of injustice upon an anything-but-paternal Heavenly Father, accusing him—blasphemously, though appropriately, given his supreme power—of "the *supreme* iniquity."

Our apology to God for his "own Duplicity" allies the poem with the most blasphemous of Omar Khayyám's quatrains addressed to God, at least as adapted by Edward Fitzgerald in a translation the Victorian world accepted with a shock of recognition:

> Oh Thou, who Man of baser Earth didst make,
> And ev'n with Paradise devise the Snake:
> For all the sin wherewith the face of Man
> Is blackened—Man's forgiveness give—and take!

The work of such writers as Carlyle, Tennyson, and Arnold and, later, Hardy and Housman, all responding in their different ways to Darwinian and other scientific and rationalist challenges to religious belief (including biblical Higher Criticism), places an imprimatur on the judgment that Fitzgerald's version of the *Rubáiyát* "reads like the latest and freshest expression of the perplexity and of the doubt of the generation to which we ourselves belong." That acute observation was made, however, not by a British Victorian but by an American—the scholar and man of letters Charles Eliot Norton, writing in 1869, a decade before Dickinson wrote "'Heavenly Father' – take to thee."

Not only the "doubt," but the "perplexity" as well, is reflected in Dickinson's poem, for the syntax of her opening lines suggests petition even more than protest. James McIntosh, identifying "humankind" as "the supreme iniquity," takes these lines to mean: "Father, take humans, who are the supreme iniquity, to thee." Perhaps; but what, then, of the poem's ironic final lines in which, as Jane Donahue Eberwein has said, a duplicitous "God rather than man is to blame for the natural finitude that prevents man from satisfying his creator"?[14] My own reading is closer to Eberwein's than to McIntosh's, and closer still to that of Magdalena Zapedowska, who believes that, in this poem, Dickinson focuses not on the Fall as original sin,

> but on the subsequent expulsion from Paradise, which she blasphemously construes as the original wrong done to humankind by a God who first offered people happiness, then distrustfully put them to the test, and finally doomed them to suffering. Undermining the dogma of God's benevolence, Dickinson contemplates the terrifying possibility that the metaphysical order is different from Calvinist teaching and that the human individual is left wholly to him/herself, unable to rely on the hostile Deity against the chaos of the universe.[15]

* * *

For all our immortal longings, we are haunted, and angered, by the death implicit in our originating dust—in the case of Emily Dickinson, what Byron called "fiery dust." And if the "Heavenly Father" who presides over this beautiful but doomed world really *is* "an Approving God," Dickinson seems to care less for him and for a posthumous, perhaps empty heaven than for this earthly paradise—the perishable beauty that must die, everything she wishes *could* "transcend the 'frost' of death." When she *does* project an earthly eternity, it is, characteristically, in the form of a blossoming season. "No fear of frost to come" would "Haunt the perennial bloom – / But certain June!" (195).

From *Emily Dickinson's Approving God: Divine Design and the Problem of Suffering* (2008), pp. 144-159. Copyright © 2008 by The Curators of the University of Missouri. Reprinted with permission of the University of Missouri Press.

Notes

L (cited parenthetically) refers to *The Letters of Emily Dickinson*, ed. Thomas H. Johnson and Theodora Ward, 3 vols. (Harvard University Press, 1958). Dickinson's poems are cited throughout (parenthetically) by poem rather than page number as numbered in Thomas H. Johnson's *Poems of Emily Dickinson* (Harvard University Press, 1955) and in *Complete Poems of Emily Dickinson* (Little, Brown and Company, 1957, and often reprinted).

1. *The House That Jack Built*, 234.

2. Keats was writing to a pious friend, Benjamin Bailey. *Letters of John Keats*, 1:184-86.

3. *Wuthering Heights*, 198-99.

4. The Brontë poem ("Last Lines," also known as "No Coward Soul was Mine") celebrates the "God within my breast" but dismisses as "vain" the "thousand creeds," all "worthless as wither'd weeds, / Or idlest froth." Brontë's God seems doubly Romantic, fusing Coleridge on the poetic imagination (which "dissolves, diffuses, dissipates, in order to recreate") with a Shelleyan fluidity: "With wide-embracing love / Thy spirit animates eternal years, / Pervades and broods above, / Changes, sustains, dissolves, creates, and rears." Wordsworth's most famous flower-poem, "I wandered lonely as a cloud," is almost as much the work of his sister (a journal entry of Dorothy provided the seed) and of his wife. In fact Mary contributed the poem's most "Wordsworthian" lines: "They flash upon that inward eye / Which is the bliss of solitude."

5. See *The Excursion* 2:710; "Tintern Abbey," lines 104-5; the "Prospectus" to *The Recluse*, lines 43-55; and *The Prelude* 11:140-44. Emerson is quoted from his Swedenborg essay in *Representative Men* (*Emerson: Essays and Lectures*, 686-87).

6. *Peter Bell*, lines 49-56. The poem has often been ridiculed—even by Wordsworth's admirers, including Emerson, who despised it, and Shelley, who parodied it. In an interview (reprinted in the *Chicago Tribune*, January 10, 1874), in which Emerson repeated his favorite bon mot about Wordsworth (that in his inspired writing of the Intimations Ode "a way was made through the void by this finer Columbus"), he added, "Wordsworth is *the* great English poet, in spite of Peter Bell." More famously, Shelley mocked the nature lover's sexual timidity in the poem: "He touched the hem of Nature's shift, / Felt faint—and never dared uplift / The closest, all-concealing tunic" ("Peter Bell the Third," lines 314-17, in *Shelley's Poetry and Prose*, 335).

7. L 195; italics in original. The editors do not catch the Miltonic echo (*Paradise Lost* 5.573-76). Whatever his archangel thought, Milton himself seemed open to the idea of heaven as a projection of earthly happiness. In his fusion of the Classical and the Christian in "Lycidas," he leaves us free to imagine the risen man as either "saint" in heaven or the "genius of the shore," drowned but now, through the power "of him that walked the waves," mounted to a place "Where *other groves* and *other streams* along, / With nectar pure his oozy locks he laves" (172-75; italics added).

8. Stevens, "Sunday Morning" (19-22); "The Man with the Blue Guitar," section 5; "Esthetique du Mal," section 15. Compare Wordsworth's "Prospectus" to *The Recluse* (42-55) and much of Emerson's *Nature*.

---

9. Habegger, *My Wars Are Laid Away in Books*, 363. With only slightly more justi-fication than critics who have attacked Wordsworth for omitting from "Tintern Abbey" any details about upstream pollution in the River Wye, Domhnall Mitchell is disturbed that Dickinson's letter reveals her insensitivity to "poor standards of health and hous-ing," which she could hardly have known at the time contributed to the ravages of fe-ver. The title of Mitchell's paper—"A Little Taste, Time, and Means"—indicates his emphasis on Dickinson's leisured elitism.

10. Farr, *Gardens of Emily Dickinson*, 126-27. Virginia Woolf, *Mrs. Dalloway*, 88.

11. Farr, *Gardens of Emily Dickinson*, 56.

12. Anderson, *Emily Dickinson's Poetry*, 169.

13. Job 25:2-6. Edwards, *The Justice of God in the Damnation of Sinners* (1734), "Application," pt. I, p. 2.

14. McIntosh, *Nimble Believing*, 47; and in correspondence, January 16, 2008; Eberwein, *Dickinson: Strategies of Limitation*, 82.

15. Zapedowska, "Wrestling with Silence," 385. Dickinson's poem would have found favor with another major American writer. In a late notebook (June-July 1896), Mark Twain proposed a deity to "take the place of the present one." Twain's "im-proved" God "would recognize in himself the Author & Inventor of Sin, & Author & Inventor of the vehicle for its commission; & would place the whole responsibility where it would of right belong: upon Himself, the only Sinner" (quoted in Ray B. Browne, *Mark Twain's Quarrel with Heaven*, 13).

Works Cited

Anderson, Charles R. *Emily Dickinson's Poetry: Stairway to Surprise*. Garden City, N.Y.: Doubleday Anchor, 1966.

Brontë, Emily. *The Complete Poems of Emily Jane Brontë*. Edited by C. W. Hat-field. New York: Columbia University Press, 1941.

_____. *Wuthering Heights*. New York: Norton, 1972.

Browne, Ray B. *Mark Twain's Quarrel with Heaven*. New York: College and Uni-versity Press, 1970.

Eberwein, Jane Donahue. *Dickinson: Strategies of Limitation*. Amherst: University of Massachusetts Press, 1985.

Edwards, Jonathan. *The Justice of God in the Damnation of Sinners*. 1734. Cornwall: Meadow Books, 2007.

Emerson, Ralph Waldo. *Emerson: Essays and Lectures*. Edited by Joel Porte. New York: Library of America, 1983.

_____. "Threnody." In *Emerson: Collected Poems and Translations*, ed. Harold Bloom and Paul Kane. New York: Library of America, 1994.

Farr, Judith. *The Gardens of Emily Dickinson*. Cambridge: Harvard Unversity Press, 2004.

Habegger, Alfred. *My Wars Are Laid Away in Books: The Life of Emily Dickinson*. New York: Random House, 2001.

Keats, John. *Letters of John Keats*. 2 vols. Edited by Hyder E. Rollins. Cambridge: Harvard University Press, 1958.

———. *The Poems of John Keats*. Edited by Jack Stillinger. Cambridge: Harvard University Press, 1978.

McIntosh, James. *Nimble Believing: Dickinson and the Unknown*. Ann Arbor: University of Michigan Press, 2004.

Milton, John. "Lycidas." In *The Portable Milton*, ed. Douglas Bush, 107-13. New York: Viking Press, 1949.

———. *Paradise Lost*. Edited by Alastair Fowler. London: Longman, 1968.

Mitchell, Domhnall. "A Little Taste, Time, and Means: Dickinson and Flowers." In *Emily Dickinson: Monarch of Perception*, 112-53. Amherst: University of Massachusetts Press, 2000.

Shelley, Percy Bysshe. *Shelley's Poetry and Prose*. Edited by Donald H. Reiman and Sharon B. Powers. New York: Norton, 1977.

Spicer, Jack. *The House That Jack Built*. Edited by Peter Gizzo. Middletown, Conn.: Wesleyan University Press, 1998.

Stevens, Wallace. *Collected Poems*. New York: Knopf, 1965.

Woolf, Virginia. *Mrs. Dalloway*. 1925. Reprint, London: Wordsworth Classics, 1996.

Wordsworth, William. *The Poems*. Edited by John O. Hayden. 2 vols. New Haven: Yale University Press, 1981.

———. *The Prelude, 1799, 1805, 1850*. Edited by Jonathan Wordsworth, M. H. Abrams, and Stephen Gill. New York: Norton, 1979.

Zapedowska, Magdalena. "Wrestling with Silence: Emily Dickinson's Calvinist God." *American Transcendental Quarterly* (March 1, 2006): 379-98.

"Often seen – but seldom felt":
Emily Dickinson's Reluctant
Ecology of Place _____

Christine Gerhardt

Arguing for the value of ecocriticism in an analysis of Emily Dickinson's poetic explorations of place, Christine Gerhardt explores the
connections between Dickinson's verse and mid-nineteenth-century
environmental debates and proto-ecological writings. "An ecocritical
analysis," writes Gerhardt, "underscores that Dickinson's poetry, for
all its elusiveness and supreme mastery of metaphor, also perceives
human-nonhuman relationships as specific to particular locations,"
and it also reveals that Dickinson's "chief concerns with language
and the Self are related to an *ecologically* suggestive attentiveness
to natural places."

Regarding "Four Trees – opon a solitary Acre –," in which nature is
typically read as a sign of the speaker's inner state, Gerhardt argues
instead that the scene described in the poem, when read from a
green perspective, is not only attentive to place but also can be read
as a "uniquely suggestive version of an ecosystem" because of the
way that it echoes the mid-nineteenth-century proto-ecological view
of nature's complexly intricate relationships. In "The Robin's my Criterion for Tune –," Dickinson, evoking the bioregional and environmental concept of living-in-place, expresses a sense of connection with
the regional New England landscape; and even in some of her cosmic
poems, such as "Perhaps I asked too large –," she reaffirms her relationship to the local and natural environment and, taking an ethical
stance that continues to be relevant, suggests an interrelationship
between nature's small particulars and its large systems and between past and present natural systems. At the same time, because
of Dickinson's "lingering uncertainty as to how to 'read' nature," her
poetry "displays a reluctant place-centeredness," and this reluctance, in turn, "prevents an inherent sense of place from turning into

self-contained complacency." Thus, for Gerhardt, what makes Dickinson's poetic explorations of the natural landscape "environmentally resonant" is her "prevailing skepticism," which prevents her sense of place from turning into a "one-dimensional, restrictive localism."   J.B.B.

In recent years, the growing recognition of Emily Dickinson's involvement with the world around her has sparked fresh interest in the links between her poetry and nineteenth-century views of nature. Domhnall Mitchell and Judith Farr have shown that Dickinson's love of flowers was part of her time's widespread preoccupation with gardening and horticulture; similarly, as Elizabeth Petrino indicates, her remarkable floral and geographical imagery responded to the period's genuine interest in the "language of flowers"; and Rachel Stein has shown that her work undermined the prevalent notion of nature's subservience as a basis for women's secondary social status. Clearly, Dickinson's "letter to the World" was centrally about "The simple News that Nature told –" (Fr519), and her interest in nature and human-nature relationships intersected in many ways with the multifaceted, often contradictory views of her "Sweet – countrymen –."

The dawning of environmental discourses that reached across the U.S. in the mid-nineteenth century is of crucial importance to understanding Dickinson's poetry about the natural world, yet has so far gone unexplored in Dickinson criticism. Recent work in environmental history underscores the significance of the cultural paradigm shift that occurred when the majority of Americans moved, as Max Oelschlaeger puts it, "from viewing wild nature as merely a valuable resource (as a means to economic ends) and obstacle (wilderness must be conquered for civilization to advance) toward a conception of wilderness as an end in its own right and an endangered species in need of preservation" (4). Starting in the 1840s and '50s more and more people became interested in serious nature study, and recreational natural history brought a heightened awareness of natural systems also and especially to white middle-class women, as Nina Baym has shown; simultaneously, the natural history essay, combining personal narratives of nature appreciation with new scientific insights, became a widely read genre; and public debates about the need to protect vanishing wilderness areas prepared the ground for national parks later in the century. This essay argues that Dickinson's nature poetry intersects in subtle but crucial ways with these early environmental discourses. In writing about place, in particular, her poetry engages with a number of proto-ecological concerns of her day and also anticipates later positions about the possibilities and limitations of human interaction with the natural world—a stance that crystallizes in the peculiar reluctance with which she approaches "Nature in chivalry – / Nature in charity – / Nature in equity –" (Fr10).

Ecocriticism provides an ideally suited conceptual angle from which to examine the links between Dickinson's explorations of place and nineteenth-century environmental debates because the field has a defining interest in how literary constructions of nature are mediated by historically specific parameters, and also because the idea of place lies at the heart of most ecocritical concerns. Lawrence Buell, while warning that to be grounded in place does not guarantee an ecocentric orientation (*The Environmental Imagination* 253), argues that "neither the imagination of environmental endangerment nor [. . .] of environmental well-being can be properly understood without a closer look at how the imagination of place-connectedness itself works" (*Writing for an Endangered World* 56). Such passionate attention to place as an environmental category can add a fresh dimension to debates about Dickinson's slippery horizontal perspectives. While it has often been noted that she had a surprisingly keen eye for capturing local natural phenomena, others, most notably Robert Weisbuch, have long considered "scenelessness," a "lack of 'outer' situations" (18), to be Dickinson's central rhetorical strategy. Jane D. Eberwein's discussion of "Dickinson's Local, Global, and Cosmic Perspectives" concludes that, "for all her awareness of local and global environments, her truest perspective remained more vertical than horizontal, more attuned to speculations on immortality [. . .] than on Amherst, America, or the wider world opened by friendships and reading" (42). An ecocritical analysis underscores that Dickinson's poetry, for all its elusiveness and supreme mastery of metaphor, also perceives human-nonhuman relationships as specific to particular locations. More importantly, it shows that her chief concerns with language and the Self are related to an *ecologically* suggestive attentiveness to natural places at a cultural moment when many of her contemporaries engaged in environmental debates with increasing rigor.

Emily Dickinson, who once wrote, "'My Country, 'tis of thee,' has always meant the Woods – to me –" (L509), spent her entire life in New England, at a time when the area suffered one of the most dramatic ecological transformations in American history. In John Opie's words, "by 1850 Connecticut and Rhode Island had consumed 70 percent of their forests; Massachusetts, 60 percent; Vermont, 55 percent; New Hampshire, 50 percent; and Maine, 25 percent" (65). It was also in her native New England that people began to express a growing ethical concern for the distressed land; according to Richard W. Judd the region "pioneered a number of conservation ideas for the rest of the nation" (5).[1] While being a witness to these changes does not suggest that Dickinson herself developed what we today would call an environmental consciousness (and her letters hardly indicate such a perspective, paralleling her deep but oblique concern with slavery and the Civil War), it is difficult to imagine that she was unaware of the gradual greening of discourses around her. In fact, there are a number of indicators that she was exposed to cultural conversations and publications that centrally participated in this development. If it is true that "only by charting Dickinson's debt to her own time can we truly be sure how she may have anticipated current aesthetic and philosophical concerns" (11), as Barton Levi St. Armand has argued, her culture's shifting environmental perspectives can shed new light on her nature poetry.

First of all, Dickinson's schooling was significantly shaped by Amherst's proximity to Boston and New York as centers of the "new" sciences. A number of these increasingly specialized fields developed insights that formed the basis for the emergence of ecology, first defined by Ernst Häckel in 1866 as "the science of the relations of living organisms to the external world, their habitat, customs, energies, parasites, etc." (Worster 192). When Dickinson famously boasted in an early letter, "I have four studies. They are Mental Philosophy, Geology, Latin, and Botany. How large they sound" (L6), she expressed excitement about two fields that were centrally involved in formulating the era's proto-ecological theories: botany and geology. Her passion for botany, in particular, has been variously noted, since Dickinson was an amateur naturalist with a remarkable herbarium, garden, and conservatory, and a poet who turned botanical terms into stunning metaphors. Yet the role of the field as a forerunner of ecological thinking has so far been overlooked in relation to her poetry. Botany encouraged students like Dickinson to pay detailed attention to their immediate natural surroundings, developed indispensable tools for cataloguing and systematizing plants, and dealt with topics later gathered together as the science of ecology. What botanists discussed under the rubric of plant geography, in particular, included the role of environmental factors in determining geographical distribution.[2] Looking at Almira H. Lincoln's *Familiar Lectures on Botany*, which according to Richard Sewall may have been "one of the most important of [Dickinson's] school books" (351), one finds that it not only stresses the value of observing native wild flowers "in their peculiar situations," but includes sections on the "habitations" and "geographical situation" of plants as well (44, 200-204). The book also repeatedly mentions geographer, meteorologist and botanist Alexander von Humboldt, the major ecologist before Darwin (203-218). Here, the field overlaps with geography, which Donald Worster has shown to be one of ecology's most "indispensable trail-blazers" (193). Dickinson's training in botany, then, brought her in touch with a whole number of proto-ecological discussions, suggesting the possibility of new implications for her poetry's thick layers of natural scenes.

Similar connections open up through Dickinson's familiarity with geology. Nineteenth-century studies of mountains, volcanoes, and fossils added an important historical edge to the era's proto-ecological debates (Worster 138), and the future poet encountered this new science primarily through the works of Edward Hitchcock, who contributed extensively to the wealth of systematic knowledge that would soon converge in ecology as a distinct discipline. His study of fossil tracks in the sandstone of the Connecticut valley brought much-needed sophistication to the discussion of natural phenomena and their relationships in large time frames, while his *Religion of Geology* (1851), with which Dickinson was most certainly familiar, tried to reconcile Biblical and scientific conceptualizations of the earth (Sewall 345). For Hitchcock, chemistry's integrative models contributed to the era's impending proto-ecological insights; Justus von Liebig's studies, in particular, led to the later formulation of a Liebig's Law in ecology. If Hitchcock's geology and astronomy "set her studies in the largest possible frame of reference," it was a framework rich with early ecological connotations (Sewall 354). This is not changed by the fact that many in Amherst's scientific community, and Lincoln and Hitchcock in particular, were still aligning their work with natural theology, using the sciences to reveal the providence of God in ways that, as Nina Baym has recently shown, were doubtful to Dickinson (143).

Apart from the sciences, Dickinson was also familiar with the popular natural history essay, a genre that helped to promote a more widespread informed and ethical relationship with nature. Through *The Atlantic Monthly* she was exposed to an impressive range of naturalist writing, including pieces by Ralph Waldo Emerson, Henry David Thoreau, and Thomas Wentworth Higginson. Barton Levi St. Armand has argued that "[i]t was because of the skillful nature essays published in the *Atlantic* in the years immediately preceding the Civil War [. . .] that Dickinson thought of Higginson as her artistic master" (187). These essays not only played a vital role for her as "a means of inducing reverie or a mood of Transcendental meditation" (St. Armand 188), but also because of their intense orientation toward specific natural phenomena in their larger geographical and historical contexts; as Midori Asahina has recently shown, Higginson's accomplishments as a naturalist played a key role in his correspondence with Dickinson and was crucial for their mutual admiration. From an ecological perspective, one of the genre's achievements lies in directing readers' attention to relationships within natural systems and between humans and specific natural environments, which is also true for Higginson's pieces. His "Water-Lilies" (1858), for example, carefully describes the species' place within the flora and fauna of New England's ponds, and comments on the region's environmental history:

> There stand in its bosom hundreds of submerged trees [. . .]. They are remnants of border wars with the axe [. . .]. [G]radually sinking in their soft ooze, and ready, perhaps, when a score of centuries has piled two more strata of similar remains of mud above them, to furnish foundations for a newer New Orleans [. . .]. The present decline in business is clear revenue to the water-lilies. (466)

"[T]he crucial point about nature writing," writes Thomas Lyon, is "the awakening of perception to an ecological way of seeing" (xiv).[3] Dickinson's familiarity with the genre suggests that she shared in the increasingly environmentally-oriented debates that washed across the U.S. at mid-century, and that her poetic interest in being "aware / Of Neighbors and the Sun" (Fr817) might involve more than mere transcendence.

Finally, Dickinson's reading of journals and newspapers also brought her in touch with early preservationist arguments, which expressed concern over nature's extensive exploitation and formulated an ethics of wilderness protection. In the *Atlantic*, such views were recurrent, ranging from sentimental warnings that, "[t]he birds long retain their tradition of old places, and strive to keep their hold upon them; but we are building them out year by year. [. . .] perhaps the last black duck has quacked on the rivers, and the last whistler taken its final flight" (Cabot 216), and asides on "the gradual disappearance of these venerable trees, which the public should have protected from the profane hands of the timberer" (Flagg 259-260), to Thoreau's explicit call for national preserves "in which the bear and panther, and some even of the hunter race, may still exist, and not be 'civilized off the face of the earth'" (Thoreau, "Chesuncook" 317). The journal also carried a review of George Perkins Marsh's key ecological study *Man and Nature; or, Physical Geography as Modified by Human Action* (1864), which discussed human-nonhuman relationships in explicitly ethical terms and warned that, "man has too long forgotten that the earth was given to him for usufruct alone, not for consumption, still less for profligate waste" (Marsh 134). It was against such a backdrop of increasing awareness of nature's fragility and alarm over its destruction that Dickinson wrote "Who robbed the Woods – / the trusting Woods?" (Fr57), a deceptively simple poem in which moral urgency and child-like ease put considerable pressure on each other, opening spaces for environmental interpretations of the speaker's ambivalent gestures of concern.

Looked at individually, the sometimes subtextual, sometimes more direct expressions of environmental awareness that kept coming up in America's and especially New England's views of "the woods" may seem twice removed from Dickinson's art. Taken together, however, they constitute more than "sweet latent events – too shy to confide –" (L619): they form a context against which the exceptional metaphorical suggestiveness of her nature poetry resounds in new and unexpected ways, especially in an era that was fascinated by a notion of correspondence between mind and world, binding symbolic insights subliminally back to the naturescapes from which they were derived. The oblique resonance with her time's environmental debates surfaces in the tension between her commitment to place and her simultaneous expression of doubt and reluctance vis-à-vis the natural world and our human capacity to relate to it.

A poem whose ambiguous engagement with the local might well constitute one of Dickinson's most ecologically sensitive contemplations of human-nonhuman relationships in particular places is "Four Trees – opon a solitary Acre" (Fr778), probably written in late 1863:

> Four Trees – opon a solitary Acre –
> Without Design
> Or Order, or Apparent Action –
> Maintain –
>
> The Sun – opon a Morning meets them –
> The Wind –
> No nearer Neighbor – have they –
> But God –
>
> The Acre gives them – Place –
> They – Him – Attention of Passer by –
> Of Shadow, or of Squirrel, haply –
> Or Boy –
>
> What Deed is Their's unto the General Nature –
> What Plan
> They severally – retard – or further –
> Unknown –

So far, the poem has been read mainly as an expression of Dickinson's sense of isolation caused by the perceived absence of nature's divine order, and as an example of linguistic fragmentation that displays the poet's inner chaos.[4] Taking a different angle, Christopher Benfey has discussed the formal placement of periods, colons, dashes, trees and human beings in the poem (115), while Rachel Stein has argued that the speaker boldly revises traditional views of nature, order, and gender (33-34). What all of these interpretations share is a primary concern with the poem's metaphorical and formal connotations in ways that remain unrelated to the evolving environmental debates of the mid-century. Yet if one looks at the poem's natural phenomena as more than emblems of the speaker's spiritual, emotional, or intellectual disposition, a different interpretation becomes possible.

First of all, "Four Trees" emerges as rooted in a specific locale, as having a place whose physical presence matters in the poem's multilayered landscape. The speaker is inspired in classic Emersonian fashion by a natural scene that catches her eye, yet rather than moving through place as a lesser aspect of poetic concern, her perspective remains grounded in geography. The trees on the acre "maintain" her attention through all four stanzas, and as she grapples with the details of what she sees, she never arrives at a conclusion that would take her fully beyond or out of the scene's immediacy, even as she ponders the neighborly presence of God and "General Nature." Douglas Anderson has argued that Dickinson was committed "to the mutable world" (207) only as a sphere where transcendence could be experienced, and that in "Four Trees," "her subject seems, merely, place" but actually is "a nearness to tremendousness" (222). While Dickinson certainly negotiates the two, place has more weight in this poem than has previously been acknowledged. The poem's "attention" to place, which it not only mentions but performs, turns place from a stepping stone for transcendence into a subject in its own right. As geographer Yi-Fu Tuan has argued, "place is whatever stable object catches our attention. As we look at a panoramic scene our eyes pause at points of interest. Each pause is time enough to create an image of place" (*Space and Place* 161).

More specifically, "Four Trees" can be read as part of Dickinson's larger New England project, a meditation on one of those typical "fields of stubble," which, as she phrased it in a later poem, are "often seen – but seldom felt, / On our New England Farms –" (Fr1419). Just like this other composition about a serene field, "Four Trees" registers New England's unpretentious, stark beauty and participates in mapping its cultural *and* natural geographies, even without clarifying the trees' species or the acre's exact location. The poem's genericism does not mean that it cannot resonate in relation to a regional landscape; as Buell remarked in a different context, "the generic quality of such images does not mean they lack 'thereness,'" rather they constitute "a form of readily recognizable spatialized experience, so recognizable as to be taken for granted" (*Writing for an Endangered World* 26). Many of the nature essays published in New England magazines described the region's birds, trees, farms and ponds without giving their exact location or identity. Similarly, Dickinson's thoroughly familiar scene does not require any further specifications to render it complete, making the poem a perfect example not of placelessness, but of Leonard Lutwack's observation that, "the imagination may thrive on the most meager materials to make a place meaningful" (33). Similar to nineteenth-century naturalist prose, her lines pay attention to a seemingly unspectacular landscape that exists on its own terms and has a right to continued existence—which is in itself a crucial prerequisite for environmental awareness in the broadest sense of the term.

Apart from the poem's sheer attention to nature in a particular place, its speaker takes a close look at the relationships among natural phenomena, betraying an eye for ecologically significant processes. Critics usually emphasize the poem's lack of connection and argue that, in Cynthia Wolff's words, "no thread of commonality holds the contents of this work together—nothing but happenstance seems to justify their inclusion in the same piece of verse" (460); to my knowledge only Cristanne Miller has addressed the interdependence and agency involved in its ambiguous subject-object relations (Miller 255-56). Read from a green perspective, the scene is full of ecologically suggestive relationships: The trees attract various "visitors"—they "meet" the sun, create a shifting shadow on the landscape as the sun travels across the sky, and they provide shelter and presumably also nourishment for the squirrel. As they break up the monotony of the surrounding fields, they turn a cultivated piece of land into a more diverse biotope. The sun provides light and energy, and the wind brings humidity and a different kind of movement and change, while the acre gives all of them "Place." What is more, the links among plants, soil, climate, and animal are not so much indeterminate as they are multiple, since each of the parts is connected with more than one other unit, so that their relationships are surprisingly multidimensional. Especially if one reads the dashes as both disruptive and connective, the poem evokes a complex and dynamic web of relationships, which undermines the initial claim that there is no "design," "order," or "action."

Before ecology took shape as a field of its own, Dickinson's poem takes her time's fascination with "the habitations of plants," "agents which effect the growth of plants," and "their geographical situations" a step further into what soon evolved as the "science" of "relations" Häckel describes (Lincoln 199-204). As it zooms in on a spatially limited constellation that is nonetheless linked to global phenomena and meaning, the poem transforms language into a network of relationships that is both stable and dynamic, where energy flows in multiple directions, and where the role of human beings as both outside observers and part of the picture is critically ambiguous. The scene can even be read as a uniquely suggestive version of an ecosystem. According to Worster, "a model of interrelatedness in nature, [an ecosystem] presents both the biological and non-biological aspects of the environment as one entity, with strong emphasis on measuring the cycling of nutrients and the flow of energy in the system—whether it be a pond, a forest, or the earth as a whole" (378).[5] As such, Dickinson's poem echoes and pushes forward her time's proto-ecological understanding of nature's intricate relationships, turning into poetic language emerging ways of seeing and relating to nature that are still relevant in today's environmental debates. What is even more remarkable than its anticipation of abiding ecological concepts is that the poem avoids precisely those early ecological notions that later turned out to be misleading. In her keen awareness of our limited human understanding and of nature's non-harmonious aspects, Dickinson stops short of evoking a natural (eco-)system that remains in balance as long as it is undisturbed by humans—an idea that was formulated by Dickinson's contemporary George Perkins Marsh and dominated ecology and modern environmentalism for decades, before it came under attack in the 1980s and 1990s for neglecting the possible positive effects of disturbances. If "Four Trees" resembles an ecosystem, it does so in a way that leaves room for change, for disruption, and for the ambiguous role of humans as ethical or destructive agents. In short, the poem's view of the interaction between wind, sun, shadows, acre, trees, and squirrel as occurring in place (rather than as a free-floating idea) corresponds closely to the growing awareness of natural life in particular locales, which was fostered by environmentally sensitive nature essays; its language of reciprocity and interdependence evokes an ecosystem before the term was coined, echoing the era's proto-ecological interest in natural relationships. Moreover, the ways in which it includes the possibility of change and (human) disturbance, and avoids misleading notions of eternal stability, make "Four Trees" ecologically suggestive even from a twenty-first century perspective.

Such a reading does not level out the profound uncertainty with which this poem approaches nature. If one considers the environmental implications of the speaker's relationship to the natural world, the poem's controlling skepticism itself rings with new connotations. Perhaps the emerging web of relationships is already a crucial part of what there is to know about the scene, maybe this is its "plan" and "deed." From such an angle, the speaker's insecurity seems partially ironic because she remains unaware that by simple observation of the most common local natural scene, she may already understand parts of its "design." More importantly, her awareness of her limited insights acknowledges a respectful distance between human and nature, which grants nature a dignified autonomy. Through this tentative take on familiar places, the natural environment assumes a presence that goes beyond its role as a "commodity" for the expanding nation or, for that matter, the observing mind.

There are a number of other poems that express a similar engagement with local environments while acknowledging nature's difference and distance. For example, the little-discussed "From Cocoon forth a Butterfly" (Fr610) juxtaposes the seemingly "Miscellaneous Enterprise" of a butterfly with the daily workings of flora, fauna, and peasants in one area, noting the transience of the scene and the movements of its individual players. Nevertheless the baffled speaker echoes the tone of "Four Trees" and deems the relationships among them "Without Design." Relating to "Four Trees" on a different level, the already mentioned poem pulls an outwardly unremarkable "Field of Stubble" into the center of attention so that this place may for once be imaginatively seen *and* felt. The poem undoes the stated lack of attention concerning a plain working landscape by turning it into New England's signature feature, yet the fact that the speaker offers several possibilities as to what exactly "Is often seen [. . .] / On our New England Farms –" and ends by claiming that it is "seldom felt" simultaneously questions the very attempt to positively "feel" place. In this sense, even "Bloom upon the Mountain – stated – " (Fr787) has hidden but relevant environmental undercurrents. The speaker's inspiration is based on careful observation of natural processes on the surface of a mountain that is both prototypical and can be linked to the hills in the Connecticut valley, and she relates to this ancient, autonomous formation without assuming a position of actual or imaginative control.

In spite of its characteristic elusiveness, then, Dickinson's poetry fosters a non-utilitarian recognition of horizontal natural systems in particular locales, at precisely the time when proto-ecological studies were first beginning to move from the description of individual organisms to the analysis of their complex relationships, and when natural history essays were directing people's attention to the inherent value of seemingly plain common landscapes. Such poems about local naturescapes show her responding to the era's growing interest in seeing and speaking about nature's elements and their intricate relationships in environmentally suggestive ways. Yet what is perhaps most noteworthy about Dickinson's evocation of local ecosystems as living communities is that she keeps questioning the notion of epistemological certainty vis-à-vis familiar landscapes as one of the bases of human presumption. Her poetry's hesitation concerning the "plan" of everyday natural places undercuts the illusion of ultimate human knowledge and control so prevalent at the time, even in the emerging discourses of the proto-ecological sciences and environmental protection.

Apart from evoking environmentally suggestive local landscapes that can be read as dynamic ecosystems, Dickinson also approaches "the woods" on a larger scale, one of them being the region as a space in which people engage with nature in culturally specific ways. In particular, it is by setting seemingly familiar geographies against other, "Remote / Or settled Regions wild –" (Fr1154), that she carves out also the region as a reliable parameter for thinking about nature. This connects with her era's evolving environmental ideas and foreshadows later, more explicitly "green" ideas about living-in-place. In the following poem, the speaker compares her actual ties to regional life in New England to her imaginary relationship to British topographies:

> The Robin's my Criterion for Tune –
> Because I grow – where Robins do –
> But, were I Cuckoo born –
> I'd swear by him –
> The ode familiar – rules the Noon –
> The Buttercup's, my whim for Bloom –
> Because, we're Orchard sprung –
> But, were I Britain born,
> I'd Daisies spurn –
>
> None but the Nut – October fit –
> Because – through dropping it,

The Seasons flit – I'm taught –
Without the Snow's Tableau
Winter, were lie – to me –
Because I see – New Englandly –
The Queen, discerns like me –
Provincially –

(Fr256)

The speaker expresses a sense of belonging by way of metaphorically identifying with a typical New England bird, while Britain serves as the Other to her specific sensibilities. George Monteiro and Barton Levi St. Armand have noted that, "for most readers [seeing 'New Englandly'] has come to mean in the broadest sense that her work should be interpreted in the context of and as part of New England's intellectual, religious, and literary history. But New England also has a social and cultural history, and it is of course only logical that Emily Dickinson should have her own place in that history, albeit an original one" (187). Yet even these approaches leave the question untouched to what degree New England's *natural* history also figures as a context in which this speaker's imagination works, and how this is environmentally relevant.

According to Elizabeth Petrino, "The Robin's my Criterion for Tune –" is a variation on the common nineteenth-century trope of a bird-song that signifies the female poetic voice (*Emily Dickinson and Her Contemporaries* 202). Yet New England denotes more than the speaker's intellectual or literary background. Between the lines, the poem also displays an appreciation of the region's natural phenomena, including such markers as the robin, daisies, buttercups, orchards, nuts, and the region's four distinct seasons, with a particularly prominent, visually dramatic winter. Unlike in many other Dickinson poems, where birds "seem to live in another world," this robin belongs to a certain place, growing in New England the same way plants do, and embodying its distinct beauty (Anderson 119). Indeed, robins began to stay in New England all year long in the mid-nineteenth century, being as characteristic of the region as the buttercup, a flower that thrives in the Northeast's colder climate. Interestingly, birding as a branch of amateur nature studies and bird essays as a subgenre of the natural history essay contributed considerably to the development of a New England sense of place in environmentally sensitive ways—that is, paying attention to the interdependence of regionally specific natural elements whose significance cannot be reduced to the sum of their parts. For instance, an 1858 *Atlantic* essay about New England's birds wonders, "[w]hy should [the crow] give himself so much trouble to subsist here?" and suggests: "The crow, it seems, is not a mere eating and drinking machine, drawn hither and thither by the balance of supply and demand, but has his motives of another sort. It is, perhaps, some *local attachment*" (Cabot 210; italics mine). In Dickinson's poem, the bird and the other species may bolster a political difference, yet their signal presence and the speaker's relationship to them create a subtext in which the region constitutes an actual natural place and where attention to regional landscape matters.

Furthermore, the poem expresses a sense of connectedness and identification with New England's nature that implies an environmentally resonant ethics of an informed and humble life with what regional landscapes have to offer. When the speaker describes herself as physically nourished by the region just as the plants and birds are, growing out of the soil together and linked to them through a collective "we," she does more than echo the era's discourses of plant geography, according to which "every country where man is to be found has its vegetation [and] some species of plants, with respect to localities are confined to narrow limits" (Lincoln 202). The poem suggests that the speaker is an equal member of the region's biotic community, and that New England is defined by interlocking cultural and natural systems. On one level, one could argue that where "Four Trees" has "place," "The Robin" expresses the speaker's "sense of place." As Tuan explains, "[p]eople demonstrate their sense of place when they apply their moral and aesthetic discernment to sites and locations," which not only depends on the ability to see but requires "close contact and long association with the environment" ("Space and Place" 446). On another level, one can also relate the poem to the more explicitly political concept of bioregionalism, an old cultural principle that has been revived by twentieth-century environmentalists. While it is simplistic to label any regionally-oriented text that pays attention to human life in and with natural systems as "bioregional," the concept helps articulate this poem's environmental implications. According to Peter Berg and Raymond F. Dasmann, bioregionalism recognizes a given region as "geographical terrain *and* a terrain of consciousness—[. . .] a place and the ideas that have developed about how to live in that place," it promotes "living-in-place" that seeks "a balance with its region of support through links between human lives, other living things, and the processes of the planet—seasons, weather, water cycles—as revealed by the place itself" (35-36), and it embraces the notion that small is beautiful. Dickinson's poem about the speaker's almost organic connection to familiar natural particulars expresses such a sense of her region's integrity, of reciprocity between humans and nature, and of living in a "small" place, which forgoes an attitude of nature's dominance and appropriation.

The poem's movement between New England and Britain in many ways strengthens this affirmative regionalism and its green implications. The way the speaker keeps distancing herself from Britain emphasizes her ties to her own region and renders the natural vectors of her home more specific: the bird with which she identifies becomes an American Robin, a large thrush not even related to the much smaller European Robin, and the daisy emerges as a common American marguerite, which stands apart from the short-stemmed flower of European origin that is often called the English daisy. Also, the back and forth between New England and Britain creates a momentary equilibrium of region and nation in which the speaker's locale becomes equal in status to the British kingdom: the juxtaposition brings to the fore that

Britain's political elite, too, "discerns provincially," that a foreign place, even if constituted by another country, is always also regional, and that in all places the national is grounded in the regional. Thus Dickinson's poem carries New England's ways of seeing nature beyond its geographical boundaries; or rather, "seeing New Englandly" already implies the need to look beyond the limits of the region without, however, severing the ties. From such a New England perspective the speaker is able to "discern" transatlantic patterns of relating to nature in place, suggesting a kind of global regionalism that is nonetheless based upon living intently in one natural-cultural situation. If this has environmental resonances today, it began to do so in Dickinson's lifetime. In an era when Marsh read regional histories of the local extinction of trees in global comparison and drew critical conclusions for America's environmental politics, and Thoreau discussed the history of British forests before calling for a more sensitive approach to the land in the U.S. ("Chesuncook" 317), an imaginary journey to European regions that involved references to people's ties to the land in different cultural constellations was not environmentally neutral.

The poem's sense of identification with a region's natural environment, however, remains undercut by the recognition that groundedness in place is a matter of chance ("But, were I Britain born"); it is defined by possibly unreliable stories ("I'm taught –") and, to a degree, interchangeable: after all, daisies and buttercups, cuckoo and robin—at least in the name—as well as the snow, all exist in New England and in Britain. Even as the speaker underscores being-in-place as her primary reference ("Because I see – New Englandly –"), apparently prioritizing region over nation, she blurs the lines between the two. From an environmental perspective, the fact that she *doubts* local affiliations even as she confirms them is perhaps the most remarkable aspect of this poem's uneasy place-centeredness. Disrupting the urge for untrammeled authenticity and "pure" native platial belonging, she offers insights into the possibilities of an impassioned nature-centered regionalism that will not lose sight of the worlds beyond the familiar, nor of its own limitations. Again, such a position resonates even with contemporary debates about the drawbacks of a restrictive local environmentalism.

Further examples for this dynamic between familiar and distant regions that only partially confirms the speaker's identification with her own natural environment can be found in some of Dickinson's poems about the wind. In "A South Wind – has a pathos" (Fr883) the speaker's fascination with the "foreignhood" of other places and their "farness" depends on her position in the North, at the New England "landing" where the voices of "Emigrants" make memories of faraway regions almost graspable; it is a culturally and naturally located, "landed" imagination that draws outward yet remains largely in place. Also, in "The Wind didn't come from the Orchard – today –" (Fr494), an uncommon aquatic breeze inspires the speaker to go imaginatively over the nearby fields and forests, recounting, in a sense, her familiarity with "Hay," "Clovers" and "Mowers." Yet in the face of the impending storm she also questions the "natural" position of well-known places ("But the Fir is Where – Declare – / Were you ever there?"), which unsettles her seemingly stable regional position of speaking.

As Dickinson explores the symbolical import of the dynamics between near and far geographies, then, she indirectly also acknowledges the significance of familiar natural environments and of people's sustaining ties to their region, suggesting that the relevance of local worlds can grow by transatlantic comparison. In such instances, her poetry values New England's natural landscapes in conjunction with small-scale, earthly forms of living often associated with regionalism. At a time when the U.S. was deeply enmeshed in the politics of westward expansion and colonialism, both at an immense cost to the land and "other" people's ties to it, such an appreciation of local life grounded in natural systems reassesses the subversive potential of a regionalist perspective in America's national framework, also with regards to its environmental implications. Yet a persistent hesitation regarding the human ability to grasp the parameters of our long-term relationships to familiar environments pulls away from a full embrace of any "green regionalism." In this way, Dickinson manages to use regional attachment to conceptualize human relationships to nature without endorsing flat environmental determinism, and especially without falling into the trap of a retrograde idealization of living in place, both of which can easily crop up in affirmative discourses of place-connectedness and bioregionalism.

Finally, even some of Dickinson's cosmic poems have a way of evoking natural places that binds the imagination back to the land. Viewed against the vastness of the cosmos, the woods' "trinkets" and the speaker's bond with them do not turn into nothingness but remain part of the immeasurable web of interrelated phenomena that she is grappling with. This position is again subtly linked to the emerging environmental discourses of her time. Here is a poem in which the speaker compares common local affiliations to the unbound perspectives of the "Firmaments":

> Perhaps I asked too large –
> I take – no less than skies –
> For Earths, grow thick as
> Berries, in my native Town –
>
> My Basket holds – just – Firmaments –
> Those – dangle easy – on my arm,
> But smaller bundles – Cram.
>
> (Fr358)

On the surface, the speaker seems to pull away from the "small," restrictive landscape of the "native Town," claiming to be interested in nothing but "skies." The "Firmaments," which Wendy Barker has read as "fine philosophy and poetry" (65), are a light burden for her whereas "smaller" issues constitute a heavy, perhaps even oppressive weight; Rachel Stein has argued in a similar vein that the titanic speaker "gath-

ers immensities of nature—'Earths,' 'skies,' 'Firmaments'—and refuses the 'smaller bundles' that would, ironically, 'Cram' her within
the constricted scope of feminine norms" (42). Even though Stein,
too, underscores the poem's movement away from small local context, she addresses the woman poet's engagement with natural elements, emphasizing its liberating import. Taking off from here, further
"green" implications of the apparent renunciation of local naturescapes can be uncovered by considering that, at the time, "cosmic"
views were an integral part of evolving proto-ecological perspectives
that were primarily explored by the more "grounded" sciences of
chemistry or botany.

The poem's appreciation of the cosmic dialectically depends upon
and indirectly reaffirms the relevance of local places. In a geographical
sense, but also regarding the structure of the poem's argument, the native territory constitutes a basis for the speaker's cosmic reach; she
takes "no less than skies" *for*, or because of, these apparently small, local "Earths," which may even have stimulated her interest in other
findings. If one reads these "Earths" as "'Babes in the Wood.' Berries"
(L615), as Dickinson once wrote, the trope retains only a faint echo of
place. Yet according to the contemporary Webster, "Earth, in its primary sense, signifies the particles which compose the mass of the
globe, but more particularly the particles which form the fine mold on
the surface of the globe," referring to the earth under our feet, the land,
soil; simultaneously, "earth" also denotes "the terraqueous globe
which we inhabit."[6] Taking account of these geographical dimensions
adds a double layer of place to the metaphorically suggestive "thick
Earths" in which the speaker's imagination is grounded even as she
pulls away from them.

This cosmic poem's somewhat inverted platial quality intersects
complexly with the speaker's relationship to earthly places. Dickinson
never fully clarifies what exactly the speaker asked for that may have
been "too large." "Perhaps" the "skies" she was after, turning away
from her native environment, are too large—but the opposition be-

tween skies and local "bundles" is destabilized at least partially by the recognition that these "bundles" constitute "thick Earths," implying that entire worlds can be found close to home. Yet perhaps these "native berries" were the objects "too large," which would again suggest not only that the skies are worth aiming for but that equally immense perspectives can open up when one looks at what is nearest. Regardless of the speaker's apparent interest in "skies" rather than "Earths," the poem's unresolved crossover of possibilities grants her relationship to local landscapes a presence that rivals her yearning for the "Firmaments." These realms are not so much exclusive of each other as they remain linked through a perception that can turn both ways, like a telescope, blurring the line between near and far, earthly and otherworldly.

This correlation between the two spheres has interesting environmental implications concerning the period's growing tensions between transcendentalist and new scientific approaches to nature, and regarding the considerable overlaps among different sciences. Botanists, for example, referred to "what Astronomers have proved" not only to confirm the perfect structure of God's creation, but also to emphasize links between the exploration of solar systems and their study of "our own little globe, and [. . .] the matter which exists upon it" as related investigations of complex natural systems (cf. Lincoln 229). Similarly, Edward Hitchcock studied fossils right behind Dickinson's "native Town" to underpin the truth of the Bible, but his geological, geographical, and botanical approach to reading the earth's history from one small place also shed new light on the intersections between nature's complex systems. Dickinson's poem is not directly concerned with these questions, but it resonates with her time's growing awareness of the unexpected *interrelatedness* of nature's small and large, past and present elements. Such a perspective involves an ethical stance toward nature that Edward O. Wilson recently embraced in his ecological manifesto *The Future of Life*: "The creature at your feet dismissed as a bug or a weed is a creation in and of itself. It has a name, a million-year history, and a place in the world. [. . .] The ethical value substantiated by close examination of its biology is that the life forms around us are too old, too complex, and potentially too useful to be carelessly discarded" (131). While Wilson harks back to the nineteenth century when he opens his study with a letter to Thoreau, Dickinson's conflicting engagement with the links between small particulars and global systems, and with the merit of close scrutiny of both, implies an ethical stance toward the environment that is still relevant today.

Yet everything the poem implies regarding nature's systems in near and far places is again undercut by the speaker's ambivalence. Despite the defiant tone of someone who takes "no less than skies" in the face of the familiar "earths" all around her, there is the nagging suspicion, condensed in the opening "Perhaps," that she may have taken on too much, even as she keeps going. When Thoreau declared in "Walking" "[m]y vicinity affords many good walks, and though I have walked almost every day for so many years, and sometimes for several days together, I have not yet exhausted them" before claiming, "my desire to bathe my head in atmospheres unknown to my feet is perennial and constant," he rejoiced in the wealth of insights that can spring from nature observation in geographically small areas (660, 671). Dickinson's poem displays a much more covert recognition of well-known natural places as potentially meaningful, and replaces Thoreau's provocative confidence with an equally provocative—and equally environmentally resonant—*reluctance* regarding our human capability to decipher the natural world in its small and large manifestations.

Other cosmic poems also engage the geographies they seem so unconcerned with and thereby participate in America's controversial debates about how to relate to the land—which included conversations about the dynamics between earthly and cosmic systems, and between the earth's ancient history and possible future effects of human action. The outwardly naïve poem which begins "What is – 'Paradise' – / Who live there – / Are they 'Farmers' – / Do they 'hoe' –" (Fr241) is as much about rural New England as about "the sky." The poem "Is Heaven a

Place – a Sky – a Tree?" (Fr476) may reject the signifying power of "Location's narrow way," yet relies on geographical paradigms that bring the otherworldly close to home. Another poem beginning "The Fact that Earth is Heaven – / Whether Heaven is Heaven or not / If not an Affidavit / Of that specific Spot" (Fr1435) embraces the physical earth even as it reminds readers that its "heavenly" qualities do not suffice as affirmation or evidence for what lies beyond it. The cautionary remark "That it is not for us / [. . .] To dwell in such a place –," which may refer to heaven, earth, or both, advocates a position toward both realms that precludes the common presumption that we are able to be authentically in or grasp our environment. Dickinson's cosmically oriented work expresses an acute awareness of the pitfalls of being solely grounded in the physical world and moves beyond a narrowing localism that only sees the familiar and specific; at the same time it suggests a remarkable restraint regarding an overconfident notion of superiority regarding our natural surroundings, which applies both to the small worlds at our feet and to the earth as part of a vast extraterrestrial system.

At a time when civilization's pressures upon American landscapes became increasingly intense, Emily Dickinson's respectful attention to natural places constitutes an important environmental gesture because it recognizes nature as a domain of its own that has value apart from its economic, recreational, or poetic benefits. More specifically, her poetic meditations on trees and acres, on New England's regional geographies, and on the rich "Earths" of a seemingly narrow territory intersect with key aspects of her time's growing green sensibilities: her visions of connectedness and interdependence test early ecological concerns as poetic perspective; her nature-oriented regionalism can be linked to living-in-place as a long-standing environmental strategy; and her exploration of cosmic yearnings that fold back into earthly landscapes suggest a basic interrelatedness of small and large, past and present natural systems that is still at the heart of ecology today. Her views of nature as a complex system with which humans interact in a variety of ways and on which they fundamentally depend was part of her complex response to the world, emblematically condensed in the view of herself as "A Guest in this stupendous place –" (Fr572). In spite of her indirection, Dickinson may well be seen as an unruly collaborator in early environmentalism's larger green foray.

Instead of directly criticizing "the destructive and annihilating sway of man over the world," as Marsh's argument was summarized in the *Atlantic* (262), Dickinson offered an ethics of careful observation and tentative conclusions that accounts for her lingering uncertainty as to how to "read" nature. As such, her poetry displays a reluctant place-centeredness whose environmental significance lies not only in the evocation of particular locales and their natural economies but also in this very reluctance, for it is this reluctance that prevents an inherent sense of place from turning into self-contained complacency. In unexpected ways, her prevailing skepticism makes her explorations of natural landscapes environmentally resonant because it challenges any one-dimensional, restrictive localism, anticipating the critical sense of place that environmentalists have only recently begun to promote. If literature is indeed instrumental in registering, revitalizing, and redirecting our engagement with nature, as Lawrence Buell has argued, Dickinson's poetry can be said to do precisely that. In its own paradoxical and elusive way, Dickinson's poetry works against the relative indifference toward natural places that was characteristic of her own time as much as it has been of ours.

From *The Emily Dickinson Journal* 15, no. 1 (2006): 56-78. Copyright © 2006 by The Johns Hopkins University Press. Reprinted with permission of The Johns Hopkins University Press.

Notes

My warmest thanks go to Neil Browne and Jon and Gail Smith for their generous comments on earlier versions of this piece. *Danke!*

1. With remarkable foresight, Susan Fenimore Cooper's popular *Rural Hours* (1850) expressed this growing concern for the "abuse" and "waste" of the Northeastern forests: "One would think that by this time, when the forest has fallen in all the valleys—when the hills are becoming more bare every day—[. . .] some forethought and care in this respect would be natural in people laying claim to common sense. [. . .] It has been calculated that 60,000 acres of pine woods are cut every year in our own State alone; and at this rate, it is said that in twenty years, or about 1870, these trees will have disappeared from our part of the country!" (132). Cooper urges Americans to overcome their purely utilitarian stance (133) and suggests a set of highly specific preservation measures: "Thinning woods and not blasting them; clearing only such ground as is marked for immediate tillage; preserving the wood on the hill-tops and rough side-hills; encouraging a coppice on this or that knoll; permitting bushes and young trees to grow at will along the brooks and water-courses" (134)—all of which indicates that the ruthless subjugation of the land met with increasing criticism during Dickinson's early years.

2. I thank David Kohn for confirming to me this crucial connection between botany and ecology.

3. In a similar vein, Scott Slovic's detailed study has shown that "nature writers both study the phenomenon of environmental consciousness and attempt to stimulate this heightened awareness among their readers" (Slovic 7). Another aspect of the genre's possible relevance to Dickinson studies is that it was at that time firmly grounded in the geographies of the Northeast, providing Dickinson and her contemporaries with detailed knowledge of their regionally specific surroundings.

4. Joanne Feit Diehl links the poem's "absence of assured meaning either in the trees' relation to other natural facts or to an ordering principle" to Dickinson's "sense of dislocation" (164-65), and Shira Wolosky stresses that it confronts a "world of radical disorder," "of discrete details without interconnection," through a syntax that is "as discontinuous as the scene it presents" (163). Similarly, E. Miller Budick argues that the poem's "confusion and fragmentation" have less to do with "external nature" than with "the human thought process," since they not only "imitate natural disunities" but "rival and surpass them" as language (16-17). Cynthia Griffin Wolff reads the poem as an example of Dickinson's view of a "demythologized world" that is "emancipated from the tyranny of God's rule," a universe that "has been evacuated of meaning and intrinsic relationships" (459).

5. Now the "the central organizing idea of ecology" (Worster 378), the ecosystem concept was discussed for several decades before Arthur Tansley coined the term in 1935.

6. I am quoting from the 1856 edition, but the entry on "Earth" to which I refer here is unchanged from the original 1828 edition.

Works Cited

The following abbreviations are used to refer to the writings of Emily Dickinson:

Fr   *The Poems of Emily Dickinson*. Ed. R. W. Franklin. 3 vols.
      Cambridge, MA: Harvard UP, 1998. Citation by poem number.

L   *The Letters of Emily Dickinson*. Ed. Thomas H. Johnson and
      Theodora Ward. Cambridge, MA: Harvard UP, 1986 (1958).
      Citation by letter number.

Anderson, Douglas. "Presence and Place in Emily Dickinson's Poetry." *The New England Quarterly* 57.2 (June 1984): 205-24.

Asahina, Midori. "'Fascination' is absolute of Clime: Reading Dickinson's Correspondence with Higginson as Naturalist." *The Emily Dickinson Journal* 14.2 (2005): 103-119.

Barker, Wendy. *Lunacy of Light: Emily Dickinson and the Experience of Metaphor*. Carbondale: Southern Illinois UP, 1987.

Baym, Nina. *American Women of Letters and the Nineteenth-Century Sciences: Styles of Affiliation*. New Brunswick, NJ: Rutgers UP, 2002.

Benfey, Christopher E. G. *Dickinson and the Problem of Others*. Amherst: U of Massachusetts P, 1984.

Berg, Peter, and Raymond F. Dasmann. "Reinhabiting California." *Home! A Bioregional Reader*. Ed. Van Andruss et al. Philadelphia: New Society, 1990. 35-38.

Budick, E. Miller. *Emily Dickinson and the Life of Language: A Study in Symbolic Poetics*. Baton Rouge: Louisiana State UP, 1985.

Buell, Lawrence. *The Environmental Imagination: Thoreau, Nature Writing, and the Formation of American Culture*. Cambridge, MA: Harvard UP, 1995.

_____. *Writing for an Endangered World. Literature, Culture, and Environment in the U.S. and Beyond*. Cambridge, MA: Belknap-Harvard UP, 2001.

Cabot, James Elliot. "Our Birds and Their Ways." *The Atlantic Monthly* 1.2 (1857): 209-216.

Capps, Jack L. *Emily Dickinson's Reading: 1836-1886*. Cambridge, MA: Harvard UP, 1966.

Cooper, Susan Fenimore. *Rural Hours*. Eds. Rochelle Johnson and Daniel Patterson. Athens: U of Georgia P, 1998.

Diehl, Joanne Feit. "Ransom in a Voice: Language as Defense in Dickinson's Poetry." *Feminist Critics Read Emily Dickinson*. Ed. Suzanne Juhasz. Bloomington: Indiana UP, 1983. 156-75.

Eberwein, Jane Donahue. "Dickinson's Local, Global, and Cosmic Perspectives." *The Emily Dickinson Handbook*. Ed. Gudrun Grabher, Roland Hagenbüchle, and Cristanne Miller. Amherst: U of Massachusetts P, 1998. 27-45.

Farr, Judith, and Louise Carter. *The Gardens of Emily Dickinson*. Cambridge, MA: Harvard UP, 2004.

Flagg, W. "Among the Trees." *The Atlantic Monthly* 6.35 (1860): 257-271.

Habegger, Alfred. *My Wars Are Laid Away in Books: The Life of Emily Dickinson*. New York: Random House, 2001.

Higginson, Thomas Wentworth. "Water-Lilies." *The Atlantic Monthly* 2.11 (1858): 465-473.

Judd, Richard W. *Common Lands, Common People: The Origins of Conservation in Northern New England*. Cambridge, MA: Harvard UP, 1997.

Kohn, David. E-mail to the author. 9 August 2005.

Lincoln, Almira H. *Familiar Lectures on Botany*. Hartford, CT: H. and F. J. Huntington, 1829.

Lutwack, Leonard. *The Role of Place in Literature*. Syracuse, NY: Syracuse UP, 1984.

Lyon, Thomas J. Preface and Ed. *This Incomperable Lande: A Book of American Nature Writing*. Ed. Lyon. New York: Penguin, 1991. x-xvi.

Rev. of *Man and Nature; or, Physical Geography as Modified by Human Action*, by George P. Marsh. *The Atlantic Monthly* 14.82 (1864): 216-218.

Marsh, George Perkins. *So Great a Vision: The Conservationist Writings of George Perkins Marsh*. Ed. Stephen C. Trombulak. Hanover, NH: UP of New England, 2001.

Miller, Cristanne. "Dickinson's Experiments in Language." *The Emily Dickinson Handbook*. Ed. Gudrun Grabher, Roland Hagenbüchle, and Cristanne Miller. Amherst: U of Massachusetts P, 1998. 240-57.

Mitchell, Domhnall. *Emily Dickinson: Monarch of Perception*. Amherst: U of Massachusetts P, 2000.

Monteiro, George, and Barton Levi St. Armand. "The Experienced Emblem: A Study of the Poetry of Emily Dickinson." *Prospects: A Journal of American Cultural Studies* 6 (1981): 187-240.

Oelschlaeger, Max. *The Idea of Wilderness: From Prehistory to the Age of Ecology*. New Haven, CT: Yale UP, 1991.

Opie, John. *Nature's Nation: An Environmental History of the United States*. Fort Worth, TX: Harcourt Brace, 1998.

Petrino, Elizabeth A. *Emily Dickinson and Her Contemporaries: Women's Verse in America, 1820-1885*. Hanover, NH: UP of New England, 1998.

_____. "Late Bloomer: The Gentian as Sign or Symbol in the Work of Dickinson and Her Contemporaries." *The Emily Dickinson Journal* 14.1 (2005): 104-25.

St. Armand, Barton Levi. *Emily Dickinson and Her Culture: The Soul's Society*. Cambridge: Cambridge UP, 1984.

Sewall, Richard. *The Life of Emily Dickinson*. New York: Farrar, Straus and Giroux, 1974.

Slovic, Scott. *Seeking Awareness in American Nature Writing: Henry David Thoreau, Annie Dillard, Edward Abbey, Wendell Berry, and Barry Lopez*. Salt Lake City: U of Utah P, 1992.

Stein, Rachel. *Shifting the Ground: American Women Writers' Revision of Nature, Gender, and Race*. Charlottesville: UP of Virginia, 1997.

Thoreau, Henry David. "Chesuncook." *The Atlantic Monthly* 2.10 (1858): 305-317.

_____. "Walking." *The Atlantic Monthly* 9.56 (1862): 657-674.

Tuan, Yi-Fu. "Space and Place: Humanistic Perspective." *Human Geography: An Essential Anthology*. Ed. J. D. N. Livingstone Agnew and A. Rogers. Oxford: Blackwell, 1996. 444-57.

_____. *Space and Place: The Perspective of Experience*. 1977. Minneapolis: U of Minnesota P, 1995.

Webster, Noah. *An American Dictionary of the English Language . . . Revised and Enlarged by Chauncey A. Goodrich*. Springfield, MA: Merriam, 1856.

Weisbuch, Robert. *Emily Dickinson's Poetry*. Chicago, IL: U of Chicago P, 1975.

Wilson, Edward O. *The Future of Life*. New York: Vintage, 2003.

Wolff, Cynthia Griffin. *Emily Dickinson*. New York: Knopf, 1987.

Wolosky, Shira. "A Syntax of Contention." *Emily Dickinson*. Ed. Harold Bloom. New York: Chelsea House, 1999. 161-85.

Worster, Donald. *Nature's Economy: The Roots of Ecology*. 1977. San Francisco: Sierra Club, 1988.

Addresses to a Divided Nation:
Images of War in Emily Dickinson and Walt Whitman_____

Faith Barrett

Countering the view of Dickinson as a reclusive and private poet who absented herself from the political debates of her day, Faith Barrett offers a comparative analysis of the responses of Dickinson and her contemporary Walt Whitman to the Civil War. If in "This is my letter to the World" Dickinson's speaker, in addressing her "Sweet countrymen" in a time of war, proceeds by indirection as she conveys to the world the "simple News" told to her by "Nature," Whitman, in "Apostroph," styling himself as a poet-bard, directly addresses an American audience as he attempts to hold together the divided nation with his poetic oratory.

Both Dickinson and Whitman respond to the horrific violence of the Civil War in poems that Barrett calls "the landscapes of war," poems in which both poets "grapple with the difficulties of representing the enormous scale of modern warfare." Dickinson, in "They dropped like Flakes –," and Whitman, in "Cavalry Crossing a Ford," use the pastoral mode to describe death on a massive scale by offering "harmonious visions of heroic bodies merging with a vital and redemptive American landscape." In contrast, Dickinson, in "The name – of it – is 'Autumn' –," and Whitman, in "Look Down Fair Moon," reveal the fraudulence of this "redemptive perspective" by suggesting that "the American landscape has been drenched with blood and that there is no secure outside position from which the war can be witnessed." For Dickinson and Whitman, "the exploration of wartime suffering leads to profound discoveries about the workings of lyric address." While both poets recognize "the impossibility of representing the experience of battle," Whitman nevertheless wants to address the nation through his poetry and bind it together as he depicts death as "redemptive and meaningful"; Dickinson, even as she feels "obligated" to represent the horrors of war, also insists that "no poem can convey the experience of war to its readers."   J.B.B.

"'Sweet Land of Liberty' is a superfluous Carol till it concern ourselves," Emily Dickinson writes in a warm and expansive letter to Mabel Loomis Todd in the summer of 1885 (*Letters* #1004).[1] Writing to her brother's mistress, who was then traveling in Europe, Dickinson touches on a subject one might not expect to encounter in her writings: the love of one's homeland, her love for America. "I saw the American Rag last Night in the shutting West," she writes, "and I felt for every exile." She signs the letter "America."

In reading Emily Dickinson, we do not expect to encounter a writer who speaks to or for the nation; rather we expect to encounter a writer who lives in internal domestic exile, absenting herself from the political discussions of her day. Yet Dickinson's poetry of the Civil War era raises important questions about speaking to and for "America"; as the ironic stance of the post-war letter to Todd suggests, these questions are invariably raised obliquely. Dickinson's work, I contend, does address the nation, though it does so skeptically and tentatively; simultaneously, her work offers an exhaustive analysis of the risks of that rhetorical platform. Dickinson's speaker thus undercuts her own position, and as a result, readers have been slow to recognize her critical engagement with nineteenth-century political debates. Following the publication of Johnson's complete edition of the poems in 1955, the first generation of scholars who read Dickinson emphasized her intellectual and physical isolation from the outside world.[2] Recent scholarship, however, urges us to consider the ways in which her work addresses both her immediate community of family and friends and the wider audience she undoubtedly reached through circulation of her work in correspondence; recent scholarship also urges us to consider the ways in which Dickinson's work addresses political and literary developments in nineteenth-century America.[3] Embracing these recent studies, my approach to Dickinson's address to the nation begins with the premise that we must attend to the ways in which her work is vitally connected to its historical and social context. My argument, however, considers the address to the nation not only as an historically determined and embedded stance but also as the means by which Dickinson articulates a critique of the limitations of the lyric self.

For Dickinson, as for Walt Whitman, the political crisis of the Civil War raises unavoidable questions about the workings of literary representation. For both poets, the dilemmas of the address to the nation are inseparable from the dilemmas of witnessing wartime violence and suffering. It is a critical commonplace that Walt Whitman is a public poet and Emily Dickinson, a private one: while Whitman's "I" addresses the whole nation, in Dickinson's poems the positing of the lyric self seems to require a privacy of address that excludes the outside world. Such a reading, however, neglects the tensions which underlie Whitman's inclusive apostrophes; it also neglects the ways in which Dickinson deliberately, though skeptically, addresses the nation. Dickinson's work suggests that the stability of the poet's platform in addressing the nation depends upon the speaker's ability to bear witness to the suffering of others; this is a stance which she profoundly mistrusts.[4] Moreover, Dickinson is not alone is displaying this mistrust; the address to the nation is undercut by anxiety and tension in the work of many American writers of the nineteenth century. I contend, however, that Dickinson foregrounds the problems of the address to the nation in a way that no other American poet of this era does. If we read American poetry of the Civil War era through the lens of Dickinson's critique of address, we find that her work illuminates changes in the stances of the lyric self, changes which result in part from the crisis of a nation divided by war.[5]

While Dickinson is invariably skeptical about the address to the nation, Whitman adopts this platform enthusiastically, self-consciously styling himself as America's bard. In order to understand Dickinson's suspicions about address, we need also to consider Whitman's enthusiasm for it.[6] An examination of address which juxtaposes Dickinson's

Civil War poetry with Whitman's will shed greater light on the range of stances available to all American poets in this period.[7] The analysis that follows then will compare scenes of the address to the nation and scenes of wartime suffering as they are depicted by both Dickinson and Whitman. The first section of this essay considers a pair of poems which explicitly describe the platform of the address to the nation; my reading of each speaker's position attends to the dilemmas such a platform poses when that nation is faced with a Civil War. The second section examines a group of poems which attempt to describe the collective suffering of the nation through depiction of battlefield landscapes. In these poems, both poets explore the limitations of Romantic poetry in representing the horror of war; both also raise urgent questions about poetic and painterly traditions which situate American identity in the wholeness of natural landscapes. Through these comparative readings, I will suggest that for both writers the exploration of wartime suffering leads to profound discoveries about the workings of lyric address: the crisis of a divided nation corresponds to the crisis of a lyric self divided both from the reader and from the suffering soldiers that the poems try to describe. The difficulty of representing the violence of war thus reveals the limitations of the lyric self in each writer's work.

1. Letters to America

In reading these poets' addresses to the nation, I will take as a paradigm for the Romantic scene of address John Stuart Mill's influential definition of lyric poetry. Mill's definition will serve particularly well for this purpose not only because it continues to be a central model in critical discussions of the lyric, but also because it foregrounds the issue of the lyric speaker's demands on his or her audience; Mill's definition also foregrounds the contrast between lyric poetry and public oratory which at first appears so prominent when we juxtapose Dickinson's stance with Whitman's.[8] Mill's model has exercised a particularly tenacious hold on the field of Dickinson studies. "Poetry and eloquence," Mill writes, "are both alike the expression or utterance of feeling. But if we may be excused the antithesis, we should say that eloquence is heard, poetry is overheard" (12). What separates poetry from oratory in Mill's scheme, then, is the kind of reader or listener each creates: in the case of poetry, both the reader and the speaker are supposed to agree tacitly to ignore that there is any bond between them. More specifically, both parties agree to ignore the fact that the poem is not a spontaneous verbal outcry, but rather a written text. The contract between speaker and reader stipulates that the reader will "eavesdrop" on the speaker's private soliloquy, and both parties agree to uphold this fiction. It is precisely by ignoring the reader that the poet achieves his or her goal of engaging the reader's attention.[9] The orator, by contrast, makes his persuasive aims—and his claims on the audience's attention—explicit.[10] In my reading of Dickinson and Whitman, I will argue that both poets critique Mill's model for the scene of address—though they approach these critiques from very different angles. Because Whitman's work obsessively addresses the reader and because his speaker makes explicit his persuasive aims, he explicitly rejects Mill's definition of poetry. In reading Dickinson's poem, however, I will suggest that she too disrupts Mill's model by pointing insistently to a failed scene of address as a central site of dramatic tension in her work.[11]

In "This is my letter to the World" (F 519), a poem deceptively simple on its surface, Dickinson offers an incisive analysis of the Romantic scene of address.[12] In two brief stanzas, the speaker seems to touch directly on Dickinson's decisions as a writer:

> This is my letter to the World
> That never wrote to Me
> The simple News that Nature told –
> With tender Majesty

Her Message is committed
To Hands I cannot see –
For love of Her – Sweet – countrymen –
Judge tenderly – of Me

Boldly declaring the lyric to be a "letter to the World," Dickinson begins the poem by disrupting the Romantic staging of voice and making textuality evident; indeed, the poem as a whole would seem to emphasize the oxymoronic status of the lyric as "written utterance." The opening line already points to the fictional nature of the scene of address by juxtaposing the deictic "this" with the idea of the poem as a "letter to the World"; the deictic foregrounds the idea of the presence and voice of the speaker, even as the "letter" points to the speaker's absence and the text of the poem on the page. Moreover, in the poem, Dickinson also presents the scene of address as one marked by triangulation: the speaker suggests that her "letter to the World" is in fact nothing more than "The simple News that Nature told – / With tender Majesty," a phrase which occurs in apposition to the "letter." According to these lines then, the speaker's task consists merely of relaying to "the World" the "simple News" told to her by "Nature."

Although the first line declares the poem to be the speaker's "letter to the World," by the second stanza the poem has become "Her Message," a message from Nature, and this message, the speaker explains, has been "committed / To Hands I cannot see –." At this point then, the identity of the recipient of the letter/message becomes unclear: the unseen "Hands" might be those of God or those of the "Sweet – countrymen –" who are subsequently addressed. In either case, the speaker has lost control over the "committ[ing]" of the message. The speaker has been shut out of the circuit of address, and the message is, at this point, definitely a text since it has been "committed" to unseen "Hands." The concluding lines of the poem, however, undercut this emphasis on the poem as text with what is for Dickinson a highly uncharacteristic moment of address. The speaker calls on her

"Sweet – countrymen –" to "Judge tenderly – of [Her]," not out of love for the speaker, but out of love for Nature, who is, the speaker insists, the actual source of the poem. In addressing her "countrymen," the speaker thus figures herself as a go-between or messenger from Nature to the World.

Yet while we can read the poem as a critique of the Romantic scene of address, if we keep in mind Franklin's hypothesis that the poem was written in the spring of 1863, it also becomes possible to read the poem as an oblique commentary on the difficulties a woman poet faces in addressing her "countrymen" in a time of war. Such a reading is also supported by the poem's position in fascicle 24, a packet that includes two poems which make explicit reference to the war: "When I was small, a woman died" (F 518) and "It feels a shame to be Alive –" (F 524). Read in this light, "This is my letter to the World" (F 519) describes not only the workings of the Romantic scene of address in general but the particular dilemmas a woman writer faces in attempting to stage such a scene. For, as we have seen, Mill declares that the skill of the poet consists in his being able to conceal the fact that he desires or expects to have a listener/reader; yet for a nineteenth-century woman poet, the question of what stances one's speakers ought to assume towards an audience is clearly a vexed and vexing one. Mill's ideal poet is too genteel to make any explicit claims on his reader; but a nineteenth-century woman poet who conceals her claims on her audience too effectively may well have no audience at all. "Eloquence supposes an audience," Mill writes; "the peculiarity of poetry seems to us to lie in the poet's utter unconsciousness of a listener. Poetry is feeling confessing itself to itself, in moments of solitude" (12). Indeed, Dickinson's literal withdrawal from the world in her own life presents an almost parodic version of the Romantic scene of address—particularly if we consider those accounts of her preferring not to receive guests directly, but rather remaining in an adjacent room to overhear conversations. Dickinson was herself an eavesdropper, and many of her poems explicitly thematize the fact that other readers will "eavesdrop" on the scenes of address presented in her poems—hundreds of which circulated among family and friends through her correspondence.[13]

"This is my letter to the World" offers a trenchant analysis of the perils of this scene of eavesdropping for a woman writer, implicitly thematizing Dickinson's literal and historical refusal to send her own "letter to the World." The deictic "This" of the opening line refers not to any message within the poem itself, but rather, implicitly, to her entire body of work. "This is my letter to the World/" the speaker declares, "That never wrote to me," and the second line points both to the lack of reciprocity in the scene of the lyric address and—perhaps more bitterly—to the invisibility of the woman writer in the eyes of the world. While the poem points to the tension between "voice" and "text" in the lyric undertaking, it also points obliquely to the difficulties a woman poet faces in trying to get her "voice" heard. In the lines that follow, then, the speaker describes herself as nothing more than an intermediary between "Nature" and the "World," which is, of course, the conventional position of the Romantic poet in the tradition of Wordsworth. Yet, in this poem, the gesture might also be read as one of feminine, self-deprecating modesty: the speaker declares her letter to be nothing more than "the simple News that Nature told." The lines effectively erase the speaker's agency as a writer, making her merely a messenger. And what could be more appropriate for a genteel woman poet—during a time of war and bloodshed, a time when the actual "News" was rarely "simple"—than to serve as conduit for the transcendent "tender Majesty" of "Nature"?

In the second stanza of the poem, then, this link between the speaker and Nature is made still stronger by means of feminine pronouns which make the speaker Nature's double. "Her Message" replaces the speaker's "letter," and "For love of Her," the speaker pleads with her "countrymen" to "judge" her "tenderly." The second stanza thus also juxtaposes the position of Nature/the speaker (both gendered feminine) with the position of the audience, the "countrymen," a masculine collective.[14] When the speaker declares that she has lost control of her "letter" ("Her Message is committed / To Hands I cannot see –"), she seems in part to allude to the loss of control over her own words which would attend publication—just as Dickinson herself effectively lost control of those few of her poems which were published during her lifetime. One thinks, for example, of Karen Dandurand's account of the 1864 publication of three Dickinson poems in a newspaper raising funds for the Union army—and of the subsequent reprinting of these poems in other publications. The poems which Dickinson allowed Richard Storrs to publish in the *Drum Beat* are universally about the "simple News that Nature told."[15] In "This is my letter to the World," then, Dickinson's speaker assumes an ironic stance towards the many perils of addressing her "Sweet – countrymen –": she writes knowing that she cannot anticipate a reply; she effaces her own position as a writer, figuring herself instead as a mere intermediary between Nature and the World; she acknowledges that her letter has been "committed" to a recipient whom she cannot see; and she worries about the critical judgments that will be passed on her work. At the same time, however, the poem points ironically to Dickinson's refusal to publish her work: just as the speaker is not permitted to "see" the "Hands" which now hold the letter, so too are we the readers not permitted to see the sealed "Message" or "letter" which the poem describes. We are ironically asked to "Judge" what we cannot see.

While Dickinson's speaker figures herself as a self-effacing messenger who has lost control over the transmission of her own textual/ epistolary message, Whitman's poems frequently present a speaker who argues, like an orator, for the powers of poetic voice—even as he is at times overcome by the power of his own lyric cries. While Dickinson's poem insistently points to its own dual status as text and as the staging of a voice, Whitman's poems frequently seek to foreground voice above all else. Examples of the direct address to the nation abound in Whitman, but, in its excesses, the poem "Apostroph" presents a particularly striking example of all that Whitman hopes to accomplish in his poetics of address. The fact that the poem appeared in only the 1860 edition of *Leaves of Grass* (though eleven of its lines do appear in the 1867 edition) signals Whitman's ambivalence about the heightened rhetorical stances of the piece. "Apostroph" consists essentially of an extraordinarily inclusive list of dramatic addresses to various persons, groups, individuals, objects and abstractions, each line beginning either with the "O" of the Romantic apostrophe ("O mater! O fils!") or with the "O" of dramatic exclamation ("O I heard, and yet hear, angry thunder") (2: 290-92). Though the poem can only unfold in the suspended temporality of its own apostrophes and dramatic exclamations, it nonetheless maps out a narrative in the present-tense immediacy of the speaker's cries: the speaker calls on various groups to awake (2: 290, ll. 1-12), witnesses a shipwreck (12-15), worries aloud that the whole world might be "a sham, a sell" (16), praises America and freedom as the only "real" thing (17-18), addresses and praises first the North and then the South (21-23; 35-37), declares the union "impossible to dissever" (53), and finally, in the last five lines, both anticipates his own death and calls on "the poets to come" to fulfill his visions for America.

If we read the poem as a whole in light of the last five lines, the drama of the poem seems to consist in the speaker's postponing his own death for as long as possible by means of his own lyric exclamations. "O present! I return while yet I may to you!" the speaker cries, and the line emphasizes the tenacity with which the speaker clings to the suspended present tenses of apostrophic time throughout the poem (64). Likewise the poem reads as an attempt to hold in abeyance the threat of the dividing of the nation: "O Libertad! O compact! O union impossible to dissever!" (53). By means of the address to the nation, the poem aims to hold the nation together. This Utopian project of unifying the nation is inseparable from Whitman's aim of using poetic voice to unite objects with their names, signifiers with signifieds, a goal which is clearly evident in "Apostroph."[16] Whitman's poetics thus leads him to privilege voice—with the promise of presence which it offers—over writing, which threatens to insert the reader into symbolic hierarchies which the poet insistently rejects as oppressive and authoritative.[17] Not surprisingly, Whitman's poetics also explicitly privileges oratory because he values both the immediacy of the orator's voice and the possibility of the efficacy of that voice in the political present. In "Apostroph," then, the "orators" and the "poets" appear to be essentially interchangeable.[18] "O voices of greater orators!" the speaker calls out, implying with the comparative that "the orators" to come will perhaps be even "greater" than the poet himself, "I pause—I listen for you!" (56). The final line of the poem then echoes this grammatical structure, thereby linking orators and poets: "O poets to come, I depend upon you!" (65).

Yet while the poem aims to conjure up the groups addressed and the scenes the speaker exclaims over, the sheer quantity of exclamations in the poem lends the speaker's voice a tone of frenzied anxiety: anxiety about the inefficacy of language, anxiety about the difficulties of addressing another person in a poem, and, perhaps most pressingly, anxiety about a nation divided from and within itself.[19] It is no coincidence that Whitman's poetry moves increasingly away from explorations of address in the aftermath of the Civil War.[20] In his wartime poetry, Whitman must confront head-on the philosophical dilemma which his exploration of the apostrophe leads to: namely, the impossibility of encountering the other—and representing the other's suffering—through the lyric address. In "Apostroph," the tension between naming and loss, between union and division, both propels the poem forward and keeps the speaker suspended in a state of feverish chatter. The proliferation of addressed groups and abstractions only points to the speaker's fear of loss: the incantatory repetition of the poetic "O" which conjures up the sound of the speaker's voice simultaneously suggests the null or zero of the loss of each person or thing named.[21] "O Libertad! O compact! O union impossible to dissever!" the speaker cries: but, writing in 1860, Whitman himself realizes that the three abstractions he addresses in this line can no longer hold true for the United States.

If we juxtapose Whitman's "Apostroph" with Dickinson's "This is my letter to the World," certain contrasts and shared concerns in their explorations of address become apparent. Dickinson's poem focuses on the speaker's status as intermediary between her "countrymen" and "Nature," while the Whitman poem presents the speaker as an intermediary between his readers and their nation. The Dickinson poem, however, erases both the speaker's position as writer and the "Message" itself, focusing instead on the roundabout circuit by means of which the Message travels. Whitman's poem, on the other hand, does convey the message—"O union impossible to dissever!"—but the voicing of the message is, in and of itself, an anxious attempt to make the message hold true. Moreover, in these poems, the two poets' opposing positions are clearly inflected—in a self-consciously exaggerated fashion—by gender. With feminine modesty, Dickinson's speaker demurs to write her own letter or to write about the war, preferring instead to relay "The simple News that Nature told –." Whitman effectively addresses a masculine figure for himself when he calls on the "bearded roughs" to awake and become "bards" (10); he also addresses "muscle and pluck," calling on a masculine strength to hold the union together (30). Yet, while the speakers' gender positions are polar opposites, what ultimately links these two poems is the implicit meditation each offers on the business of addressing an American audience. For while the Dickinson poem undermines the position of the speaker as writer, it also undermines the position of the reader as audience, by teasingly refusing to relay the short-circuited "Message." "This is my letter to the World," the speaker declares, but as readers we are not given access to it; rather we are only permitted to watch it being handed off. Though the speaker addresses her "Sweet – countrymen," the poem effectively enacts the impossibility of such an address: the poem describes both the impossibility of writing such a letter and the impossibility of receiving it. Dickinson's poem suggests that the circuit of the address to the nation is subject to both slippage and disruption: in the logic of her poem, the writer's "Message" can never travel directly to a waiting reader. In its insistent catalogue of apostrophes, Whitman's poem, like Dickinson's, points to the impossibility of addressing the fictional audience whom it nonetheless posits. Calling out to a nation soon to be sundered, Whitman's speaker tries to invent the kind of poetry audience that might prevent such a catastrophe: "O union impossible to dissever!"[22] But the "bearded roughs" whom he calls on to become "bards" will soon have little time for reading and writing and will instead have to use their "muscle and pluck" in a bloody war (10, 30).

As these readings begin to suggest, the position of the speaker in each of these poems offers a larger statement about each writer's stance towards the task of addressing the nation. The speaker of "This is my letter to the World" promises to address the nation only obliquely, demurely, and in a roundabout fashion; she will not address her "Sweet countrymen" in a direct apostrophe again. What she will do, however, is serve as a go-between between her "countrymen" and "Nature," and that "Nature," as Dickinson sees it during the years of Civil War, is often a bloody and violent place. Profoundly distrustful of the authoritative posture which the apostrophe requires—and equally distrustful of both the public taste and the institutions of literary publication—Dickinson proceeds to address the nation by indirection.[23] Yet the poems about violence and suffering during the Civil War, many of which circulated among her family and friends, must necessarily be read as addresses to her fellow Americans. The argument which follows will focus on a pair of Civil War era poems which are implicitly addressed to an American readership.

Whitman, however, will take a very different approach to the dilemmas of addressing a nation at war, as the insistent use of the figure in "Apostroph" suggests. Though few of his Civil War poems will use the apostrophe quite so obsessively as this one, Whitman's speaker nonetheless persists in using direct addresses to his audience in his representations of war; the speaker also persists in describing the kind of audience he needs. For Whitman such descriptions are part of the poet's obligations: styling himself as the bard who will chronicle the war for the nation, he attempts to reunite a war-torn country with poetry. When his attempt to hold the Union together with apostrophes fails, Whitman turns his hand to the related task of linking those at home with those on the front-lines, linking the observers of the war with the soldiers fighting and dying in it.

2. Landscapes of War

For Dickinson and Whitman, the task of writing poetry in a time of war leads to a crisis of faith in the imagery and stances of the Romantic lyric poem. In confronting this crisis, their work travels along parallel trajectories of exploration. Both writers present themselves as intermediaries who can represent the violence of war to those not on the front lines; both envision poetry as a place where one might bear witness to the suffering of others. At the same time, however, both rigorously examine the philosophical dilemmas of the intermediary's position and the attendant dilemmas of representing the violence of war—modern war, in particular. When these poets take up the task of representing death on the battlefield, they also take up the question of whether or not it is possible for poetry to represent another human being's suffering. This question is, for both writers, an ethical one, and it is the central question of their Civil War poems.

In view of their very different approaches to the address to the nation, it is not surprising that they offer very different responses to this question. Just as Whitman persists in addressing the nation even as that nation is on the brink of dissolution, so too will he aim to bind the nation together again—paradoxically—through his depiction of the war's violence. Although Whitman feels he has a moral obligation to render in poetry as accurately as he can the horror of the suffering he has witnessed, he also believes he has a moral commitment—as a poet addressing the nation—to represent that suffering in a way that justifies the violence and the eventual outcome of the war. Faced with the conflict of these two obligations, Whitman most often chooses to argue that the loss of life served the moral purpose of reuniting the nation. At the same time, however, the conflict between these two commitments in his work discloses the inadequacy of poetic language in representing violence; this conflict threatens the stability of the speaker's position as witness—and the stability of the lyric self.[24]

In Dickinson's work, by contrast, the speaker's profound ambivalence about the rhetorical platform of the address to the nation corresponds to a very different approach to the representation of wartime violence. While Whitman's poems display his commitment to envisioning the reuniting of the nation in the aftermath of violence, Dickinson avoids having to connect her depiction of violence to a fixed political position of support for either side by means of the oblique stance from which she describes the war. While Dickinson, like Whitman, believes that a writer has a moral obligation to look unflinchingly at violence and to seek to represent it, her work points insistently to the impossibility of fulfilling that obligation and the inadequacy of poetic language for such a task. While Whitman portrays suffering as part of the heroism necessary to reunite a divided nation, Dickinson insistently represents death and violence as events which must necessarily sunder the bond between the witness and the suffering individual—as well as the bond between the lyric speaker and her audience. In order to examine in more detail each poet's confrontation with the dilemmas of representing the violence of the Civil War, I will turn next to a group of Dickinson and Whitman poems which offer descriptions of battlefield scenes through detailed descriptions of landscapes and the natural world.

If we choose to read Dickinson's "This is my Letter to the World" as a commentary on the difficulties of being a woman writer during a time of war, then the speaker's insistence that her work conveys nothing but "the simple News that Nature told" takes on a particular irony in light of some of Dickinson's Civil War poems. A number of Dickinson poems which offer descriptions of landscapes simultaneously offer representations of death on the battlefield. In their strangely seamless blending of landscape and carnage, these poems suggest that the "News that Nature told –" could never, at least during the years of the war, be "simple." One strategy that Dickinson adopts then is to write about the war obliquely, so that her war poems will not be immediately recognizable as such. This strategy, however, is not merely an instance of a female writer being coy about her choice of topic; rather, by representing the horror of war through landscape description, Dickinson points to the limitations of the pastoral tradition in both poetry and painting of the nineteenth century.[25]

In Whitman's work, by contrast, the pastoral mode becomes an essential part of the poet's strategy for reuniting the nation;[26] and if at times, the horror of the violence the speaker must represent threatens to destabilize that pastoral structure, the poems nonetheless usually insist on the moral certainties which the recuperative force of the pastoral provides. In their Civil War poems, both Dickinson and Whitman experiment with representing panoramic views of battle, writing poems which offer what might be called "the landscapes of war." In these poems, which showcase contemporary interest in panoramic vistas in literature, painting and photography, both poets grapple with the difficulties of representing the enormous scale of modern warfare.[27] What these poems suggest is that each poet's perspective on the representation of landscape has been irrevocably marked by the Civil War.

Dickinson's "They dropped like Flakes –" (F 545) and "The name – of it – is 'Autumn' –" (F 465) both employ descriptions of pastoral scenes in order to evoke the horrors of war. They do so, however, with very different effects. "They dropped like Flakes –" represents a battlefield massacre by means of metaphors for nature's harmonious cycles; deliberately rejecting these kinds of metaphoric links, "The name – of it – is 'Autumn' –" represents natural cycles themselves as inherently violent and destructive. In "They dropped like Flakes –," which Franklin dates in the spring of 1863, Dickinson's speaker begins by likening soldiers falling in battle to falling flakes of snow. In the first stanza, the poem then goes on to change the central metaphor two more times, comparing the falling men to shooting stars and falling rose petals:

> They dropped like Flakes –
> They dropped like stars –
> Like Petals from a Rose –
> When suddenly across the June
> A Wind with fingers – goes –
>
> (F 545)

The proliferation of metaphors and the rapidity with which each replaces the one that came before suggests both the speed with which the dying men fall and the speed with which fresh soldiers step in to replace the dead. The stanza suggests both that an infinite number of soldiers will die and that death is an extraordinarily passive process. The sequence of images—from the falling snows of winter to the falling "Petals" of June—suggests that the rapid accumulation of dead bodies is as inevitable as the rapid changing of the seasons. The images used to describe the men—the snow, the stars, the petals—belong to the conventional poetic repertoire for landscape description; yet the vision which they present—of death on a massive scale in the context of modern warfare—is an unsettling match for this repertoire.

Although the conventional metaphors seem to collide with the poem's content, this collision is not powerful enough to disrupt the soothing, dream-like effect of the poetic imagery. The overall effect of the first stanza is to represent death as part of the cycles and events of the natural world, even though the sheer numbers of deaths involved would seem to undermine such a claim.[28] The falling soldiers are in harmony with the natural landscape which surrounds them. Only in the second stanza does the speaker begin to address death as loss, and even here the vision of death is a redemptive, relatively reassuring one:

They perished in the Seamless Grass –
No eye could find the place –
But God can summon every face
On his Repealless – List.

(F 545)

Just as the images in the first stanza seamlessly wove death into the representation of the landscape itself, so are the individual dead here represented as blending into the "Seamless Grass –." The blades of grass emphasize the abundance of the dead bodies, even as they suggest that each dead man is identical to the next; individual deaths are subsumed into the totality of death on a massive scale. The final two lines of the poem, however, present a God who records and maintains individuality in his tally of the dead. Unlike the human "eye," God can "summon every face." Even as the verb "repeal" in Dickinson's adjective "Repealless" suggests the idea of being "called back" to God, the word "Repealless" simultaneously underlines the irrevocable nature of death: once one's name has been entered on the list of the dead, that entry can never be revoked or annulled. Significantly, the speaker herself seems removed from the perils of the battlefield landscape. Throughout the poem, the speaker's position as witness to the scene seems both authoritative and secure; there is no risk that she herself will be among the fallen.

Where "They dropped like Flakes –" succeeds in making human death seem part of nature's cycles, the poem "The name – of it – is 'Autumn' –" (F 465), which Franklin assigns to late 1862, makes natural cycles the site of bloody carnage.[29] If "They dropped like flakes" rewrites death on the battlefield as a natural event, "The name – of it – is 'Autumn' –" rewrites the change of nature's seasons as the scene of a massacre.[30] The poem first appeared (under the title "Autumn") in *Youth's Companion* in September of 1892, where it was presumably read as a description of an autumnal landscape. However, if the poem was written in the fall of 1862, it was written during the same fall in which the battle of Antietam took place, with its massive toll of 26,000 dead and wounded. The poem describes a landscape transformed not by the color of blood, but by blood itself:

> The name – of it – is "Autumn" –
> The hue – of it – is Blood –
> An Artery – opon the Hill –
> A Vein – along the Road –
>
> Great Globules – in the Alleys –
> And Oh, the Shower of Stain –
> When Winds – upset the Basin –
> And spill the Scarlet Rain –
>
> It sprinkles Bonnets – far below –
> It gathers ruddy Pools –
> Then – eddies like a Rose – away –
> Opon Vermillion Wheels
>
> (F 465)

Where "They dropped like Flakes –" erases the gore of death with its array of poetic metaphors, in "The name – of it – is 'Autumn' –" conventional poetic metaphors repeatedly go awry and always in gory fashion. The opening line of the poem suggests that we ought to read the "Blood" as a metaphor for the "hue" of the autumn landscape, but the details which accumulate around this central metaphor make such a reading untenable. Ultimately, the "Blood" which the poem offers as a metaphor can only be read as literal blood. To describe a landscape in relation to the human body is to follow the English lyric tradition; yet to make the "Artery" and the "Vein" a central part of such a comparison is to emphasize the fragility of the human body and thus the violence which underpins these metaphors. Where "They dropped like Flakes –" links death "Seamless[ly]" with the snow, the "Stars" and the

"Grass," "The name – of it – is 'Autumn' –" points to the violence erased by the other poem's metaphoric links. There is no blood in the former and nothing but blood in the latter.

While "They dropped like Flakes –" describes a battlefield in the terms of a rural landscape, "The name – of it – is 'Autumn' –" ranges from the battlefield on "Hill" and "Road" to the "Alleys" of the cities and towns—where fighting also took place—to the "Basin" of blood in the hospital and the "Vermillion Wheels" of the trains and wagons which bore the dead and the wounded away from the scene of the fighting. The movement which each stanza describes is the movement of blood, first implicitly through the "Artery" and "Vein," then explicitly with the "Shower of Stain" and the verbs "spill," "sprinkles," "gathers," and "eddies." Stanzas one and three are built around an emphatic use of the pronoun "it," which is set off by dashes in stanza one and which starts the first two lines of stanza three; though the first line of the poem establishes "Autumn" as a referent for "it," the pronoun might also refer to "war" which remains unnamed in the poem. While the poem includes words which belong to the conventional repertoire for describing the natural world—the "Hill," the "Shower," the "Winds," the "Rain," the "Pools" and the "Rose," for example—the poem consistently disrupts the workings of these images. For example, the strongly alliterative phrase which opens stanza two—"Great Globules"—jars the poem's imagery with its sudden and graphic specificity about the quality of the blood. The dramatic "Oh" in this stanza's second line ("And Oh, the Shower of Stain –") seems to mock the use of the exclamation in lyric poetry: the "Oh" here might be read as an ironic echo of a cry of pain.

In the final stanza, then, the poem's two metaphoric registers, which might be called the poetic and the medical, collide with each other decisively:

It sprinkles Bonnets – far below –
It gathers ruddy Pools –
Then – eddies like a Rose – away –
Opon Vermillion Wheels –

As part of the conventional poetic register, the word "Bonnets" also introduces a feminine figure—by way of metonymy—into the poem. Yet the two meanings of "sprinkle" allow for two alternate readings of "Bonnets": in the first possibility, it is "Autumn" which scatters red "Bonnets" or leaves across the landscape. In this reading, then, the "Bonnets" have replaced the "Globules" as the central noun of the poem's grammar, which is, at best, a startling substitution. In the second possible reading, however, the "Bonnets" are themselves "sprinkled" or stained with the drops or "Globules" of blood shed in the war: read symbolically, the line might seem to suggest that women, too, have inevitably been touched by the war's violence. The poem then goes on to conclude with a climactic moment of metaphoric disjunction. In the third line of this stanza, Dickinson's speaker introduces a simile for the first time in a poem that has otherwise relied on unstated metaphorical links; the speaker insists that the blood "eddies *like* a Rose" (emphasis added). Yet the explicit statement of the metaphoric link only serves to underline the disconnection of the metaphor's two parts: the simile compares blood to the conventional "Rose," a comparison which seems deliberately and jarringly unsuccessful. While the spilling blood might well "edd[y]," it is more difficult to imagine an "edd[ying]" Rose. The poem's metaphoric structure founders, and this collapse would ultimately seem to point to the impossibility of rendering such a scene in poetic imagery.

In "This is my letter to the World" (F 519), Dickinson's speaker represents herself as a self-effacing feminine go-between between "Nature" and her "Sweet – countrymen –"; in "They dropped like Flakes –" and "The Name – of it – is 'Autumn' –," Dickinson's speaker relays "the simple News that Nature told –," innocently offering up landscape descriptions which simultaneously comment on the carnage of war. While "They dropped like Flakes –" erases the bloodshed of the war, "The name – of it – is 'Autumn' –" emphatically rejects the possibility of such an erasure, suggesting that poetic imagery is inadequate to the task of representing war's violence. Nowhere does Dickinson's speaker suggest that a woman writer might be too removed from the war to represent it; the "Bonnets" too have been spattered with blood. Rather, read as a pair, the two poems would seem to suggest that conventional poetic metaphors, if not the genre of the lyric itself, are inadequate for the task of representing modern war. Exposing the pastoral vision of "They dropped like Flakes –" as fraudulent and deceptive, "The name – of it – is 'Autumn' –" emphasizes both the bloodshed and suffering in war and the impossibility of describing them.

If we look for parallel representations of battlefields in Whitman's *Drum-Taps*, we find that he, too, responds to pastoral models in representing the landscapes of war. Reading *Drum-Taps*, Timothy Sweet argues that the pastoral mode performs significant symbolic work in relation to the representation of violence, providing "a powerful, typifying structure of recuperation" (77). In the poetry of the war years, Whitman's poetics of the pastoral works to erase the political complexity of the dead bodies on the battlefields in order "to legitimate the outcome of the war and provide a vision of the future" (77).[31] Perhaps the most obvious example of this strategy of legitimation in *Drum-Taps* is the poem "Pensive on Her Dead Gazing," which offers the symbolic figure of the "Mother of All," walking the battlefields and mourning the dead even as she calls on the earth to reabsorb and thus to recover their bodies. After the opening frame structure of the first four lines, in which the speaker describes overhearing the Mother's soliloquy, the remaining thirteen lines of the poem are devoted to the Mother's words. The figure's posture is dramatic and her speech, high-literary:

> Absorb them well O my earth, she cried, I charge you lose
>> not my sons, lose not an atom . . .
> My dead absorb or South or North—my young men's bodies
>> absorb, and their precious blood. . . .

$$(2: 527)$$

As so often in Whitman's work, however, an example of a particular stance is accompanied by a counter example. The "Mother of All" is a figure of mourning who makes possible the recuperation of the dead through their reintegration into the natural world. In "Come Up from the Fields Father," however, Whitman describes a mother who cannot accept the loss of her son and whose continued mourning thus disrupts the pastoral idyll described in stanzas two and three of the poem. While I agree with Sweet's claim that the pastoral is fundamentally a recuperative mode in Whitman's *Drum-Taps*, in juxtaposing Whitman's battlefield landscapes with Dickinson's, I want to attend in particular to passages in Whitman where the recuperative force of the pastoral threatens to collapse, undermining the metaphoric link between wartime bloodshed and nature's cycles of autumnal harvest and vernal renewal.

Two short poems from *Drum-Taps* might be read as companion pieces to one another insofar as they depict landscape scenes both before and after battle.[32] In both "Cavalry Crossing a Ford" and "Look Down Fair Moon," poetic gestures collide with journalistic description, and the speaker seems caught between these two stances. The result in each poem is an unresolved tension between pastoral symbolism and journalistic detail. In "Cavalry Crossing a Ford," which first appeared in 1865, Whitman's speaker offers a panoramic and picturesque scene—presumably prior to battle—in which soldiers and landscape seem to blend harmoniously:

A line in long array where they wind betwixt green islands,
They take a serpentine course, their arms flash in the sun—
    hark to the musical clank,
Behold the silver river, in it splashing horses loitering stop
    to drink,
Behold the brown-faced men, each group, each person a
    picture, the negligent rest on the saddles,
Some emerge on the opposite bank, others are just entering
    the ford—while,
Scarlet and blue and snowy white,
The guidon flags flutter gayly in the wind.

                                  (2: 457)

While the poem at first glance offers a photographic image of a cavalry unit on the march, the image is both carefully framed and artfully presented.[33] The opening line of the poem, "A line in long array where they wind betwixt green islands," presumably refers to the lines of soldiers, yet might also be read as referring to the river and its winding tributaries. The first three lines of the poem establish emphatic parallels between the movements and sounds of the soldiers and the movement and sounds of the river itself. The men "take a serpentine course." Their weapons, which "flash in the sun," provide a visual complement to the "silvery river"; their "musical clank" mingles pleasantly with the sound of "the splashing horses." The speaker's stance is that of a journalist insofar as the poem offers a detailed photographic description, yet the harmonious aural and visual blending of the soldiers with the natural world reveals the artistic intervention of the poet-speaker.[34] The imperatives to the reader emphasize that this is a literary presentation of the scene: "hark to the musical clank," "Behold the silvery river," and "Behold the brown-faced men." The imperatives have the paradoxical effect of drawing the reader's attention away from the horsemen, towards the speaker who is not merely witnessing but in fact staging the described scene.

In the poem "Look Down Fair Moon," as in "Cavalry Crossing a Ford," poetic imagery collides with journalistic detail. In "Look Down Fair Moon," however, which describes a gruesome night-time scene in the aftermath of battle, the tension between these two registers is more pronounced and the position of the speaker-witness is as a result less stable. I cite the strikingly brief poem in full:

> Look down fair moon and bathe this scene,
> Pour softly down night's nimbus floods on faces ghastly,
> swollen, purple,
> On the dead on their backs with arms toss'd wide,
> Pour down your unstinted nimbus sacred moon.
>
> (2: 519-20)

The high-literary trope of the address to the moon both opens and closes the poem and thus serves as a framework to contain the horrifying realism of the phrase which is at the poem's core: "faces ghastly, swollen, purple." This reliance on high-literary tropes appears elsewhere in *Drum-Taps*, particularly in the poems of the Sequel which Whitman added after Lincoln's death. In reading Whitman's elegies for Lincoln, Justin Kaplan describes the poet's return to a more conventionally poetic diction as evidence of "a retreat from the idiomatic boldness and emotional directness of [his] earlier work" (309-10). The apostrophe in "Look Down Fair Moon" also presents a retreat: transfixed by what he sees, the speaker effectively excludes the reader from the scene. Whitman has abandoned the easy confidence of the imperatives to the reader which we saw in "Cavalry Crossing a Ford."

Although the apostrophe to the moon represents a retreat from Whitman's stylistic innovations, in "Look Down Fair Moon" that retreat does not offer the same kind of resolution it provides in the Lincoln elegies. In "O Captain! My Captain!," for example, Whitman responds to the crisis of Lincoln's death by writing an elegy which reverts to the formal constraints of the lyric tradition both in its metrical regularity and in its repeated use of the apostrophe.[35] The catalogue of poetic techniques employed in "O Captain! My Captain!" has the cumulative effect of erasing the historical specificity of Lincoln's death and inserting the poem into the timeless elegiac tradition of "Lycidas" and "Adonais." The poem thus provides resolution by establishing Lincoln's death as a heroic one through association with the elegiac tradition.

In "Look Down Fair Moon," however, the gesture of the apostrophe seems incommensurate with the scene of carnage which the poem describes. While the speaker calls on the moon to "bathe this scene" with its "unstinted nimbus," the scene which the poem presents is horrifying in its detail and specificity: the "faces" are "ghastly, swollen, purple" and the "dead" are "on their backs with arms toss'd wide." The poem does not capture "night's nimbus floods" softening such a gruesome sight; rather it presents a speaker who, transfixed by the horror before him, calls on the moon to do so. While the speaker in "Cavalry Crossing a Ford" insists on representing a harmonious blending of soldiers with the natural world, in "Look Down Fair Moon," the relationship between the natural world and the battlefield is more ambiguous symbolically. Does the speaker call on the moon to shed light on the horror of wartime slaughter? Or does he call on the moon to cast an aura or nimbus of heroism around each dead man's face? Will nature reveal all the horror of human violence? Or will the moon recreate harmony between the human and natural worlds? While the speaker seems to call on the moon to soften the scene ("Pour softly down"), the poem offers no guarantee that the gesture of the apostrophe will be an effective or redemptive one: rather, the drama of the poem lies in its presentation of a speaker who wields the poetic apostrophe without evident success. The brevity of the poem only heightens the drama of this uncertainty.

In these poems then, Dickinson and Whitman examine the possibilities for representing violence by means of images drawn from the natural world. "They dropped like Flakes –" and "Cavalry Crossing a Ford" offer harmonious visions of heroic bodies merging with a vital and redemptive American landscape; in these poems, the speaker's position as witness is secure and authoritative. In "The name – of it – is 'Autumn' –" and "Look Down Fair Moon," however, this redemptive perspective is revealed to be fraudulent and deceptive. While "Look Down Fair Moon" relies on the high-literary apostrophe to control the horror of the faces of the dead, the balance the poem establishes between the literary trope and the gruesome description of the dead is a precarious one; the speaker's position is precarious as well. Though the poems in Whitman's *Drum-Taps* frequently rely on pastoral symbolism to imagine reconciliation and harmony after the war, "Look Down Fair Moon" points out that such a reconciliation will require the wholesale erasure of the collective memory of violence and death. In "The name – of it – is 'Autumn' –," Dickinson explicitly rejects the possibility of such an erasure. Simultaneously, she suggests that the poetic register of the pastoral is inadequate to representing the horrors of the scene. "Look Down Fair Moon" and "The name – of it – is 'Autumn' –" suggest both that the American landscape has been drenched with blood and that there is no secure outside position from which the war can be witnessed.

I want to conclude with a brief comparison of the stances of address in these Civil War battlefield poems. In these poems, both writers probe the limits of the lyric speaker's position as witness to suffering; simultaneously through their exploration of the Romantic scene of address, Dickinson and Whitman consider the dilemmas an American writer faces in addressing the nation in a time of war. As I have suggested, the speaker's stance in "Look Down Fair Moon" represents a stylistic retreat for Whitman—a retreat from the easy confidence with which his speaker commands the reader in "Cavalry Crossing a Ford." In "Look Down Fair Moon," Whitman reverts to the Romantic apostrophe to nature, placing his readers in the position of eavesdroppers as his speaker turns away from the audience. The brevity of the poem speaks both to the speaker's horror at the scene and to Whitman's uneasiness with this speaker's stance. The contrast between "Look Down

Fair Moon" and "Cavalry Crossing a Ford" suggests that Whitman is conflicted about whether to continue the bold innovation of his direct addresses to the readers or to return to the Romantic fiction of the solitary lyric speaker who is seemingly unaware of his audience.

Dickinson's two battlefield landscape poems offer an indirect critique of the Romantic scene of address by sustaining the fiction of a soliloquizing speaker who is wrapt in solitary contemplation of nature's wonders: after all, both poems explicitly represent the changing of the seasons. Yet by taking on the subject of the war in these poems, Dickinson calls on her readers to look for her satirical critique both of the Romantic scene of address and of the Romantic repertoire of nature imagery. The contrast between "They dropped like Flakes –" and "The name – of it – is 'Autumn' –" suggests that a poet of war can no longer observe the suffering of others from a safe distance as the Romantic poet conventionally did; the contrast between the two poems also foregrounds the instability of the lyric self who serves as Dickinson's speaker-witness.

Reading Dickinson's Civil War poetry in relation to Whitman's illuminates both poets' anxiety about their rapport with their readers. While the Civil War prompts an outpouring of American poetry which will be read by a growing American audience, the war also challenges writers to reexamine their obligations to that readership. Both Whitman and Dickinson recognize the impossibility of representing the experience of battle. For Whitman, however, this recognition is trumped by his desire to address the nation and to bind it together again through a poetry which represents death as redemptive and meaningful. Acutely aware of the challenges a woman writer faces both in addressing the nation and in representing war, Dickinson chooses not to publish her work via the conventional print means. This choice gives her the freedom not to compromise her own vision: though she feels obligated to represent war's horrors, she also feels obliged to insist that no poem can convey the experience of war to its readers.

From *Arizona Quarterly* 6, no. 4 (Winter 2005): 67-99. Copyright © 2005 by Arizona Board of Regents. Reprinted with permission of Faith Barrett.

Notes

I would like to thank Nancy Ruttenburg, Susan Schweik, Samuel Otter, and Tenney Nathanson for their responses to earlier versions of this essay.

1. All references to Dickinson's letters are cited from Johnson and Ward according to the letter numbers assigned in this edition.

2. Lynen's position, while strongly stated, is nonetheless largely representative of this first wave of Dickinson criticism. In an article published in 1966, Lynen writes: "Emily Dickinson is a baffling poet because she seems to bear little or no relation to the historical period within which she worked. She stands apart, as indifferent to the literary movements of her day as to its great events" (126). While Lynen's position is representative of much of the criticism from this period, Jay Leyda had already offered a counter-argument, suggesting in his 1960 biography that Dickinson "wrote more *in time*, that she was much more involved in the conflicts and tensions of her community than we have thought" (1: xx). Emphasis on Dickinson's isolation from her nineteenth-century surroundings also appears in more recent scholarship, however. In an article which examines Dickinson's class position, Erkkila argues that Dickinson's comfortable middle-class background allows her the luxury of refusing to participate in the political and literary debates of her day ("Emily Dickinson and Class").

3. Two of these studies analyze Dickinson's work in the context of relationships between and among women. Petrino reads Dickinson's work in relation to that of other nineteenth-century American women poets. Smith examines exchanges of letters and poems between Dickinson and her correspondents, particularly her beloved sister-in-law, and argues that such exchanges are themselves a form of publication. On the subject of Dickinson's response to the Civil War, a recent article by Miller offers an astute analysis of Dickinson's use of the word "liberty" in the context of Republican rhetoric; Marcellin provides a thematic survey of Dickinson's Civil War-related poems ("'Singing'"). For an analysis of Dickinson's political commitments in relation to the war, see Erkkila ("Dickinson and the Art") and Hutchinson. Reading Melville and Dickinson poems comparatively, Lee points out that both writers maintain a skeptical and oblique position in relation to dominant Northern wartime ideologies. To date, the only book-length study of Dickinson's response to the Civil War is Wolosky's, which argues that Dickinson's work offers a philosophical meditation on war's violence; Wolosky suggests that Dickinson's extraordinary rate of productivity during the war years cannot be dismissed as mere coincidence. R. W. Franklin's dating of Dickinson's manuscripts would suggest that she wrote an astonishing 937 poems between 1861 and 1865. My approach to Dickinson's representation of the Civil War is deeply indebted to Wolosky's analysis. While Wolosky begins by examining responses to the war in Dickinson's work, her analysis eventually leads away from the historical context of the war and its attendant problems of audience towards poems which focus on theological

and metaphysical questions about language. My account reads the poems which represent the war as poems that are fundamentally about the dilemmas of the address to the nation. In a recent article, Wolosky reframes some of her arguments in more historical terms; noting parallels between "radical experimentation in twentieth-century poetics" and Dickinson's work, she describes the context in which Dickinson wrote as a time when "long-standing traditional assumptions regarding the basic frameworks for interpreting the world [were] challenged"; she asserts, "Dickinson's work is among the first directly to register the effects on poetic language of such a breakdown" (126), and she notes that Dickinson "not only explores her world in her world in her work but also addresses it" (127). Although Dickinson's critique of the address to the nation is not Wolosky's central concern, her claims run parallel to mine.

4. As these opening remarks begin to suggest, my approach to Dickinson's address to the nation fundamentally rejects the premise with which Sanchez-Eppler's analysis begins. Reading a letter which Dickinson wrote near the end of the Civil War, Sanchez-Eppler argues that "Dickinson claims freedom for herself by forfeiting any engagement with the nation, and even more radically, by forfeiting her own body" (105). I claim, on the contrary, that Dickinson does address the nation in her work, but that she does so from an oblique and skeptical position. This oblique position results, I will argue, not from her forfeiture of her body, but rather from her rejection of sentimental models for identification with the body of the suffering other. Sanchez-Eppler's analysis does not address those Dickinson poems which seek to represent the violence of the Civil War, nor does it address those poems in which Dickinson seeks to represent the racialized body in the terms of the abolition debate.

5. In a recent study, Jackson analyzes how twentieth-century critical lenses have classified (and effectively reified) Dickinson's work as lyric poetry; Jackson suggests that our insistence on reading Dickinson's pieces as lyrics works to obscure our understanding of the nineteenth-century context and communities in which the poems were produced. Though we approach the genre of the lyric from different critical angles, my concerns parallel Jackson's insofar as I, too, argue that Dickinson's poems resist and critique the boundaries of the lyric poem.

6. Two important studies of Whitman offer detailed analyses of the rhetoric of address in his work. Larson examines the relationship between Whitman's poetics of address and his political commitments. Nathanson offers a reading of the relationship between voice, writing, and lyric address. Both of these accounts influenced my approach to address in Whitman.

7. Wilson dismisses much of the poetry written during the Civil War as "versified journalism" in which the aims of propaganda were writ large (487); I would argue that Dickinson's Civil War poetry offers a counter example to this claim. For a discussion of a broad spectrum of poets' responses to Civil War ideologies and rhetoric, see my Introduction in *"Words for the Hour."*

8. Hosek and Parker offer a number of accounts of the position of Mill's model in contemporary theories of the lyric. See, for example, Culler's argument about the importance of Mill's model. Tucker takes Mill's model as a point of departure in analyzing the relationship between historical time and the lyric moment in Browning's work. Culler also emphasizes the centrality of Mill's model in his influential essay "Apostro-

---

phe." For a critique of the shaping influence Mill's model of the scene of address has had on twentieth-century readings of the lyric in general and Dickinson in particular, see Jackson (129-33).

9. Responding to Michael Fried's *Absorption and Theatricality*, Bernstein considers the differences between the "absorptive" text and the "antiabsorptive" one, suggesting that "both require artifice, but the former may hide / this while the latter may flaunt / it" (20). Bernstein also notes that "absorption may be a quality that characterizes specifically Romantic works" (13). In the poems in which they address America, Dickinson and Whitman both foreground the artifice of address in ways that disrupt the possibility of an absorptive reading.

10. Whitman's interest in public speaking is often mentioned in critical studies of his work, and his frequent use of dramatic apostrophes lends itself to comparative analyses between poetry and oratory. By contrast, Dickinson rarely uses the figure and uses the apostrophe to a reading public only ironically; her work might seem like an improbable place to look for ideas about the relationship between the lyric and the public speaking circuit. Dickinson's work, however, clearly responds to a range of nineteenth-century oratorical modes. Two recent studies of Dickinson argue for the connections between her poetry and sermon rhetoric. Lease examines the relationship between Dickinson's poetry and Wadsworth's sermons. Doriani explores the relationship between sermon rhetoric and Dickinson's poetics (see in particular Chapter 3). Reading Dickinson's work in relation to contemporary political oratory would no doubt also prove to be a fruitful field of inquiry. Any analysis of the lyric voice in Dickinson's work must, of course, attend to the impact of both religious and political oratory on her poems. Dickinson, like Whitman, writes not only with Emerson's writerly essays in mind, but also with years of public speeches, debates and sermons ringing in her ears. Even before she began in her thirties to keep increasingly to her home, Dickinson would have had the opportunity to hear countless lectures, sermons, talks and discussions at civic and university events in Amherst and South Hadley, at church services, and in her father's and brother's homes. Doriani calculates that Dickinson would have heard "well over fifteen hundred sermons during her period of regular attendance at church" (45).

11. Larson claims that Whitman's work provides a noteworthy exception to Mill's definition insofar as the poetry makes plain its demands on the reader (5-6). I would argue, however, that this claim neglects the extent to which the rhetoric of the apostrophe—throughout the lyric tradition—inevitably disrupts Mill's theory; the apostrophe insistently points to the circuit of communication which links the speaker and the reader. In other words, it is not only Whitman's poetics which disrupts Mill's scheme, but any poetics which emphasizes the scene of address.

12. References to Dickinson's poems are cited from R. W. Franklin's variorum edition using the initial "F" and the numbers assigned by Franklin.

13. Franklin notes that Dickinson sent poems to more than forty people. He estimates that she sent 250 to Susan Gilbert Dickinson, 100 to Higginson, 71 to Louise and Frances Norcross, and 40 to Samuel Bowles (3: 1547). If we assume that some of these poems were circulated among a wider group of readers by their intended recipients (as was common practice with correspondence at this time), then hundreds of Dickinson's

unpublished poems could have been read by hundreds of readers. In analyzing the rhetoric of address in nineteenth-century American poetry, then, it is essential to consider the influence both of reading practices and of epistolary communities on these writers' poetics: it is essential that we ask how writers and readers might have experienced the idea of lyric voice in a culture in which both poems and letters were routinely read aloud and circulated among friends.

14. In 1863, of course, the phrase "Sweet – countrymen –" would have made a collective whole out of what was in fact a divided nation. Moreover, the line breaks and spacing in the handwritten version of this poem (Manuscript 1: 548) work to heighten the gender divide: the word "men" is the penultimate line. Franklin moves "men" to the end of the preceding line, but the manuscript offers another reading: "For love of her [nature], sweet country, men judge tenderly of me." In this variant, Dickinson's speaker addresses not her "countrymen," but her "sweet country"; her male readers "judge" her "tenderly" because of their love of nature—and for women poets who choose to write about nature.

15. As Dandurand notes, the three poems which appeared in the *Drum Beat* are: "Blazing in Gold and quenching in Purple" (F 321), "Flowers – well, if anybody" (F 95), and "These are the days when Birds come back –" (F 122).

16. In his suggestive analysis of the rhetoric of address in Whitman, Nathanson writes: "Performative declarations that suggest the magical efficacy of the word abound in Whitman's early work. At their most dramatic, Whitman's performatives claim to produce actual presences, disposing creatures and objects by intoning their names as easily as the poet conjures up his own presence by declaring it" (7).

17. Pointing to the connection between Whitman's development of the open line and his commitment to the ideal of freedom, Grossman suggests that Whitman's work calls for the rejection of symbolic hierarchies: "The rewriting of hierarchies—soul/ body, collective/individual, nation/state—as equalities, and the rewriting of identities as conventional dualities, above all the self and the other, is the task of the 'translator,' whose goal is union as the fraternalization of the community" (194).

18. Analyzing voice in Whitman's work, Pease argues that Whitman mistrusts the extraordinary power which the nineteenth-century orator's voice often had over the masses: "For Whitman, any orator who put the masses into bondage to his tropes supported slavery" (147). Pease suggests that Whitman seeks to create a different kind of oratorical voice in his poetry, not a voice which brings the masses into submission, but rather a voice which expresses "the relation between the individual and the mass" (150). It is this Utopian and participatory ideal of oratorical voice which Whitman reaches for in "Apostroph."

19. While such divisions prove anxious ones for the speaker in Whitman's poems, they also, of course, prove to be tremendously productive ones for Whitman's poetic imagination. Responding to both Larson's and Erkkila's (*Whitman*) accounts of the importance of union to Whitman's poetics, Maslan notes that "these critics hesitate to express what their opinions effectively assume: that division is a vital principle of Whitman's poetics" ("Whitman and His Doubles" 136). Maslan continues, "Rethinking division in this manner—as enabling rather than debilitating—would involve reexamining a whole series of relationships in Whitman in which critics have seen

union as the organizing principle" (136). Breitwieser makes a similar claim in arguing that Whitman's poems present a dialogue between two speakers, "one timid, gentle, frequently disconsolate, the other large, all-inclusive" (121). Breitwieser contends that "Whitman's great poems . . . are crisis poems that concern themselves with being between these possibilities" (142). Focusing on Whitman's work in Civil War hospitals, Davis suggests that the poet-nurse in Whitman's wartime writings is able to occupy a liminal position, hovering on the boundaries between living and dead and thereby "proposing an alternative concept of Union," one that resists "the binary deadlock of secession and civil war" (6-7).

20. Two analyses argue that the poetry Whitman wrote during and after the Civil War considerably complicates his earlier pronouncements about the poetics of presence in his work. Moon describes how later editions of *Leaves of Grass* complicate the first edition's account of the relationship between the world of the body and discourses of the body. Maslan argues that "the identification of text and body in Whitman requires that the body [itself] become representational" ("Whitman's 'Strange Hand'" 938).

21. Pointing to the power of the apostrophe in Whitman's work, Pease argues: "Whitman experiences language not as a deprivation but as a plenipotential force" (155). "Living apostrophaically," Pease writes, "entails living for the sake of the activity which the apostrophe calls forth. An apostrophe has no existence apart from the activity it motivates. Hence death can have no dominion over it" (153). I would counter that the frenzied list of apostrophes in this poem reveals the speaker's fear of death, his terror at the prospect of the splitting of the nation, and his awareness that the language of the poem cannot prevent that splitting.

22. Analyzing Whitman's vision of the American subject, Altieri points to the limitations of the formulas for describing American identity that dominate contemporary discourses of the left and center. Such slogans, which emphasize both multiculturalism and the ideology of the melting-pot's shared culture, tend to avoid the tensions of difference, Altieri suggests, rather than confronting them. Altieri goes on to argue that Whitman's poetics "can help us both analyze the problem and develop a good deal more intensity of will than we can get from this bureaucratically seductive formula" (59-60). While Altieri's point is well-taken, his analysis does not address those passages in Whitman's work where the tensions of difference within the nation come to the fore. Altieri does not address Whitman's response to the violence of the war; nor does he examine Whitman's attempts to conceive of America as a nation which includes many races.

23. Wolosky points to the ways in which Dickinson's demurrals are part of a deliberate stance: "Dickinson is an assertive and determined poet . . . whose retirement is a stance of attack, whose timidity is aggressive" (*Emily Dickinson* xiii).

24. Just as the war threatens the stability of the lyric self, so too did it threaten Whitman's own psychic stability, as Aaron argues: "Given his personal expectations and his prophecies of American promise, [Whitman] had to insist on the providentiality of the War and to wring optimistic conclusions from its horrors" (68).

25. Two studies read Dickinson's work in relation to nineteenth-century painting. Fair examines Dickinson's painterly interest in the sublime, and St. Armand reads

Dickinson's work in relation to both the Victorian painterly aesthetic of the sublime and popular forms of folk art. Neither study, however, considers Dickinson's painterly depictions of battlefield landscapes.

26. I am drawing here on Sweet, who argues that Whitman's poetics relies on a recuperative aesthetics of pastoralism in order to imagine the reuniting of North and South.

27. The landscape paintings of Thomas Cole, which were enormously popular with the public, offer just one example of the contemporary fascination with panoramic representation. Miller and Parry offer analyses of Cole's work and of American landscape painting. Dougherty examines the ways in which Whitman uses a visual vocabulary to "serve as the base of communion" between the poet and his readers (xiv). Drawing on Martin Buber's formulation of the "I-Thou" relationship, Dougherty's study argues that Whitman's poetics of the visual enables the poet and his citizen readers to share "a common space" (xvi). Dougherty's argument thus relies on a belief in the bond between poet and reader which my argument aims to unsettle. Folsom examines the relationship between Whitman's poetics and the development of photography; his analysis, however, touches only briefly on the dilemmas of representing war.

28. I would thus disagree with the emphasis Wolosky places, in her reading of this poem, on the violence inherent in Dickinson's vision of nature. Wolosky writes: "The comparison of battle to snow and wind, far from making the death of soldiers seem more natural, makes nature seem sudden and frightening" (*Emily Dickinson* 37). I would instead offer the poem "The Name – of it – is 'Autumn' –" (F 465) as an instance of Dickinson's reckoning with the violence of nature.

29. Paglia argues that criticism continues to neglect and downplay violence in Dickinson's work. She also notes the frequency with which Dickinson offers descriptions of blood or relies on a palette of reds. Yet while Paglia cites "The name – of it – is 'Autumn' –" among other examples, she fails to consider the possibility that the violence of Dickinson's poetics offers a commentary on the violence of the Civil War. In a recent article, Cody reads "The name – of it – is 'Autumn' –" in relation to the Civil War, juxtaposing the poem with possible source texts both from tourist literature and from the Bible.

30. Like "The name – of it – is 'Autumn' –" (F 465), "Whole Gulfs – of Red, and Fleets – of Red –" (F 468) appears in fascicle 22 and clearly responds to the war's violence.

31. Reading Whitman's representation of violence in relation to Lincoln's, Erkkila makes a similar point: "As in Lincoln's Gettysburg Address, Whitman's urge to naturalize the unnatural bloodiness of the Civil War, by mingling blood and grass in a redemptive teleology, fed willy-nilly the national myth of regeneration through violence that marked, and still does mark, the course of American history" (*Whitman* 210).

32. *Drum-Taps* first appeared as a separate volume in 1865, and this edition included fifty-three poems; these poems were subsequently incorporated as an annex into the 1867 version of *Leaves of Grass*. In reading *Drum-Taps* in its historical context, it is important to keep in mind, as Asselineau notes, that many of the poems which first appeared in this volume were most likely written before the start of the war or during its first few months; more specifically, many of the poems may well have been

written before Whitman became directly involved with the war through his work as a nurse (308-9). See also Chapter 5 in Moon.

33. Sweet agrees with Wilson's characterization of this poem as a realistic "sketch from life" (Wilson 482, Sweet 209 n.3). I would argue, however, that the poem is as deliberately artful in its presentation of detail as any of the poems in *Drum-Taps*.

34. Erkkila notes that the relaxed and casual postures of the soldiers "contradict traditional notions of military order, discipline, and hierarchy, thereby projecting the figure of a democratic army" (*Whitman* 215). The artfully casual posture of the soldiers thus corresponds to the artfully casual air of the reportage provided by the speaker.

35. "O Captain! My Captain!" first appeared in print in the *New York Saturday Press*, November 4, 1865, and was included in the *Sequel to Drum-Taps* of 1865.

Works Cited

Aaron, Daniel. *The Unwritten War: American Writers and the Civil War*. Madison: University of Wisconsin Press, 1987.

Altieri, Charles. "Spectacular Antispectacle: Ecstasy and Nationality in Whitman and His Heirs." *American Literary History* 11 (1999): 34-62.

Asselineau, Roger. *The Evolution of Walt Whitman: The Creation of a Personality*. Cambridge: Harvard University Press, 1960.

Barrett, Faith. Introduction. *"Words for the Hour": A New Anthology of American Civil War Poetry*. Ed. Faith Barrett and Cristanne Miller. Amherst: University of Massachusetts Press, 2005. 1-22.

Bernstein, Charles. "Artifice of Absorption." *Artifice & Indeterminacy: An Anthology of New Poetics*. Ed. Christopher Beach. Tuscaloosa: University of Alabama Press, 1998. 3-23.

Breitwieser, Mitchell. "Who Speaks in Whitman's Poems?" *Bucknell Review* 28. *The American Renaissance: New Dimensions*. Ed. Harry Garvin and Peter Carafiol. Lewisburg, PA: Bucknell University Press, 1983. 121-43.

Cody, David. "Blood in the Basin: The Civil War in Emily Dickinson's 'The Name – of it – is "Autumn" –.'" *Emily Dickinson Journal* 12 (2003): 25-52.

Culler, Jonathan. "Apostrophe." *The Pursuit of Signs*. Ithaca: Cornell University Press, 1981. 135-54.

_____. "Changes in the Study of the Lyric." Hosek and Parker 38-54.

Dandurand, Karen. "New Dickinson Civil War Publications." *American Literature* 56 (1984): 17-27.

Davis, Robert Leigh. *Whitman and the Romance of Medicine*. Berkeley: University of California Press, 1997.

Dickinson, Emily. *The Letters of Emily Dickinson*. 3 vols. Ed. Thomas Johnson and Theodora Ward. Cambridge: Belknap-Harvard University Press, 1958.

_____. *The Manuscript Books of Emily Dickinson*. 2 vols. Ed. R. W. Franklin. Cambridge: Belknap-Harvard University Press, 1981.

_____. *The Poems of Emily Dickinson: The Variorum Edition.* 3 vols. Ed. R. W. Franklin. Cambridge: Belknap-Harvard University Press, 1998.

Doriani, Beth Maclay. *Emily Dickinson, Daughter of Prophecy.* Amherst: University of Massachusetts Press, 1996.

Dougherty, James. *Walt Whitman and the Citizen's Eye.* Baton Rouge: Louisiana State University Press, 1993.

Erkkila, Betsy. "Dickinson and the Art of Politics." Pollak 133-74.

_____. "Emily Dickinson and Class." *American Literary History* 4 (1992): 1-27.

_____. *Whitman: The Political Poet.* New York: Oxford University Press, 1989.

Farr, Judith. *The Passion of Emily Dickinson.* Cambridge: Harvard University Press, 1992.

Folsom, Ed. *Walt Whitman's Native Representations.* New York: Cambridge University Press, 1994.

Grossman, Allen. "The Poetics of Union in Whitman and Lincoln: An Inquiry toward the Relationship of Art and Policy." *The American Renaissance Reconsidered.* Ed. Walter Benn Michaels and Donald Pease. Baltimore: Johns Hopkins University Press, 1985. 183-208.

Hosek, Chaviva, and Patricia Parker, eds. *Lyric Poetry: Beyond New Criticism.* Ithaca: Cornell University Press, 1985.

Hutchinson, Coleman. "'Eastern Exiles': Dickinson, Whiggery, and War. *Emily Dickinson Journal* 13 (2004): 1-26.

Jackson, Virginia. *Dickinson's Misery: A Theory of Lyric Reading.* Princeton: Princeton University Press, 2005.

Kaplan, Justin. *Wait Whitman: A Life.* New York: Simon and Schuster, 1980.

Larson, Kerry. *Whitman's Drama of Consensus.* Chicago: University of Chicago Press, 1988.

Lease, Benjamin. *Emily Dickinson's Readings of Men and Books: Sacred Soundings.* New York: St. Martin's, 1990.

Lee, Maurice. "Writing through the War: Melville and Dickinson after the Renaissance." *PMLA* 115 (2000): 1124-28.

Leyda, Jay. *The Years and Hours of Emily Dickinson.* 2 vols. New Haven: Yale University Press, 1960.

Lynen, John. "The Uses of the Present: The Historian's, the Critic's, and Emily Dickinson's." *College English* 28 (1966): 126-36.

Marcellin, Leigh-Anne Urbanowicz. "'Singing off the Charnel Steps': Soldiers and Mourners in Emily Dickinson's War Poetry." *Emily Dickinson Journal* 9 (2000): 64-74.

Maslan, Mark. "Whitman and His Doubles: Division and Union in *Leaves of Grass* and Its Critics." *American Literary History* 6 (1994): 119-39.

_____. "Whitman's 'Strange Hand': Body as Text in *Drum-Taps.*" *ELH* 58 (1991): 935-55.

Mill, John Stuart. *Essays on Poetry.* Ed. F. Parvin Sharpless. Columbia: University of South Carolina Press, 1976.

Miller, Angela. *Empire of the Eye*. Ithaca: Cornell University Press, 1993.

Miller, Cristanne. "Pondering 'Liberty': Emily Dickinson and the Civil War." *American Vistas and Beyond: A Festschrift for Roland Hagenbüchle*. Ed. Marietta Messmer and Josef Raab. Trier: Wissenschaftlicher Verlag Trier, 2002. 45-64.

Moon, Michael. *Disseminating Whitman: Revision and Corporeality in* Leaves of Grass. Cambridge: Harvard University Press, 1991.

Nathanson, Tenney. *Whitman's Presence: Body, Voice, and Writing in* Leaves of Grass. New York: New York University Press, 1992.

Paglia, Camille. "Amherst's Madame de Sade: Emily Dickinson." *Sexual Personae: Art and Decadence from Nefertiti to Emily Dickinson*. New Haven: Yale University Press, 1990. 623-73.

Parry, Ellwood C. *The Art of Thomas Cole: Ambition and Imagination*. Newark: University of Delaware Press, 1988.

Pease, Donald. *Visionary Compacts: American Renaissance Writings in Cultural Context*. Madison: University of Wisconsin Press, 1987.

Petrino, Elizabeth. *Emily Dickinson and Her Contemporaries: Women's Verse in America*. Hanover, NH: University Press of New England, 1998.

Pollak, Vivian, ed. *A Historical Guide to Emily Dickinson*. New York: Oxford University Press, 2004.

St. Armand, Barton Levi. *Emily Dickinson and Her Culture: The Soul's Society*. Cambridge: Cambridge University Press, 1984.

Sanchez-Eppler, Karen. *Touching Liberty: Abolition, Feminism, and the Politics of the Body*. Berkeley: University of California Press, 1993.

Smith, Martha Nell. *Rowing in Eden: Rereading Emily Dickinson*. Austin: University of Texas Press, 1992.

Sweet, Timothy. *Traces of War: Poetry, Photography, and the Crisis of the Union*. Baltimore: Johns Hopkins University Press, 1990.

Tucker, Herbert. "Dramatic Monologue and the Overhearing of Lyric." Hosek and Parker 226-46.

Whitman, Walt. *Leaves of Grass: A Textual Variorum of the Printed Poems*. 3 vols. Ed. Sculley Bradley, Harold Blodgett, Arthur Golden, and William White. New York: New York University Press, 1980.

Wilson, Edmund. *Patriotic Gore: Studies in the Literature of the American Civil War*. New York: Oxford University Press, 1962.

Wolosky, Shira. *Emily Dickinson: A Voice of War*. New Haven: Yale University Press, 1984.

_____. "Public and Private in Dickinson's War Poetry." Pollak 103-33.

"The Inner Brand":
Emily Dickinson, Portraiture, and the Narrative of Liberal Interiority_____

Sarah E. Blackwood

When Thomas Wentworth Higginson, in a well-known episode from Dickinson's life, asked for her portrait, she replied, "Could you believe me – without?" While Dickinson's reluctance to send a daguerreotype portrait has been explained as a sign of her "proper feminine recoil from the increasingly vulgar visual mass market," Sarah E. Blackwood contends that Dickinson's unease with visual portraiture also actively critiques an idea that is fundamental to American literary studies: that each individual has an "inviolable interior life." As Dickinson explores the relationship between an individual's external appearance and interior life in poems such as "Portraits are to daily faces," "A Charm invests a face," and "The Outer – from the Inner," she challenges accepted nineteenth-century wisdom that portraiture or outer appearance reflects interiority. Indeed, "Dickinson recognizes the impossibility of ever gaining a direct knowledge, unmediated by sensual perception, of anything, including one's own inner life. No meaning exists before representation creates it." Offering a "fascinating challenge" to traditional liberal ideals, Dickinson's poetics are anti-liberal in their acknowledgment that "interiority does not exist without its representation." Fearless in her recognition of the "unstable and oftentimes anti-liberal nature of an individual's interior world," Dickinson, without the "liberal interior to project itself upon and structure the external world," turns to the "complexities of perception and representation to evince a keenly-felt uneasiness with the liberal dominion of the self." J.B.B.

The enduring opposition between the "private" Emily Dickinson, the reclusive bread baker and gardener, and the "public" Emily Dickinson, the letter writer and self-published author, has long shaped critical work on the poet.[1] Though she is perhaps no longer the madwoman in the attic, Dickinson's rich interior world is often still cast as a thing of brilliance that becomes oxidized and tarnished upon contact with the public. I contend that figuring Dickinson's poetics in this manner— private versus public, inner versus outer, personal versus political—is not only to mischaracterize these terms as polar opposites but also to put one's faith in a historically-specific ideal of interiority. Further, this ideal of interiority is inextricably connected with the narrative of liberalism. That narrative, according to Elizabeth Maddock Dillon, has fashioned the liberal subject as one and the same as the private subject: "The unencumbered liberal agent emerges with the help of a powerful narrative, one that defines the liberal subject's agency as grounded in his possessive relation to privacy" (25).[2] While recent scholarship on Dickinson's engagement with national politics has made great strides in challenging the mythos of withdrawal and privacy that has structured Dickinson studies, this scholarship has often situated her politics within the comfortably wide margins of the liberal tradition.[3]

The idea that each person has an inviolable interior life is a foundational one for American literary studies. The full emergence of the field during the Cold War demanded an exceptionalist theory of American literature to set it apart from the "anti-democratic" literatures of Britain and Europe.[4] This exceptionalism emphasized the importance of individualism and self-determination and has ineluctably shaped the way we read American literature today. The psychological offspring of liberal individualism, the liberal interior is the kernel inside each human. It is an authentic core self, bearing rights and privileges, striving always for self-determination, and entitled, by the simple tautological fact of its existence, to freedom.[5] This essay will argue that Dickinson's exploration of interiority—what it is and how it comes to mean— complicates the promises of liberalism by confounding its ideals of individual expression. The impersonality with which Dickinson approaches her poetics is decidedly anti-liberal in its acknowledgement of the extent to which interiority does not exist without its representation. My argument will center on a reading of Dickinson's complicated response to Thomas Wentworth Higginson's well-known request for her portrait. This episode is neither mere anecdote nor evidence of the poet's pathological reclusiveness, but instead evidence that Dickinson was actively critiquing an ideal of interiority that has since come to seem both natural and ahistorical. Emily Dickinson's engagement with forms of visual portraiture reevaluates the relevance of the narrative of liberal interiority to questions of freedom and liberty. Her canny exploration of the epistemology of vision—how one comes to know what one sees and see what one knows—emerges as a fascinating challenge to liberal definitions of subjectivity and interiority.

The narrative of liberal interiority fetishizes the possession of that interiority; the mere *expression* of inner life becomes an aesthetic goal in and of itself.[6] It is in this context that the question Dickinson posed in reply to Higginson's request for her portrait—"Could you believe me – without" (L268)—is profoundly startling. She wonders, on the page, whether or not he can believe that she exists without visual evidence. Her pause is short-lived, however, as she proceeds to paint a verbal picture of herself for him, a synaesthetic sketch of her "bold" hair and "Sherry"-tinted eyes. With typical Dickinsonian resourcefulness, the poet creates her own version of publicity; dissatisfied with the public forms available to her—saying of the daguerreotype that "I noticed the Quick wore off those things, in a few days"—she creates her own. Yet her verbal self-portrait cannot undo the unsettling effect of the letter's opening query. Dickinson's question to Higginson is crucial not because it displays the wincing self of a woman unfamiliar with the tenets and promises of liberalism, but because it displays so well the fearlessness with which she identifies what the theory of liberal interiority is loath to acknowledge: the unstable and oftentimes anti-liberal nature of an individual's interior world. Her question is phrased starkly, not "would you" but "could you," the difference being the one between a polite request for forbearance and a frightening acknowledgement of the possibility of nonexistence.

In the mid-nineteenth century, one's portrait was one's calling card and public persona.[7] The cultural currency attached to the circulation of an individual's portrait bears out the critical consensus that Dickinson was intensely private and unwilling to expose herself within the public sphere. Her reluctance to send a portrait has been noted as doubly odd when placed in relation to her avowed fondness for portraits of other writers.[8] One explanation for the reluctance is certainly her proper feminine recoil from the increasingly vulgar visual mass market. The poet famously exclaims elsewhere:

> How dreary – to be – Somebody!
> How public – like a Frog –
> To tell one's name – the livelong June –
> To an admiring Bog!
>
> (Fr260)

Herman Melville expressed a similar antipathy toward the circulation of portraits in an 1851 letter to Evert Duyckinck, observing, "The fact is, almost everybody is having his 'mug' engraved nowadays; so that this test of distinction is getting to be reversed; and therefore, to see one's 'mug' in a magazine, is presumptive evidence that he's a nobody. . . . I respectfully decline being oblivionated by a Daguerretype [sic]" (12 February 1851). Dickinson's pose in her letter is a familiar one in her time; it is not at all becoming for a genius to allow her picture to be circulated in public as if she were some music hall singer.

And yet, Dickinson's skepticism toward the daguerreotype does more than just confirm her increasingly keen awareness of her genius, and is more than just the expected pose of a precocious writer. After refusing Higginson's request for her portrait, Dickinson writes, "When I state myself, as the Representative of the Verse – it does not mean – me – but a supposed person" (L268). It is crucial that her only comment on the lyric "I" she used throughout her thirty-five-year career employs the liberal language of political representation to make its point about authorship. After denying Higginson's request for her portrait, Dickinson makes herself both senator and state, representative and represented, individual and collective. The letter marks the fascinating intersection of portraiture and political representation, the point at which the self is both subjected to and dependent upon the process of representational abstraction. *Subjected to*, because, as Dickinson so clearly intimates through her alternative verbal self-portrait, representational portraiture will always fail to capture a self fully without "dishonor[ing]" (L268) the original.[9] Yet the self is also *dependent on* this process of abstraction to make recognizable its existence. The usefully redundant utterance, "When I state myself," illuminates this tension in two ways. It is both an active expression and a transitive creation through which Dickinson simultaneously claims a self capable of expression—the "I"—while also highlighting the extent to which that self does not exist prior to the utterance—"state myself." We might read "state" not simply as an active verb connoting expression and declaration, but as also possessing an adverbial dimension in describing how an action is performed by "I" upon "myself." Dickinson's language makes it impossible to separate a "real" self from its "constructed" representation.

The remarkable daguerreotype letter entwines interior and exterior, the thing and its representation, in explicit contradiction to the ideals of liberal interiority. Her representations of interiority are based neither solely on a depth model of psychology, where a truth about a person is hidden deep inside the self, nor solely on an expressive model, where the surface reveals what lies beneath. In a number of poems, Dickinson considers how a person's inner life may or may not become visible, often taking "the face"—and, by extension, the portrait—as a figure through which to explore this epistemological problem. From the first, the poet probes accepted wisdom about portraiture and interiority:

> Portraits are to daily faces
> As an Evening West,
> To a fine – pedantic sunshine –
> In a satin vest!
>
> (Fr174)

In this, one of Dickinson's modest set pieces, the poet begins by making the expected comparison between a portrait and a daily face. Like a spectacular sunset, a portrait depicts a heightened reality, the implication being that the portrait is somehow unfaithful to the real thing, "daily faces." Then, Dickinson plays upon this art versus life sophistry by describing the true light of day as "pedantic," clad "In a satin vest." Her delightful characterization of the everyday person as a frivolous blowhard, all finery and glare, suggests that Dickinson was not working with a model of the self that is at all separate from its representation. The "daily faces" in this unassuming poem are, apparently, always playing themselves, always both sitter and daguerreotypist.

In 1862, Dickinson first wrote to Higginson, entered treatment for an eye affliction that has been variously diagnosed as exotropia or anterior uveitis, and began considering an epistemological problem that had also preoccupied her distant colleagues Nathaniel Hawthorne and Herman Melville: is a person's inner life revealed in his or her appearance? And, furthermore, can anyone trust her own eyes to detect this expression of interiority accurately? Of a lady's prerogative to produce desire in others by remaining veiled, the poet writes, "A Charm invests a face / Imperfectly beheld –" (Fr430). More importantly, it emerges in this poem that this lady recognizes the danger inherent in the human drive to know by seeing:

> But peers beyond her mesh –
> And wishes – and denies –
> Lest Interview – annul a want
> That Image satisfies –

Just as Dickinson prefers to deny Higginson the satisfaction of the image, here a coquettish woman hedges her bets on the possibility that she will appear more charming and intriguing if she keeps herself slightly out of focus. The power of the image far outstrips the person; it is simultaneously the means and the end of this momentary courtship. Using a logical rhetorical move for a poet living with an eye affliction that forced her into an increasingly more antagonistic relationship to light and the visual, this poem disconnects the person from the image.

It seems the poet wants to conclude that there *is* something more than the satisfaction of the image,

> Before I got my eye put out –
> I liked as well to see
> As other creatures that have eyes –
> And know no other way –

but she is continually drawn to the seduction of vision, content yet cognizant that she has sacrificed visual euphoria for safety and concludes:

> So safer – guess – with just my soul
> Upon the window pane
> Where other creatures put their eyes –
> Incautious – of the Sun –
>
> (Fr336)

This poem is often read as an assertion of a poetic vision that goes beyond biologically-conscripted eyesight. The speaker has learned to look in an "other way," with her "soul" as opposed to her fallible and failing "eyes." Yet I am intrigued by the poem's final turn where we learn that those who continue to look with their eyes act injudiciously. The speaker offers the soul up to the blinding rays of "the Sun" in an attempt to protect the "eyes." What presumably resides inside the speaker, "my soul," is transmuted into something that exists outside,

---

incautiously placed "Upon the window pane," while the precious eyes are secreted away inside. What does it mean to drag the soul into the bright light of day? What would the soul look like? And, conversely, what then does the emptied interior look like?

Dickinson actively works through these questions about the relationship between an individual's interior life and exterior appearance. In a world consumed with curiosity and anxiety over hucksterism, fakery, and imposture, the concern that rouged cheeks covered a blackened soul was a pressing one.[10] Upon first glance, the following poem seems to move in lockstep with nineteenth-century sentimental culture in asserting that one's appearance is an expression of one's interior life:

> The Outer – from the Inner
> Derives it's magnitude –
> 'Tis Duke, or Dwarf, according
> As is the central mood –
>
> The fine – unvarying Axis
> That regulates the Wheel –
> Though Spokes – spin – more conspicuous
> And fling a dust – the while.
>
> The Inner – paints the Outer –
> The Brush without the Hand –
> It's Picture publishes – precise –
> As is the inner Brand –
>
> On fine – Arterial Canvas –
> A Cheek – perchance a Brow –
> The Star's whole secret – in the Lake –
> Eyes were not meant to know.
>
> (Fr450)

Things seem to be in their place. Modest cheeks blush exactly as *Godey's Lady's Book* insists they should, and a rationalized and predictable machinery ensures the constancy of expression. At the center of each person is a "fine – unvarying Axis / That regulates the Wheel." But a few words stand out against this interpretation: "mood," "conspicuous," "publishes," "Brand," "Canvas." Something is interfering with the unmediated expression of the individual's inner life. Blinding dust is flung, the conspicuous spokes distract the viewer from the "unvarying Axis," an "inner Brand" is violently stamped upon the artificial "Arterial Canvas," and the "unvarying Axis" is governed by that nineteenth-century psychological villain, "mood." For a poem that first appears to answer the epistemological problem in the affirmative—"Yes, inner life is clearly writ upon the outer, and, yes, we can trust what our eyes see in others"—the final line, cast unambiguously in the negative, is a surprise. The poem's speaker becomes both the viewing "eye" looking upon another, and in a play on words, the "I" deep in frustrated self-analysis. In both cases, the eye/I cannot know "The Star's whole secret."

Crucially, the play on eye/I brings together the issue of interiority and visuality. In a poetic reprise of her question to Higginson, Dickinson writes:

> I felt my life with both my hands
> To see if it was there –
> I held my spirit to the Glass
> To prove it possibler –
>
> (Fr357)

This time the speaker asks the question—"Could you believe me – without?" (L268)—of herself. Is the there there even during those times when we can neither feel nor see any evidence of interiority? Or to rephrase the question more positively, what is in "the Glass" that allows for possibility? Far from finding a perversion or distortion of an interior truth, Dickinson here accepts that sometimes all we can know is what we see. As she writes a few years later:

> The Object absolute, is nought –
> Perception sets it fair
> And then upbraids a Perfectness
> That situates so far –
>
>   (Fr1103)

Dickinson recognizes the impossibility of ever gaining a direct knowledge, unmediated by sensual perception, of anything, including one's own inner life. No meaning exists before representation creates it. Yet we must not smooth over the jagged edges of this possibility, for it may ultimately reveal an absence, a nothingness at the center of the self. By repeatedly turning to the visual, Dickinson's poetic philosophy makes the inner life a material thing, a thing that in its materiality is subject to the same forces of destruction as all matter.

Dickinson's juxtaposition of interiority and the visual is remarkable in its continual return to the epistemological problem of how both to represent and to apprehend the inner life. The "inner Brand" that is stamped upon "Arterial Canvas" emerges as a fascinating answer to this problem. This "Brand" is wielded in two directions at once. Following traditional liberal-sentimental ideals, an inner truth is stamped upon each individual for all to survey. Yet this "Arterial Canvas" is intriguing; as a canvas, the self might be shaded, erased, and painted over. Even further, the canvas is not always fresh and unsullied, but oftentimes already writ upon with the crimson paint of one's "Arterial" blood. What does it mean for one's physical body to be understood as canvas, one's blood as crimson paint? In "Arterial" one hears the contraction of "art" and "material," a play on words that highlights the aesthetic construction of body, mind, and soul. The "Brand" and "Canvas" work in concert with one another; what is outside seeps in, what is inside often pours forth. This complex exchange does not seem to fulfill a liberal ideal of individual self-determination, where the self stands inviolate, guided by an interior compass that always points North. Instead, it emerges as a strong argument for a re-evaluation of this very ideal.

Lionel Trilling argued that the imagination creates the ultimate paradox for liberalism: the liberal democratic tradition vaunted by critics such as Matthiessen failed to produce literature of "lasting interest" not because liberal democratic ideals are weak in themselves but because these ideals fail to allow for the possibility that the imagination had the capacity "to deteriorate and become corrupt and to work harm" (283). By celebrating the moral complexities of writers such as Henry James and Mark Twain over and against the propagandistic morality of writers such as Theodore Dreiser and John Dos Passos, Trilling called for an American writing that fulfilled the political promises of liberalism by investigating, in James's phrase, "the imagination of disaster" (58). Dickinson often imagined disaster: the poet investigated the ramifications of self-disidentity in works such as "I felt a Funeral, in my Brain" (Fr340), "There's a certain Slant of light" (Fr320), "One need not be a Chamber – to be Haunted –" (Fr407), "The first Day's Night had come –" (Fr423), "I heard a Fly buzz – when I died –" (Fr591), and "I felt a Cleaving in my Mind –" (Fr867). Yet Dickinson goes beyond Trilling's idealized "imagination of disaster" where an autonomous agent engages in a struggle with the interior self only and always to come out on top. Dickinson's poetics do not contemplate an interior wracked by the pains of Hawthorne's "bosom serpent," a contemplation that, while dark, still asserts an interior presence. But the poetics also contemplate the far more frightening possibility that the human interior is characterized by nothing so much as nothing.

This conclusion is perhaps not as nihilistic as it at first appears. Shira Wolosky has argued that Dickinson's resistance to the liberal democratic tradition is inextricably connected to her status as a woman in the nineteenth century: "[T]he Emersonian, liberal tradition of autonomous selfhood contrasts not only against female social realities. . . .

It may run counter to fundamental conditions in the world, and fundamental needs of society" ("Dickinson's Emerson" 136). Dickinson had a profound commitment to the investigation of both abstract and structural freedoms. For Dickinson, the inner world of the imagination was the place where it most mattered to be free. She worked through this theme in poems such as "No Rack can torture me –" (Fr649), "They shut me up in Prose" (Fr445), and "Publication – is the Auction" (Fr788), repeatedly insisting that there is an inner truth, a place inside the self that must, at all costs, be free. And yet she notes, "Captivity is Consciousness – / So's Liberty –" (Fr649). With typical economy, Dickinson's aphorism elides captivity and liberty to highlight how consciousness—or as she has termed it before, "perception"—engenders both freedom and constraint. Whereas American Renaissance writers such as Emerson and Thoreau and their later Cold War critical champions believed in a coherent interior that continually projected itself upon the world, indeed, that the world's meaning and logic emanated from such an individual self, Dickinson explored the possibility that a dialectical relationship exists between the self and the world. Without the liberal interior to project itself upon and structure the external world, Dickinson turned to the complexities of perception and representation to evince a keenly-felt uneasiness with the liberal dominion of the self.

From *The Emily Dickinson Journal* 14, no. 2 (2005): 48-59. Copyright © 2005 by The Johns Hopkins University Press. Reprinted with permission of The Johns Hopkins University Press.

Notes

My thanks to Betsy Erkkila, Jay Grossman, Carl Smith, Katy Chiles, Peter Jaros, and Sarah Mesle for their advice with this article.

1. Thomas H. Johnson's early evaluation of the poet concluded that Dickinson lived outside history and had no subject or reference points exterior to her self: "[T]he fact is that she did not live in history and held no view of it, past or current" (xiv). Critics subsequently trained in the lessons of feminism and historicism eschewed

Johnson's New Critical assessment, instead contextualizing Dickinson's poetics of privacy within a nineteenth-century culture of domesticity and sentimentalism, as well as within the tradition of Calvinist self-examination. See, for example, Jane Eberwein, Joanne Dobson, and Barton St. Armand. More recently, critics have highlighted how Dickinson's rigorous turn inward might be better understood as a subtle and savvy technique for engaging with, critiquing, and thus redefining both "private" and "public." See especially Erkkila, Diana Fuss, Martha Nell Smith, and Shira Wolosky, "Public and Private in Dickinson's War Poetry." I understand Dickinson's poetics of privacy as a speculative, self-consciously epistemological project. In other words, I believe that Dickinson knew what she was doing when she, as Suzanne Juhasz has put it, "chose to keep to her house, to her room, to live in her mind rather than in the external world, in order to achieve certain goals" (4).

2. Throughout this essay, I will be working with C. B. Macpherson's characterization of liberalism, traced through John Locke, as "possessive individualism." He argues that the liberal subject is defined as one who owns property, most importantly, property in the self. I am interested in asking how committed Dickinson was to the aspiration to self-ownership, an obviously vexed category in the mid-nineteenth century.

3. See Erkkila, Coleman Hutchison, and Cristanne Miller.

4. See F. O. Matthiessen's 1941 *American Renaissance: Art and Expression in the Age of Emerson and Whitman*.

5. See Gray for a useful overview of the development of liberal political theory from the early modern period through the twentieth century. He notes that the liberal tradition, while varied, can generally be characterized as committed to individualism, egalitarianism, universalism, and meliorism. These liberal ideals were regularly and necessarily denied to non-white, non-upper-class, non-male citizens throughout the eighteenth and nineteenth centuries (see especially Gillian Brown, Linda Kerber, and Elizabeth Dillon).

6. See, for example, Johnson's introduction to the *Selected Letters*, which claims that Dickinson's letters are great not because they display a rigorous mind at work, but more simply (and merely) because they are an "expression" of a self: "[The letters] are the expression of her unique personality. . . . Though she never wrote about herself after adolescence, the letters nevertheless are always self-portraits, written by one who has observed herself frankly and with no self-pity or regrets" (xv).

7. Introduced in the United States in 1860, the *carte de visite* was a portrait photograph mounted on card stock backing. Reproduced in multiple copies from a negative, the *carte de visite* was more easily exchanged than the one-of-a-kind daguerreotype. These miniature photographs were often used as calling cards, tucked into letters to friends and relatives, and collected as souvenirs, especially when the sitter was a celebrity. The *carte de visite*'s popularity heralded the end of the daguerreotype era. See Robert Taft, 138-152, and William Welling, 143-148.

8. Dickinson had portraits of George Eliot, Elizabeth Barrett Browning, and Thomas Carlyle hanging in her bedroom. See Fuss, 59, and Polly Longsworth, 80.

9. Indeed, most critics have read Dickinson's verbal self-portrait as an attempt to escape traditional forms of representation like the daguerreotype portrait. See, for example, Susan Williams, who claims Dickinson probably felt that "A real portrait leaves

a cold record, while a verbal portrait encapsulates the ambiguity that is a hallmark of [her] poetry" (133).

10. See, for example, Karen Halttunen, who claims that nineteenth-century values of sincerity took the form of a "sentimental typology of conduct" characterized by "visible outward signs of inner moral qualities" (40). This emphasis on transparency was often in direct conflict with the interest in theatricality and posing that permeated the popular culture of the day.

Works Cited

The following abbreviations are used to refer to the writings of Emily Dickinson:

Fr *The Poems of Emily Dickinson.* Ed. R. W. Franklin. 3 vols. Cambridge, MA: Harvard UP, 1998. Citation by poem number.

L   *The Letters of Emily Dickinson.* Ed. Thomas H. Johnson and Theodora Ward. 3 vols. Cambridge, MA: Harvard UP, 1958. Citation by letter number.

Brown, Gillian. *Domestic Individualism: Imagining Self in Nineteenth-Century America.* Berkeley: U of California P, 1990.

Dillon, Elizabeth Maddock. *The Gender of Freedom: Fictions of Liberalism and the Literary Public Sphere.* Stanford: Stanford UP, 2004.

Dobson, Joanne. *Dickinson and the Strategies of Reticence: The Woman Writer in Nineteenth-Century America.* Bloomington: Indiana UP, 1989.

Eberwein, Jane Donahue. *Dickinson: Strategies of Limitation.* Amherst: U of Massachusetts P, 1987.

Erkkila, Betsy. "Dickinson and the Art of Politics." *A Historical Guide to Emily Dickinson.* Ed. Vivian Pollak. Oxford: Oxford UP, 2004. 133-74.

Fuss, Diana. *The Sense of an Interior: Four Writers and the Rooms That Shaped Them.* New York: Routledge, 2004.

Gray, John. *Liberalism.* Minneapolis: U of Minnesota P, 1986.

Halttunen, Karen. *Confidence Men and Painted Women: A Study of Middle-Class Culture in America, 1830-1870.* New Haven: Yale UP, 1982.

Hutchison, Coleman. "'Eastern Exiles': Dickinson, Whiggery and War." *The Emily Dickinson Journal* 13.2 (2004): 1-26.

Johnson, Thomas H. Introduction. *The Selected Letters of Emily Dickinson.* Cambridge, MA: Harvard UP, 1996.

Juhasz, Suzanne. *The Undiscovered Continent: Emily Dickinson and the Space of the Mind.* Bloomington: Indiana UP, 1983.

Kerber, Linda. *No Constitutional Right to Be Ladies: Women and the Obligations of Citizenship.* New York: Hill and Wang, 1998.

Longsworth, Polly. *The World of Emily Dickinson.* New York: Norton, 1990.

Macpherson, C. B. *The Political Theory of Possessive Individualism: Hobbes to*

Locke. London: Oxford UP, 1975.

Matthiessen, F. O. *American Renaissance: Art and Expression in the Age of Emerson and Whitman*. Oxford: Oxford UP, 1941.

Melville, Herman. *Correspondence*. Ed. Lynn Horth. Evanston: Northwestern UP; Chicago: Newberry Library, 1993. Vol. 14 of *The Writings of Herman Melville*. Harrison Hayford, Hershel Parker, G. Thomas Tanselle, gen. ed. 15 vols. 1968-1989.

Miller, Cristanne. "Pondering 'Liberty': Emily Dickinson and the Civil War." *American Vistas and Beyond*. Ed. Marietta Messmer and Josef Raab. Trier: Wissenschaftlicher Verlag Trier, 2002. 45-64.

St. Armand, Barton Levi. *Emily Dickinson and Her Culture: The Soul's Society*. New York: Cambridge UP, 1984.

Smith, Martha Nell. *Rowing in Eden: Rereading Emily Dickinson*. Austin: U Texas P, 1992.

Taft, Robert. *Photography and the American Scene: A Social History, 1839-1889*. New York: Macmillan Co., 1938.

Trilling, Lionel. *The Liberal Imagination: Essays on Literature and Society*. New York: Harcourt Brace Jovanovich, 1979.

Welling, William. *Photography in America: The Formative Years, 1839-1900*. New York: Crowell, 1978.

Williams, Susan S. *Confounding Images: Photography and Portraiture in Antebellum American Fiction*. Philadelphia: U of Pennsylvania P, 1997.

Wolosky, Shira. "Dickinson's Emerson: A Critique of American Identity." *The Emily Dickinson Journal* 9.2 (2000): 123-41.

_____. "Public and Private in Dickinson's War Poetry." *A Historical Guide to Emily Dickinson*. Ed. Vivian Pollak. Oxford: Oxford UP, 2004. 103-132.

RESOURCES

1830	Emily Elizabeth Dickinson is born in Amherst, Massachusetts, on December 10 to Edward and Emily Norcross Dickinson.
1833	Sister Lavinia is born. Edward Dickinson sells the family house, the Homestead, and the Dickinsons share the house with its new owners until 1840.
1840-1847	Dickinson attends Amherst Academy.
1840	Edward Dickinson buys another house in Amherst, and the family moves.
1847-1848	Dickinson attends Mount Holyoke Female Seminary.
1852	A Dickinson poem, "A Valentine," appears in the *Springfield Republican* in February.
1853	Benjamin Newton, a law student in Edward Dickinson's office and a close friend of Emily, dies.
1855	During February and March, Dickinson travels to Washington, D.C., with Lavinia to visit their father, who is serving as a congressman. The two stop in Philadelphia on their return trip and likely hear Reverend Mr. Charles Wadsworth preach. Dickinson forms a strong attachment to him and the two correspond until his death in 1882. After the owner of the Homestead dies, Edward Dickinson repurchases the house, where Emily and Lavinia will live for the rest of their lives. Dickinson's mother's long illness begins.
1856	Dickinson's brother, Austin, marries one of Emily's childhood friends, Susan Gilbert. The couple settles next door to the Homestead in a house called the Evergreens.
1858	Samuel Bowles, editor of the *Springfield Republican* and friend of Austin, begins to visit the Dickinsons regularly. Dickinson's extant correspondence with Bowles begins. The first Master letter is dated to this year.

1861-1865	Dickinson's "flood" years, during which she writes roughly half of her 1,789 extant poems.
1861	"I taste a liquor never brewed –" appears in the *Springfield Republican* in May. The second and third Master letters are dated to this year.
1862	"Safe in their Alabaster Chambers" appears in the *Springfield Republican* in March. In April, Dickinson writes to Thomas Wentworth Higginson—the pastor of a Worcester, Massachusetts, church, a regular contributor to *The Atlantic Monthly*, and ardent abolitionist and supporter of women's rights—to ask his opinion of four of her poems, sparking a lifelong friendship and correspondence.
1864	Dickinson travels to Cambridge, Massachusetts, to be treated for an eye ailment by a Boston doctor. After returning home, she never again leaves Amherst and withdraws gradually into her house and its surrounding gardens. "Some keep the Sabbath going to Church –" is published in *The Round Table*; "Blazing in Gold and quenching in Purple," "Flowers – well, if anybody," and "These are the days when Birds come back –" are published in *Brooklyn Drum Beat*.
1866	"A Narrow Fellow in the Grass" is published in the *Springfield Republican* in an edited form.
1870	Higginson visits Amherst, and he and Dickinson meet for the first time.
1873	Higginson makes his second visit to Dickinson.
1874	Dickinson's father dies.
1875	Dickinson's mother is paralyzed.
1877	Dickinson begins a steady correspondence with Otis Phillips Lord, a Massachusetts Supreme Judicial Court judge and friend of the Dickinson family, after the death of his wife. The two become close.
1878	Bowles dies.
1882	Wadsworth dies in April; Dickinson's mother dies in November.

1883	Dickinson's nephew, Gilbert, of whom she is very fond, dies in October.
1884	Judge Lord dies in March.
1886	Dickinson dies on May 15.

Works by Emily Dickinson

Poetry

Poems: First Series, 1890 (Mabel Loomis Todd and T. W. Higginson, editors)
Poems: Second Series, 1891 (Mabel Loomis Todd and T. W. Higginson, editors)
Poems: Third Series, 1896 (Mabel Loomis Todd, editor)
The Single Hound, 1914 (Martha Dickinson Bianchi, editor)
Further Poems, 1929 (Martha Dickinson Bianchi, editor)
Unpublished Poems, 1936 (Martha Dickinson Bianchi and Alfred Leete Hampson, editors)
Bolts of Melody, 1945 (Mabel Loomis Todd and Millicent Todd Bingham, editors)
The Poems of Emily Dickinson, 1955 (3 volumes; Thomas H. Johnson, editor)
The Complete Poems of Emily Dickinson, 1960 (Thomas H. Johnson, editor)
The Manuscript Books of Emily Dickinson, 1981 (2 volumes; R. W. Franklin, editor)
The Poems of Emily Dickinson: Variorum Edition, 1998 (3 volumes; R. W. Franklin, editor)
The Poems of Emily Dickinson: Reading Edition, 1999 (R. W. Franklin, editor)

Nonfiction

Letters, 1894 (2 volumes; Mabel Loomis Todd, editor)
The Letters of Emily Dickinson, 1958 (3 volumes; Thomas H. Johnson and Theodora Ward, editors)
Emily Dickinson: Selected Letters, 1986 (Thomas H. Johnson, editor)
The Master Letters of Emily Dickinson, 1986 (R. W. Franklin, editor)
Emily Dickinson's Herbarium: A Facsimile Edition, 2006

Bibliography

Allen, R. C. *Emily Dickinson: Accidental Buddhist.* Victoria, BC: Trafford, 2007.

Anderson, Charles R. *Emily Dickinson's Poetry: Stairway of Surprise.* New York: Holt, Rinehart and Winston, 1960.

Barker, Wendy. *Lunacy of Light: Emily Dickinson and the Experience of Metaphor.* Carbondale: Southern Illinois University Press, 1987.

Barnstone, Aliki. *Changing Rapture: Emily Dickinson's Poetic Development.* Hanover, NH: University Press of New England 2006.

Bennett, Paula. *Emily Dickinson: Woman Poet.* Iowa City: University of Iowa Press, 1990.

Bianchi, Martha Dickinson. *Emily Dickinson Face to Face.* Boston: Houghton Mifflin, 1932.

_____. *The Life and Letters of Emily Dickinson.* Boston: Houghton Mifflin, 1924.

Blake, Caesar R., and Carlton F. Wells, eds. *The Recognition of Emily Dickinson: Selected Criticism Since 1890.* Ann Arbor: University of Michigan Press, 1968.

Buckingham, Willis J., ed. *Emily Dickinson's Reception in the 1890s: A Documentary History.* Pittsburgh: University of Pittsburgh Press, 1989.

Cameron, Sharon. *Choosing Not Choosing: Dickinson's Fascicles.* Chicago: University of Chicago Press, 1992.

_____. *Lyric Time: Dickinson and the Limits of Genre.* Baltimore: Johns Hopkins University Press, 1979.

Cody, John. *After Great Pain: The Inner Life of Emily Dickinson.* Cambridge, MA: Harvard University Press, 1971.

Crumbley, Paul. *Inflections of the Pen: Dash and Voice in Emily Dickinson.* Lexington: University Press of Kentucky, 1997.

Davinroy, Elise. "Tomb and Womb: Reading Contexture in Emily Dickinson's 'Soft Prison.'" *Legacy* 23.1 (2006): 1-13.

Delli Carpini, John. *Poetry as Prayer: Emily Dickinson.* Boston: Pauline Books & Media, 2002.

Dickenson, Donna. *Emily Dickinson.* Oxford, England: Berg, 1985.

Duchac, Joseph. *The Poems of Emily Dickinson: An Annotated Guide to Commentary Published in English, 1890-1977.* New York: G. K. Hall, 1979.

_____. *The Poems of Emily Dickinson: An Annotated Guide to Commentary Published in English, 1978-1989.* Boston: G. K. Hall, 1993.

Eberwein, Jane Donahue. *Dickinson: Strategies of Limitation.* Amherst: University of Massachusetts Press, 1985.

_____, ed. *An Emily Dickinson Encyclopedia.* Westport, CT: Greenwood Press, 1998.

Farr, Judith. *The Passion of Emily Dickinson*. Cambridge, MA: Harvard University Press, 1992.

Ferlazzo, Paul, ed. *Critical Essays on Emily Dickinson*. Boston: G. K. Hall, 1984.

Ford, Thomas W. *Heaven Beguiles the Tired: Death in the Poetry of Emily Dickinson*. Tuscaloosa: University of Alabama Press, 1966.

Garbowsky, Maryanne M. *The House Without the Door: A Study of Emily Dickinson and the Illness of Agoraphobia*. Rutherford, NJ: Fairleigh Dickinson University Press, 1989.

Gelpi, Albert. *Emily Dickinson: The Mind of the Poet*. Cambridge, MA: Harvard University Press, 1965.

Grabher, Gudrun, Roland Hagenbüchle, and Cristanne Miller, eds. *The Emily Dickinson Handbook*. Amherst: University of Massachusetts Press, 1998.

Griffith, Clark. *The Long Shadow: Emily Dickinson's Tragic Poetry*. Princeton, NJ: Princeton University Press, 1964.

Guthrie, James R. *Emily Dickinson's Vision: Illness and Identity in Her Poetry*. Gainesville: University Press of Florida, 1998.

Habegger, Alfred. *My Wars Are Laid Away in Books: The Life of Emily Dickinson*. New York: Random House, 2001.

Heginbotham, Eleanor Elson. *Reading the Fascicles of Emily Dickinson: Dwelling in Possibilities*. Columbus: Ohio State University Press, 2003.

Jackson, Virginia. *Dickinson's Misery: A Theory of Lyric Reading*. Princeton, NJ: Princeton University Press, 2005.

Jenkins, Macgregor. *Emily Dickinson, Friend and Neighbor*. Boston: Little, Brown, 1930.

Juhasz, Suzanne. *The Undiscovered Continent: Emily Dickinson and the Space of the Mind*. Bloomington: Indiana University Press, 1983.

_____, ed. *Feminist Critics Read Emily Dickinson*. Bloomington: Indiana University Press, 1983.

Juhasz, Suzanne, Cristanne Miller, and Martha Nell Smith. *Comic Power in Emily Dickinson*. Austin: University of Texas Press, 1993.

Keane, Patrick J. *Emily Dickinson's Approving God: Divine Design and the Problem of Suffering*. Columbia: University of Missouri Press, 2008.

Keller, Karl. *The Only Kangaroo Among the Beauty: Emily Dickinson and America*. Baltimore: Johns Hopkins University Press, 1979.

Leyda, Jay. *The Years and Hours of Emily Dickinson*. 2 vols. New Haven, CT: Yale University Press, 1960.

Lindberg-Seyersted, Brita. *The Voice of the Poet: Aspects of Style in the Poetry of Emily Dickinson*. Cambridge, MA: Harvard University Press, 1968.

Loeffelholz, Mary. *Dickinson and the Boundaries of Feminist Theory*. Urbana: University of Illinois Press, 1991.

Lowenberg, Carlton. *Emily Dickinson's Textbooks*. Ed. Territa A. Lowenberg and Carla L. Brown. Berkeley, CA: West Coast Print Center, 1986.

Lubbers, Klaus. *Emily Dickinson: The Critical Revolution*. Ann Arbor: University of Michigan Press, 1962.

Lundin, Roger. *Emily Dickinson and the Art of Belief*. Grand Rapids, MI: Wm. B. Eerdmans, 1998.

Mackenzie, Cynthia. *Concordance to the Letters of Emily Dickinson*. Boulder: University Press of Colorado, 2000.

McNeil, Helen. *Emily Dickinson*. New York: Virago, 1986.

Mamunes, George. *"So Has a Daisy Vanished": Emily Dickinson and Tuberculosis*. Jefferson, NC: McFarland, 2008.

Martin, Wendy, ed. *The Cambridge Companion to Emily Dickinson*. New York: Cambridge University Press, 2008.

Messmer, Marietta. *A Vice for Voices: Reading Emily Dickinson's Correspondence*. Amherst: University of Massachusetts Press, 2001.

Miller, Cristanne. "Controversy in the Study of Emily Dickinson." *Literary Imagination* 6.1 (2004): 39-50.

_____. *Emily Dickinson: A Poet's Grammar*. Cambridge, MA: Harvard University Press, 1987.

Mitchell, Domhnall. "'A Foreign Country': Emily Dickinson's Manuscripts and Their Meanings." *Legacy* 17.2 (2000): 174-86.

_____. *Measures of Possibility: Emily Dickinson's Manuscripts*. Amherst: University of Massachusetts Press, 2005.

Mossberg, Barbara Antonina Clarke. *Emily Dickinson: When the Writer Is a Daughter*. Bloomington: Indiana University Press, 1982.

Mudge, Jean McClure. *Emily Dickinson and the Image of Home*. Amherst: University of Massachusetts Press, 1975.

Oberhaus, Dorothy Huff. *Emily Dickinson's Fascicles: Method and Meaning*. University Park: Pennsylvania State University Press, 1995.

Pollak, Vivian R., ed. *A Historical Guide to Emily Dickinson*. New York: Oxford University Press, 2004.

Pollitt, Josephine. *Emily Dickinson: The Human Background of Her Poetry*. New York: Harper & Brothers, 1930.

Porter, David T. *The Art of Emily Dickinson's Early Poetry*. Cambridge, MA: Harvard University Press, 1966.

_____. *Dickinson: The Modern Idiom*. Cambridge, MA: Harvard University Press, 1981.

Robinson, John. *Emily Dickinson: Looking to Canaan*. Winchester, MA: Faber & Faber, 1986.

Rosenbaum, S. P. *A Concordance to the Poems of Emily Dickinson*. Ithaca, NY: Cornell University Press, 1964.

Rosenthal, M. L., and Sally M. Gall. *The Modern Poetic Sequence: The Genius of Modern Poetry*. New York: Oxford University Press, 1983.

St. Armand, Barton Levi. *Emily Dickinson and Her Culture: The Soul's Society.* New York: Cambridge University Press, 1985.

Salska, Agnieszka. *Walt Whitman and Emily Dickinson: Poetry of the Central Consciousness.* Philadelphia: University of Pennsylvania Press, 1985.

Sewall, Richard B. *The Life of Emily Dickinson.* New York: Farrar, Straus and Giroux, 1974.

_____, ed. *Emily Dickinson: A Collection of Critical Essays.* Englewood Cliffs, NJ: Prentice-Hall, 1963.

Sherwood, William R. *Circumference and Circumstance: Stages in the Mind and Art of Emily Dickinson.* New York: Columbia University Press, 1968.

Small, Judy Jo. *Positive as Sound: Emily Dickinson's Rhyme.* Athens: University of Georgia Press, 1990.

Smith, Martha Nell. *Rowing in Eden: Rereading Emily Dickinson.* Austin: University of Texas Press, 1992.

Smith, Martha Nell, and Mary Loeffelholz, eds. *A Companion to Emily Dickinson.* Malden, MA: Blackwell, 2008.

Spencer, Theodore. "Concentration and Intensity." *The Recognition of Emily Dickinson: Selected Criticism Since 1890.* Ed. Caesar R. Blake and Carlton F. Wells. Ann Arbor: University of Michigan Press, 1968. 131-33. Reprinted from *New England Quarterly* 2 (July 1929).

Stonum, Gary Lee. *The Dickinson Sublime.* Madison: University of Wisconsin Press, 1990.

Taggard, Genevieve. *The Life and Mind of Emily Dickinson.* New York: Alfred A. Knopf, 1930.

Tate, Allen. "New England Culture and Emily Dickinson." 1932. *The Recognition of Emily Dickinson: Selected Criticism Since 1890.* Ed. Caesar R. Blake and Carlton F. Wells. Ann Arbor: University of Michigan Press, 1968. 153-67.

Todd, John Emerson. *Emily Dickinson's Use of the Persona.* The Hague: Mouton, 1973.

Weisbuch, Robert. *Emily Dickinson's Poetry.* Chicago: University of Chicago Press, 1975.

Werner, Marta L. *Emily Dickinson's Open Folios: Scenes of Reading, Surfaces of Writing.* Ann Arbor: University of Michigan Press, 1995.

Whicher, George Frisbie. *This Was a Poet: A Critical Biography of Emily Dickinson.* New York: Charles Scribner's Sons, 1938.

White, Fred D. *Approaching Emily Dickinson: Critical Currents and Crosscurrents Since 1960.* Rochester, NY: Camden House, 2008.

Wolff, Cynthia Griffin. *Emily Dickinson.* New York: Alfred A. Knopf, 1986.

Wolosky, Shira. *Emily Dickinson: A Voice of War.* New Haven, CT: Yale University Press, 1984.

CRITICAL
INSIGHTS

About the Editor

J. Brooks Bouson is a Professor of English at Loyola University in Chicago whose area of specialization is women's literature. She has published essays and book chapters on a variety of authors (including Dorothy Allison, Saul Bellow, Emily Dickinson, Ted Hughes, Franz Kafka, Jamaica Kincaid, Toni Morrison, Edwin Muir, George Orwell, Richard Russo, and Christa Wolf), and she is the author of five books: *Embodied Shame: Uncovering Female Shame in Contemporary Women's Writings* (2009), *Jamaica Kincaid: Writing Memory, Writing Back to the Mother* (2005), *Quiet As It's Kept: Shame, Trauma, and Race in the Novels of Toni Morrison* (2000), *Brutal Choreographies: Oppositional Strategies and Narrative Design in the Novels of Margaret Atwood* (1993), and *The Empathic Reader: A Study of the Narcissistic Character and the Drama of the Self* (1989). In addition, she is the editor of the Critical Insights series volume on *The Handmaid's Tale*, by Margaret Atwood (2010), and of *Margaret Atwood: "The Robber Bride," "The Blind Assassin," and "Oryx and Crake"* (2010).

About *The Paris Review*

The Paris Review is America's preeminent literary quarterly, dedicated to discovering and publishing the best new voices in fiction, nonfiction, and poetry. The magazine was founded in Paris in 1953 by the young American writers Peter Matthiessen and Doc Humes, and edited there and in New York for its first fifty years by George Plimpton. Over the decades, the *Review* has introduced readers to the earliest writings of Jack Kerouac, Philip Roth, T. C. Boyle, V. S. Naipaul, Ha Jin, Ann Patchett, Jay McInerney, Mona Simpson, and Edward P. Jones, and published numerous now classic works, including Roth's *Goodbye, Columbus*, Donald Barthelme's *Alice*, Jim Carroll's *Basketball Diaries*, and selections from Samuel Beckett's *Molloy* (his first publication in English). The first chapter of Jeffrey Eugenides's *The Virgin Suicides* appeared in the *Review*'s pages, as well as stories by Rick Moody, David Foster Wallace, Denis Johnson, Jim Crace, Lorrie Moore, and Jeanette Winterson.

The Paris Review's renowned Writers at Work series of interviews, whose early installments include legendary conversations with E. M. Forster, William Faulkner, and Ernest Hemingway, is one of the landmarks of world literature. The interviews received a George Polk Award and were nominated for a Pulitzer Prize. Among the more than three hundred interviewees are Robert Frost, Marianne Moore, W. H. Auden, Elizabeth Bishop, Susan Sontag, and Toni Morrison. Recent issues feature conversations with Salman Rushdie, Joan Didion, Norman Mailer, Kazuo Ishiguro, Marilynne Robinson, Umberto Eco, Annie Proulx, and Gay Talese. In November 2009, Picador published the final volume of a four-volume series of anthologies of *Paris Review* interviews. *The New York Times* called the Writers at Work series "the most remarkable and extensive interviewing project we possess."

The Paris Review is edited by Philip Gourevitch, who was named to the post in 2005, following the death of George Plimpton two years earlier. A new editorial team has published fiction by André Aciman, Colum McCann, Damon Galgut, Mohsin Hamid, Uzodinma Iweala, Gish Jen, Stephen King, James Lasdun, Padgett Powell, Richard Price, and Sam Shepard. Poetry editors Charles Simic, Meghan O'Rourke, and Dan Chiasson have selected works by John Ashbery, Kay Ryan, Billy Collins, Tomaž Šalamun, Mary Jo Bang, Sharon Olds, Charles Wright, and Mary Karr. Writing published in the magazine has been anthologized in *Best American Short Stories* (2006, 2007, and 2008), *Best American Poetry*, *Best Creative Non-Fiction*, the Pushcart Prize anthology, and *O. Henry Prize Stories*.

The magazine presents two annual awards. The Hadada Award for lifelong contribution to literature has recently been given to Joan Didion, Norman Mailer, Peter Matthiessen, and, in 2009, John Ashbery. The Plimpton Prize for Fiction, awarded to a debut or emerging writer brought to national attention in the pages of *The Paris Review*, was presented in 2007 to Benjamin Percy, to Jesse Ball in 2008, and to Alistair Morgan in 2009.

The Paris Review was a finalist for the 2008 and 2009 National Magazine Awards in fiction, and it won the 2007 National Magazine Award in photojournalism. The *Los Angeles Times* recently called *The Paris Review* "an American treasure with true international reach."

Since 1999 *The Paris Review* has been published by The Paris Review Foundation, Inc., a not-for-profit 501(c)(3) organization.

The Paris Review is available in digital form to libraries worldwide in selected academic databases exclusively from EBSCO Publishing. Libraries can contact EBSCO at 1-800-653-2726 for details. For more information on *The Paris Review* or to subscribe, please visit: www.theparisreview.org.

Contributors

J. Brooks Bouson is a Professor of English at Loyola University in Chicago whose area of specialization is women's literature. She has published essays and book chapters on a variety of authors, including Emily Dickinson, and is the author of five books, among them *Embodied Shame: Uncovering Female Shame in Contemporary Women's Writings* (2009) and *The Empathic Reader: A Study of the Narcissistic Character and the Drama of the Self* (1989).

Gerhard Brand was Professor Emeritus, Department of English and Comparative Literature, at California State University, Los Angeles.

Jascha Hoffman has written for *Nature* and *The New York Times*. He lives in San Francisco, where he occasionally sets an Emily Dickinson poem to music.

Elizabeth Petrino is Associate Professor of English at Fairfield University in Fairfield, Connecticut. Her books include *Emily Dickinson and Her Contemporaries: American Women's Verse, 1820-1885* (1998) and *Jesuit and Feminist Education: Intersections in Teaching and Learning for the Twenty-first Century*, coedited with Jocelyn Boryczka (2010). A Scholar in Residence at New York University in 2002 and a Reese Fellow at the American Antiquarian Society in 2007, she is currently researching how nineteenth-century women's writing entered into popular national discourses on topics such as abolition, the Civil War, and Native American removal in antebellum print culture.

Fred D. White is Professor of English at Santa Clara University in Northern California, where he teaches poetry, nonfiction writing, and an undergraduate seminar on Emily Dickinson. In 1997 he received the Louis and Dorina Brutocao Award for Teaching Excellence. His books include *Approaching Emily Dickinson: Critical Currents and Crosscurrents Since 1960* (2008), *The Daily Writer: 366 Meditations for a Productive and Meaningful Writing Life* (2008), *The Daily Reader: 366 Selections of Great Poetry and Prose to Inspire Great Writing* (2009), and *Essential Muir: A Selection of John Muir's Best Writings* (2006).

Margaret H. Freeman is Professor Emeritus of Los Angeles Valley College and a Co-Director of Myrifield Institute for Cognition and the Arts, a think tank for research in the cognitive sciences and the creative arts located in Heath, Massachusetts. She helped to found the Emily Dickinson International Society and served as its first president from 1988 to 1992. She has published many articles in journals and anthologies in the area of cognitive poetics, which she applies to the poetry of Dickinson (among others). She is currently at work on two books: *Poetic Iconicity* and *Reading Emily Dickinson: A Cognitive Guide*. She resides at Myrifield, where she hosts monthly meetings of the Emily Dickinson Reading Circle, with her husband, Don, and Moss, a border collie.

Matthew J. Bolton is Professor of English at Loyola School in New York City, where he also serves as Dean of Students. He received his doctor of philosophy degree in English from the Graduate Center of the City University of New York (CUNY) in 2005. His dissertation was titled "Transcending the Self in Robert Browning and T. S. Eliot." Prior to attaining his Ph.D. at CUNY, he earned a master of philosophy degree in English (2004) and a master of science degree in English education (2001). His undergraduate work was done at the State University of New York at Binghamton, where he studied English literature.

Jane Donahue Eberwein is Distinguished Professor of English and Coordinator of American Studies at Oakland University. Recognized worldwide as an authority on Emily Dickinson's poetry, she has published fifty literary essays and eighteen reviews on the poet's work. Her first book, *Early American Poetry* (1978), is considered a standard in the field. She is also the editor of *An Emily Dickinson Encyclopedia* (1998).

Helen Vendler is A. Kingsley Porter University Professor at Harvard University, where she has taught for more than twenty-five years. She is recognized as one of the leading American critics of poetry and has focused much of her attention on Pope, Whitman, Dickinson, and Keats. She is credited with more than twenty-eight books, including *Our Secret Discipline: Years and Lyric Form* (2007), *Coming of Age as a Poet: Milton, Keats, Eliot, Plath* (2003), and *Anthology of Contemporary American Poetry* (2003).

Jed Deppman is Director of Comparative Literature and Associate Professor of Comparative Literature and English at Oberlin College. He is the author of *Trying to Think with Emily Dickinson* (2008) and coeditor of *Genetic Criticism: Texts and Avant-Textes* (2004). His teaching interests include modernism, postmodernism, philosophy, and literary theory.

Joanne Feit Diehl is Professor of English at the University of California, Davis. Feminist literary theory, contemporary theory, and American poetry are among her fields of study. Her books include *Elizabeth Bishop and Marianne Moore: The Psychodynamics of Creativity* (1993), *Women Poets and the American Sublime* (1990), and *Dickinson and the Romantic Imagination* (1981).

Suzanne Juhasz is Professor of English at the University of Colorado, Boulder. Her publications include *The Women and Language Debate: A Sourcebook* (1995), *Reading from the Heart: Women, Literature, and the Search for True Love* (1995), *Comic Power in Emily Dickinson* (1993), and *The Undiscovered Continent: Emily Dickinson and the Space of the Mind* (1983). She is also the founding editor of *The Emily Dickinson Journal*.

Shira Wolosky is Professor of English and American Literature at the Hebrew University of Jerusalem. A former Associate Professor of English at Yale University, she received a Guggenheim Fellowship in 2001 and was Drue Heinz Visiting Professor at Oxford University in 2008. Her publications include *Defending Identity* (2008), *The Art of Poetry* (2001), *Language Mysticism: The Negative Way of Language in Eliot, Beckett, and Celan* (1995), and *Emily Dickinson: A Voice of War* (1984).

Nancy Mayer is Professor of English at Northwest Missouri State University as well as associate editor of *The Laurel Review*. She holds particular interest in the poetry of Emily Dickinson. Her various essays and articles have appeared in *Midwest Quarterly*, *The Hudson Review*, *The Emily Dickinson Journal*, and *Clackamas Literary Review*.

Patrick J. Keane is Professor Emeritus of English at Le Moyne College, where he concentrates his teaching on the Romantic period, the Irish Renaissance, and literature and history. He has published several books, including *Coleridge's Submerged Politics* (1994) and *Yeats's Interactions with Tradition* (1987).

Christine Gerhardt is Assistant Professor at the University of Dortmund, Germany. Teaching mostly in American literature of the nineteenth and twentieth centuries, she specializes in Walt Whitman, Emily Dickinson, and southern literature. Her publications include *Rituale des Scheiterns: Die Reconstruction-Periode im US-amerikanischen Roman* [*Rituals of Failure: The Reconstruction Period in American Novels*] (2002) and essays in *Profession, Mississippi Quarterly, The Emily Dickinson Journal*, and *Forum for Modern Language Studies*.

Faith Barrett is Assistant Professor of English at Lawrence University in Wisconsin, where she specializes in nineteenth-century American literature. She is coeditor of *"Words for the Hour": A New Anthology of American Civil War Poetry* (2005), and she is at work on two books: *"To Fight Aloud Is Very Brave": American Poets and the Civil War* and *Letters to the World: Emily Dickinson and the Lyric Address*. Her work can also be found in *A Companion to Emily Dickinson* (2008), *The Emily Dickinson Journal, Arizona Quarterly*, and *Leviathan: A Journal of Melville Studies*.

Sarah E. Blackwood earned her doctorate in English literature from Northwestern University in 2009 with a dissertation titled "The Portrait's Subject: Picturing Psychology in American Literary and Visual Culture, 1839-1900." Her research focuses on nineteenth-century American literature, in particular representations of interiority and psychological portraiture. Her essay "The Aesthetics of Psychology" appears in *Henry James in Context* (2010), and she has published other work in *The Emily Dickinson Journal*.

Contributors

Acknowledgments

"Emily Dickinson" by Gerhard Brand. From *Dictionary of World Biography: The 19th Century*. Copyright © 1999 by Salem Press, Inc. Reprinted with permission of Salem Press.

"The *Paris Review* Perspective" by Jascha Hoffman. Copyright © 2011 by Jascha Hoffman. Special appreciation goes to Christopher Cox, Nathaniel Rich, and David Wallace-Wells, editors at *The Paris Review*.

"Dickinson's Local, Global, and Cosmic Perspectives" by Jane Donahue Eberwein. From *The Emily Dickinson Handbook*, edited by Gudrun Grabher, Roland Hagenbüchle, and Cristanne Miller (1998), pp. 27-43. Copyright © 1998 by The University of Massachusetts Press. Reprinted with permission of The University of Massachusetts Press.

"Emily Dickinson Thinking" by Helen Vendler. From *Parnassus: Poetry in Review* 26, no. 1 (2001): 34-56. Copyright © 2001 by Poetry in Review Foundation. Reprinted with permission of the author.

"Trying to Think with Emily Dickinson" by Jed Deppman. From *The Emily Dickinson Journal* 14, no. 1 (2005): 84-103. Copyright © 2005 by The Johns Hopkins University Press. Reprinted with permission of The Johns Hopkins University Press.

"The Ample Word: Immanence and Authority in Dickinson's Poetry" by Joanne Feit Diehl. From *The Emily Dickinson Journal* 14, no. 2 (2005): 1-11. Copyright © 2005 by The Johns Hopkins University Press. Reprinted with permission of The Johns Hopkins University Press.

"The Irresistible Lure of Repetition and Dickinson's Poetics of Analogy" by Suzanne Juhasz. From *The Emily Dickinson Journal* 9, no. 2 (2000): 23-31. Copyright © 2000 by The Johns Hopkins University Press. Reprinted with permission of The Johns Hopkins University Press.

"Emily Dickinson: Reclusion Against Itself" by Shira Wolosky. From *Common Knowledge* 12, no. 3 (Fall 2006): 443-459. Copyright © 2006 by Duke University Press. All rights reserved. Reprinted with permission of Duke University Press.

"The Back Story: The Christian Narrative and Modernism in Emily Dickinson's Poems" by Nancy Mayer. From *The Emily Dickinson Journal* 17, no. 2 (2008): 1-23. Copyright © 2008 by The Johns Hopkins University Press. Reprinted with permission of The Johns Hopkins University Press.

"Dickinson's Death-Haunted Earthly Paradise" by Patrick J. Keane. From *Emily Dickinson's Approving God: Divine Design and the Problem of Suffering* (2008), pp. 144-159. Copyright © 2008 by The Curators of the University of Missouri. Reprinted with permission of the University of Missouri Press.

"'Often seen – but seldom felt': Emily Dickinson's Reluctant Ecology of Place" by Christine Gerhardt. From *The Emily Dickinson Journal* 15, no. 1 (2006): 56-78. Copyright © 2006 by The Johns Hopkins University Press. Reprinted with permission of The Johns Hopkins University Press.

"Addresses to a Divided Nation: Images of War in Emily Dickinson and Walt Whitman" by Faith Barrett. From *Arizona Quarterly* 61, no. 4 (Winter 2005): 67-99. Copyright © 2005 by the Arizona Board of Regents. Reprinted with permission of the author.

"'The Inner Brand': Emily Dickinson, Portraiture, and the Narrative of Liberal Interiority" by Sarah E. Blackwood. From *The Emily Dickinson Journal* 14, no. 2 (2005): 48-59. Copyright © 2005 by The Johns Hopkins University Press. Reprinted with permission of The Johns Hopkins University Press.